# The Date-A-Base Book

# 2026

# The Date-A-Base Book

# 2026

**Compiled by Dave Haslett**

**ideas4writers**

First published in Great Britain in 2022 by
ideas4writers
19 Crow Green
Cullompton
Devon
EX15 1EW

Telephone image by Factumquintus\Resonances, 2004
United Airlines image by N509FZ, 2020
Creative Commons via Wikimedia

**If you would like this series to continue, please tell people about it.**

# Contents

# Introduction

Welcome to the nineteenth edition of *The Date-A-Base Book* series.

As always, every entry has been cross-checked with official sources and reputable websites. And, as always, this was not an easy process as there's an awful lot of 'disinformation' out there. Whenever there was any doubt, I tried to find the original source. Even so, you are advised to double-check each entry before using it, and satisfy yourself that it is 100% correct. If you come across any mistakes please let me know.

I'll post any corrections I hear about on our blog at ideas4writers.com

As far as possible, and where appropriate, I've used New Style (NS) dates from the Gregorian calendar. Dates from the Julian calendar are marked (OS) for Old Style.

With such a vast number of worthy people to choose from, I elected to list only those who are included in *Encyclopaedia Britannica*, or those I've heard of. I apologise if a few non-British household names didn't make the final cut.

I have not included any births of living people, except for royalty.

In the case of wars, it was impossible to include every significant event. I've chosen what I think are the main ones, but if I've left out something you think should have been included please let me know.

# How to use this book

The **Ann.** column gives the anniversary of each entry, so 1100 means the 1100th anniversary of that event. The date on which the event took place is listed next, followed by a brief description.

The most obvious way to use this book is to choose the entries that interest you, then write news reports, newspaper and magazine articles, TV/radio features, short stories, novels, essays, stage plays, screenplays, poems, jokes, non-fiction books, guidebooks, biographies, and so on about them.

But how about thinking outside the box? For example, you might try to see the event through the eyes of someone who was there at the time. Or think about how the world might have been different if that person hadn't been born, or if he had done something else, or if the event hadn't taken place, or if it had happened in a different way or at a different time or to someone else.

You could also use an event, or a series of them, as background detail in a novel or screenplay. Perhaps your characters could think about the events, and discuss them. Perhaps they could influence an event, or be influenced by it.

What most editors, publishers, broadcasters and producers are looking for is something original; something that hasn't been done before. They don't (necessarily) want a summary of a person's life, or a history and timeline of an event. They can probably write that in-house anyway, using their own staff writers – though it's always worth enquiring, just in case they can't.

But you'll probably have more success if you provide them with something different, more compelling, a new angle; something that ties in with the date of the event, but which can run alongside the more general features.

If you're writing about a person, don't just focus on his accomplishments. Have a look at the other things going on in his life: problems, rivalries, disputes, legal issues, patent and copyright issues, interests, hobbies, associations, relatives and relationships, fans and detractors, and so on. See if you can tie that in with one of your own areas of interest. You probably already read publications and visit websites related to those interests, so those are good markets to aim for.

See if you can relate the item to something from your own life, or use it to trigger memories and reminiscences that might lead you to a new writing project.

If you haven't written much before, or if you've never had anything published, use the item as a starting point and write a letter about it, which you can send to your local newspaper or your favourite magazine. You'll find it much easier to get published if the item is relevant to the geographic area the publication covers. Perhaps the famous person was born there, or went to school there, or worked there, or spent his holidays there, or made his big discovery there. You don't have to live there yourself: pick items that interest you, search online for publications that cover those areas, and tailor your letters and articles for their readers.

After you've had a few letters published, see if can get the coveted 'star letter' slot in one of the publications. Then, once you've achieved that, try writing some short articles.

Don't limit yourself to printed publications. There are thousands upon thousands of online publications that need writers – and some of them will even pay you.

Similarly, don't limit yourself to your own country – there's a whole world out there that's keen to hear what you have to say.

Timing is important too, of course. You need to start work well in advance of the anniversary, so that your finished piece of writing appears in print – or on stage or screen or radio – at the time of the anniversary. That's where *The Date-A-Base Book* can help you.

It's also important to bear in mind that magazines work several months in advance. For example, most monthly publications prepare their Christmas issues during the summer so they can be sure everything is ready in time. If you're writing for the stage or screen you might need to have your script ready at least two years before the anniversary occurs. That will allow time for things like casting, rehearsals, set design and building, filming, editing, post-production, promotion, and so on. So you should look at getting the next edition of *The Date-A-Base Book* as soon as it becomes available!

The currently available books are listed at ideas4writers.com and can be purchased from there.


**Dave Haslett**

**Contact me at: mail@ideas4writers.com**

# JANUARY 2026

| Ann. | Date | Event |
|------|------|-------|
| 1100 | 8 Jan 926 | Death of Athelm, Archbishop of Canterbury and first Bishop of Wells. |
| 900 | 18 Jan 1126 | Emperor Huizong of the Song dynasty in China abdicated in favour of his son, Emperor Qinzong, took the title Taishang Huang (Retired Emperor) and fled to the countryside after forces from the Jin Empire invaded the Song Empire. |
| 750 | 10 Jan 1276 | Death of Pope Gregory X. Succeeded by Innocent V (who died in June). |
| 500 | 14 Jan 1526 | The Treaty of Madrid was signed by the Holy Roman Emperor, Charles V, and his prisoner, Francis I, King of France. France renounced its claims in Italy, surrendered Burgundy, and abandoned its sovereignty over Flanders and Artois. Once the treaty was signed, the King was released (on 6th March) and allowed to return to France. |
| 500 | 19 Jan 1526 | Death of Isabella of Austria, Queen consort of Denmark. Wife of King Christian II. |
| 500 | 20 Jan 1526 ? | Birth of Rafael Bombelli, Italian mathematician. Best known for his work on the understanding of imaginary numbers. (Baptised on this date.) |
| 500 | 25 Jan 1526 | Birth of Adolf, Duke of Holstein-Gottorp. Son of King Frederick I of Denmark. |
| 400 | 24 Jan 1626 | Death of Samuel Argall, English adventurer and naval officer. He discovered the shorter northern route across the Atlantic Ocean from England to Virginia, and was Governor of the Virginia Colony. He also kidnapped Pocohontas, daughter of the Chief of the Powhatan Confederacy. |
| 300 | 25 Jan 1726 | Death of Guillaume Delisle, French cartographer. Noted for his accurate maps of Europe and the Americas. |
| 250 | 1 Jan 1776 | American Revolution: according to tradition, George Washington raised the first American flag, the Grand Union Flag, at Prospect Hill in Charlestown, Somerville, Massachusetts on this date. |
| 250 | 1 Jan 1776 | American Revolutionary War: British ships shelled Norfolk, Virginia while British forces and Patriots started fires in the city. More than 800 buildings were destroyed – around two-thirds of the city at that time. |
| 250 | 5 Jan 1776 | New Hampshire adopted the first state constitution in what would become the USA. |
| 250 | 10 Jan 1776 | American Revolution: political activist Thomas Paine published *Common Sense*, a 47-page pamphlet that called for the thirteen colonies' complete independence from Great Britain. It was hugely influential, and inspired the patriots to declare independence. |
| 250 | 10 Jan 1776 | Birth of George Birkbeck, British physician, academic and philanthropist. A pioneer of adult education. Founder of Birkbeck, University of London. He helped create one of the first chemistry laboratories for students, and created mechanics' institutes. |
| 250 | 14 Jan 1776 | Death of Edward Cornwallis, British military officer and politician. Governor of Nova Scotia (1749–52), Governor of Gibraltar (1761–76). |

**JANUARY 2026**

| Ann. | Date | Event |
|---|---|---|
| 250 | 24 Jan 1776 | Birth of E. T. A. Hoffmann, German fantasy/Gothic horror writer, composer, artist and judge.<br>Offenbach's opera *The Tales of Hoffman* is based on his stories.<br>Tchaikovsky's ballet *The Nutcracker* is also based on one of his stories. |
| 200 | 17 Jan 1826 | Death of Juan Crisóstomo Arriaga, Spanish composer. Known as 'the Spanish Mozart'. (Tuberculosis and/or exhaustion, aged 19.) |
| 200 | 26 Jan 1826 | Birth of Julia Grant, First Lady of the United States (1869–77).<br>Wife of U.S. President Ulysses S. Grant. |
| 200 | 30 Jan 1826 | The Menai Suspension Bridge was opened in the UK.<br>It links the island of Anglesey to mainland Wales.<br>It was the world's first major suspension bridge. |
| 175 | 7 Jan 1851 | French physicist Léon Foucault set up the first Foucault pendulum in the cellar of his home to demonstrate the rotation of the Earth.<br>On 3rd February he gave a public demonstration of a larger pendulum at the Paris Observatory.<br>On 31st March he created his most famous pendulum, hanging a 28-kilogram (62-pound) lead weight from a 67-metre (220-foot) wire from the dome of the Panthéon in Paris. |
| 175 | 15 Jan 1851 | Mariano Arista became President of Mexico (until 1853). |
| 175 | 16 Jan 1851 | Birth of Sir William Hall-Jones, British-born New Zealand politician.<br>Interim Prime Minister of New Zealand (1906 for two months following the death of Richard Seddon). |
| 175 | 19 Jan 1851 | Birth of Jacobus Kapteyn, Dutch astronomer.<br>Best known for discovering galactic rotation. He was also one of the first astronomers to suggest the existence of dark matter. |
| 175 | 27 Jan 1851 | Death of John James Audubon, Haitian-born American ornithologist and artist. He discovered and named 25 species of bird, and is known for his book *The Birds of America* in which he documented and illustrated every known species of bird in North America. |
| 175 | 28 Jan 1851 | Northwestern University was established in Evanston, Illinois, USA. |
| 150 | 3 Jan 1876 | Birth of Wilhelm Pieck, first President of East Germany (1946–50). |
| 150 | 5 Jan 1876 | Birth of Konrad Adenauer, first Chancellor of West Germany (1949–63). |
| 150 | 9 Jan 1876 | Death of Samuel Gridley Howe, American physician, abolitionist, social activist and philanthropist. An advocate of education for the blind.<br>Husband of the poet and writer Julia Ward Howe. |
| 150 | 11 Jan 1876 | Birth of Elmer Flick, American baseball player (Philadelphia Phillies, Philadelphia Athletics, Cleveland Bronchos/Naps). |
| 150 | 12 Jan 1876 | Birth of Fevzi Çakmak, Prime Minister of Turkey (1921–22). |
| 150 | 12 Jan 1876 | Birth of Jack London, American novelist and journalist.<br>A pioneer of commercial fiction and science fiction.<br>Best known for his novels *The Call of the Wild* and *White Fang*. |
| 150 | 12 Jan 1876 | Birth of Ermanno Wolf-Ferrari, Italian composer of comic operas. |

## JANUARY 2026

| Ann. | Date | Event |
|------|------|-------|
| 150 | 14 Jan 1876 | Death of Jean-Auguste-Dominique Ingres, French Neoclassical artist. His works influenced modern artists including Picasso and Matisse. |
| 150 | 15 Jan 1876 | The first Afrikaans-language newspaper, *Die Afrikaanse Patriot*, was published in Paarl, South Africa. It ceased publication in 1904. |
| 150 | 15 Jan 1876 | Death of Eliza McCardle Johnson, First Lady of the United States (1865–69). Wife of U.S. President Andrew Johnson. |
| 150 | 15 Jan 1876 | Birth of Claude Buckenham, British cricketer (Essex and England) and football player (gold medallist at the 1900 Olympics). |
| 125 | 1 Jan 1901 | The Commonwealth of Australia was established when the six British colonies of New South Wales, Northern Territory, Queensland, South Australia, Victoria, and Western Australia were federated. |
| 125 | 1 Jan 1901 | The first official Mummers Parade was held in Philadelphia, Pennsylvania, USA. |
| 125 | 2 Jan 1901 | Birth of Bob Marshall, American forester, writer and wilderness activist. Co-founder of The Wilderness Society. |
| 125 | 3 Jan 1901 | Birth of Ngô Đình Diệm, President of South Vietnam (1955–63 – assassinated). |
| 125 | 7 Jan 1901 to 12th | The first national bowling tournament sanctioned by the American Bowling Congress (now the United States Bowling Congress) was held in Chicago, Illinois. |
| 125 | 9 Jan 1901 | Birth of Chic Young, American cartoonist who created the comic strip *Blondie*. |
| 125 | 10 Jan 1901 | The first major oil field in the USA was discovered at Spindletop in Beaumont, Texas. It marked that beginning of the U.S. oil industry. |
| 125 | 16 Jan 1901 | Birth of Fulgencio Batista, President of Cuba (1940–44), President/dictator of Cuba (1952–59). |
| 125 | 16 Jan 1901 | Birth of Frank Zamboni, American inventor of the ice resurfacer. Founder of the Zamboni Company. |
| 125 | 21 Jan 1901 | Death of Elisha Gray, American electrical engineer. Co-founder of Western Electric. Regarded by many as the true inventor of the telephone rather than Alexander Graham Bell. |
| 125 | 22 Jan 1901 | Death of Queen Victoria of the United Kingdom. Succeeded by her son, Edward VII. |
| 125 | 27 Jan 1901 | Birth of Art Rooney, American football executive. Founder, chairman and owner of the Pittsburgh Steelers (1933–88). |
| 125 | 27 Jan 1901 | Death of Giuseppe Verdi, Italian composer. Best known for his operas, including *Aida*, *Requiem*, *Otello* and *Falstaff*. |
| 125 | 28 Jan 1901 | The American League of Professional Baseball Clubs (commonly known as the American League) was founded. It is one of the two leagues that make up Major League Baseball in North America. (The National League was founded in 1876.) The first American League game was played on 24th April 1901, between Chicago and Cleveland. |

**JANUARY 2026**

| Ann. | Date | Event |
|------|------|-------|
| 100 | 3 Jan 1926 | Birth of George Martin, British record producer, arranger, composer, musician and audio engineer. Best known for producing the Beatles' records, and sometimes referred to as the 'Fifth Beatle'. (Died 2016.) |
| 100 | 5 Jan 1926 | Birth of Hosea Williams, American civil rights leader, minister, entrepreneur and philanthropist. He led many of Martin Luther King Jr.'s protest campaigns and was a close associate. (Died 2000.) |
| 100 | 6 Jan 1926 | Birth of Ralph Branca, American baseball pitcher (Brooklyn Dodgers, Detroit Tigers, New York Yankees). (Died 2016.) |
| 100 | 6 Jan 1926 | Birth of Kid Gavilán, Cuban boxer. Undisputed world welterweight champion 1951–54. (Died 2003.) |
| 100 | 8 Jan 1926 | Bảo Đại became the last Emperor of Vietnam. The monarchy was abolished in 1945. |
| 100 | 8 Jan 1926 | Abdul-Aziz ibn Saud became King of Nejd and Hejaz. In 1932 he united four regions and established the Kingdom of Saudi Arabia, with himself as its first King. |
| 100 | 8 Jan 1926 | Birth of Soupy Sales, American comedian, actor and radio/television personality. Best known for the children's TV series *Lunch with Soupy Sales* (later known as *The Soupy Sales Show*). He also appeared as a panellist on several game shows, including *What's My Line?* (Died 2009.) |
| 100 | 12 Jan 1926 | The first episode of the radio sitcom *Sam 'n' Henry* was broadcast on WGN in Chicago, Illinois, USA. It is considered the first-ever sitcom. It ran until 1928, and was then redeveloped into the long-running sitcom *Amos 'n' Andy*. |
| 100 | 13 Jan 1926 | Birth of Michael Bond, British children's writer who created the characters Paddington Bear and Monsieur Pamplemousse. (Died 2017.) |
| 100 | 14 Jan 1926 | Birth of Warren Mitchell, British radio, television, stage and film actor. Best known for his role as Alf Garnett in the TV sitcoms *Till Death Us Do Part* and *In Sickness and in Health*. (Died 2015.) |
| 100 | 14 Jan 1926 | Birth of Tom Tryon, American stage, film and television actor and novelist. Best known for his roles in the films *The Cardinal*, *The Longest Day* and *In Harm's Way*, and for the TV series *Texas John Slaughter*. (Died 1991.) |
| 100 | 17 Jan 1926 | Birth of Moira Shearer, Scottish ballet dancer and actress. Best known for her roles in the films *The Red Shoes* and *Peeping Tom*. (Died 2006.) |
| 100 | 17 Jan 1926 | Birth of Clyde Walcott, West Indian cricketer and cricket administrator. Regarded as the best batsman in the world in the mid-1950s. He later became the first non-English chairman of the International Cricket Council. (Died 2006.) |
| 100 | 20 Jan 1926 | Birth of Patricia Neal, American stage, film and television actress Best known for her roles in the films *The Day the Earth Stood Still*, *A Face in the Crowd*, *Breakfast at Tiffany's* and *Hud*. (Died 2010.) |
| 100 | 21 Jan 1926 | Death of Camillo Golgi, Italian biologist and pathologist. Joint winner of the 1906 Nobel Prize in Physiology or Medicine for his work on the structure of the nervous system. Several structures in the human body are named in his honour. |

## JANUARY 2026

| Ann. | Date | Event |
|------|------|-------|
| 100 | 26 Jan 1926 | Scottish engineer and inventor John Logie Baird gave the first demonstration of his television system to members of the Royal Institution and a reporter from *The Times* newspaper, at his laboratory in London. |
| 100 | 29 Jan 1926 | Violette Anderson became the first African American woman to practice law before the U.S. Supreme Court. |
| 90 | 4 Jan 1936 | *Billboard* magazine published the first music hit parade in the USA. |
| 90 | 6 Jan 1936 | Barbara Hanley became mayor of Webwood, Ontario, Canada. She was the first woman in Canada to be elected mayor. |
| 90 | 8 Jan 1936 | The Shah of Iran issued the Kashf-e hijab decree, which banned the wearing of Islamic veils in public. Iranians were encouraged to adopt European dress. |
| 90 | 9 Jan 1936 | The U.S. Army adopted the M1 Garand semi-automatic rifle as its standard service rifle (until 1958). Most Army units did not receive theirs until September 1937 because of production delays. It was widely used in WWII, and more than five million were produced. |
| 90 | 10 Jan 1936 | Birth of Stephen Ambrose, American biographer and historian. Best known for his biographies of U.S. Presidents Eisenhower and Nixon. (Died 2002.) |
| 90 | 15 Jan 1936 | The Ford Foundation, a charitable organisation, was established in the USA by Edsel Ford, the President of the Ford Motor Company, and his father, Henry Ford. The foundation aims to advance human achievement, reduce poverty and injustice, strengthen democratic values, and promote international cooperation. |
| 90 | 15 Jan 1936 | The first building to be made entirely from glass blocks was completed: the Owens–Illinois Glass Company's Research Laboratory in Toledo, Ohio, USA. It was built using the company's own *Insulux* blocks. |
| 90 | 16 Jan 1936 | Death of Albert Fish, American serial killer, kidnapper, rapist, child molester and cannibal. One of the most notorious murderers in U.S. history. He was convicted of killing three children, but is suspected of killing more. (Executed.) |
| 90 | 18 Jan 1936 | Death of Rudyard Kipling, British writer and poet (*The Jungle Book, Kim, If* and many more). Winner of the 1907 Nobel Prize in Literature. |
| 90 | 19 Jan 1936 | Birth of Ziaur Rahman, President of Bangladesh (1976–81 – assassinated). |
| 90 | 20 Jan 1936 | Death of King George V of the United Kingdom. Succeeded by his son Edward VIII, who abdicated in December. |
| 90 | 22 Jan 1936 | Birth of Ong Teng Cheong, the first directly elected President of Singapore (1993–99). (Died 2002.) |
| 90 | 24 Jan 1936 | Albert Sarraut became Prime Minister of France (until June) following Pierre Laval's resignation over the Abyssinia crisis. |
| 90 | 27 Jan 1936 | Birth of Troy Donahue, American actor. A teen idol of the 1950s and 60s. (Died 2001.) |

## JANUARY 2026

| Ann. | Date | Event |
|------|------|-------|
| 90 | 29 Jan 1936 | The first inductees into the Baseball Hall of Fame were announced: Ty Cobb, Walter Johnson, Christy Mathewson, Babe Ruth, and Honus Wagner. (The Hall of Fame opened in 1939.) |
| 90 | 29 Jan 1936 | Birth of Patrick Caulfield, British Pop Art artist and printmaker. (Died 2005.) |
| 90 | 29 Jan 1936 | Birth of James Jamerson, American bass guitarist who played on most of the Motown hits of the 1960s and early 70s. (Died 1983.) |
| 90 | 31 Jan 1936 | *The Green Hornet* radio show was first broadcast on WXYZ in Detroit, USA. From April 1938 it was broadcast on the Mutual Broadcasting System network, and later on NBC and ABC. It ran until 1952. It also spawned a film series, feature film, TV series and comic book series. |
| 80 | 1 Jan 1946 | The first civil flight took off from London's Heathrow Airport, heading to Buenos Aires, Argentina. |
| 80 | 1 Jan 1946 | Emperor Hirohito of Japan released the Imperial Rescript, declaring that he was not a living god. |
| 80 | 2 Jan 1946 | King Zog I of Albania abdicated as he was unable to resume the throne following WWII. He had been in exile in the UK since 1939.<br>Prime Minister Enver Hoxha declared Albania a republic on 11th January. |
| 80 | 3 Jan 1946 | Death of William Joyce, ('Lord Haw-Haw'), British fascist politician who broadcasted Nazi propaganda from Germany during WWII. (Hanged for treason.) |
| 80 | 4 Jan 1946 | Death of George Woolf, Canadian jockey. Best known for riding the Thoroughbred champion Seabiscuit to several victories in 1938.<br>(Fell from a horse during a race, aged 35.)<br>The annual George Woolf Memorial Jockey Award was created in his honour. |
| 80 | 6 Jan 1946 | The first general election was held in North Vietnam, to elect members of the National Assembly. The communist-led Việt Minh won the most seats. The National Assembly held its first session on 2nd March. |
| 80 | 6 Jan 1946 | Birth of Syd Barrett, British rock singer, guitarist and songwriter (Pink Floyd). Noted for his secluded lifestyle and drug abuse. (Died 2006.) |
| 80 | 7 Jan 1946 | Suzanne Degnan, aged six, was kidnapped from her home in Chicago, Illinois, USA. A ransom note demanded $20,000 for her return.<br>Her dismembered body was found nearby shortly afterwards.<br>William Heirens confessed to killing her and two others, and was sentenced to life imprisonment. He later withdrew his confession and said he was a victim of police brutality and coercive investigation.<br>(He died in prison in 2012.) |
| 80 | 8 Jan 1946 | American singer Elvis Presley received his first guitar for his 11th birthday. (Apparently he would have preferred a bicycle or a rifle.) |
| 80 | 10 Jan 1946 | The United Nations General Assembly convened for the first time, in Westminster Central Hall, London, UK. (See also: 17th January 1946.) |
| 80 | 10 Jan 1946 | Project Diana: The U.S. Army Signal Corps successfully bounced radar signals off the Moon and received the reflected signals. |

## JANUARY 2026

| Ann. | Date | Event |
|------|------|-------|
| 80 | 11 Jan 1946 | Following King Zog I of Albania's abdication (see 2nd January 1946) Prime Minister Enver Hoxha declared the People's Republic of Albania with himself as leader/dictator. |
| 80 | 14 Jan 1946 | Birth of Harold Shipman, British doctor who was one of the most prolific serial killers in history. Estimated to have killed 250 people. (Died 2004.) |
| 80 | 17 Jan 1946 | The United Nations Security Council met for the first time, in London. On 24th January it passed its first resolution, establishing the United Nations Atomic Energy Commission. |
| 80 | 19 Jan 1946 | U.S. General Douglas MacArthur ordered the establishment of the International Military Tribunal for the Far East to try Japanese war criminals following WWII. It convened for the first time on 29th April. |
| 80 | 21 Jan 1946 | The first episode of the detective drama radio series *The Fat Man* was broadcast on ABC in the USA. It ran until 1951. It was adapted into a film of the same name in 1951. |
| 80 | 21 Jan 1946 | Birth of Johnny Oates, American baseball player, coach and manager. Best known for managing the Texas Rangers (1995–2001). (Died 2004.) |
| 80 | 22 Jan 1946 | U.S. President Harry S. Truman created the Central Intelligence Group. The interim authority was the direct predecessor of the Central Intelligence Agency (CIA) and was disestablished in September 1947. |
| 80 | 22 Jan 1946 | Birth of Malcolm McLaren, British rock/punk impresario, singer and businessman. Best known as the manager/promoter of the Sex Pistols and the New York Dolls, and for popularising punk and hip-hop. (Died 2010.) |
| 80 | 24 Jan 1946 | The United Nations Atomic Energy Commission was established. |
| 80 | 26 Jan 1946 | Félix Gouin became President of the Provisional Government of France (for six months). |
| 80 | 28 Jan 1946 | Canada's most famous ship, *Bluenose* (a racing and fishing schooner) struck a reef off Haiti, and was abandoned. It later broke apart. It was regarded as an important symbol of Canada, and was an icon for Nova Scotia. |
| 80 | 31 Jan 1946 | The Socialist Federal Republic of Yugoslavia was established, based on the model of the Soviet Union. It was comprised of six constituent republics: Bosnia-Herzegovina, Croatia, Macedonia, Montenegro, Serbia, and Slovenia. It was dissolved in 1992. |
| 80 | 31 Jan 1946 | Birth of Terry Kath, American rock singer, guitarist and songwriter (Chicago). (Died 1978.) |
| 75 | 1 Jan 1951 | Phonevision, the first pay television service in the USA, was launched by the Zenith Radio Corporation in Chicago, Illinois. Three hundred subscribers could order Hollywood films over the phone, then watch them for $1 each using a de-scrambling device connected to their televisions. The service was not financially sustainable, and was discontinued when the three-month trial ended. |
| 75 | 4 Jan 1951 | Korean War: North Korean and Chinese forces captured Seoul, the capital of South Korea. |

## JANUARY 2026

| Ann. | Date | Event |
|---|---|---|
| 75 | 6 Jan 1951 to 8th | The Ganghwa massacre, South Korea.<br>South Korean police and militiamen killed between 212 and 1,300 unarmed civilians. They were accused of being communist sympathisers who collaborated with the Korean People's Army of North Korea. |
| 75 | 9 Jan 1951 | The United Nations headquarters in New York City, USA was officially opened. |
| 75 | 9 Jan 1951 | The beginning of the jet age – the world's first passenger jet flight.<br>A U.S. de Havilland Comet flew from Chicago, Illinois to New York City. The Comet officially entered service with BOAC (now British Airways) on 2nd May 1952. |
| 75 | 10 Jan 1951 | Death of Sinclair Lewis, American novelist, short story writer and playwright. Winner of the 1930 Nobel Prize in Literature. |
| 75 | 11 Jan 1951 | The USA established the Nevada Test Site (now the Nevada National Security Site) for testing nuclear devices.<br>The first test was carried out on 27th January when a 1-kiloton bomb was dropped on Frenchman Flat, a dry lake bed. |
| 75 | 12 Jan 1951 | The Convention on the Prevention and Punishment of the Crime of Genocide (the Genocide Convention) came into effect. |
| 75 | 12 Jan 1951 | The first X-rated (adults only) film was screened in the UK:<br>*La Vie Commence Demain* (Life Begins Tomorrow) at the Regent Street Cinema in London. |
| 75 | 13 Jan 1951 to 17th | First Indochina War – the Battle of Vinh Yên.<br>French Union forces secured their first major victory of the war. |
| 75 | 14 Jan 1951 | The first National Football League (NFL) Pro Bowl game was played, in Los Angeles, California, USA. |
| 75 | 15 Jan 1951 | Ilse Koch, wife of Nazi concentration camp commandant Karl-Otto Koch, was sentenced to life imprisonment for her extreme cruelty against prisoners during WWII. She was known by various nicknames, including the Bitch/Witch of Buchenwald. She hanged herself in prison in 1967. |
| 75 | 17 Jan 1951 | The Beveridge Committee report on radio and television broadcasting in the UK was published. It led to an expansion of television broadcasting and the further development of regional broadcasting. |
| 75 | 18 Jan 1951 | Mount Lamington volcano in Papua New Guinea erupted.<br>About 3,000 people were killed. |
| 75 | 22 Jan 1951 | Death of Karl Nessler, German-born American hairdresser who invented the permanent wave (perm). |
| 75 | 25 Jan 1951 | Birth of Steve Prefontaine, American long-distance runner.<br>He helped to inspire the 1970s running boom.<br>(Killed in a car crash in 1975, aged 24.) |
| 75 | 27 Jan 1951 | Nuclear testing began at the Nevada Test Site in the USA.<br>The first test was Operation Ranger (the USA's fourth series of nuclear tests) which comprised of five bombs dropped between 27th January and 6th February. 928 nuclear tests have been carried out at the site since testing began there. |

# JANUARY 2026

| Ann. | Date | Event |
|---|---|---|
| 75 | 27 Jan 1951 | Death of Carl Gustaf Mannerheim, President of Finland (1944–46). |
| 75 | 29 Jan 1951 | British-American film actress Elizabeth Taylor was granted the first of her eight divorces (from Conrad Hilton Jr.). |
| 75 | 30 Jan 1951 | Birth of Bobby Stokes, British football player (Southampton, Portsmouth). (Died 1995.) |
| 75 | 30 Jan 1951 | Death of Ferdinand Porsche, Austrian automotive engineer who designed the Volkswagen Beetle and the Tiger tank and founded the Porsche sports car company. |
| 70 | 1 Jan 1956 | Sudan gained its independence from the United Kingdom and Egypt. |
| 70 | 1 Jan 1956 | Birth of Mark Reynolds Hughes, American entrepreneur. Founder of Herbalife. (Died 2000.) |
| 70 | 3 Jan 1956 | The top of the Eiffel Tower in Paris, France was damaged by a fire in the television transmitter. It took a year to repair it. |
| 70 | 3 Jan 1956 | Death of Joseph Wirth, Chancellor of Germany (1921–22). |
| 70 | 5 Jan 1956 | Death of Mistinguett, French singer and entertainer. The world's highest-paid female entertainer. Noted for her beautiful legs and lively stage persona. |
| 70 | 8 Jan 1956 | Operation Auca: five American Evangelical Christian missionaries were killed by members of the savage and isolated Huaorani tribe in Ecuador. The missionaries were attempting to bring Christianity to the Huaorani people, and had spent several months dropping gifts from an aircraft. They established a camp a few miles from the Huaorani's settlements on 6th January, and were killed within two days. |
| 70 | 9 Jan 1956 | The first *Dear Abby* advice column appeared in the *San Francisco Chronicle* in the USA. It is now syndicated to about 1,400 newspapers worldwide. |
| 70 | 18 Jan 1956 | Death of Konstantin Päts, first President of Estonia (1938–40). |
| 70 | 22 Jan 1956 | The Redondo Junction train wreck, Los Angeles, California, USA. A passenger train on the Santa Fe Railroad derailed at a junction while travelling at excessive speed. The two carriages tipped over on their sides. 30 people were killed and 117 injured. |
| 70 | 22 Jan 1956 | The first episode of the Western radio series *Fort Laramie* was broadcast on CBS in the USA. It ran for 41 episodes until October. |
| 70 | 23 Jan 1956 | The city of Cleveland in Ohio, USA banned children under the age of eighteen from dancing in public unless they were accompanied by an adult. The law aimed to suppress the growth of rock and roll music. |
| 70 | 23 Jan 1956 | Death of Sir Alexander Korda, Hungarian-born British film director and producer. Founder of London Films. Owner of British Lion Films. |
| 70 | 26 Jan 1956 to 5 Feb | The 1956 Winter Olympics were held in Cortina d'Ampezzo, Italy. |
| 70 | 27 Jan 1956 | Elvis Presley's song *Heartbreak Hotel* was released. It topped the U.S. *Billboard* chart in April and became his first record to sell over 1 million copies. It also became his first UK hit in May. |

## JANUARY 2026

| Ann. | Date | Event |
|------|------|-------|
| 70 | 27 Jan 1956 | The first episode of the radio anthology series *CBS Radio Workshop* was broadcast in the USA. It featured Aldous Huxley reading *Brave New World*. The series ran until September 1957 and featured some of the biggest names in science fiction. It paved the way for other science fiction radio and television series such as *The Twilight Zone*. |
| 70 | 28 Jan 1956 | Elvis Presley made his first appearance on national television in the USA, on the Dorsey Brothers' variety show *Stage Show*. |
| 70 | 29 Jan 1956 | Death of H. L. Mencken, American journalist, essayist, satirist, critic and magazine editor. The most influential American literary critic of the 1920s. |
| 70 | 30 Jan 1956 | During the Montgomery bus boycott in Alabama, USA, civil rights leader Martin Luther King Jr.'s home was bombed by a white supremacist. No one was injured, but it outraged the community. |
| 70 | 31 Jan 1956 | Juscelino Kubitschek became President of Brazil (until 1961). |
| 70 | 31 Jan 1956 | Death of A. A. Milne, British writer, poet, humourist and playwright. Best known for his children's stories about *Winnie the Pooh*. |
| 65 | 3 Jan 1961 | The first nuclear power plant fatalities in the USA. The U.S. Army's experimental Stationary Low-Power Reactor Number One (SL-1) in Idaho underwent a steam explosion and meltdown, killing three men. (Cause: the central control rod was withdrawn too far – reason unknown, possible murder, suicide, sabotage or accident.) |
| 65 | 4 Jan 1961 | Death of Erwin Schrödinger, Austrian physicist. He made numerous contributions to physics, and is best known for his 'Schrödinger's cat' thought experiment. Winner of the 1933 Nobel Prize in Physics. |
| 65 | 5 Jan 1961 | The first episode of the television sitcom *Mister Ed* was broadcast in the USA. It aired in syndication until July, and was then broadcast on CBS from 1st October. It ran for six seasons until 1966. |
| 65 | 7 Jan 1961 | British security services arrested the five core members of the Portland Spy Ring in London. The spies had been leaking information to the Soviet Union since the late 1950s. They received prison sentences ranging from fifteen to twenty years. Their story has been adapted into a film, stage play, television drama, radio play, and a novel. |
| 65 | 8 Jan 1961 | In a referendum, the citizens of France voted in favour of granting Algeria its independence. Algeria gained its independence from France in July 1962. |
| 65 | 10 Jan 1961 | Death of Dashiell Hammett, American novelist, short story writer, screenwriter and activist. Known for his hard-boiled detective stories. Creator of Sam Spade. Best known for *The Maltese Falcon*, *The Thin Man* and *Red Harvest*. |
| 65 | 15 Jan 1961 | The Supremes (then known as the Primettes) were signed to Motown Records. A condition of signing was that they changed their name. |
| 65 | 17 Jan 1961 | U.S. President Dwight D. Eisenhower gave his farewell address, three days before leaving office. He warned the nation to guard against the military-industrial complex, and warned of the dangers of massive spending. |

## JANUARY 2026

| Ann. | Date | Event |
|------|------|-------|
| 65 | 17 Jan 1961 | Death of Patrice Lumumba, first Prime Minister of the Democratic Republic of the Congo. (Assassinated by state authorities.) |
| 65 | 20 Jan 1961 | John F. Kennedy was inaugurated as the 35th President of the United States. |
| 65 | 20 Jan 1961 | American actress Marilyn Monroe travelled to Mexico, where she was granted a divorce from her third husband, the playwright Arthur Miller. It was much easier to obtain a divorce in Mexico than in the USA, and she chose this date because the media was focused on John F. Kennedy's inauguration as U.S. President. |
| 65 | 23 Jan 1961 | Portuguese terrorists hijacked the cruise ship *Santa Maria*. They planned to sail it to Angola and establish a renegade Portuguese government in opposition to the official one. Their leader, Henrique Galvão, released the hostages after being offered political asylum in Brazil. |
| 65 | 24 Jan 1961 | Goldsboro B-52 crash, North Carolina, USA. A U.S. Air Force bomber broke up in mid-air while carrying two nuclear bombs. Three of the eight crew were killed. Neither bomb detonated, though it was later revealed that one of them almost did. |
| 65 | 24 Jan 1961 | Death of Alfred Carlton Gilbert, American athlete, inventor, toy-maker and businessman. Inventor of the Erector Set. Founder of the A. C. Gilbert Company. Gold medallist in the 1908 Olympics (pole vault). |
| 65 | 25 Jan 1961 | U.S. President John F. Kennedy gave the first live televised presidential news conference. |
| 65 | 25 Jan 1961 | Walt Disney's animated film *101 Dalmatians* was released in the USA. UK: 25th July. |
| 65 | 31 Jan 1961 | Project Mercury: Mercury-Redstone 2: Ham the Chimp became the first hominid to travel into space. He was launched by NASA to test its *Mercury* capsule, and returned to Earth safely after a sixteen-minute flight. |
| 65 | 31 Jan 1961 | The U.S. première of the Western drama film *The Misfits*. It was Clark Gable's and Marilyn Monroe's last completed film. Released: 1st February 1961. UK première: 8th April 1961. |
| 60 | 1 Jan 1966 | Jean-Bédel Bokassa became President of the Central African Republic after seizing power from David Dacko in a coup. He was also the self-proclaimed Emperor of Central Africa (1976–79), though this was not recognised internationally. |
| 60 | 1 Jan 1966 | The Federal Cigarette Labeling and Advertising Act came into effect in the USA. It established national standards for cigarette packaging and labelling, and forced manufacturers to include the statement 'Caution: cigarette smoking may be hazardous to your health' on packaging. |
| 60 | 1 Jan 1966 | Death of Vincent Auriol, President of France (1947–54) – the first president of the French Fourth Republic. |
| 60 | 2 Jan 1966 | Rio de Janeiro flood and landslides, Brazil. A massive storm hit the city and surrounding area, causing record rainfall. 250 people were killed, and a further 70 died from disease afterwards. |

## JANUARY 2026

| Ann. | Date | Event |
|------|------|-------|
| 60 | 3 Jan 1966 | The President of Upper Volta (now Burkina Faso), Maurice Yaméogo, was forced to resign following widespread protests over his single-party rule. He was succeeded by Sangoulé Lamizana, who led a provisional military government until a new constitution was approved in June 1970. |
| 60 | 7 Jan 1966 to 8th | The current world record for the most rain in 24 hours was set: 71.9 inches (1,825 mm) at Foc-Foc, Réunion, Indian Ocean, during tropical cyclone Denise. The current record for the most rain in 12 hours was also set. |
| 60 | 7 Jan 1966 | Birth of Carolyn Bessette-Kennedy, American publicist. Wife of John F. Kennedy Jr. (They were both killed in a plane crash in 1999.) |
| 60 | 8 Jan 1966 to 14th | Vietnam War – Operation Crimp (the Battle of the Ho Bo Woods). U.S. and Australian forces targeted a key Viet Cong headquarters, believed to be concealed underground. U.S.–Australian tactical victory. |
| 60 | 10 Jan 1966 | The Tashkent Declaration was signed by India and Pakistan. The peace agreement marked the official end of the Indo–Pakistan War of 1965 (also called the Second Kashmir War). |
| 60 | 11 Jan 1966 | The first episode of the African-based children's drama TV series *Daktari* was broadcast on CBS in the USA. It ran for four seasons until 1969. |
| 60 | 11 Jan 1966 | Death of Alberto Giacometti, Swiss sculptor and artist. Noted for his attenuated, isolated figures. |
| 60 | 11 Jan 1966 | Death of Hannes Kolehmainen, Finnish long-distance runner. The first of the 'Flying Finns'. Gold medallist in the 5,000 m, 10,000 m and cross-country at the 1912 Olympics. The Olympic marathon winner in 1920. |
| 60 | 12 Jan 1966 | Vietnam War: in his State of the Union address, U.S. President Lyndon B. Johnson said U.S. forces should continue fighting in Vietnam until communist aggression there was ended. |
| 60 | 12 Jan 1966 | The first episode of the television series *Batman* was broadcast on ABC in the USA. It ran for three seasons until 1968. |
| 60 | 14 Jan 1966 | David Bowie's first single, *Can't Help Thinking About Me*, was released. The song failed to chart. His first hit was *Space Oddity* in 1969. (He had released previous singles in 1964 and 1965 as Davy/Davie Jones.) |
| 60 | 14 Jan 1966 | Death of Bill Carr, American athlete. Gold medallist in the 400 m and 4 x 400 m relay at the 1932 Olympics. |
| 60 | 14 Jan 1966 | Death of Sergei Korolev, Soviet rocket engineer and spacecraft designer. Considered the father of practical astronautics. |
| 60 | 15 Jan 1966 | The Prime Minister of Nigeria, Abubakar Tafawa Balewa, was overthrown and executed in a military coup. He was succeeded (as Head of the Federal Military Government) by Major General Johnson Aguiyi-Ironsi. |
| 60 | 17 Jan 1966 | The Palomares Incident, Spain. A U.S. Air Force B-52 bomber carrying four hydrogen bombs collided with a Boeing Stratotanker over the Mediterranean Sea. The Stratotanker exploded, killing all four crew. Three of the B-52's seven crew were killed. Three of the bombs landed near Palomares and were recovered – the non-nuclear explosives in two of them had detonated, contaminating the area with plutonium. The fourth bomb was recovered safely on 7th April. |

## JANUARY 2026

| Ann. | Date | Event |
|------|------|-------|
| 60 | 17 Jan 1966 | The album *Sounds of Silence* by Simon and Garfunkel was released. |
| 60 | 18 Jan 1966 | Robert C. Weaver became the USA's first Secretary of Housing and Urban Development (until December 1968). <br> He was the first African American appointed to the U.S. Cabinet. |
| 60 | 20 Jan 1966 | The song *The Ballad of the Green Berets* by Staff Sergeant Barry Sadler was released. It became an international hit in March. |
| 60 | 24 Jan 1966 | Air India Flight 101 crash, Mont Blanc, France. <br> The plane was flying from Mumbai, India to London, UK. <br> It flew into the mountain after the pilot misunderstood an instruction from the radar operator. All 117 passengers and eleven crew were killed. |
| 60 | 24 Jan 1966 | Indira Gandhi became Prime Minister of India for the first time (until 1977). (She was Prime Minister again from 1980 until her assassination in 1984.) |
| 60 | 27 Jan 1966 to 29th | North American blizzard of 1966. <br> The blizzard swept across the USA and Canada bringing record low temperatures, heavy snow and high winds. <br> At least 201 people were killed, either directly from the storm or from heart attacks while clearing snow or pushing cars, or in traffic accidents. |
| 60 | 29 Jan 1966 | The musical *Sweet Charity* opened on Broadway. |
| 60 | 31 Jan 1966 | The Soviet Union launched its spacecraft *Luna 9* to the Moon. <br> On 3rd February it became the first spacecraft to achieve a soft landing on another planetary body, and the first to send back photos from the surface of another planetary body. |
| 50 | 1 Jan 1976 | Middle East Airlines Flight 438 was destroyed by a terrorist bomb over Saudi Arabia while flying from Beirut, Lebanon to Muscat, Oman. <br> All 66 passengers and fifteen crew were killed. <br> The perpetrators were never identified. |
| 50 | 1 Jan 1976 | Venezuela nationalised its oil industry. <br> All foreign oil companies were replaced by Venezuelan ones, and the state-owned petroleum company Petróleos de Venezuela was established. |
| 50 | 1 Jan 1976 | The United Nations Centre Against Apartheid was established. |
| 50 | 2 Jan 1976 to 5th | The Gale of January 1976 (also known as the Capella storm) caused widespread flooding and wind damage in western and central Europe. <br> Between 82 and 100 people were killed (24 in the UK) and it caused £1 billion ($1.3 billion) in damage. |
| 50 | 3 Jan 1976 | The International Covenant on Economic, Social and Cultural Rights came into effect. |
| 50 | 4 Jan 1976 | The Troubles in Northern Ireland – the Reavey and O'Dowd killings, County Armagh. Six unarmed Catholic civilians were shot dead by members of the Ulster Volunteer Force (UVF). <br> This led to a revenge attack (the Kingsmill massacre) on 5th January. |
| 50 | 5 Jan 1976 | The Troubles in Northern Ireland – the Kingsmill massacre, County Armagh. Ten Protestant workmen travelling in a minibus were shot dead by members of the South Armagh Republican Action Force in revenge for the Reavey and O'Dowd killings the previous day (see 4th January 1976). |

## JANUARY 2026

| Ann. | Date | Event |
|---|---|---|
| 50 | 5 Jan 1976 | Pol Pot's communist Khmer Rouge regime in Cambodia proclaimed a new constitution and renamed the country Democratic Kampuchea.<br>The regime collapsed in 1979 and the country was renamed the People's Republic of Kampuchea until May 1989 when it became the State of Cambodia. |
| 50 | 5 Jan 1976 | A nationwide television service was launched in South Africa.<br>It was a colour service from the outset, though there was only one channel. A second channel was launched in 1981. |
| 50 | 5 Jan 1976 | Death of John A. Costello, Taoiseach of Ireland (1948–51, 1954–57). |
| 50 | 5 Jan 1976 | Death of Georges Migot, French composer, poet and artist. |
| 50 | 8 Jan 1976 | Death of Zhou Enlai, the first Premier of China (1949–76). |
| 50 | 10 Jan 1976 | Death of Howlin' Wolf, American Chicago Blues singer, guitarist, harmonica player and composer. |
| 50 | 11 Jan 1976 | The Acting President of Ecuador, Guillermo Lara, was ousted in a military coup and succeeded by Interim President Alfredo Poveda (until 1979). |
| 50 | 11 Jan 1976 | Stephen Sondheim's musical *Pacific Overtures* opened on Broadway. |
| 50 | 12 Jan 1976 | Death of Dame Agatha Christie, British crime novelist, short story writer and playwright. Best known for creating the characters Hercule Poirot and Miss Marple, and for the world's longest-running play *The Mousetrap*. |
| 50 | 13 Jan 1976 | American inventor Raymond Kurzweil unveiled the Kurzweil Reading Machine – a flatbed scanner that could read pages of text out loud in a synthesised voice. It enabled blind people to understand written text. |
| 50 | 13 Jan 1976 | Death of Margaret Leighton, British stage, film and television actress. |
| 50 | 14 Jan 1976 | The first episode of the science fiction television series *The Bionic Woman* was broadcast on ABC in the USA. It was a spin-off show from *The Six Million Dollar Man* and ran for three seasons. |
| 50 | 18 Jan 1976 | The Scottish Labour Party was formed, as a breakaway party from the UK Labour Party. It was dissolved in 1979. |
| 50 | 19 Jan 1976 to 9 Feb | Swine flu outbreak, Fort Dix, New Jersey, USA.<br>One person died and thirteen were hospitalised.<br>The outbreak prompted a mass immunisation programme in the USA.<br>There were multiple reports of side-effects from the immunisation.<br>500 people may have contracted Guillain–Barré syndrome, which can cause paralysis, and 25 of them died. |
| 50 | 19 Jan 1976 | The U.S. Food and Drug Administration (FDA) banned the food colouring Red Dye No. 2 (amaranth), which had been in use for over 100 years.<br>There were fears it could cause cancer in high doses.<br>Red Dye No. 4 was also banned shortly afterwards.<br>As a result, certain products became unavailable for several years, including red M&M candies.<br>The dyes remained legal in other countries, including the UK. |
| 50 | 21 Jan 1976 | The supersonic airliner Concorde went into commercial service in Britain and France, with simultaneous take-offs from London to Bahrain and Paris to Rio de Janeiro. |

## JANUARY 2026

| Ann. | Date | Event |
|------|------|-------|
| 50 | 23 Jan 1976 | The first episode of the television variety series *Donny & Marie* was broadcast on ABC in the USA. It was hosted by brother and sister pop singers Donny and Marie Osmond. It ran until 1979. |
| 50 | 23 Jan 1976 | Death of Paul Robeson, American actor, singer and civil rights activist. |
| 50 | 27 Jan 1976 | The first episode of the television sitcom *Laverne and Shirley* was broadcast on ABC in the USA. It was a spin-off from the sitcom *Happy Days*. It ran for eight seasons until 1983. |
| 50 | 29 Jan 1976 | Twelve small IRA bombs exploded in the West End of London during the night. One person was injured. |
| 50 | 29 Jan 1976 | A former male model, Norman Scott, claimed in court that he was the homosexual lover of British Liberal Party leader Jeremy Thorpe during the 1960s. The scandal lead to Thorpe resigning as party leader, losing his seat as a Member of Parliament (MP), and being charged with conspiracy to murder Scott. He was later acquitted, but his career was ruined. |
| 50 | 30 Jan 1976 | George H. W. Bush (later U.S. President) became the Director of Central Intelligence in the USA (until January 1977). |
| 50 | 31 Jan 1976 | Death of Ernesto Miranda, American labourer whose conviction for kidnapping, rape and armed robbery was reversed when it was revealed that he had been interrogated by police and signed a confession without being told he had the right to remain silent or to have a lawyer present. This landmark case led to the police having to give 'Miranda warnings' to everyone they arrested, to inform them of their rights. |
| 40 | 1 Jan 1986 | Portugal and Spain joined the European Union. |
| 40 | 1 Jan 1986 | Aruba became autonomous from the Netherlands Antilles, though it remained part of the Kingdom of the Netherlands. |
| 40 | 2 Jan 1986 | Death of Bill Veeck, American baseball executive and promoter. Particularly noted for his publicity stunts. |
| 40 | 4 Jan 1986 | Death of Christopher Isherwood, British-born American novelist. |
| 40 | 4 Jan 1986 | Death of Phil Lynott, British-born Irish rock singer and musician (Thin Lizzy). (Alcohol- and drug-related septicaemia, pneumonia and heart failure, aged 36.) |
| 40 | 7 Jan 1986 | The USA imposed economic sanctions against Libya, banning all trade, commercial contracts, and travel. The sanctions were lifted in 2004. |
| 40 | 7 Jan 1986 | Death of Juan Rulfo, Mexican novelist, short story writer and photographer. Considered one of Latin America's finest writers. |
| 40 | 8 Jan 1986 | *The Hacker Manifesto* (also known as *The Conscience of a Hacker*) was published. |
| 40 | 9 Jan 1986 | Britain's Defence Secretary Michael Heseltine resigned from the Cabinet following a row with Prime Minister Margaret Thatcher over the Westland helicopter affair. The Trade and Industry Secretary, Leon Brittan, also resigned on 24th January. |
| 40 | 9 Jan 1986 | Kodak ceased making instant cameras and film after losing a patent battle with Polaroid. |

## JANUARY 2026

| Ann. | Date | Event |
|------|------|-------|
| 40 | 11 Jan 1986 | The Gateway Bridge in Brisbane, Australia was officially opened. |
| 40 | 13 Jan 1986 to 24th | South Yemen Civil War.<br>An ideological/tribal dispute between two factions of the ruling Yemeni Socialist Party developed into an attempted coup and then a full-scale civil war. Thousands of people were killed, including former president Abdel Fattah Ismail.<br>President Ali Nasir Muhammad was deposed on 24th January and fled to North Yemen. He was succeeded by Haidar Abu Bakr al-Attas (as Chairman of the Presidium of the Supreme People's Council)<br>The war led to the unification of North and South Yemen in 1990. |
| 40 | 14 Jan 1986 | Vinicio Cerezo became President of Guatemala (until 1991). |
| 40 | 14 Jan 1986 | Death of Donna Reed, American film and television actress. |
| 40 | 15 Jan 1986 | The National Center for Supercomputing Applications (NCSA) opened at the University of Illinois at Urbana-Champaign. It provided high-performance computing resources to researchers across the USA. |
| 40 | 16 Jan 1986 | The Internet Engineering Task Force (IETF) was established.<br>It creates voluntary standards to maintain and improve the usability and interoperability of the internet. |
| 40 | 18 Jan 1986 | The soft rock song *These Dreams* by Heart was released. |
| 40 | 19 Jan 1986 | The first computer virus to affect IBM-compatible personal computers appeared. The virus, called (c) Brain, was created by two brothers from Pakistan, and spread via infected floppy disks.<br>The very first computer virus was Creeper, which appeared in 1971 and infected DEC PDP-10 mainframe computers.<br>The first virus to infect personal computers was Elk Cloner which appeared in 1982 and infected Apple II computers. |
| 40 | 20 Jan 1986 | Military coup in Lesotho. Prime Minister Leabua Jonathan was ousted and replaced by Justin Lekhanya as Chairman of the Military Council and Minister of Defence. He remained in office until 1991. |
| 40 | 20 Jan 1986 | Martin Luther King Day was celebrated as a federal holiday in the USA for the first time. |
| 40 | 23 Jan 1986 | The first members were inducted into the Rock and Roll Hall of Fame: Chuck Berry, James Brown, Ray Charles, Fats Domino, The Everly Brothers, Buddy Holly, Jerry Lee Lewis, and Elvis Presley. |
| 40 | 24 Jan 1986 | The U.S. space probe *Voyager 2* made its closest approach to Uranus.<br>The images it sent back led to the discovery of ten new moons and several new rings. It was the first (and, so far, only) spacecraft to visit Uranus.<br>It also visited Neptune in August 1989. |
| 40 | 24 Jan 1986 to 5 Feb 1987 | The Wapping Dispute. Six thousands newspaper workers in London began a year-long strike against News International. There were several outbreaks of violence during the strike and over 1,000 arrests.<br>The strike ultimately failed, ending restrictive trade union practices in the British newspaper publishing industry. |

## JANUARY 2026

| Ann. | Date | Event |
|------|------|-------|
| 40 | 24 Jan 1986 | Death of L. Ron Hubbard, American science fiction writer who developed the Dianetics self-help system and founded the Scientology religion. |
| 40 | 24 Jan 1986 | Death of Gordon MacRae, American actor and singer. Best known for his roles in the Rodgers and Hammerstein musicals *Oklahoma!* and *Carousel*. |
| 40 | 26 Jan 1986 | Yoweri Museveni declared himself President of Uganda after his National Resistance Movement toppled Tito Okello's government.<br>He was sworn in on 29th January. He is still in office at the time of writing. |
| 40 | 27 Jan 1986 | Death of Lilli Palmer, German film and television actress.<br>Wife of the American actor Rex Harrison. |
| 40 | 28 Jan 1986 | The Space Shuttle *Challenger* disaster.<br>The U.S. space shuttle *Challenger* exploded shortly after lift-off from Cape Canaveral, Florida. All seven astronauts were killed, including the first teacher in space, Christa McAuliffe. |
| 40 | 29 Jan 1986 | The U.S. première of the teen comedy drama film *Pretty in Pink*.<br>Released: 28th February 1986. UK: 25th April 1986. |
| 40 | 29 Jan 1986 | Death of Leif Erickson, American actor. Best known for playing Big John Cannon in the Western television series *The High Chaparral*. |
| 40 | 31 Jan 1986 and 2 Feb | Liechtenstein general election.<br>The first election in Liechtenstein in which women were allowed to vote. |
| 30 | 2 Jan 1996 | The first convoy of U.S. peacekeeping troops arrived in Northern Bosnia following the end of the Bosnian War.<br>This was the USA's first military involvement in Europe since WWII. |
| 30 | 3 Jan 1996 | The Motorola StarTAC mobile phone was released.<br>It was one of the first clamshell flip phones, and one of the first mobile phones to gain mainstream popularity. |
| 30 | 6 Jan 1996 to 8th | North American blizzard. One of the largest blizzards in U.S. history paralysed the eastern states. More than 150 people were killed and it caused over $1 billion of damage. |
| 30 | 8 Jan 1996 | The deadliest plane crash in African history.<br>An overloaded Air Africa plane failed to take off from N'Dolo Airport in Kinshasa, Zaire (now the Democratic Republic of the Congo) and ploughed into a local street market. Between 225 and 348 people were killed and 500 were injured. Two of the plane's six crew were killed. |
| 30 | 8 Jan 1996 | Netgear, the computer networking equipment manufacturer, was founded in San Jose, California, USA. |
| 30 | 8 Jan 1996 | Death of François Mitterrand, President of France (1981–95). |
| 30 | 9 Jan 1996 to 18th | First Chechen War – the Kizlyar–Pervomayskoye hostage crisis.<br>Chechen separatist guerrillas attacked a military airbase near Kizlyar and took thousands of civilians hostage.<br>In the ensuing battle with Russian forces, the village of Pervomayskoye was completely destroyed by artillery fire. Chechen separatist victory. |
| 30 | 10 Jan 1996 | Following the signing of the Israel–Jordan peace treaty in 1994, King Hussein of Jordan made a historic first public visit to Tel Aviv in Israel. |

## JANUARY 2026

| Ann. | Date | Event |
|---|---|---|
| 30 | 12 Jan 1996 | The first Malaysian communications satellite *MEASAT-1* was launched. |
| 30 | 12 Jan 1996 | U.S. and Russian forces launched a peacekeeping mission in Bosnia – their first joint military operation since WWII. |
| 30 | 14 Jan 1996 | Álvaro Arzú became President of Guatemala (until 2000). |
| 30 | 15 Jan 1996 | Death of Minnesota Fats (Rudolf Wanderone), American pool player. |
| 30 | 15 Jan 1996 | Death of Moshoeshoe II, Paramount Chief (King) of Lesotho (1966–90, 1995–96). Succeeded by his son Letsie III. |
| 30 | 17 Jan 1996 | Death of Amber Hagerman, American child who was kidnapped and murdered, aged nine, leading to the introduction of the 'Amber Alert' child abduction alert system. |
| 30 | 19 Jan 1996 | North Cape oil spill, Rhode Island, USA. Approximately 828,000 gallons (3.1 million litres) of heating oil was spilled in Block Island Sound and the Trustom Pond National Wildlife Refuge when a barge ran aground. It was the first major oil spill in the USA since the 1990 Oil Pollution Act was passed. |
| 30 | 19 Jan 1996 | The overloaded Indonesian ferry *Gurita* tipped over and sank during a storm off the coast of Sumatra. Between 260 and 340 people were killed. |
| 30 | 20 Jan 1996 | The first Palestinian general election. Yasser Arafat was elected President of the Palestinian National Council in a landslide victory. |
| 30 | 20 Jan 1996 | Death of Gerry Mulligan, American jazz saxophonist, clarinetist, composer and arranger. He helped to popularise cool jazz. |
| 30 | 22 Jan 1996 | Bosnian War: a mass grave was discovered near Brcko, Bosnia that contained the bodies of nearly 3,000 victims of Serb ethnic cleansing. They had been killed in May – June 1992. |
| 30 | 24 Jan 1996 | Polish Prime Minister Jozef Oleksy resigned over alleged connections with the Soviet KGB. |
| 30 | 25 Jan 1996 | The Off-Broadway première of Jonathan Larson's musical *Rent*. Larson died suddenly the same day, but the performance went ahead with his parents' permission. The show opened on Broadway on 29th April. It was a rock musical update of Puccini's opera *La Bohème*. |
| 30 | 25 Jan 1996 | Death of Billy Bailey, American convicted murderer. The last person to be hanged in the USA. |
| 30 | 25 Jan 1996 | Death of Jonathan Larson, American composer and playwright. Best known for the Pulitzer Prize-winning rock musical *Rent*. |
| 30 | 26 Jan 1996 | Whitewater scandal: Hillary Clinton testified before a grand jury regarding her investments in the Whitewater Development Corporation. This was the first time in U.S. history that a First Lady had been subpoenaed to testify before a grand jury. |
| 30 | 26 Jan 1996 | Death of Dave Schultz, American Olympic and world champion freestyle wrestler. Olympic gold medallist 1984. (Shot dead by his team's sponsor, who was declared mentally ill.) |

## JANUARY 2026

| Ann. | Date | Event |
|------|------|-------|
| 30 | 27 Jan 1996 | The first democratically elected President of Niger, Mahamane Ousmane, was overthrown in a military coup. He was succeeded by Ibrahim Baré Maïnassara (who was overthrown and assassinated in April 1999). |
| 30 | 27 Jan 1996 | The first Holocaust Remembrance Day was observed in Germany. It became International Holocaust Remembrance Day in 2005 when it was adopted by the United Nations. It marks the day (27th January 1945) when the Auschwitz–Birkenau concentration/death camp was liberated during WWII. |
| 30 | 27 Jan 1996 | Surgeons in San Diego, California, USA separated conjoined twins Sarah and Sarahi Morales, who were joined at the chest and abdomen. Sarahi died shortly after the operation, but Sarah survived. |
| 30 | 28 Jan 1996 | Death of Joseph Brodsky, Russian-born American poet. Winner of the 1987 Nobel Prize in Literature. U.S. Poet Laureate (1991). |
| 30 | 28 Jan 1996 | Death of Jerry Siegel, American comic book writer. Co-creator of Superman. |
| 30 | 28 Jan 1996 | Death of San Yu, President of Burma (Myanmar) (1981–88). |
| 30 | 29 Jan 1996 | France announced that it would no longer test nuclear weapons. It carried out six tests (of a planned series of eight) at Moruroa Atoll and Fangataufa Atoll in the Pacific between September 1995 and January 1996, leading to international protests and boycotts of French products. |
| 30 | 29 Jan 1996 | La Fenice opera house in Venice, Italy was destroyed in an arson attack by two electricians. They were facing heavy fines over delays in repair work. Rebuilding began in 2001. The new opera house opened in December 2003. |
| 30 | 30 Jan 1996 | Death of Gino Gallagher, Chief of Staff of the Irish National Liberation Army. (Shot dead by a member of a rival political faction, aged 32.) |
| 30 | 31 Jan 1996 | Central Bank bombing, Colombo, Sri Lanka. A suicide bomber from the Tamil Tigers militant organisation crashed a truck full of explosives through the bank's main gate and detonated it. 91 people were killed and 1,400 injured. |
| 30 | 31 Jan 1996 | Comet Hyakutake was discovered by Yuji Hyakutake, a Japanese amateur astronomer. It made its closest approach to the Earth on 25th March and was easily visible to the naked eye, though only for a few days. |
| 25 | 1 Jan 2001 | Death of Ray Walston, American stage, film and television actor and comedian (*My Favorite Martian*, *South Pacific*, *Damn Yankees*, *The Sting*, *Fast Times at Ridgemont High*, *Of Mice and Men*, *Picket Fences*, and more). |
| 25 | 2 Jan 2001 | Sila María Calderón became the first female Governor of Puerto Rico. |
| 25 | 2 Jan 2001 | Death of William P. Rogers, U.S. Secretary of State (1969–73), U.S. Attorney General (1957–61). |
| 25 | 3 Jan 2001 | Former U.S. First Lady Hillary Rodham Clinton became the first female Senator from New York. She was the first former First Lady to be elected to public office. |
| 25 | 7 Jan 2001 | John Kufuor was inaugurated as President of Ghana (until 2009). It was the first peaceful transfer of power since Ghana gained its independence in 1957. |

**JANUARY 2026**

| Ann. | Date | Event |
|---|---|---|
| 25 | 7 Jan 2001 | The National Geographic television channel was launched in the USA. (UK: September 1997.) |
| 25 | 9 Jan 2001 | DNA analysis of Mungo Man (ancient human remains found in New South Wales, Australia) showed it was the earliest human specimen ever found in Australia. It challenged the theory that all modern humans evolved in Africa, as it appeared to have evolved from a separate genetic line. The findings are controversial as the remains were in poor condition and the indigenous people have refused to allow further testing. |
| 25 | 9 Jan 2001 | Apple launched iTunes, its digital media player/media management software. |
| 25 | 9 Jan 2001 | China launched its *Shenzhou 2* spacecraft on a mission to test its life-support systems. It carried a monkey, a dog and a rabbit, and several scientific experiments. The re-entry module returned to Earth after seven days in space, but its parachutes failed and it crashed in Inner Mongolia. |
| 25 | 11 Jan 2001 | AOL and Time Warner merged to form AOL Time Warner. The merger was not a success. AOL was dropped from the name in 2003, spun off as a separate company in 2009, and purchased by Verizon in 2015. Time Warner was renamed WarnerMedia in 2018. |
| 25 | 11 Jan 2001 | Scientists from the Oregon Health Sciences University in the USA announced that they had created a fluorescent monkey. The three-month-old rhesus monkey, named ANDi, was created by inserting a gene from a fluorescent jellyfish into an unfertilised monkey egg. The egg was then fertilised and allowed to develop. ANDi looked normal, but his skin and hair glowed green under fluorescent light. |
| 25 | 11 Jan 2001 | Death of Sir Denys Lasdun, British architect. Best known for designing the Royal National Theatre in London. |
| 25 | 11 Jan 2001 | Death of Michael Williams, British stage, film, television and radio actor. Best known for his role in the TV sitcom *A Fine Romance*, in which he starred with his real-life wife, Judi Dench. |
| 25 | 12 Jan 2001 | Swedish football manager Sven Goran Eriksson became the first non-Briton to coach the England national football team. |
| 25 | 12 Jan 2001 | Death of Affirmed, American Thoroughbred race horse. Winner of the 1978 Triple Crown. |
| 25 | 12 Jan 2001 | Death of Bill Hewlett, American engineer and businessman. Co-founder of Hewlett-Packard (HP). |
| 25 | 13 Jan 2001 | El Salvador earthquake and landslide. More than 800 people were killed. A second earthquake struck a month later. |
| 25 | 15 Jan 2001 | Wikipedia, the online collaborative encyclopaedia, was officially launched. |
| 25 | 16 Jan 2001 | The Ecuadoran oil tanker *MV Jessica* ran aground in the Galapagos Islands. Containment measures failed, and about 132,000 gallons of diesel and fuel oil spilled into the sea. It was one of the worst environmental disasters to affect the islands. |

# JANUARY 2026

| Ann. | Date | Event |
|------|------|-------|
| 25 | 15 Jan 2001 | U.S. President Bill Clinton awarded former President Theodore Roosevelt the Medal of Honor posthumously. The medal was awarded for Roosevelt's actions in the Battle of San Juan Hill in Cuba during the SpanishAmerican War. He is the only President to win a Medal of Honor. |
| 25 | 16 Jan 2001 | Death of Auberon Waugh, British journalist. Son of the novelist Evelyn Waugh. |
| 25 | 17 Jan 2001 | The report *Youth Violence: A Report of the Surgeon General* was published in the USA. It studied the signs, causes and effects of youth violence, and strategies for combatting it. The study was commissioned following the Columbine High School massacre in April 1999. |
| 25 | 17 Jan 2001 to 18th | The U.S. state of California instituted rolling blackouts to combat a shortage in the supply of electricity. It cut the supply to hundreds of thousands of domestic customers and businesses. The shortage was caused by droughts, delays in the approval of new power stations, and an 800 percent increase in the wholesale price of electricity due to market manipulation (by Enron). There were further blackouts in March and May. |
| 25 | 18 Jan 2001 | Death of Laurent Kabila, President of the Democratic Republic of the Congo (1997–2001). Assassinated by one of his bodyguards during an attempted coup. Succeeded by his son, Joseph Kabila. |
| 25 | 18 Jan 2001 | Death of Al Waxman, American stage, film, radio and television actor. Best known for his role as Lieutenant Samuels in the TV crime drama series *Cagney and Lacey*. |
| 25 | 19 Jan 2001 | The internet twins case. American twin baby girls were seized from a hotel in Wales and taken into care. They had been 'sold' by an adoption broker and adopted over the internet by a British couple, Alan and Judith Kilshaw. The couple became infamous after selling their story to a national newspaper. The twins were later returned to the USA after a judge ruled they were not safe in the couple's care. |
| 25 | 20 Jan 2001 | George W. Bush was inaugurated as the 43rd President of the USA. |
| 25 | 20 Jan 2001 | The Second EDSA Revolution, Philippines. The President of the Philippines, Joseph Estrada, was ousted after four days of mass protests over corruption. Vice-President Gloria Macapagal Arroyo was sworn in as his replacement. |
| 25 | 21 Jan 2001 to 23rd | Six members of the Texas Seven, who escaped from a maximum-security prison in Texas, USA in December 2000, were recaptured after being featured on the television show *America's Most Wanted*. The seventh member committed suicide before he could be arrested. The surviving six were sentenced to death for killing a police officer during a robbery they committed after they escaped. At the time of writing, four of them had been executed. |
| 25 | 22 Jan 2001 | The British government launched a campaign to convince parents that the triple Measles-Mumps-Rubella (MMR) vaccine was safe, after a flawed study suggested it could cause autism. Despite the campaign, uptake of the vaccine fell significantly over the following years. |

## JANUARY 2026

| Ann. | Date | Event |
|---|---|---|
| 25 | 24 Jan 2001 | Britain's Secretary of State for Northern Ireland, Peter Mandelson, was forced to resign from the government for a second time following accusations that he had used his position to influence a passport application. He had previously resigned from his roles as Secretary of State for Trade and Industry, and President of the Board of Trade, in December 1998 after failing to declare an interest-free home loan from fellow cabinet member, Geoffrey Robinson. |
| 25 | 26 Jan 2001 | Gujarat earthquake (also called the Bhuj earthquake), India and Pakistan. Up to 20,000 people were killed and 167,000 injured. 400,000 homes and buildings were destroyed, including the main hospital. |
| 25 | 31 Jan 2001 | A Scottish court in the Netherlands convicted Abdelbaset al-Megrahi of the bombing of Pan Am Flight 103 over Lockerbie, Scotland in 1988. He was the head of airport security for Libyan Arab Airlines and a suspected Libyan intelligence officer. He was sentenced to life imprisonment but was released on medical grounds in 2009 and died in 2012. A second Libyan was acquitted. |
| 20 | 1 Jan 2006 | The Pirate Party was founded as a political party in Sweden. It is currently the third-largest party in Sweden (by membership) and aims to reform copyright and patent laws. Other Pirate Parties have since been established in other countries. |
| 20 | 4 Jan 2006 | The Prime Minister of Israel, Ariel Sharon, suffered a stroke that left him in a persistent vegetative state until his death in 2014. He was succeeded by Ehud Olmert. |
| 20 | 4 Jan 2006 | Death of Sheikh Maktum ibn Rashid al-Maktum (also spelled Maktoum bin Rashid Al Maktoum), Emir of Dubai (1990–2006), Prime Minister of the United Arab Emirates (1971–79, 1990–2005) |
| 20 | 5 Jan 2006 | Death of Lord Merlyn-Rees, Welsh-born Labour politician. Secretary of State for Northern Ireland (1974–76), Home Secretary (1976–79). |
| 20 | 6 Jan 2006 | Death of Lou Rawls, American gospel/R&B/soul/jazz/blues singer, actor, voice actor, songwriter and record producer. |
| 20 | 8 Jan 2006 | Death of Tony Banks, Baron Stratford, British Labour politician. Minister for Sport (1997–99). Noted for his outspoken comments and his passion for sport and animal welfare. |
| 20 | 12 Jan 2006 | At least 346 people were killed in a stampede during the annual Hajj pilgrimage in Mina, Saudi Arabia. |
| 20 | 12 Jan 2006 | Nikon announced that its was discontinuing all but two of its film cameras and would focus on digital models. On 19th January, Konica Minolta announced that it was discontinuing all of its film and digital cameras and was exiting the camera market. |
| 20 | 14 Jan 2006 | Death of Shelley Winters, American stage, film and television actress (*The Diary of Anne Frank, A Patch of Blue, A Place in the Sun, The Big Knife, Lolita, The Night of the Hunter, Alfie, The Poseidon Adventure*, and more). |

## JANUARY 2026

| Ann. | Date | Event |
|---|---|---|
| 20 | 15 Jan 2006 | The sample return capsule from NASA's *Stardust* space probe successfully returned to Earth with a cargo of dust collected from the comet Wild 2. |
| 20 | 15 Jan 2006 | Death of Sheikh Jaber Al-Ahmad Al-Jaber Al-Sabah, Emir of Kuwait (1977–2006). Succeeded by Sabah Al-Ahmad Al-Jaber Al-Sabah (on 29th January). |
| 20 | 16 Jan 2006 | Ellen Johnson-Sirleaf became President of Liberia (until 2018). She was the first female elected head of state in Africa. |
| 20 | 19 Jan 2006 | NASA launched its *New Horizons* space probe to study the dwarf planet Pluto and its moons. It reached Pluto in July 2015, successfully returned close-up photos, and then continued onwards to study the Kuiper Belt. |
| 20 | 19 Jan 2006 | Death of Wilson Pickett, American soul/R&B/rock and roll singer and songwriter. His hit songs include *In the Midnight Hour*, *Mustang Sally* and *Funky Broadway*. |
| 20 | 21 Jan 2006 | Death of Ibrahim Rugova, first President of Kosovo (1992–2000, 2002–06). |
| 20 | 22 Jan 2006 | Evo Morales was inaugurated as President of Bolivia (until 2019). He was the first member of Bolivia's indigenous population to become president. |
| 20 | 24 Jan 2006 | Death of Chris Penn, American film and television actor (*Reservoir Dogs*, *Footloose*, *Rush Hour* and more). Brother of the actor Sean Penn. |
| 20 | 25 Jan 2006 | Independent observers confirmed the discovery of OGLE-2005-BLG-390Lb, the first 'super-Earth' rocky extrasolar planet. It is thought to be about five times larger than the Earth with a surface temperature of around -220°C (-370°F). |
| 20 | 27 Jan 2006 | The end of the telegram. Western Union discontinued its telegram service. It was the last company in the USA to offer a telegram service. Telegrams were introduced in 1851. |
| 20 | 27 Jan 2006 | Death of Gene McFadden, American singer, songwriter, musician and record producer (McFadden and Whitehead). Best known for the song *Ain't No Stoppin' Us Now*. |
| 20 | 27 Jan 2006 | Death of Johannes Rau, President of Germany (1999–2004). |
| 20 | 28 Jan 2006 | Katowice Trade Hall roof collapse, Poland. The roof of one of the buildings housing the Katowice International Fair collapsed, probably due to the weight of snow on it. 65 people were killed and more than 170 injured. |
| 20 | 28 Jan 2006 | Death of Henry McGee, British comedy actor. Best known for *The Benny Hill Show* and the *Sugar Puffs* commercials featuring the honey monster. |
| 20 | 30 Jan 2006 | Death of Coretta Scott King, American civil rights activist and writer. Wife of Martin Luther King Jr. |
| 20 | 31 Jan 2006 | Samuel Alito became an Associate Justice of the U.S. Supreme Court, succeeding Sandra Day O'Connor. |
| 20 | 31 Jan 2006 | Death of Moira Shearer, Scottish ballet dancer and actress. Best known for her performance in the film *The Red Shoes*. Wife of the journalist and broadcaster Ludovic Kennedy. |

## JANUARY 2026

| Ann. | Date | Event |
|---|---|---|
| 15 | 1 Jan 2011 | Dilma Rousseff became the first female President of Brazil (until 2016). |
| 15 | 1 Jan 2011 | The Oprah Winfrey Network (OWN) television channel was launched in the USA. |
| 15 | 4 Jan 2011 | The standard rate of Value Added Tax (VAT) in the UK was raised from 17.5 percent to 20 percent. |
| 15 | 5 Jan 2011 | John Boehner became Speaker of the U.S. House of Representatives (until 2015). |
| 15 | 9 Jan 2011 to 15th | South Sudanese independence referendum. More than 98 percent of the population voted in favour of independence from Sudan. South Sudan became an independent state on 9th July 2011. |
| 15 | 12 Jan 2011 to 14th | Victoria floods, Australia. Heavy rainfall caused major flooding across western and central Victoria. 51 communities were affected, thousands of people were evacuated and homes, businesses and farms were flooded. Two people were killed, and it caused around A$2 billion ($1.4 billion/£1.1 billion) worth of damage. |
| 15 | 24 Jan 2011 | Domodedovo International Airport bombing, Moscow, Russia. A suicide bomber from the North Caucasus killed 37 people and injured 173 in the international arrivals hall. |
| 15 | 25 Jan 2011 to 11 Feb | Egyptian revolution. Millions of protestors demanded President Hosni Mubarak's resignation over allegations of corruption, abuse of power, and increasing police brutality. He resigned on 11th February. Presidential power was transferred to the Supreme Military Council. (Mubarak was convicted of corruption in 2012 and again at a retrial in 2015, but he was acquitted following an appeal.) |
| 15 | 27 Jan 2011 to 27 Feb 2012 | Arab Spring: the Yemeni Revolution. The government was overthrown, the prime minister and members of the ruling party resigned (in December 2011), and the military was restructured. |
| 15 | 28 Jan 2011 | The American mass media conglomerate NBC Universal merged with the telecommunications conglomerate Comcast. NBC Universal became a subsidiary of Comcast. |
| 10 | 8 Jan 2016 | Operation Black Swan: Mexican drug trafficker Joaquín Guzmán ('El Chapo'), the leader of the Sinaloa Cartel, was recaptured by U.S. and Mexican forces after escaping from a maximum-security prison in Mexico in July 2015. He was extradited to the USA, convicted of several criminal charges, and sentenced to life imprisonment. |
| 10 | 10 Jan 2016 | Death of David Bowie, British pop/rock singer, songwriter and actor. |
| 10 | 14 Jan 2016 | Death of Alan Rickman, British stage, film and television actor and director. |
| 10 | 18 Jan 2016 | Death of Glenn Frey, American rock singer, songwriter, musician and actor. A founding member of the Eagles, and a successful solo artist. |

# JANUARY 2026

| Ann. | Date | Event |
|------|------|-------|
| 10 | 19 Jan 2016 | Death of Sheila Sim, British stage and film actress. Wife of the actor and director Richard Attenborough. |
| 10 | 22 Jan 2016 | Death of Cecil Parkinson, British politician. A member of Margaret Thatcher's cabinet. He was forced to resign from his role as Secretary of State for Trade and Industry after it was revealed that his former secretary was pregnant with his child. He later became Secretary of State for Energy, and for Transport, and was Chairman of the Conservative Party (1997–98). |
| 10 | 24 Jan 2016 | Death of Marvin Minsky, American computer scientist. Best known for his work on artificial intelligence. |
| 10 | 31 Jan 2016 | Death of Terry Wogan, Irish radio and television broadcaster. Known for his long-running BBC Radio 2 show, and for presenting the TV series *Wogan*, *Blankety Blank*, *Come Dancing*, the *Children in Need* fundraisers, and for his commentaries on the *Eurovision Song Contest*. |

## FEBRUARY 2026

| Ann. | Date | Event |
|------|------|-------|
| 500 | 27 Feb 1526 | The League of Torgau, an alliance of Lutheran princes, was formed by Hesse and Saxony.<br>It opposed the Edict of Worms, but was unable to achieve its aims. |
| 400 | 5 Feb 1626 | Birth of Marie de Rabutin-Chantal, marquise de Sévigné, French aristocrat and writer. Best known for the letters she wrote to her daughter.<br>She is regarded as one of the greatest French writers of the 17th century. |
| 400 | 7 Feb 1626 | Death of William V, (William the Pious), Duke of Bavaria (1579–97 – abdicated). |
| 400 | 20 Feb 1626 ? | Death of John Dowland, English Renaissance composer, lute player and singer. Known for his melancholy songs and his instrumentals for lute and guitar. |
| 300 | 13 Feb 1726 | The Mapuche uprising of 1723 ended with the Parliament of Negrete, a diplomatic meeting and peace treaty that was signed in what is now Chile. The Mapuche people had rebelled against the Spanish Empire in western South America. |
| 300 | 20 Feb 1726 | Birth of William Prescott, American colonel in the American Revolutionary War. Commander of the patriot forces in the Battle of Bunker Hill.<br>Best known for his order, 'Don't fire until you see the whites of their eyes.' |
| 300 | 26 Feb 1726 | Death of Maximilian II Emanuel, Elector of Bavaria (1679–1726). Succeeded by his son, Charles Albert (later Charles VII, the Holy Roman Emperor). |
| 250 | 11 Feb 1776 | Birth of Ioannis Kapodistrias, Greek statesman. First Governor of Greece (1828–31), Foreign Minister of the Russian Empire (1816–22). |
| 250 | 17 Feb 1776 | Volume I of Edward Gibbon's *The History of the Decline and Fall of the Roman Empire* was published. Volumes II and III were published in 1781 and Volumes IV, V and VI in 1788–89. |
| 250 | 23 Feb 1776 | Birth of John Walter II, British newspaper editor. Second proprietor and editor of *The Times* (1803–47), which was founded by his father. |
| 250 | 27 Feb 1776 | American Revolutionary War: the Battle of Moore's Creek Bridge, Wilmington, North Carolina. North Carolina victory over Great Britain. |
| 200 | 4 Feb 1826 | James Fenimore Cooper's historical romance novel *The Last of the Mohicans* was published. |
| 200 | 11 Feb 1826 | University College London (UCL) was founded (as London University). |
| 200 | 13 Feb 1826 | The American Temperance Society was established in Boston, Massachusetts. |
| 200 | 16 Feb 1826 | Birth of Franz von Holstein, German composer. |
| 200 | 24 Feb 1826 | The First Anglo–Burmese War ended with the signing of the Treaty of Yandabo. British victory, which led to the establishment of British rule in India. (The war began in March 1824.) |
| 200 | 27 Feb 1826 | Biela's Comet was discovered by German-Austrian military officer Wilhelm von Biela.<br>It split into two in about 1845, and has not been seen since 1852, so it is believed to have been destroyed. |

**FEBRUARY 2026**

| Ann. | Date | Event |
|---|---|---|
| 175 | 1 Feb 1851 | Death of Mary Shelley, British novelist.<br>Best known for her Gothic novel *Frankenstein; or, The Modern Prometheus*. Wife of the poet Percy Bysshe Shelley. (Brain tumour, aged 53.) |
| 175 | 6 Feb 1851 | Black Thursday bushfires, Victoria, Australia.<br>Around 12 million acres (a quarter of the state) was burned. Twelve people, a million sheep, and thousands of cattle and other animals were killed. |
| 175 | 12 Feb 1851 | Gold prospector Edward Hargraves discovered gold in Lewis Ponds Creek in New South Wales, Australia. This led to the Australian gold rush. |
| 150 | 2 Feb 1876 | The National League of Professional Baseball Clubs (commonly known as the National League) was founded in the USA.<br>It is one of the two Major League Baseball leagues in the USA and Canada – the other league is the American League, founded in 1901.<br>The first National League game was played on 22nd April 1876 between the Philadelphia Athletics and Boston Baseball Club. It is generally regarded as the first game in the history of Major League Baseball. |
| 150 | 3 Feb 1876 | Spalding, the American sporting goods manufacturing company, was founded by baseball pitcher Al Spalding in Chicago, Illinois. |
| 150 | 8 Feb 1876 to 1877 | The Great Sioux War, USA.<br>Following the discovery of gold in the Black Hills of South Dakota and Wyoming, the USA announced that it would take possession of the hills, remove the Native Americans, and relocate them to smaller reservations. The Native Americans refused to cede their lands to the USA and launched a series of battles. U.S. Victory. |
| 150 | 12 Feb 1876 | Birth of the 13th Dalai Lama (Thubten Gyatso). |
| 150 | 13 Feb 1876 | Birth of Fritz Buelow, German-born American baseball catcher (St. Louis Perfectos, St. Louis Cardinals, Detroit Tigers, Cleveland Naps, St. Louis Browns). |
| 150 | 14 Feb 1876 | Electrical engineers Alexander Graham Bell and Elisha Gray both filed U.S. patents for the invention of the telephone on the same day.<br>There is considerable debate as to whose patent was filed first.<br>Bell was awarded the patent on 7th March (U.S. Patent 174,465), but Gray challenged it and said Bell had stolen his design. An examiner concluded that although Gray had invented some of the essential components of the telephone, and had discussed them with Bell, Bell was the first to put them together as a telephone, test them, and write the idea down. |
| 150 | 16 Feb 1876 | Birth of G. M. Trevelyan, British historian, academic and writer.<br>Regius Professor of History at the University of Cambridge (1927–43). Master of Trinity College, Cambridge (1940–51), Chancellor of Durham University (1950–57). |
| 150 | 19 Feb 1876 | Birth of Constantin Brâncuşi, Romanian sculptor, artist and photographer. A pioneer of Modernism. One of the most influential sculptors of the 20th century. |
| 150 | 21 Feb 1876 | Britain and New Zealand were directly connected by the Imperial telegraph service when the New Zealand–Sydney cable began operating. |

## FEBRUARY 2026

| Ann. | Date | Event |
|---|---|---|
| 150 | 22 Feb 1876 | Johns Hopkins University was founded in Baltimore, Maryland, USA. |
| 150 | 24 Feb 1876 | Henrik Ibsen's play *Peer Gynt* was performed for the first time, in Oslo, Norway. |
| 150 | 24 Feb 1876 | Death of Joseph Jenkins Roberts, first and seventh President of Liberia (1848–56, 1872–76). |
| 150 | 26 Feb 1876 | Japan and Korea signed the Japan–Korea Treaty of 1876.<br>Korea was forced to sign the unequal treaty, which gave Japan extra-territorial rights in Korea, and allowed it to open three ports there.<br>(Japan annexed Korea in 1910.) |
| 150 | 26 Feb 1876 | Birth of Agustín Pedro Justo, President Argentina (1932–38). |
| 125 | 1 Feb 1901 | Birth of Clark Gable, American film actor. MGM's biggest male star. Known as 'The King of Hollywood'. His films include *Gone with the Wind*, *Mutiny on the Bounty*, *It Happened One Night*, and many more. |
| 125 | 2 Feb 1901 | The funeral of Queen Victoria of the United Kingdom. |
| 125 | 2 Feb 1901 | The U.S. Army Nurse Corps was established. |
| 125 | 2 Feb 1901 | Birth of Jascha Heifetz, Russian-born American violin virtuoso and teacher. |
| 125 | 9 Feb 1901 | Birth of Brian Donlevy, American stage, film and television actor. Best known for his film noir supporting roles (*Beau Geste*, *The Great McGinty*, and *Wake Island*.) |
| 125 | 10 Feb 1901 | Birth of Stella Adler, American actress and acting teacher.<br>Founder of the Stella Adler Studio of Acting in New York City. |
| 125 | 11 Feb 1901 | Death of Milan I, King of Serbia (1882–89). |
| 125 | 12 Feb 1901 | The Netherlands passed the 1901 Penal Children's Act. It required delinquent children to be rehabilitated, required youth to be taken into account in sentencing, and abolished the death penalty for juveniles. |
| 125 | 14 Feb 1901 | Death of Edward Stafford, Prime Minister of New Zealand (1856–61, 1865–69, 1872). |
| 125 | 15 Feb 1901 | Birth of Christmas Humphreys, British barrister, judge and writer.<br>A prosecutor in several controversial cases in the 1940s and 50s.<br>He later became a judge at the Old Bailey.<br>He was also a noted Buddhist and founded the London Buddhist Society.<br>His former home in London is now a Buddhist temple. |
| 125 | 16 Feb 1901 | Birth of Wayne King, ('the Waltz King'), American musician, songwriter and bandleader. He performed on numerous NBC and CBS radio shows. |
| 125 | 16 Feb 1901 | Birth of Chester Morris, American stage and film actor.<br>Best known for the film *Alibi* and the *Boston Blackie* film series. |
| 125 | 18 Feb 1901 | British engineer Hubert Cecil Booth patented his invention of the vacuum cleaner. His system was too large for domestic use. It, and was taken to people's homes on a horse-drawn carriage, where employees sucked dust out of the building using hoses. He founded the British Vacuum Cleaner and Engineering Co. He also founded Goblin Vacuum Cleaners in the 1930s. (He also designed Ferris wheels, suspension bridges and factories.) |

## FEBRUARY 2026

| Ann. | Date | Event |
|---|---|---|
| 125 | 19 Feb 1901 | Birth of Mohamed Naguib, first President of Egypt (1953–54), Prime Minister of Egypt (1954). Along with Gamal Abdel Nasser he led the Egyptian Revolution of 1952, which ended the monarchy of Egypt and Sudan, and led to the establishment of the Republic of Egypt and the independence of Sudan. |
| 125 | 20 Feb 1901 | Birth of Cecil Harmsworth King, British newspaper publisher and executive. Chairman of Daily Mirror Newspapers, Sunday Pictorial Newspapers, and the International Publishing Corporation. Director of the Bank of England (1965–68). |
| 125 | 22 Feb 1901 | Birth of Charles Evans Whittaker, Associate Justice of the U.S. Supreme Court (1957–62). |
| 125 | 25 Feb 1901 | Birth of Zeppo Marx, American actor and comedian (the Marx Brothers). He later became a theatrical agent and engineer. |
| 125 | 28 Feb 1901 | Birth of Linus Pauling, American chemist, biochemist, chemical engineer, peace activist, writer and educator. One of the most important scientists in history. Winner of the 1954 Nobel Prize in Chemistry for his research into chemical bonds, and the 1962 Nobel Peace Prize for his campaign against nuclear weapons testing. |
| 100 | 2 Feb 1926 | Birth of Valéry Giscard d'Estaing, President of France (1974–81). (Died 2020.) |
| 100 | 8 Feb 1926 | The Disney Brothers Cartoon Studio (founded in 1923) was renamed Walt Disney Studios. |
| 100 | 9 Feb 1926 | Birth of Garret FitzGerald, Taoiseach (Prime Minister) of Ireland (1981–82, 1982–87). (Died 2011.) |
| 100 | 9 Feb 1926 | The Atlanta Board of Education in Georgia, USA banned the teaching of the theory of evolution in schools. The ban was lifted in May when legal advisers said they had no authority to ban the textbooks they had listed. |
| 100 | 10 Feb 1926 | Birth of Danny Blanchflower, Northern Irish football player and manager. (Died 1993.) |
| 100 | 11 Feb 1926 | The British colony of Tokelau (previously known as the Union Islands) was transferred to New Zealand. It was known as the Tokelau Islands until 1976. |
| 100 | 11 Feb 1926 | Birth of Leslie Nielsen, Canadian-American film and television actor and comedian (*Airplane!*, *Police Squad*, *The Naked Gun* (and sequels), *The Poseidon Adventure*, *Forbidden Planet*, *Mr. Magoo* and more). (Died 2010.) |
| 100 | 12 Feb 1926 | Birth of Charles Van Doren, American writer and editor. Best known for his involvement in the television quiz show scandal of the 1950s. He testified before Congress that the producers of NBC's quiz show *Twenty-One* had supplied him with the correct answers when he took part in it. He later worked for *Encyclopaedia Britannica*. (Died 2019.) |
| 100 | 15 Feb 1926 | The Brooks Atkinson Theatre opened in New York City, USA (as the Mansfield Theatre). |

## FEBRUARY 2026

| Ann. | Date | Event |
|---|---|---|
| 100 | 16 Feb 1926 | Birth of Margot Frank, German-Dutch holocaust victim. Elder sister of the Jewish diarist Anne Frank. (Died of typhus in Bergen–Belsen concentration camp in 1945.) |
| 100 | 16 Feb 1926 | Birth of John Schlesinger, British stage, film and television director (*Midnight Cowboy, Sunday Bloody Sunday, The Day of the Locust, Marathon Man* and more). (Died 2003.) |
| 100 | 22 Feb 1926 | Birth of Kenneth Williams, British comedy actor and comedian. Star of numerous radio and television shows and 26 *Carry On…* films. (Died 1988.) |
| 90 | 1 Feb 1936 | Birth of Azie Taylor Morton, Treasurer of the United States (1977–81). The first African American to hold this office. (Died 2003.) |
| 90 | 3 Feb 1936 | The National Wildlife Federation was founded in the USA. |
| 90 | 4 Feb 1936 | Radium E, the first radioactive element to be made synthetically in the USA, was produced by Dr John Jacob Livingood at the University of California, Berkeley. |
| 90 | 4 Feb 1936 | Birth of Claude Nobs, Swiss founder and general manager of the Montreux Jazz Festival. (Died 2013.) |
| 90 | 5 Feb 1936 | The Japanese Baseball League was founded. It operated until 1949, and reorganised as Nippon Professional Baseball in 1950. |
| 90 | 5 Feb 1936 | Charlie Chaplin's film *Modern Times* was released. It was the last major silent film. (The sound era had become well established since 1929.) |
| 90 | 6 Feb 1936 to 16th | The 4th Winter Olympics were held in Garmisch-Partenkirchen, Germany. |
| 90 | 7 Feb 1936 | The first official flag of the Vice President of the USA was established. The current design was adopted in 1975. |
| 90 | 8 Feb 1936 | The National Football League (NFL) in the USA held its first draft (a two-day event where teams recruit new players from the college system). The first player to be selected was Jay Berwanger, who joined the Philadelphia Eagles. |
| 90 | 8 Feb 1936 | Death of Charles Curtis, Vice-President of the USA (1929–33), Senate Majority Leader (1925–29). The first Native American to hold either post. |
| 90 | 9 Feb 1936 | Birth of Clive Swift, British stage, film and television actor. Best known for his role as Hyacinth Bucket's husband Richard in the television sitcom *Keeping Up Appearances*. Husband of the novelist Margaret Drabble. (Died 2019.) |
| 90 | 10 Feb 1936 to 19th | Second Italo–Abyssinian War – the Battle of Amba Aradam (Ethiopia). Italian tactical victory. |
| 90 | 11 Feb 1936 | Birth of Burt Reynolds, American film and television actor and director (*Smokey and the Bandit, The Cannonball Run, The Best Little Whorehouse in Texas*, and many more). (Died 2018.) |
| 90 | 17 Feb 1936 | The Phantom, the first fictional costumed superhero, made his first appearance in a daily newspaper strip in the USA. Unlike later superheroes, he does not have any superpowers. |

## FEBRUARY 2026

| Ann. | Date | Event |
|------|------|-------|
| 90 | 19 Feb 1936 | Death of Billy Mitchell, U.S. Army officer and aviation pioneer. Regarded as the father of the U.S. Air Force. |
| 90 | 20 Feb 1936 | Birth of Larry Hovis, American actor and singer. Best known for his role as Sergeant Andrew Carter in the television sitcom *Hogan's Heroes*. (Died 2003.) |
| 90 | 21 Feb 1936 | Birth of Barbara Jordan, American politician. The first African American Congresswoman to come from the Deep South. (Died 1996.) |
| 90 | 26 Feb 1936 to 29th | The February 26 Incident, Japan. An attempted coup against the government by young military officers. Several senior politicians were killed. |
| 90 | 27 Feb 1936 | Death of Ivan Pavlov, Russian physiologist. Best known for developing the concept of the conditioned reflex. Winner of the 1904 Nobel Prize in Physiology or Medicine. |
| 80 | 1 Feb 1946 | The Kingdom of Hungary was dissolved, the monarchy abolished, and the Second Hungarian Republic proclaimed. It was dissolved in August 1949 and succeeded by the People's Republic of Hungary (until 1989). |
| 80 | 1 Feb 1946 | Birth of Elisabeth Sladen, British television actress. Best known for her role as Sarah Jane Smith in *Doctor Who*, *K-9 and Company* and *The Sarah Jane Adventures*. (Died 2011.) |
| 80 | 2 Feb 1946 | Trygve Lie of Norway became the first Secretary-General of the United Nations (until 1952). |
| 80 | 2 Feb 1946 | The first episode of the radio quiz show *Twenty Questions* was broadcast on the Mutual Broadcasting System in the USA. A television version was launched in November 1949. |
| 80 | 4 Feb 1946 | RCA gave the first U.S. demonstration of an all-electronic colour television system. The first public demonstration was on 30th October. |
| 80 | 5 Feb 1946 | Death of George Arliss, British stage and film actor, writer, playwright and filmmaker. The first British actor to win an Academy Award. Best known for his biopics (*Disraeli*, *Volitaire*, *Cardinal Richlieu*) and light comedies. |
| 80 | 7 Feb 1946 | Birth of Pete Postlethwaite, British stage, film and television actor (*In the Name of the Father*, *Brassed Off*, *The Usual Suspects*, *Amistad*, *Clash of the Titans*, *Inception* and more). (Died 2011.) |
| 80 | 8 Feb 1946 | The Provisional People's Committee of North Korea was established. It was the provisional government of North Korea, which was established in 1948. |
| 80 | 8 Feb 1946 | The Chondoist Chongu Party, a popular front political party, was founded in North Korea. |
| 80 | 8 Feb 1946 | Hungarian composer Béla Bartók's *Piano Concerto No. 3* was performed for the first time, in Philadelphia, Pennsylvania, USA. It was unfinished when he died in September 1945, and was completed by his friend, Tibor Serly. |
| 80 | 9 Feb 1946 | The Labour Party, a social-democratic political party, was established in the Netherlands. |

## FEBRUARY 2026

| Ann. | Date | Event |
|---|---|---|
| 80 | 11 Feb 1946 | The Revised Standard Version of the New Testament was published. It was the first major English-language update of the Bible since the King James version was published in 1611. |
| 80 | 11 Feb 1946 | World War II – Operation Deadlight ended. This was a British Royal Navy operation to scuttle 116 U-boats surrendered by Germany at the end of the war. The submarines were sunk off north-west Ireland – though many of them sank before reaching the designated area. |
| 80 | 14 Feb 1946 | The Bank of England was nationalised. |
| 80 | 14 Feb 1946 | Birth of Bernard Dowiyogo, President of Nauru (1976–78, 1989–95, 1996, 1998–99, 2000–01, 2003). (Died 2003.) |
| 80 | 15 Feb 1946 | ENIAC (the Electronic Numerical Integrator and Computer) was dedicated at the Moore School of Electrical Engineering at the University of Pennsylvania in the USA. It was proclaimed as the world's first large-scale general-purpose digital computer. (It was not actually the first, but it was the first to be made public. Britain's Colossus and Germany's Z3 already existed, but were secret at that time. ) |
| 80 | 16 Feb 1946 | The first commercial helicopter, the Sikorsky S-51, made its first flight. It was certified by the Civil Aviation Agency in the USA in March and entered service in August. |
| 80 | 18 Feb 1946 to 23rd | The Royal Indian Navy mutiny. Indian sailors began a general strike and revolt in Bombay harbour, protesting against British rule. It quickly spread throughout British India, eventually involving 20,000 sailors. It was repressed by the British Royal Navy. Seven people were killed. |
| 80 | 19 Feb 1946 | British mathematician and cryptanalyst Alan Turing presented a detailed paper to the National Physical Laboratory that gave the first reasonably complete design of a stored-program computer. This led to the development of the Pilot ACE computer, which ran its first program in 1951. It was sold commercially as the English Electric DEUCE in 1955. |
| 80 | 19 Feb 1946 | Birth of Karen Silkwood, American trade union activist. Best known as a nuclear safety whistle-blower who testified to the Atomic Energy Commission about her concerns for workers' safety. She was killed in a 1974 car crash in unclear circumstances. The film *Silkwood* tells her story. |
| 80 | 20 Feb 1946 | Birth of J. Geils, American rock guitarist, singer and songwriter (The J. Geils Band). (Died 2017.) |
| 80 | 21 Feb 1946 | Birth of Alan Rickman, British stage, film and television actor and director. (Died 2016.) |
| 80 | 27 Feb 1946 | The U.S. première of the musical comedy film *Road to Utopia*. The fourth film in the *Road to…* series. Released 22nd March. UK première: November 1945, released: December 1945. |
| 80 | 28 Feb 1946 | Birth of Robin Cook, Scottish Labour politician. British Foreign Secretary (1997–2001). (Died 2005.) |
| 80 | 28 Feb 1946 | Birth of Syreeta Wright, American R&B/soul singer and songwriter. First wife of Stevie Wonder. (Died 2004.) |

# FEBRUARY 2026

| Ann. | Date | Event |
|---|---|---|
| 75 | 1 Feb 1951 | The first live television broadcast of an atomic explosion. KTLA in Los Angeles, California, USA broadcast an atomic test at Frenchman Flats in Nevada, filming it from a mountain 250 miles away. |
| 75 | 1 Feb 1951 | The United Nations General Assembly condemned China for its intervention in the Korean War. It was the first time that the UN condemned a country. |
| 75 | 3 Feb 1951 | Tennessee Williams' play *The Rose Tattoo* opened on Broadway. It ran until October. It was adapted into a film in 1955. |
| 75 | 6 Feb 1951 | The Woodbridge train derailment, New Jersey, USA. One of the worst rail disasters in U.S. history. 86 people were killed and more than 500 injured. |
| 75 | 9 Feb 1951 to 11th | Korean War: the Geochang massacre. South Korean capitalist forces killed 719 unarmed citizens that it said were communist sympathisers. |
| 75 | 13 Feb 1951 to 15th | Korean War – the Battle of Chipyong-ni. Chinese forces made their deepest incursion into South Korea. United Nations victory. |
| 75 | 15 Feb 1951 | An atomic reactor was used for medical purposes for the first time, to treat a patient suffering from brain cancer. The boron neutron capture therapy was performed at the Brookhaven National Laboratory in Upton, New York, USA. |
| 75 | 16 Feb 1951 | Korean War: Soviet leader Joseph Stalin denounced the United Nations, calling it 'a weapon of aggressive war'. |
| 75 | 19 Feb 1951 | Death of André Gide, French writer. Winner of the 1947 Nobel Prize in Literature. |
| 75 | 20 Feb 1951 | Birth of Randy California, American rock guitarist, singer and songwriter. A member of the band Spirit and a successful solo artist. (Died 1997.) |
| 75 | 25 Feb 1951 to 9 Mar | The first Pan American Games were held, in Buenos Aires, Argentina. |
| 75 | 26 Feb 1951 | American author James Jones's novel *From Here to Eternity* was published. |
| 75 | 26 Feb 1951 | Birth of Lee Atwater, American political consultant. An adviser to U.S. Presidents Ronald Reagan and George H. W. Bush. Noted for his aggressive election campaign tactics. (Died 1991 – brain tumour, aged 40.) |
| 75 | 27 Feb 1951 | The 22nd Amendment to the U.S. Constitution was ratified. It limits the U.S. President to a maximum of two terms in office. |
| 70 | 2 Feb 1956 | The world première of Eugene O'Neill's play *Long Day's Journey into Night*, in Stockholm, Sweden. It opened on Broadway on 7th November. (O'Neill had died in 1953. He was posthumously awarded the 1957 Pulitzer Prize for Drama for this play.) |
| 70 | 8 Feb 1956 | Death of Connie Mack, American baseball team manager and owner (Philadelphia Athletics). The longest-serving manager in Major League Baseball history. |

## FEBRUARY 2026

| Ann. | Date | Event |
|---|---|---|
| 70 | 11 Feb 1956 | Two members of the Cambridge spy ring, British diplomats Guy Burgess and Donald Maclean, announced they had defected to the Soviet Union. They had both vanished in mysterious circumstances in 1951.<br>(Russian leader Nikita Khrushchev had denied they were in the Soviet Union when questioned two weeks earlier.) |
| 70 | 16 Feb 1956 | McMurdo Station, a U.S. Antarctic research station, was established on Ross Island. It is now the largest community in Antarctica, and can support up to 1,258 residents. |
| 70 | 18 Feb 1956 | Death of Gustave Charpentier, French composer.<br>Best known for his opera *Louise*. |
| 70 | 25 Feb 1956 | At the 20th Congress of the Communist Party of the Soviet Union in Moscow, Soviet leader Nikita Khruschev's gave a secret speech entitled *On the Cult of Personality and Its Consequences*. He condemned and denounced former leader Josef Stalin as a brutal despot.<br>This led to the de-Stalinisation of the Soviet Union. |
| 70 | 28 Feb 1956 | American computer engineer Jay Wright Forrester from the Massachusetts Institute of Technology was granted a U.S. patent for the magnetic memory core. It became the standard random access memory device for digital computers for the next twenty years, until it was replaced by solid state RAM. (U.S. Patent 2,736,880.) |
| 70 | 29 Feb 1956 | Death of Elpidio Quirino, President of the Philippines (1948–53). |
| 65 | 3 Feb 1961 | The U.S. Air Force's Strategic Air Command launched Operation Looking Glass (the Airborne National Command Post).<br>The airborne command and control centre for the USA's nuclear forces will take over if ground-based command centres are rendered inoperable. |
| 65 | 3 Feb 1961 | Death of William Morrison, 1st Viscount Dunrossil, British politician. Speaker of the House of Commons (1951–59), Governor-General of Australia (1960–61), Postmaster General (1940–43), Minister of Agriculture (1936–39), Minister of Food (1939–40). |
| 65 | 4 Feb 1961 to 25 Apr 1974 | Angolan War of Independence.<br>Result: Angolan independence from Portugal in 1975, leading to the Angolan Civil War (1975–2002). |
| 65 | 5 Feb 1961 | The first edition of the *Sunday Telegraph* newspaper was published in the UK. |
| 65 | 9 Feb 1961 | British rock band the Beatles played at the Cavern Club in Liverpool for the first time. They became the Cavern's house band in August. |
| 65 | 10 Feb 1961 | The Niagara Falls hydroelectric project (official name: the Robert Moses Niagara Hydroelectric Power Station) went online and began generating electricity. |
| 65 | 12 Feb 1961 | The Soviet Union launched its *Venera 1* space probe on a mission to Venus. It flew past Venus in May, but radio contact had been lost and it failed to return any data. |
| 65 | 14 Feb 1961 | The chemical element lawrencium (Lr, atomic number 103) was synthesised for the first time at the University of California, Berkeley, USA. |

## FEBRUARY 2026

| Ann. | Date | Event |
|------|------|-------|
| 65 | 15 Feb 1961 | Sabena Flight 548 crash, Brussels, Belgium.<br>73 people were killed, including the entire U.S. figure skating team. |
| 65 | 16 Feb 1961 | NASA launched *Explorer 9*, a 12-foot (3.6-metre) reflective balloon, into orbit around the Earth. It remained in orbit for three years before burning up in the atmosphere. Scientists monitoring the balloon's position were able to create a seasonal model of the Earth's upper atmosphere |
| 65 | 17 Feb 1961 | Death of Nita Naldi, American stage and silent film actress. |
| 65 | 19 Feb 1961 | Birth of Justin Fashanu, British football player.<br>The first openly gay professional footballer.<br>(Died 1998 – suicide after being accused of sexual assault in the USA.) |
| 65 | 20 Feb 1961 | Death of Percy Grainger, Australian-born American composer, pianist and conductor. |
| 65 | 25 Feb 1961 | Birth of Davey Allison, American NASCAR racing driver.<br>(Died 1993 – helicopter crash, aged 32.) |
| 65 | 26 Feb 1961 | Death of Mohammed V, King of Morocco (1957–61).<br>Succeeded by his son, Hassan II. |
| 60 | 1 Feb 1966 | Death of Hedda Hopper, American gossip columnist and actress. |
| 60 | 1 Feb 1966 | Death of Buster Keaton, American silent film actor, comedian and director. Noted for his physical comedy and deadpan 'stone face' expression. |
| 60 | 3 Feb 1966 | The Soviet Union's space probe *Luna 9* became the first craft to achieve a soft landing on the Moon. (The USA's *Surveyor 1* achieved the same feat four months later, on 2nd June.) |
| 60 | 3 Feb 1966 | NASA launched the *ESSA-1* satellite, which captured cloud-cover photographs for the National Meteorological Center.<br>(Its camera system failed after eight months in orbit.<br>There were six ESSA satellites, operating for a total of about four years.) |
| 60 | 4 Feb 1966 | All Nippon Airways Flight 60 crashed into Tokyo Bay, Japan.<br>(Cause: unknown, but witnesses reported that it was on fire before it crashed, and the pilot reported that his cockpit instruments had failed.)<br>All 126 passengers and seven crew were killed. |
| 60 | 4 Feb 1966 | Death of Gilbert Hovey Grosvenor, American geographer, writer and magazine editor. President of the National Geographic Society.<br>Editor of *National Geographic* magazine (1899–1954). |
| 60 | 5 Feb 1966<br>to 8th | Vietnam War: the Hawaii Conference was held in the USA.<br>U.S. President Lyndon B. Johnson and South Vietnamese Premier Nguyen Cao Ky signed the Declaration of Honolulu, in which the USA pledged its ongoing support to South Vietnam against North Vietnamese aggression, and to help develop its economy |
| 60 | 9 Feb 1966 | Death of Sophie Tucker, Russian-born American singer, actress and entertainer. She was hugely popular on the vaudeville and music hall circuit. Noted for her flamboyant stage persona and comical and risqué songs. |

## FEBRUARY 2026

| Ann. | Date | Event |
|---|---|---|
| 60 | 10 Feb 1966 | Death of Billy Rose, American lyricist, Broadway producer and theatrical impresario. He wrote over 400 songs, including *Me and My Shadow*. Owner of the Diamond Horseshoe nightclub and the Ziegfeld Theatre. |
| 60 | 14 Feb 1966 | Australia's currency was decimalised, replacing the British system of pounds, shillings and pence. |
| 60 | 20 Feb 1966 | Death of Chester W. Nimitz, Fleet Admiral of the United States Navy. Commander-in-chief of U.S. forces in the Pacific during WWII. |
| 60 | 22 Feb 1966 | The Soviet Union launched its *Kosmos 110* spacecraft, which carried two dogs, Veterok and Ugolok, as well as several species of plants. The spacecraft remained in orbit for 22 days before returning safely. The dogs were severely dehydrated and suffered from muscle loss and other issues, but fully recovered after several weeks. Some of the plants grew better in space than they did on Earth. |
| 60 | 23 Feb 1966 | The President of Syria, Amin al-Hafiz, was ousted in a military coup. He was succeeded by Nureddin al-Atassi (who was considered a ceremonial figurehead – the real power was held by the Deputy General Secretary of the Ba'ath Party, Salah Jadid). |
| 60 | 24 Feb 1966 | The President of Ghana, Kwame Nkrumah, was deposed by the National Liberation Council. He went into exile in Guinea. He was succeeded by Joseph Arthur Ankrah as Military Head of State (until 1969). |
| 60 | 26 Feb 1966 | NASA launched *AS-201*, the first unmanned test flight of the Apollo command/service module system and the first flight of the Saturn IB rocket. There were a few minor problems, but most of the mission's objectives were successful, including a demonstration of the heat shield's ability to withstand re-entry into the Earth's atmosphere. |
| 60 | 28 Feb 1966 | NASA T-38 crash, Lambert Field, St. Louis, Missouri, USA. Two Project Gemini astronauts, Elliot See and Charles Bassett, were killed when their aircraft crashed into the McDonnell Aircraft building during poor weather. (Cause: pilot error.) |
| 60 | 28 Feb 1966 | The Federal Communications Commission (FCC) in the USA banned eavesdropping on private conversations using radio devices. |
| 50 | 1 Feb 1976 | Death of Werner Heisenberg, German theoretical physicist and philosopher. Best known for his uncertainty principle. Winner of the 1932 Nobel Prize in Physics for developing the field of quantum mechanics. |
| 50 | 1 Feb 1976 | Death of George Whipple, American pathologist. Joint winner of the 1934 Nobel Prize in Physiology or Medicine for his discovery that the previously fatal disease anaemia could be successfully treated by feeding the patient liver. |
| 50 | 4 Feb 1976 | Guatemala earthquake. 23,000 people were killed, 76,000 injured and approximately 1.2 million left homeless |
| 50 | 4 Feb 1976 to 15th | The 1976 Winter Olympics were held in Innsbruck, Austria. |
| 50 | 4 Feb 1976 | Hua Guofeng became Premier of the People's Republic of China (until 1980.) He was also Chairman of the Communist Party of China throughout this period, as the successor to Mao Zedong. |

**FEBRUARY 2026**

| Ann. | Date | Event |
|------|------|-------|
| 50 | 5 Feb 1976 | Death of Rudy Pompilli, American saxophonist (Bill Haley and His Comets). |
| 50 | 6 Feb 1976 | Death of Vince Guaraldi, American jazz pianist. Best known for his music for the television adaptations of the *Peanuts* comic strip, and for his innovative compositions and arrangements. (Heart attack, aged 47.) |
| 50 | 7 Feb 1976 | The current National Hockey League (NHL) record for most points scored in one game: Darryl Sittler of the Toronto Maple Leafs (10 points). |
| 50 | 9 Feb 1976 | Death of Percy Faith, Canadian orchestrator, composer, bandleader and conductor. Known for his easy listening music. |
| 50 | 11 Feb 1976 | John Curry won Britain's first-ever Olympic gold medal in figure skating. It was also Britain's first medal at the Winter Olympics for twelve years. |
| 50 | 11 Feb 1976 | Death of Lee J. Cobb, American stage, film and television actor. Best known for the films *12 Angry Men*, *On the Waterfront* and *The Exorcist*, the Broadway play *Death of a Salesman*, and the TV series *The Virginian*. |
| 50 | 11 Feb 1976 | Death of Alexander Lippisch, German-born aircraft designer and aerodynamics pioneer. He made major contributions to the development of the delta wing, and designed the only rocket-powered fighter plane ever to be put into operation: the Messerschmitt Me 163 Komet. |
| 50 | 12 Feb 1976 | Death of Sal Mineo, American stage, film and television actor, singer and director. His films include *Rebel Without a Cause*, *Giant*, *Exodus*, *The Longest Day*, and *Escape from the Planet of the Apes*. (Stabbed by a mugger, aged 37.) |
| 50 | 13 Feb 1976 | Death of Murtala Mohammed, Head of the Federal Military Government of Nigeria (1975–76). (Assassinated.) |
| 50 | 13 Feb 1976 | Death of Lily Pons, French-born American operatic soprano. Best known for her association with the Metropolitan Opera in New York City, where she performed for more than thirty years. |
| 50 | 19 Feb 1976 | U.S. President Gerald Ford rescinded Executive Order 9066, under which Japanese Americans were held in internment camps during WWII. |
| 50 | 19 Feb 1976 | Cod War: Iceland broke off diplomatic relations with Britain. |
| 50 | 22 Feb 1976 | Death of Florence Ballard, American singer (The Supremes). |
| 50 | 23 Feb 1976 | Death of L. S. Lowry, British artist. Known for his bleak industrial landscapes of north-west England, populated with 'matchstick men'. |
| 50 | 24 Feb 1976 | The current Constitution of Cuba came into effect. It declared that there was only one political party in Cuba: the Communist Party of Cuba. |
| 50 | 27 Feb 1976 | The Sahrawi Arab Democratic Republic was proclaimed. It claims sovereignty over the entire Western Sahara territory, but is only partially recognised. (Morocco also claims sovereignty over the territory, though this is not recognised by any UN member state.) |
| 40 | 1 Feb 1986 | Death of Dick James, British music publisher. Best known for founding Northern Songs, the Beatles' publisher, with Brian Epstein. He also founded DJM Records. |

**FEBRUARY 2026**

| Ann. | Date | Event |
|------|------|-------|
| 40 | 6 Feb 1986 | Death of Dandy Nichols, British stage and television actress.<br>Best known for her role as Elsie, the long-suffering wife of Alf Garnett, in the sitcoms *Till Death Us Do Part* and *In Sickness and in Health*. |
| 40 | 6 Feb 1986 | Death of Minoru Yamasaki, American architect who designed the twin towers of the World Trade Center in New York City (destroyed by terrorists on 11th September 2001). |
| 40 | 7 Feb 1986 | The President of Haiti, Jean-Claude Duvalier, left the country and went into exile in France following a popular uprising.<br>He was succeeded by Henri Namphy. |
| 40 | 8 Feb 1986 | Hinton train collision, Dalehurst, Alberta, Canada. A passenger train and a freight train collided – probably due to crew error/fatigue. 23 people were killed – the worst rail accident in Canadian history at that time (until 2013). |
| 40 | 10 Feb 1986 to Dec 1987 | The Maxi Trial, Palermo, Sicily – the largest-ever criminal trial of the Sicilian Mafia. 474 defendants faced multiple charges, 119 of whom were tried in their absence as they were still on the run. 360 were convicted and 114 were acquitted (of whom 18 were later killed by the Mafia). |
| 40 | 11 Feb 1986 | Death of Frank Herbert, American science fiction writer.<br>Best known for his *Dune* series of novels. |
| 40 | 12 Feb 1986 | The Treaty of Canterbury was signed by Britain and France.<br>It was the agreement to construct the Channel Tunnel linking the two countries. The tunnel opened in 1994. |
| 40 | 19 Feb 1986 | The Akkaraipattu massacre, Sri Lanka.<br>The Sri Lankan Army allegedly shot and killed 80 Tamil farm workers in Sri Lanka's Eastern Province, and burned their bodies. |
| 40 | 19 Feb 1986 | The U.S. Senate finally voted to ratify the Genocide Convention (the Convention on the Prevention and Punishment of the Crime of Genocide) after a 37-year deadlock.<br>The Convention was adopted by the United Nations in 1948 and came into effect in January 1951. The USA ratified it on 25th November 1988. |
| 40 | 20 Feb 1986 | The Soviet Union launched the *Mir* space station.<br>It remained in orbit until 2001. |
| 40 | 21 Feb 1986 | Nintendo released the fantasy action-adventure video game *The Legend of Zelda*. It was the first game in a series that continues to this day.<br>Several games in the series are regarded as being among the greatest video games of all time. |
| 40 | 21 Feb 1986 | Death of Helen Hooven Santmyer, American writer. Best known for her best-selling novel *And Ladies of the Club*, published when she was 88. |
| 40 | 22 Feb 1986 | The first Swedish satellite, *Viking*, was launched.<br>It explored plasma processes in the magnetosphere and ionosphere and remained in operation until May 1987. |
| 40 | 25 Feb 1986 | The President of the Philippines, Ferdinand Marcos, fled the country and went into exile in Hawaii, USA, after being ousted for election fraud.<br>He was succeeded by Corazon Aquino, the first female President of the Philippines. |

## FEBRUARY 2026

| Ann. | Date | Event |
|---|---|---|
| 40 | 26 Feb 1986 | Robert Penn Warren became the USA's first Poet Laureate. |
| 40 | 27 Feb 1986 | The U.S. Senate agreed to allow its debates to be televised (initially on a trial basis, but it later became permanent). |
| 40 | 27 Feb 1986 | Death of Jacques Plante, Canadian ice hockey player.<br>The first professional goaltender to wear a protective face mask |
| 40 | 28 Feb 1986 | Death of Olof Palme, Prime Minister of Sweden (1969–76, 1982–86). (Assassinated.) |
| 30 | 1 Feb 1996 | U.S. President Bill Clinton met Sinn Féin President Gerry Adams at the White House to discuss the Northern Ireland peace process. |
| 30 | 2 Feb 1996 | Following a $61 million loss, Apple's board of directors ousted CEO Michael Spindler and replaced him with Gil Amelio.<br>Losses continued despite cuts and reorganisation, and Amelio brought former CEO Steve Jobs back into the company in February 1997. |
| 30 | 2 Feb 1996 | Death of Gene Kelly, American dancer, actor, choreographer and film director. |
| 30 | 3 Feb 1996 | The Lijiang earthquake, China. 322 people were killed and 14,000 injured. Nearly 200,000 houses collapsed and 300,000 more were badly damaged. |
| 30 | 3 Feb 1996 | Death of Audrey Meadows, American actress. Best known for her role as Alice Kramden in the television comedy series *The Honeymooners*. |
| 30 | 5 Feb 1996 | The first genetically modified food went on sale in the UK: tomato purée made from tomatoes which had had the 'rotting gene' removed.<br>The product was withdrawn in 1999 following strong opposition. |
| 30 | 6 Feb 1996 | The Willamette Valley flood of 1996, Oregon, USA.<br>This was one of a series of floods that affected the Pacific Northwest in the USA in January–February 1996. The floods caused more than $500 million in damage. Eight people were killed. |
| 30 | 6 Feb 1996 | Birgenair Flight 301 crashed into the sea shortly after taking off from Gregorio Luperón International Airport in Puerto Plata, Dominican Republic. All 176 passengers and 13 crew were killed.<br>(Cause: probably instrument error due to a wasp nest blocking a tube. As a result, the pilot received incorrect airspeed information.) |
| 30 | 8 Feb 1996 | The Communications Decency Act was signed into law by U.S. President Bill Clinton. It was Congress's first serious attempt to regulate internet pornography. (The U.S. Supreme Court overturned it and declared it unconstitutional in June 1997 because it infringed the right to free speech.) |
| 30 | 8 Feb 1996 | 24 Hours in Cyberspace was held.<br>It was the largest one-day online event at that time. 1,000 photographers, editors, programmers and designers created a real-time digital time capsule showing life online and the impact of the internet on people's lives. The website received four million hits during the event. |
| 30 | 9 Feb 1996 | The IRA exploded a bomb in London's Docklands.<br>It caused massive damage. Two people were killed. |

# FEBRUARY 2026

| Ann. | Date | Event |
|---|---|---|
| 30 | 9 Feb 1996 | The chemical element copernicium (Cn, atomic number 112) was created for the first time by a team at GSI in Darmstadt, Germany.<br>It is extremely radioactive, can only be created in the laboratory, and is named after the Polish scientist and astronomer Nicolaus Copernicus. |
| 30 | 10 Feb 1996 | IBM's supercomputer *Deep Blue* defeated the reigning world chess champion, Garry Kasparov, in the first of their six games. It was the first time a computer beat a world champion under tournament conditions. Kasparov won the tournament 4–2. But he was defeated when he played Deep Blue again the following year. |
| 30 | 13 Feb 1996 to 21 Nov 2006 | Nepalese Civil War. The Communist Party of Nepal (Maoist) launched a war against government forces with the aim of overthrowing the monarchy and establishing a People's Republic.<br>The war ended with the signing of a Comprehensive Peace Accord.<br>The monarchy was abolished in May 2008 and Nepal became a democratic republic. |
| 30 | 13 Feb 1996 | Death of Martin Balsam, American film and television actor (*Twelve Angry Men, Psycho, Breakfast at Tiffany's, A Thousand Clowns* and the TV sitcom *Archie Bunker's Place*). |
| 30 | 14 Feb 1996 | The launch of the *Intelsat 708* satellite in Xichang, China ended in tragedy when the rocket carrying it veered off course and crashed into a nearby village. Approximately 500 people were killed. |
| 30 | 14 Feb 1996 | Death of Bob Paisley, British football player, and manager of Liverpool FC. |
| 30 | 15 Feb 1996 | *The Scott Report* on Britain's sale of arms to Iraq during the 1980s was published. It was highly critical of the ministers involved and stated that they had misled Parliament and the general public. |
| 30 | 15 Feb 1996 | The oil tanker *Sea Empress* ran aground near Milford Haven in Wales, causing a major oil spill along the coastlines of Wales and Ireland. |
| 30 | 17 Feb 1996 | NASA launched its *NEAR Shoemaker* spacecraft.<br>It successfully orbited and landed on the near-Earth asteroid Eros in 2001.<br>(See also: 12th February 2001.) |
| 30 | 17 Feb 1996 | The Biak earthquake and tsunami, Indonesia.<br>166 people were killed, 423 injured and more than 5,000 made homeless. |
| 30 | 18 Feb 1996 | An IRA terrorist was killed when a home-made bomb he was carrying exploded prematurely on a bus in London, UK.<br>Eight people were injured, including his accomplice. |
| 30 | 21 Feb 1996 | Death of Morton Gould, American composer, conductor, arranger and pianist. |
| 30 | 26 Feb 1996 | The American supercomputer manufacturer Cray Research was purchased by Silicon Graphics Inc. (SGI).<br>SGI sold it to the Tera Computer Company in 2000, and Tera changed its name to Cray. Cray was purchased by Hewlett Packard in 2019. |
| 30 | 26 Feb 1996 | Death of Haing S. Ngor, Cambodian-born American physician, actor and writer. Best known for his role in the film *The Killing Fields*.<br>(Shot dead in Los Angeles, California, USA, aged 55.) |

**FEBRUARY 2026**

| Ann. | Date | Event |
|---|---|---|
| 30 | 27 Feb 1996 | The Pokémon media franchise was launched by Japanese video game designer Satoshi Tajiri. |
| 30 | 28 Feb 1996 | Diana, Princess of Wales announced that she had agreed to divorce Prince Charles. |
| 30 | 29 Feb 1996 | Bosnian War – the Siege of Sarajevo ended. |
| 30 | 29 Feb 1996 | A court ruled that British actress and novelist Joan Collins was entitled to keep a $1.3 million advance from the publisher Random House, plus a further $1.3 million for delivering her manuscripts on time.<br>Random House had claimed that her two books were unpublishable and had demanded their money back. |
| 25 | 7 Feb 2001 | Death of Dale Evans, American actress, singer and songwriter.<br>Wife of the Western actor and singer Roy Rogers. |
| 25 | 7 Feb 2001 | Death of Anne Spencer Morrow Lindbergh, American writer and aviator. |
| 25 | 8 Feb 2001 | Disney's California Adventure opened in Anaheim, California, USA. |
| 25 | 11 Feb 2001 | The Anna Kournikova computer worm was released. It spread via email messages, rapidly infecting tens of thousands of computers.<br>Many organisations shut down their mail servers as a precaution.<br>(Its creator, a Dutch computer programmer, handed himself in to police three days later. He was sentenced to 150 hours' community service.) |
| 25 | 12 Feb 2001 | NASA's *NEAR Shoemaker* spacecraft landed on Eros, becoming the first spacecraft to land on an asteroid. It continued to transmit data for 16 days. |
| 25 | 12 Feb 2001 | The Human Genome Project announced the publication of the first complete working draft of the human genome.<br>The project was declared complete in April 2003, although it was unable to sequence certain regions as the technology did not exist at that time.<br>All of the gaps were found and filled in by May 2021.<br>The complete sequence that was published contains a small number of errors that were still being corrected at the time of writing. |
| 25 | 12 Feb 2001 | Google created Google Groups after acquiring Deja News and its Usenet archive. |
| 25 | 13 Feb 2001 | El Salvador was hit by a second earthquake, exactly a month after the previous one (see 13th January 2001).<br>The two earthquakes killed more than 1,000 people and damaged or destroyed approximately twenty percent of the country's housing |
| 25 | 16 Feb 2001 | Death of Howard W. Koch, American film and TV producer and director. |
| 25 | 18 Feb 2001 | One of the USA's most senior Russian-counterintelligence experts, Robert Hanssen, was arrested for spying for Russia.<br>He later admitted he had been spying for Russia for fifteen years.<br>He was sentenced to life imprisonment. |
| 25 | 18 Feb 2001 to Dec | The Sampit conflict, Central Kalimantan, Indonesia.<br>An outbreak of ethnic violence that began in the town of Sampit spread throughout the province. More than 500 people were killed and 100,000 Madurese people were displaced from their homes. |

# FEBRUARY 2026

| Ann. | Date | Event |
|---|---|---|
| 25 | 18 Feb 2001 | Death of Balthus, French artist. |
| 25 | 18 Feb 2001 | Death of Dale Earnhardt, American stock car racing driver. The dominant NASCAR driver of the 1980s and 90s. (Killed in a crash at the Daytona 500, aged 49.) |
| 25 | 19 Feb 2001 | The first case of foot-and-mouth disease in the 2001 UK outbreak was detected at an abattoir in Essex. On 21st February the European Commission banned all British milk, meat and livestock exports. |
| 25 | 19 Feb 2001 | Death of Stanley Kramer, American film producer and director (*High Noon, Death of a Salesman, The Caine Mutiny, It's a Mad Mad Mad Mad World, Guess Who's Coming to Dinner*, and many more). |
| 25 | 19 Feb 2001 | Death of Charles Trenet, French jazz/easy listening singer and songwriter. |
| 25 | 24 Feb 2001 | Death of Claude Shannon, American mathematician, cryptographer, and electrical engineer. Known as 'the father of information theory'. |
| 25 | 25 Feb 2001 | Death of Don Bradman, Australian cricketer. |
| 25 | 26 Feb 2001 | Bosnian Croat political leader Dario Kordic was convicted of war crimes against the Bosniak people during the Bosnian War. He was sentenced to 25 years in prison (released June 2014). In the same trial, military commander Mario Cerkez was convicted and received a six-year sentence. |
| 25 | 28 Feb 2001 | The Selby rail crash, North Yorkshire, UK. A Land Rover crashed off the M62 motorway onto a railway track. It was hit by a passenger train, which veered into the path of an oncoming goods train. Ten people were killed and more than eighty seriously injured. |
| 20 | 3 Feb 2006 | The Egyptian ferry *MS Al-Salam Boccaccio 98* sank in the Red Sea during bad weather. It was carrying about 1,400 passengers and crew from Duba in Saudi Arabia to Safaga in southern Egypt. 1,031 people were killed. |
| 20 | 3 Feb 2006 | Death of Al Lewis, American actor. Best known for his role as Grandpa in the television sitcom *The Munsters*. |
| 20 | 6 Feb 2006 | Stephen Harper became Prime Minister of Canada (until 2015). |
| 20 | 9 Feb 2006 | Death of Sir Freddie Laker, British entrepreneur. Founder of Laker Airways, which introduced the first low-cost 'no frills' transatlantic flights, but collapsed in 1982 after other airlines slashed their prices. British courts ruled that those airlines had engaged in predatory pricing. Laker's successful legal battle paved the way for similar airlines, including easyJet and RyanAir. |
| 20 | 10 Feb 2006 to 26th | The 20th Winter Olympics were held in Turin, Italy. |
| 20 | 10 Feb 2006 | Death of J Dilla, (also known as Jay Dee), American hip-hop record producer, rapper and DJ. One of the most influential hip-hop producers. (Thrombosis and lupus, aged 32.) |
| 20 | 11 Feb 2006 | American adventurer Steve Fossett broke the record for the longest non-stop flight. He set off from Florida, USA flying east, flew right around the world, and then crossed the Atlantic a second time to land in Bournemouth, England. Distance: 25,766 miles. Time: 76 hours 45 minutes. |

**FEBRUARY 2026**

| Ann. | Date | Event |
|------|------|-------|
| 20 | 11 Feb 2006 | Dick Cheney, the Vice President of the USA, accidentally shot an acquaintance, Harry Whittington, during a quail hunt in Texas. Whittington suffered a minor heart attack three days later when some of pellets lodged in his heart. |
| 20 | 11 Feb 2006 | Death of Peter Benchley, American novelist and environmentalist. Best known for his blockbuster novel *Jaws*. (The film that was based on his novel helped launch director Steven Spielberg's film career.) |
| 20 | 14 Feb 2006 | Death of Lynden David Hall, British Nu-Soul/R&B singer, songwriter, musician, arranger and record producer. (Hodgkin's lymphoma, aged 31.) |
| 20 | 16 Feb 2006 | The U.S. Army decommissioned its last Mobile Army Surgical Hospital (MASH) unit. It was replaced by the Combat Support Hospital. A fictional MASH unit was depicted in the television series *M*A*S*H*. |
| 20 | 16 Feb 2006 | The first computer virus to attack Apple's Mac OS X system was discovered. OSX/Leap-A (or Oompa-A) spread via instant messaging systems, but posed a minimal threat. Many Mac owners were taken by surprise as they believed their machines were immune to such attacks. |
| 20 | 17 Feb 2006 | The Southern Leyte mudslide, Philippines. The mudslide followed ten days of heavy rain and a small earthquake. There was widespread damage and the village of Guinsaugon was completely buried. 1,126 people were killed, including 245 students at an elementary school. |
| 20 | 18 Feb 2006 | American speed skater Shani Davis became the first black athlete to win an individual gold medal at the Winter Olympics. |
| 20 | 18 Feb 2006 | British rock band the Rolling Stones played the world's largest free rock concert on Copacabana Beach, Rio de Janeiro, Brazil. An estimated two million people attended. |
| 20 | 19 Feb 2006 | The Pasta de Conchos mine disaster, near Nueva Rosita, Mexico. 65 coal miners were killed in a methane explosion. |
| 20 | 21 Feb 2006 to 22nd | The largest cash robbery in British history took place at a Securitas depot in Tonbridge, Kent. A gang abducted the manager and his family and took them at gunpoint to the depot. Fourteen staff were tied up. Over £53 million ($85 million) in bank notes was stolen. About £20 million was later recovered. |
| 20 | 22 Feb 2006 | The Al-Askari Mosque in Samarra, Iraq was bombed and severely damaged (probably by the terrorist organisation Al-Qaeda). No one was injured, but at least 1,000 people were killed during retaliatory violence over the following days. |
| 20 | 24 Feb 2006 | Death of Dennis Weaver, American film and television actor (*Gunsmoke*, *McCloud*, *Gentle Ben*). |
| 20 | 27 Feb 2006 | Death of Linda Smith, British comedian and comedy writer. A regular guest on radio and television comedy panel shows. (Ovarian cancer, aged 48.) |

# FEBRUARY 2026

| Ann. | Date | Event |
|---|---|---|
| 15 | 6 Feb 2011 | Jhala Nath Khanal became Prime Minister of Nepal (until August). |
| 15 | 11 Feb 2011 | Arab Spring: the President of Egypt, Hosni Mubarak, resigned after eighteen days of protests during the Egyptian Revolution.<br>He was succeeded by Mohamed Morsi in June 2012.<br>Mohamed Hussein Tantawi, the Chairman of the Supreme Council of the Armed Forces, acted as head of state in the interim. |
| 15 | 14 Feb 2011 to 18 Mar | Arab Spring: the Bahraini uprising.<br>Anti-government protests inspired by the wider Arab Spring protests developed into a sustained campaign of civil disobedience.<br>Military forces from Saudi Arabia and the UAE ended the uprising, and the King declared a three-month state of emergency.<br>As a result of the uprising, the government increased social spending, gave each family 1,000 Bahrani dinar (approximately £2,000/$2,650), and instituted the Bahrani National Dialogue. |
| 15 | 14 Feb 2011 to 16th | IBM's supercomputer Watson beat two champions of the U.S. television game show *Jeopardy!* in three special episodes (*Jeopardy!'s IBM Challenge*) and won a $1 million prize, which IBM donated to two charities. |
| 15 | 15 Feb 2011 to 23 Oct | Arab Spring: the First Libyan Civil War.<br>Large scale protests broke out in Libya against Muammar Gaddafi's regime. The Libyan Revolution began on 17th February.<br>Rebel forces launched an anti-government offensive in August.<br>Gaddafi was captured and killed on 20th October.<br>The National Transitional Council declared the war over and Libya liberated on 23rd October. |
| 15 | 22 Feb 2011 | The Canterbury earthquake, New Zealand.<br>185 people were killed and up to 2,000 injured, and there was widespread damage across the city. |
| 10 | 4 Feb 2016 | Death of Edgar Mitchell, American astronaut.<br>Lunar Module pilot of *Apollo 14*. The sixth person to walk on the Moon.<br>Co-founder of the Institute of Noetic Sciences, which investigates paranormal phenomena. |
| 10 | 7 Feb 2016 | North Korea launched *Kwangmyŏngsŏng-4*, a military reconnaissance satellite. |
| 10 | 13 Feb 2016 | Death of Antonin Scalia, Associate Justice of the U.S. Supreme Court (1986–2016). Succeeded by Neil Gorsuch in April 2017. |
| 10 | 16 Feb 2016 | Death of Boutros Boutros-Ghali, Egyptian politician and diplomat.<br>Secretary-General of the United Nations (1992–96). |
| 10 | 19 Feb 2016 | Death of Umberto Eco, Italian historical novelist, cultural critic and philosopher. Best known for his novels *The Name of the Rose* and *Foucault's Pendulum*. |
| 10 | 19 Feb 2016 | Death of Harper Lee, American novelist<br>Best known for *To Kill a Mockingbird*. |

**MARCH 2026**

| Ann. | Date | Event |
|------|------|-------|
| 900 | 8 Mar 1126 | Death of Urraca, Queen of León, Castile and Galicia. Succeeded by her son, Alfonso VII. |
| 800 | 7 Mar 1226 | Death of William Longespée, 3rd Earl of Salisbury, English nobleman. Best known for commanding the English forces at the Battle of Damme during the Anglo–French War. |
| 700 | 5 Mar 1326 | Birth of Louis I, King of Hungary (1342–82), King of Poland (1370–82). |
| 400 | 12 Mar 1626 | Birth of John Aubrey, English historian, natural philosopher, archaeologist and writer. Known for his biographical collection *Brief Lives*. He documented numerous megalithic monuments in southern England. The Aubrey holes at Stonehenge were named in his honour. |
| 400 | 21 Mar 1626 | Birth of Saint Peter of Saint Joseph de Betancur, Spanish saint and missionary in Guatemala. Known as the 'Saint Francis of Assisi of the Americas'. |
| 300 | 8 Mar 1726 | Birth of Richard Howe, 1st Earl Howe, British Admiral of the Fleet and politician. He commanded fleets in the Seven Years' War, the American Revolutionary War, the French Revolutionary Wars, and other wars. |
| 300 | 26 Mar 1726 | Death of Sir John Vanbrugh, British architect and playwright. Best known for designing Blenheim Palace and Castle Howard. He is also known for his two Restoration comedies, *The Relapse* and *The Provoked Wife*. |
| 250 | 2 Mar 1776 to 3rd | American Revolutionary War – the Battle of the Rice Boats, Georgia. Colonial rebels arrested the Governor of Georgia, James Wright, and tried to prevent the British from removing supply ships from Savannah. The British seized most of the ships. Governor Wright escaped and departed on one of the ships, marking the end of Britain's control of Georgia for that part of the war. He returned as Governor from 1779 until 1782 when the British finally withdrew. |
| 250 | 3 Mar 1776 to 4th | American Revolutionary War – the Battle of Nassau, Bahamas. The U.S. Marine Corps staged their first-ever amphibious landing. They seized two forts and a large quantity of gunpowder and other military supplies, occupied Nassau for two weeks, then returned to Connecticut. |
| 250 | 9 Mar 1776 | Scottish economist and philosopher Adam Smith's book *The Wealth of Nations* was published. It is now regarded as one of the fundamental works of classical economics. |
| 250 | 10 Mar 1776 | Birth of Louise of Mecklenburg–Strelitz, Queen consort of Prussia and Electress consort of Brandenburg (1797–1810). Wife of King Frederick William III. Mother of Frederick William IV of Prussia and the German Emperor William I. |
| 250 | 17 Mar 1776 | American Revolutionary War – the Siege of Boston ended after more than ten months. American victory: the British were forced to evacuate Boston. |
| 250 | 24 Mar 1776 | Death of John Harrison, British carpenter and clockmaker who invented the marine chronometer, which enabled sailors to calculate longitude at sea. |

## MARCH 2026

| Ann. | Date | Event |
|------|------|-------|
| 250 | 28 Mar 1776 | The Presidio of San Francisco was established in California, USA. It became a fortified U.S. Army post and is now a park and a National Historic Landmark. |
| 250 | 31 Mar 1776 | American Revolution: Abigail Adams wrote a letter to her husband, John Adams, urging him and the other members of the Continental Congress to 'remember the ladies' as they fought for America's independence from Britain. She said, 'do not put such unlimited power into the hands of husbands', and 'all men would be tyrants if they could'. |
| 200 | 4 Mar 1826 | Birth of Theodore Judah, American civil engineer and railway pioneer. Chief Engineer for the Central Pacific Railroad. |
| 200 | 10 Mar 1826 | Death of John VI, King of Portugal (1816–26), King of Brazil (1816–22), Emperor of Brazil (1825–26). Succeeded by his son, Pedro IV of Portugal (Pedro I of Brazil). |
| 200 | 21 Mar 1826 | Ludwig van Beethoven's *String Quartet No. 13* (Opus 130) was performed for the first time in Vienna, Austria. The finale was poorly received, and he substituted a shorter, lighter finale in the final version, which was performed for the first time in November 1826. It was the last piece of music he wrote before his death in March 1827. |
| 200 | 24 Mar 1826 | Birth of Matilda Gage, American writer and activist. She campaigned for women's suffrage, Native American rights, and the abolition of slavery. |
| 175 | 3 Mar 1851 | The U.S. Congress authorised the three-cent coin (also known as a *trime*). It remained in circulation until 1873. |
| 175 | 11 Mar 1851 | The première of Italian composer Giuseppe Verdi's opera *Rigoletto*, in Venice, Italy. |
| 175 | 11 Mar 1851 | Death of Marie-Louise Coidavid, Queen consort of Haiti (1811–20). Wife of King Henri I. |
| 175 | 19 Mar 1851 | Birth of Roque Sáenz Peña, President of Argentina (1910–14). |
| 175 | 27 Mar 1851 | The first recorded sighting of Yosemite Valley in California, USA by non-Native Americans (the Mariposa Battalion). |
| 175 | 28 Mar 1851 | Birth of Bernardino Machado, President of Portugal (1915–17, 1925–26). |
| 150 | 2 Mar 1876 | The U.S. Secretary of War, William W. Belknap resigned suddenly. He faced impeachment for corruption. At his impeachment trial in the U.S. Senate in April, the majority of Senators voted to impeach him, but not the two-thirds needed for his impeachment, and he was acquitted. |
| 150 | 2 Mar 1876 | Birth of Pope Pius XII (1939–58). |
| 150 | 5 Mar 1876 | Birth of Thomas Inskip, 1st Viscount Caldecote, British politician. Lord Chief Justice of England (1940–46), Leader of the House of Lords (1940), Lord High Chancellor (1939–40), Attorney General (1932–35). |
| 150 | 7 Mar 1876 | Scottish-born American inventor Alexander Graham Bell was granted a U.S patent for the telephone. The patent application was hotly contested by Elisha Gray, who had filed his own patent on the same day as Bell (14th February). (U.S. Patent 174,465.) (See also: 10th March 1876.) |
| 150 | 7 Mar 1876 to 9th | Ethiopian–Egyptian War – the Battle of Gura (Eritrea). Ethiopian victory in the decisive battle of the war, which ended on 9th March. |

**MARCH 2026**

| Ann. | Date | Event |
|---|---|---|
| 150 | 10 Mar 1876 | The world's first telephone call.<br>Alexander Graham Bell used his telephone to call his assistant, Thomas Watson, after spilling acid in his laboratory. The first words spoken by telephone were: 'Mr Watson, come here. I want you.' |
| 150 | 11 Mar 1876 | Birth of Carl Ruggles, American composer and artist. |
| 150 | 16 Mar 1876 | The first women's boxing match in the USA: Nelly Saunders v. Rose Harland in New York City. Saunders won the match.<br>(Women's boxing began in the UK in the 1720s.) |
| 125 | 1 Mar 1901 | The Australian Army was founded. |
| 125 | 2 Mar 1901 | U.S. Steel (the United States Steel Corporation) was founded by J. P. Morgan when the Carnegie Steel Company merged with the Federal Steel Company and the National Steel Company.<br>Andrew Carnegie announced his retirement on 13th March and said he would become a philanthropist and give away his fortune. |
| 125 | 3 Mar 1901 | The National Institute of Standards and Technology (NIST) was established in the USA (as the National Bureau of Standards). |
| 125 | 4 Mar 1901 | Birth of Wilbur R. Franks, Canadian scientist. Best known for inventing the anti-gravity suit (G-suit) worn by pilots and astronauts to counter the effects of high G forces. |
| 125 | 4 Mar 1901 | Birth of Charles Goren, American bridge player and writer who helped develop and popularise the game. |
| 125 | 5 Mar 1901 | Birth of Louis Kahn, Estonian-born American architect and educator. Known for his monumental and monolithic buildings, including the Yale University Art Gallery and the Salk Institute in San Diego, California. |
| 125 | 13 Mar 1901 | Death of Benjamin Harrison, 23rd President of the USA (1889–93). |
| 125 | 23 Mar 1901 | Philippine–American War: American forces captured the President of the Philippines, Emilio Aguinaldo. He subsequently swore an oath of allegiance to the USA and accepted the USA's authority over the Philippines. However, General Miguel Malvar took over the leadership of the Philippines government, and the war continued until July 1902. |
| 125 | 24 Mar 1901 | Birth of Ub Iwerks, American cartoonist and animator. Best known for creating Oswald the Lucky Rabbit and for co-creating Mickey Mouse with Walt Disney. He won multiple Academy Awards for his cartoons. |
| 125 | 25 Mar 1901 | Birth of Ed Begley, American stage, film, radio and television actor (*Sweet Bird of Youth, 12 Angry Men, The Unsinkable Molly Brown*).<br>Father of the actor Ed Begley Jr. |
| 125 | 29 Mar 1901 and 30th | The first federal elections were held in Australia, to elect members of the first Parliament of Australia. |
| 100 | 1 Mar 1926 | Birth of Pete Rozelle, American businessman and football executive. Commissioner of the National Football League (NFL) (1960–89).<br>(Died 1996.) |
| 100 | 3 Mar 1926 | Birth of James Merrill, American poet. Best known for *The Changing Light at Sandover* and *Divine Comedies*. (Died 1995.) |

## MARCH 2026

| Ann. | Date | Event |
|---|---|---|
| 100 | 4 Mar 1926 | Birth of Richard DeVos, American businessman and sports team owner. Co-founder of Amway. Owner of the Orlando Magic basketball team. (Died 2018.) |
| 100 | 7 Mar 1926 | The first transatlantic telephone call was made, from London, UK to New York City, USA. The commercial transatlantic telephone service began on 7th January 1927. |
| 100 | 10 Mar 1926 | The Book of the Month Club was established in the USA and chose its first selection: *Lolly Willowes; or The Loving Huntsman* by British novelist Sylvia Townsend Warner. |
| 100 | 11 Mar 1926 | Birth of Ralph Abernathy, American pastor and civil rights activist. Martin Luther King Jr.'s chief aide. President of the Southern Christian Leadership Conference following King's assassination in 1968. (Died 1990.) |
| 100 | 13 Mar 1926 | Birth of Raúl Alfonsín, President of Argentina (1983–89). (Died 2009.) |
| 100 | 13 Mar 1926 | Birth of Carlos Roberto Reina, President of Honduras (1994–98). (Died 2003.) |
| 100 | 14 Mar 1926 | The El Virilla train accident, Costa Rica. An overcrowded train derailed after hitting a weakly fastened rail on a bridge. It fell 190 feet (58 metres) into the Virilla River Canyon. 248 people were killed and 93 injured. |
| 100 | 16 Mar 1926 | American physicist and inventor Robert H. Goddard launched the world's first successful liquid-fuelled rocket, in Auburn, Massachusetts. It reached a height of 41 feet (12.5 metres) and landed 184 feet (56 metres) away, demonstrating that liquid propellants were possible. (The site is now a National Historic Landmark: the Goddard Rocket Launching Site.) |
| 100 | 16 Mar 1926 | Birth of Jerry Lewis, ('the King of Comedy'), American comedian and film actor. He began his career with a ten-year comedy partnership with Dean Martin. He also helped develop the video assist, which allowed film directors to view what had been shot without waiting for the film to be developed. (Died 2017.) |
| 100 | 17 Mar 1926 | The musical comedy *The Girl Friend* by Richard Rodgers and Lorenz Hart opened on Broadway. It ran until December. |
| 100 | 18 Mar 1926 | Birth of Peter Graves, American film and television actor. Best known for his roles as Jim Phelps in the television series *Mission: Impossible* and airline pilot Clarence Oveur in the comedy film *Airplane!* (Died 2010.) |
| 100 | 24 Mar 1926 | Birth of Dario Fo, Italian playwright, actor and theatrical director. Winner of the 1997 Nobel Prize in Literature. (Died 2016.) |
| 100 | 26 Mar 1926 ? | The world's first lip-reading tournament was held in Philadelphia, Pennsylvania, USA. It was won by a fifteen-year-old girl. (Some sources give the date as 23rd June 1926.) |
| 100 | 26 Mar 1926 | Death of Constantin Fehrenbach, Chancellor of Germany (1920–21 – resigned over war reparation payments to the Allies). |
| 100 | 27 Mar 1926 | Death of Georges Vezina, Canadian ice hockey goaltender (Montreal Canadiens). (Tuberculosis, aged 39.) |
| 100 | 30 Mar 1926 | Birth of Ingvar Kamprad, Swedish businessman who founded the furniture retail company IKEA. (Died 2018.) |

## MARCH 2026

| Ann. | Date | Event |
|------|------|-------|
| 100 | 31 Mar 1926 | Birth of John Fowles, British novelist (*The French Lieutenant's Woman*). (Died 2005.) |
| 90 | 1 Mar 1936 | Construction work on the Hoover Dam was completed. It stands on the Colorado River on the border between the U.S. states of Arizona and Nevada. |
| 90 | 1 Mar 1936 | The world's first public videophone service was launched at the Leipzig Trade Fair in Germany. Calls could be made between the fair and Augustplatz post office in Berlin, 100 miles away. |
| 90 | 1 Mar 1936 to 4th | A strike aboard the American ocean liner *S.S. California* (which was docked in San Pedro, California) led to the demise of the International Seamen's Union. It was replaced by the National Maritime Union, which merged with the Seafarers International Union of North America in 2001. |
| 90 | 1 Mar 1936 | The U.S. première of the horror film *The Walking Dead*. Released: 14th March. |
| 90 | 4 Mar 1936 | The German airship *Hindenburg* made its first flight. It was the largest airship ever constructed. It was destroyed in a fire in May 1937, ending the era of airship travel. |
| 90 | 4 Mar 1936 | Birth of Jim Clark, Scottish racing driver. Formula One world champion in 1963 and 1965. (Killed in a Formula Two accident in 1968.) |
| 90 | 5 Mar 1936 | The Supermarine Spitfire fighter plane made its first flight, in Eastleigh, Southampton, UK. |
| 90 | 5 Mar 1936 | Birth of Canaan Banana, first President of Zimbabwe (1980–87). (Died 2003.) |
| 90 | 6 Mar 1936 | Birth of Marion Barry, American politician and civil rights activist. Mayor of Washington D. C. (1979–91, 1995–99). He was infamously arrested for smoking crack cocaine in 1990 and served six months in prison. (Died 2014.) |
| 90 | 7 Mar 1936 | In the prelude to WWII, Germany reoccupied the Rhineland and other regions along the Rhine, violating the Treaty of Versailles. (See also: 29th March.) |
| 90 | 8 Mar 1936 | The first stock car race was held at Daytona Beach, Florida, USA. |
| 90 | 11 Mar 1936 | Birth of Antonin Scalia, Associate Justice of the U.S. Supreme Court (1986–2016). (Died 2016.) |
| 90 | 11 Mar 1936 | Death of David Beatty, 1st Earl Beatty, British Admiral of the Fleet and First Sea Lord. |
| 90 | 13 Mar 1936 | Death of Francis Bell, Prime Minister of New Zealand (1925 for two weeks). The first New Zealand-born Prime Minister. |
| 90 | 17 Mar 1936 to 18th | The Great St. Patrick's Day flood, Pittsburgh, Pennsylvania, USA. Warm weather melted snow and ice, and combined with torrential rain to flood the city. About 100,000 buildings were destroyed, steel mills were devastated and workers were made unemployed. The flood caused $250 million worth of damage (equivalent to around $4.75 billion today). |
| 90 | 18 Mar 1936 | Birth of F. W. de Klerk, State President of South Africa (1989–94). He and his government ended apartheid and freed future president Nelson Mandela from prison. Joint winner of the 1993 Nobel Peace Prize (with Nelson Mandela). (Died 2021.) |

## MARCH 2026

| Ann. | Date | Event |
|------|------|-------|
| 90 | 20 Mar 1936 | Birth of Lee 'Scratch' Perry, Jamaican singer, songwriter and record producer. A pioneer of dub music. Noted for his innovative studio and production techniques. (Died 2021.) |
| 90 | 29 Mar 1936 | German parliamentary elections and referendum.<br>Voters were asked to back Nazi Germany's occupation of the Rhineland and choose candidates who were all members of the Nazi Party (other political parties had been abolished).<br>Turnout was officially 99 percent, with over 98 percent expressing their support for the Nazi Party.<br>Any Jews who attempted to vote risked being arrested. |
| 80 | 1 Mar 1946 | The Bank of England was nationalised and taken under government control. It had been a private institution for more than 250 years. |
| 80 | 2 Mar 1946 | The National Assembly of North Vietnam held its first session.<br>(See also: 6th March 1946.) |
| 80 | 4 Mar 1946 | The President of Finland, Carl Gustaf Emil Mannerheim, resigned due to his declining health.<br>He was succeeded (on 11th March) by Juho Kusti Paasikivi. |
| 80 | 5 Mar 1946 | Winston Churchill gave his famous 'Iron Curtain' speech in Fulton, Missouri, USA. He used the term to describe the separation between the Soviet Union/Eastern Bloc and Western countries. |
| 80 | 9 Mar 1946 | The Burnden Park football stadium disaster, Bolton, UK.<br>33 people were killed and hundreds injured in a crush during a match between Bolton Wanderers and Stoke City. The crush was caused by over-crowding, and led to a control on crowd sizes being introduced. |
| 80 | 9 Mar 1946 | Birth of Alexandra Bastedo, British actress and animal welfare campaigner. Best known for her role as Sharron Macready in the television series *The Champions*. (Died 2014.) |
| 80 | 11 Mar 1946 | Rudolf Höss, the former commandant of Auschwitz concentration camp, was captured by British forces in Germany. He was disguised as a gardener named Franz Lang.<br>At the Nuremberg tribunals in April, he admitted being responsible for the deaths of 2.5 million people who had been killed at Auschwitz.<br>He denied any responsibility for a further 1 million who had died of starvation. He went on trial in Poland in March 1947, and was sentenced to death. He was executed on 16th April 1947. |
| 80 | 12 Mar 1946 | The U.S. Civil Aeronautics Administration issued the first commercial helicopter license to the Bell Aircraft Corporation for its Model 47. |
| 80 | 15 Mar 1946 | Birth of Bobby Bonds, American baseball player. (Died 2003.) |
| 80 | 19 Mar 1946 | French Guiana, Guadeloupe, Martinique and Réunion became overseas departments of France. |
| 80 | 20 Mar 1946 | The Aracaju train crash, Brazil.<br>A passenger train derailed while descending a steep incline.<br>185 people were killed and 300 injured.<br>The train conductors and the surviving engineer were forced to flee when grief-stricken relatives of the casualties arrived and attacked them. |

**MARCH 2026**

| Ann. | Date | Event |
|------|------|-------|
| 80 | 24 Mar 1946 | Birth of Kitty O'Neil, American racing driver and stuntwoman. Known as 'the fastest woman in the world'. She held the women's land speed record from 1976 to 2019. (Died 2018.) |
| 80 | 24 Mar 1946 | Death of Alexander Alekhine, Russian-French chess player. World Chess Champion (1927–35, 1937–46). |
| 80 | 25 Mar 1946 | London's Heathrow Airport was opened (as London Airport – it was renamed Heathrow Airport in 1966). |
| 80 | 25 Mar 1946 | Russian composer Igor Stravinsky's *Ebony Concerto* was performed for the first time, by the Woody Herman Band in New York City, USA. Stravinsky wrote the concerto specially for band. |
| 80 | 25 Mar 1946 | Birth of Maurice Krafft, French volcanologist who worked with his wife Katia Krafft. (Both killed in Japan in 1991 when Mount Unzen erupted.) |
| 80 | 28 Mar 1946 | The U.S. State Department published the Acheson–Lilienthal Report (the Report on the International Control of Atomic Energy). It proposed an international control on nuclear weapons, and the avoidance of any future nuclear warfare. Bernard Baruch created a plan (the Baruch Plan) which was presented to the United Nations Atomic Energy Commission. It was rejected by the Soviet Union, who said the USA should scrap its own nuclear weapons before it would consider the plan. |
| 80 | 29 Mar 1946 | Instituto Tecnológico Autónomo de México (ITAM) was founded. It is one of the leading universities in Mexico. |
| 80 | 31 Mar 1946 to May 1950 | The Chinese Civil War resumed after WWII. Communist victory. |
| 75 | 2 Mar 1951 | The U.S. Navy's first hunter-killer submarine, the *USS K-1*, was launched. It was designed to hunt and destroy enemy submarines. It entered service on 10th November. (It was renamed the *Barracuda* in 1955.) |
| 75 | 2 Mar 1951 | The first NBA All-Star basketball game was played, in Boston, Massachusetts, USA. |
| 75 | 3 Mar 1951 | The first rock and roll record, *Rocket 88*, was recorded by Jackie Brenston and his Delta Cats in Memphis, Tennessee, USA. (The Delta Cats were actually Ike Turner's Kings of Rhythm). The record was released in April. |
| 75 | 6 Mar 1951 to 29th | The trial of Julius and Ethel Rosenberg took place in New York City, USA. On 29th March the couple were convicted of conspiring to supply classified atomic information to the Soviet Union. In June 1953 they became the first American civilians to be executed for espionage. |
| 75 | 6 Mar 1951 | Death of Ivor Novello, Welsh composer, playwright, actor, songwriter, entertainer and manager. |
| 75 | 7 Mar 1951 to 4 Apr | Korean War – Operation Ripper (Chuncheon, South Korea). United Nations victory. |
| 75 | 7 Mar 1951 | Death of Haj Ali Razmara, Prime Minister of Iran. (Assassinated in Tehran by a Shiite fundamentalist who was executed for the crime in 1955.) |

## MARCH 2026

| Ann. | Date | Event |
|---|---|---|
| 75 | 8 Mar 1951 | American serial killers Martha Beck and Raymond Fernandez (known as the 'Lonely Hearts Killers' or the 'Honeymoon Killers') were executed. They robbed and murdered up to twenty women who had placed lonely hearts ads in newspapers. |
| 75 | 12 Mar 1951 | Hank Ketcham's comic strip *Dennis the Menace* first appeared in sixteen newspapers in the USA. (Not to be confused with the British comic strip of the same name – see 15th March 1951.) |
| 75 | 15 Mar 1951 | Dennis the Menace first appeared in the British children's comic *The Beano*. (Issue dated 17th March. On sale from 15th March.) |
| 75 | 19 Mar 1951 | The novel *The Caine Mutiny* by American author Herman Wouk was published. Wouk was awarded the Pulitzer Prize for the book, and it was adapted into a film of the same name in 1954. |
| 75 | 20 Mar 1951 | The city of Fujiyoshida in Japan was founded when the towns of Fujikamiyoshida, Shimoyoshida and Akemi were merged. |
| 75 | 20 Mar 1951 | The National Iranian Oil Company was founded. |
| 75 | 23 Mar 1951 to 28th | First Indochina War – the Battle of Mạo Khê, Vietnam. French Union victory. |
| 75 | 25 Mar 1951 | Death of Eddie Collins, ('Cocky'), American baseball player (Philadelphia Athletics, Chicago White Sox), manager and executive. |
| 75 | 26 Mar 1951 | The Flag of the United States Air Force was adopted. |
| 75 | 29 Mar 1951 | The musical *The King and I* by Richard Rodgers and Oscar Hammerstein II opened on Broadway. It ran until 1954. It was adapted into a film of the same name in 1956. |
| 75 | 31 Mar 1951 | UNIVAC I was unveiled. It was the first commercial computer built in the USA that was designed for business and administrative use (rather than scientific/ military use). It was built by the Sperry Rand Corporation for the U.S. Census Bureau. It was officially dedicated on 14th June. |
| 70 | 1 Mar 1956 | East Germany's army, the National People's Army, was established. It was disbanded in 1990. |
| 70 | 1 Mar 1956 | The Arab Legion became the Jordanian Armed Forces. King Hussein of Jordan dismissed its British commander John Bagot Glubb (Glubb Pasha) and replaced him with Radi Annab in order to distance himself from the British and strengthen his position in the Arab world. |
| 70 | 1 Mar 1956 | The NATO phonetic alphabet (also known as the International Radiotelephony Spelling Alphabet) was adopted by the International Civil Aviation Organisation. It was later adopted by many other civil and military organisations, including the International Telecommunication Union in 1959 and the International Maritime Organisation in 1965. |
| 70 | 1 Mar 1956 | Urho Kekkonen became President of Finland (until 1982). |
| 70 | 4 Mar 1956 | Chinese-born American inventor An Wang sold his patent on ferrite core memory to IBM for $500,000. He used the money to expand Wang Laboratories. (Magnetic memory core was invented by Jay Wright Forrester – see 29th February 1956.) |

## MARCH 2026

| Ann. | Date | Event |
|------|------|-------|
| 70 | 5 Mar 1956 | Birth of Teena Marie, American R&B singer, musician, songwriter and record producer. (Died 2010.) |
| 70 | 9 Mar 1956 | Archbishop Makarios III of Cyprus, a prominent nationalist, was arrested by the British and deported to the Seychelles. He spent a year there in exile before leaving to continue his work in Athens, Greece. His arrest sparked riots in Cyprus. (He became the first President of Cyprus in 1960.) |
| 70 | 11 Mar 1956 | Birth of Helen Rollason, British sports journalist and television presenter. She raised £5 million for charity after being diagnosed with terminal cancer. (Died 1999.) |
| 70 | 15 Mar 1956 | The musical *My Fair Lady* opened on Broadway. |
| 70 | 17 Mar 1956 | Death of Irène Joliot-Curie, French physical chemist. Joint winner (with her husband) of the 1935 Nobel Prize in Chemistry for their discovery of artificially prepared radioactive isotopes. Daughter of the scientists Marie and Pierre Curie (who were also Nobel Prize winners). |
| 70 | 20 Mar 1956 | Tunisia gained its independence from France. |
| 70 | 22 Mar 1956 | American civil rights leader Martin Luther King Jr. was convicted of organising an illegal boycott of buses by black passengers in Alabama. He was fined $500, which was later converted into a suspended prison sentence. The boycott continued until December. |
| 70 | 22 Mar 1956 | The musical *Mr. Wonderful* opened on Broadway. It was written by Jerry Bock, Larry Holofcener and George David Weiss to showcase the talents of the entertainer Sammy Davis Jr. It ran until February 1957. |
| 70 | 23 Mar 1956 | Pakistan became the world's first Islamic Republic. |
| 70 | 25 Mar 1956 | The MedicAlert Foundation was founded in the USA. Members wear a bracelet or necklace engraved with their medical information in case of emergency. |
| 70 | 27 Mar 1956 | The BBC made its final television transmission from its studios in Alexandra Palace, London – regarded as the birthplace of television. The following day, broadcasting switched to Lime Grove studios (until 1960), using a new, more powerful transmitter at Crystal Palace. In 1960 it moved into the new Television Centre in White City (until 2013). |
| 70 | 28 Mar 1956 | U.S. Airman D. F. Smith spent 24 hours sealed inside a space cabin simulator at the U.S. Air Force School of Aviation Medicine in Texas. The cabin replicated a real space capsule, and contained an aircraft seat, mock control panel, an oxygen supply, carbon dioxide absorption system, and a urine recycling system. The Air Force later conducted longer studies lasting several days, and also tested two-man simulators. |
| 70 | 31 Mar 1956 | Death of Ralph DePalma, Italian-born American racing driver who won more than 2,000 races. Winner of the Indianapolis 500 in 1915. He was also the world land speed record holder in 1919 (149.875 mph). |

**MARCH 2026**

| Ann. | Date | Event |
|---|---|---|
| 65 | Mar 1961 | The American Basketball League was established.<br>Eight teams were recruited and play began in October.<br>The league collapsed at the end of December 1962.<br>(Three other leagues have used the same name, most recently in 2013–15.) |
| 65 | 1 Mar 1961 | The Peace Corps was established in the USA. |
| 65 | 3 Mar 1961 | The coronation of King Hassan II of Morocco. |
| 65 | 6 Mar 1961 | The first minicabs were introduced in London, UK. |
| 65 | 6 Mar 1961 | Death of George Formby, the 'ukulele king', British comedian, singer and actor. Known for his comic songs, including *When I'm Cleaning Windows*. |
| 65 | 8 Mar 1961 | American aviator Max Conrad set a world record for flying around the world in a light aircraft.<br>He landed in Miami, Florida, USA after flying westward around the world in his Piper Aztec plane in eight days, 18 hours and 49 minutes. |
| 65 | 8 Mar 1961 | Death of Sir Thomas Beecham, British conductor and impresario.<br>He founded several major orchestras and transformed the operatic and orchestral scene in Britain. |
| 65 | 9 Mar 1961 | The Soviet Union launched its *Sputnik 9* spacecraft on a test flight.<br>It carried a mannequin cosmonaut, a dog named Chernushka (meaning 'Blackie'), some mice and a guinea pig.<br>It completed one orbit of the Earth before landing safely. During the descent, the mannequin was ejected and returned to Earth by parachute. |
| 65 | 10 Mar 1961 | Birth of Laurel Clark, American astronaut.<br>(Killed in the space shuttle *Columbia* disaster in 2003, aged 41.) |
| 65 | 13 Mar 1961 | U.S. President John F. Kennedy launched the Alliance for Progress, a ten-year aid programme for Latin America.<br>The programme failed because Latin Americans were unwilling to implement the necessary reforms, later U.S. Presidents were less supportive of the programme, and the amount of money put into the programme was too low to make a significant difference. |
| 65 | 14 Mar 1961 | The Yuba City B-52 crash, California, USA.<br>A bomber aircraft crashed after running out of fuel. It was carrying two (some sources say four) nuclear weapons. Safety devices prevented the weapons from detonating, and no radioactive material was released.<br>The crew ejected safely before the crash. |
| 65 | 17 Mar 1961 | Death of Susanna M. Salter, American politician and prohibition advocate. The first female mayor in the USA (Argonia, Kansas, 1887–88). |
| 65 | 23 Mar 1961 | Death of Jack Russell, ('The Master'), British cricket player (Essex and England 1908–30). One of the greatest batsmen in cricketing history. |
| 65 | 29 Mar 1961 | The 23rd Amendment to the U.S. Constitution was ratified.<br>It allowed residents of Washington, DC to vote in presidential elections. |
| 65 | 30 Mar 1961 | The Single Convention on Narcotic Drugs was signed.<br>It regulated the production and supply of opioid drugs.<br>It did not come into effect until 1975. |

## MARCH 2026

| Ann. | Date | Event |
|------|------|-------|
| 60 | 1 Mar 1966 | The Soviet space probe *Venera 3* probably crash-landed on Venus. It was the first spacecraft to land on the surface of another planet. Its communications system had failed before it reached Venus. |
| 60 | 1 Mar 1966 | The folk-pop song *Monday, Monday* by the Mamas & the Papas was released. |
| 60 | 3 Mar 1966 | Death of Alice Pearce, American stage, film and television comedy actress. Best known for her role as neighbour Gladys Kravitz in the TV sitcom *Bewitched*. (Ovarian cancer, aged 48.) |
| 60 | 4 Mar 1966 | British rock musician John Lennon famously said the Beatles were 'more popular than Jesus' in an interview for the *London Evening Standard*. His comment drew no complaints in the UK, but generated huge controversy when it was reprinted in the USA in July. In August, many U.S. radio stations staged public burnings of the Beatles' records and memorabilia. |
| 60 | 5 Mar 1966 | BOAC Flight 911, a round-the-world flight, crashed near Mount Fuji, Japan, killing all 124 people on board. It is thought that the plane encountered fierce winds near the summit when the pilot tried to give passengers a better view of the landmark. |
| 60 | 5 Mar 1966 | Death of Anna Akhmatova, Russian Modernist poet. Regarded as the greatest female poet in Russian literature. |
| 60 | 8 Mar 1966 | Nelson's Pillar in Dublin, Ireland was destroyed by an IRA bomb. The 134-foot (41-metre) monument to Lord Horatio Nelson had stood for 158 years. |
| 60 | 9 Mar 1966 to 10th | Vietnam War – the Battle of A Shau (A Shau Valley Special Forces Camp, South Vietnam). North Vietnamese victory. |
| 60 | 10 Mar 1966 | France withdrew from NATO's integrated military command in protest at the USA's dominance. It re-joined in 2009, but refused to join NATO's Nuclear Planning Group. |
| 60 | 10 Mar 1966 | Princess Beatrix of the Netherlands (later Queen Beatrix) married German diplomat Claus von Amsberg. |
| 60 | 11 Mar 1966 | Three members of the Nation of Islam were convicted of murdering the American black nationalist leader Malcolm X in February 1965. They all received life sentences. |
| 60 | 12 Mar 1966 | The American rock band Love released their self-titled first album, *Love*. |
| 60 | 15 Mar 1966 | Death of Abe Saperstein, American basketball coach and executive. Founder, owner and coach of the Harlem Globetrotters. |
| 60 | 16 Mar 1966 | NASA launched its *Gemini 8* spacecraft, manned by Neil Armstrong and David Scott. It took part in the first docking of two spacecraft in orbit but suffered a malfunction shortly afterwards and the mission was aborted. It returned to Earth safely the same day after completing six orbits. |

## MARCH 2026

| Ann. | Date | Event |
|------|------|-------|
| 60 | 20 Mar 1966 | The FIFA World Cup Trophy (the Jules Rimet Trophy) was stolen from Central Hall in London where it was on display. It was found (by a dog named Pickles) a week later. It was permanently awarded to Brazil in 1970, but it was stolen again in 1983 and never recovered. |
| 60 | 21 Mar 1966 | The Beach Boys' hit song *Sloop John B* was released in the USA. (UK: 15th April.) |
| 60 | 24 Mar 1966 | The U.S. Supreme Court ruled that state poll taxes were unconstitutional. (Five states required their citizens to pay a poll tax in order to be eligible to vote. This practice was outlawed.) |
| 60 | 25 Mar 1966 | Birth of Jeff Healey, blind Canadian blues-rock/jazz guitarist and singer (the Jeff Healey Band, Blue Direction, the Jazz Wizards). (Died 2008.) |
| 60 | 26 Mar 1966 to 8 Jun | Buddhist Uprising, South Vietnam. Buddhist monks led a civil and military uprising against the military junta ruling South Vietnam. South Vietnamese government victory |
| 60 | 30 Mar 1966 | Death of Maxfield Parrish, American artist and illustrator. The most popular commercial artist in the USA during first half of the 20th century. Known for his fantasy landscapes featuring attractive young women, meticulously defined outlines, detailed backgrounds and unusual colours. |
| 60 | 31 Mar 1966 | British General Election. Prime Minister Harold Wilson's Labour Party won the election with an increased majority of 96. The election was called because Labour's majority of four in the 1964 election had proved unworkable. |
| 60 | 31 Mar 1966 | The Soviet Union launched its *Luna 10* spacecraft. It became the first spacecraft to orbit the Moon. It studied the gravity, magnetism, and solar and cosmic radiation levels in the Moon's environment. It operated until May. |
| 50 | 4 Mar 1976 | The Northern Ireland Constitutional Convention was dissolved after it failed to achieve cross-party support for power-sharing. Northern Ireland remained under the direct rule of the British Parliament. |
| 50 | 4 Mar 1976 | The 'Maguire Seven' were convicted of possessing explosives, which they allegedly passed to the IRA to make the bombs used in the Guildford pub bombings of October 1974. They received prison sentences totalling 73 years. (Their convictions were quashed by the Court of Appeal in 1991.) |
| 50 | 4 Mar 1976 | Pan Am became the first airline to be charged with criminal negligence. It related to the crash of Pan Am Flight 160, a cargo plane that crashed at Logan International Airport in Boston, Massachusetts, USA in November 1973 after the cockpit filled with smoke. Pan Am pleaded no contest. |
| 50 | 9 Mar 1976 | The Cavalese cable car disaster, Dolomite mountains, northern Italy. A steel cable snapped and a cable car fell 660 feet (200 metres) down a mountainside. A three-ton overhead carriage assembly fell on top of the car, crushing it. 43 of the 44 people inside were killed. Four officials later received prison sentences. |
| 50 | 14 Mar 1976 | Death of Busby Berkeley, American film director and choreographer. Known for his elaborate musical production numbers, which often featured large numbers of dancing girls forming kaleidoscopic patterns. |

## MARCH 2026

| Ann. | Date | Event |
|---|---|---|
| 50 | 15 Mar 1976 | An IRA bomb exploded on a London Underground train at West Ham station. No one was injured, but the train driver was shot dead when he chased the bomber. |
| 50 | 16 Mar 1976 | British Prime Minister Harold Wilson announced his resignation (effective from 5th April), saying he was exhausted and had always intended retiring at the age of 60. He was succeeded by James Callaghan. |
| 50 | 17 Mar 1976 | Birth of Stephen Gately, Irish pop singer and actor. Best known as a member of the boy band Boyzone. (Died 2009.) |
| 50 | 17 Mar 1976 | Death of Luchino Visconti, Italian film and stage director and opera producer. Known as the father of Neorealism. Best known for the films *The Leopard* and *Death in Venice*. |
| 50 | 19 Mar 1976 | Buckingham Palace announced the separation of Princess Margaret and the Earl of Snowdon after sixteen years of marriage. |
| 50 | 19 Mar 1976 | Death of Paul Kossoff, British rock guitarist (Free). |
| 50 | 20 Mar 1976 | American newspaper heiress Patricia ('Patty') Hearst was convicted of robbing a San Francisco bank with members of the Symbionese Liberation Army who had kidnapped her. She was sentenced to 35 years imprisonment (reduced to two years by U.S. President Jimmy Carter). She served 22 months. She was granted a full pardon in 2001. |
| 50 | 23 Mar 1976 | The International Covenant on Civil and Political Rights came into effect. |
| 50 | 24 Mar 1976 | The President of Argentina, Isabel Perón, was deposed and arrested by the Argentine military. She was succeeded by military dictator Jorge Rafael Videla on 29th March. |
| 50 | 24 Mar 1976 | Death of Bernard Montgomery, 1st Viscount Montgomery of Alamein, British field marshal. |
| 50 | 25 Mar 1976 to 28th | The First Annual World Altair Computer Convention was held in Albuquerque, New Mexico, USA. It was the first microcomputer convention, and was for developers and users of the MITS Altair 8800 computer. Bill Gates (aged 20), the co-founder of Microsoft, gave the opening address. |
| 50 | 26 Mar 1976 | Queen Elizabeth II sent the first royal email, from the Royal Signals and Radar Establishment in Malvern, England, which had just been connected to the ARPANET. (The ARPANET later became the internet). |
| 50 | 27 Mar 1976 | The first section of the Washington Metro opened, in Washington, D.C., USA. |
| 50 | 28 Mar 1976 | Death of Arthur Crudup, American Delta blues singer, songwriter and guitarist. Several of his songs were covered by other artists, including Elvis Presley. |
| 50 | 31 Mar 1976 | The New Jersey Supreme Court in the USA ruled that 22-year-old Karen Anne Quinlan could be disconnected from her respirator. She had fallen into a coma after taking Valium and drinking alcohol while on a crash diet. She was disconnected from her respirator in May, but to everyone's surprise, she continued breathing unaided. She remained in a persistent vegetative state until her death in 1985. |

## MARCH 2026

| Ann. | Date | Event |
|------|------|-------|
| 50 | 31 Mar 1976 | Death of Paul Strand, American Modernist photographer and filmmaker who helped establish photography as an art form. |
| 40 | 3 Mar 1986 | Queen Elizabeth II signed the Australia Act, severing Australia's remaining legal ties with Britain and granting it full independence. |
| 40 | 4 Mar 1986 | The British tabloid newspaper *Today* was launched. It was the first national British newspaper to use computer photo-typesetting and full-colour offset printing. (It ceased publication in November 1995.) |
| 40 | 4 Mar 1986 | Death of Howard Greenfield, American songwriter, especially for Neil Sedaka and Connie Francis. |
| 40 | 4 Mar 1986 | Death of Richard Manuel, Canadian singer, pianist, drummer and composer (The Band). (Suicide, aged 42.) |
| 40 | 4 Mar 1986 | Death of Elizabeth Smart, Canadian poet and novelist. Best known for her prose poem/novel *By Grand Central Station I Sat Down and Wept*. |
| 40 | 6 Mar 1986 | The Soviet space probe *Vega 1* flew past Halley's Comet and sent back the first photos and measurements of its nucleus and coma. (See also: 14th March 1986.) |
| 40 | 6 Mar 1986 | Death of Georgia O'Keeffe, American artist. |
| 40 | 7 Mar 1986 and 8th | The U.S. Navy located the crew compartment of the Space Shuttle *Challenger* on the floor of the Atlantic Ocean. *Challenger* exploded shortly after launch on 28th January. The compartment was largely intact but heavily damaged. The bodies of the seven astronauts were still inside. Any astronauts who survived the explosion would have been killed instantly when the compartment hit the surface of the ocean. The compartment and bodies were recovered. |
| 40 | 9 Mar 1986 | Mário Soares became President of Portugal (until 1996). |
| 40 | 10 Mar 1986 | Death of Ray Milland, Welsh-born American film actor and director (*Reap the Wild Wind*, *The Lost Weekend*, *Dial M for Murder*, *Love Story*). |
| 40 | 11 Mar 1986 | The National Football League (NFL) in the USA adopted instant replay. It allowed disputed calls to be instantly reviewed. It was used for the first time on 7th September in a game between the Chicago Bears and the Cleveland Browns. |
| 40 | 12 Mar 1986 | The first CeBIT (the world's largest computer exposition) opened in Hanover, Germany. It began life as the computer section of the Hanover Fair in 1970, but from 1986 it became a separate trade show. |
| 40 | 13 Mar 1986 | Microsoft went public, holding its Initial Public Offering (IPO), ten years after it was founded. Bill Gates became the world's youngest billionaire. |
| 40 | 14 Mar 1986 | The European Space Agency's *Giotto* space probe made its closest approach to Halley's Comet and sent back photos of its nucleus. (It also visited the comet Grigg–Skjellerup in July 1992.) |
| 40 | 15 Mar 1986 | Cosmonauts Leonid Kizim and Vladimir Solovyev became the first occupants of the Soviet Union's *Mir* space station. They remained onboard for 50 days. |

## MARCH 2026

| Ann. | Date | Event |
|------|------|-------|
| 40 | 17 Mar 1986 | Buckingham Palace announced the engagement of Prince Andrew, Duke of York and Sarah Ferguson.<br>They were married on 23rd July 1986 and divorced in 1996. |
| 40 | 17 Mar 1986 | Death of Sir John Bagot Glubb, (Glubb Pasha), British Army officer.<br>Commander of the Arab Legion in Transjordan/Jordan (1939–56). |
| 40 | 18 Mar 1986 | Death of Bernard Malamud, American novelist and short story writer.<br>One of the best known American Jewish authors of the 20th century. |
| 40 | 20 Mar 1986 | The highest official wind speed ever recorded in the UK: 173 mph at Cairngorm Summit in Scotland.<br>Higher wind speeds have been recorded, but the records are unofficial.<br>The highest was 197 mph in Shetland on 1st January 1992, during a storm that destroyed the measuring equipment. |
| 40 | 21 Mar 1986 | Debi Thomas became the first African American to win the World Figure Skating Championships. |
| 40 | 24 Mar 1986 | Action in the Gulf of Sidra, Mediterranean Sea.<br>Following Libya's claim that the Gulf was its territory, U.S. aircraft carriers crossed the 'Line of Death' into the Gulf and began operating there.<br>They were attacked by Libyan aircraft and patrol boats. U.S. Forces responded, and destroyed numerous Libyan ships and radar stations. |
| 40 | 25 Mar 1986 | Iran–Contra affair: U.S. President Ronald Reagan announced that he was sending emergency military aid to Honduras to repel attacks by Nicaraguan government forces (Sandinistas) on camps housing Nicaraguan rebels (Contras). |
| 40 | 27 Mar 1986 | The Russell Street Police Headquarters Bombing, Melbourne, Australia.<br>A bomb hidden in a stolen car exploded at the police headquarters, injuring 23 people, one of whom later died. Constable Angela Taylor was the first Australian policewoman killed in the line of duty.<br>Three men were convicted of carrying out the bombing. They had all served previous prison sentences, and the bombing was apparently their revenge against the police. |
| 40 | 29 Mar 1986 | Death of Harry Ritz, American singer, dancer, comedian and actor (the Ritz Brothers). |
| 40 | 30 Mar 1986 | Death of James Cagney, American stage and film actor and dancer.<br>Best known for his tough-guy film roles (*The Public Enemy*, *Taxi!*, *Angels with Dirty Faces*, *The Roaring Twenties*, *White Heat*, and more). |
| 40 | 31 Mar 1986 | The Greater London Council (GLC) was abolished after 97 years, along with six other English metropolitan county councils: Greater Manchester, Merseyside, South Yorkshire, Tyne and Wear, West Midlands, and West Yorkshire. |
| 40 | 31 Mar 1986 | The 17th century King's Apartments at Hampton Court Palace in Richmond, London were severely damaged by fire.<br>It caused about £5 million ($8 million) worth of damage. |
| 40 | 31 Mar 1986 | Death of Kelly Isley, American R&B/rock/soul singer (The Isley Brothers).<br>(Heart attack, aged 48.) |

## MARCH 2026

| Ann. | Date | Event |
|------|------|-------|
| 30 | 2 Mar 1996 | Death of Jacobo Majluta, President of the Dominican Republic (1982 for six weeks), Vice President of the Dominican Republic (1978–82) |
| 30 | 4 Mar 1996 | Death of Minnie Pearl, American country music entertainer and comedian. She performed at the Grand Ole Opry for more than fifty years and appeared on the television show *Hee Haw* for more than twenty years. |
| 30 | 6 Mar 1996 | Death of Simon Cadell, British actor. Best known for his role as holiday camp entertainments manager Jeffrey Fairbrother in the television sitcom *Hi-de-Hi!* (Lung cancer from heavy smoking, aged 47.) |
| 30 | 7 Mar 1996 | The first democratically elected Palestinian Parliament (the Palestinian Legislative Council) was inaugurated. |
| 30 | 9 Mar 1996 | Jorge Sampaio became President of Portugal (until 2006). |
| 30 | 9 Mar 1996 | Death of George Burns, American comedian, actor and comedy writer. He performed for more than 70 years in vaudeville, radio, film and television, often with his wife and comedy partner Gracie Allen. He continued performing until well into his late-90s, and died aged 100. |
| 30 | 11 Mar 1996 | John Howard became Prime Minister of Australia (until 2007). |
| 30 | 13 Mar 1996 | The Dunblane massacre, Scotland. Thomas Hamilton, a former scout leader, entered Dunblane Primary School, shot dead sixteen children and a teacher, and wounded fifteen others. He then committed suicide. As a result, the private ownership of handguns was banned in the UK. |
| 30 | 13 Mar 1996 | The Summit of the Peacemakers was held in Egypt in an attempt to put the Israeli–Palestinian peace process back on track. |
| 30 | 15 Mar 1996 | The Dutch aircraft manufacturer Fokker went out of business. |
| 30 | 16 Mar 1996 | British world heavyweight boxing champion Frank Bruno lost his title to American boxer Mike Tyson. Bruno retired soon afterwards after being warned by doctors that he risked permanent blindness if he boxed again. |
| 30 | 18 Mar 1996 | The Ozone Disco fire, Quezon City, Philippines. The worst fire in Philippine history broke out in the nightclub. There were around 350 patrons and 40 staff inside the club at the time, though it was only licensed to hold 35 people. The only exit was a small door that opened inwards, fire extinguishers were defective, and the sprinklers did not work. 162 people were killed and 95 injured. (Cause: electrical fire in the DJ's booth.) The club's owners and numerous government officials were subsequently convicted of negligence. |
| 30 | 20 Mar 1996 | The British government reported that variant Creutzfeldt-Jakob disease (vCJD) in humans was linked to BSE ('mad cow disease') and could be transmitted to humans who ate infected beef. On 25th March, the European Union banned the export of British beef (until 2006). Beef from cattle over 30 months old was also banned from human consumption in the UK (until 2005). (BSE does not fully develop in cattle until they are over 30 months old.) |
| 30 | 22 Mar 1996 | Göran Persson became Prime Minister of Sweden (until 2006). |

**MARCH 2026**

| Ann. | Date | Event |
|---|---|---|
| 30 | 23 Mar 1996 | Taiwan held its first democratic election.<br>The incumbent President, Lee Teng-hui, was re-elected. |
| 30 | 25 Mar 1996 | The Labour Party was founded in Turkey.<br>The Marxist-Leninist Socialist organisation was banned almost immediately, and re-established as the Party of Labour.<br>The original name was reinstated in 2005 after the European Court of Human Rights ruled that the ban violated human rights. |
| 30 | 26 Mar 1996 | The International Monetary Fund (IMF) approved a three-year $10.2 billion loan to Russia to help it transform its economy, provided that it implemented structural reforms. |
| 30 | 26 Mar 1996 to 27th | Algerian Civil War: seven Trappist monks (the Martyrs of Atlas) were kidnapped from the Notre-Dame de l'Atlas monastery in Tibhirine.<br>They were found dead on 21st May. The circumstances of their deaths remains controversial. The Armed Islamic Group claimed to have executed them, but they may have been accidentally killed when an Algerian Army helicopter attacked the camp where they were being held. |
| 30 | 26 Mar 1996 | Death of Edmund Muskie, U.S. Secretary of State (1980–81). |
| 30 | 26 Mar 1996 | Death of David Packard, American electrical engineer and businessman. Co-founder of Hewlett-Packard. |
| 25 | 2 Mar 2001 | Death of John Diamond, British journalist and broadcaster.<br>Husband of TV cook Nigella Lawson. (Cancer, aged 47.) |
| 25 | 4 Mar 2001 | The Real IRA detonated a car bomb outside the BBC Television Centre in London. One person was injured.<br>Five men were later arrested, convicted and imprisoned for up to 22 years. Three of them had been involved in other bombing operations. |
| 25 | 4 Mar 2001 | Death of Glenn Hughes, American singer (Village People).<br>(Cancer, aged 50.) |
| 25 | 4 Mar 2001 | Death of Fred Lasswell, American cartoonist. Best known for his *Snuffy Smith* comic strip, which ran for nearly sixty years. |
| 25 | 7 Mar 2001 | Ariel Sharon became Prime Minister of Israel (until 2006 when he suffered a stroke and fell into a coma). |
| 25 | 8 Mar 2001 | British racing driver Donald Campbell's speedboat *Bluebird* was recovered from the bottom of Coniston Water in Cumbria. It crashed and sank there during a record attempt in January 1967 in which he was killed.<br>His body was recovered in May 2001. |
| 25 | 8 Mar 2001 | Death of Edward Winter, American stage, film and television actor.<br>Best known for his role as Colonel Samuel Flagg in the TV series *M\*A\*S\*H*. |
| 25 | 12 Mar 2001 | Death of Morton Downey Jr., American television talk show host. |
| 25 | 12 Mar 2001 | Death of Robert Ludlum, American thriller novelist.<br>Best known for *The Bourne Identity* and its sequels. |
| 25 | 15 Mar 2001 | Death of Ann Sothern, American stage, film, radio and television actress. Known for *Maisie Ravier* (ten films and a radio series), *Private Secretary*, *The Ann Sothern Show* and *The Whales of August*. |

# MARCH 2026

| Ann. | Date | Event |
| --- | --- | --- |
| 25 | 16 Mar 2001 | The Shijiazhuang bombings, China. Several bombs exploded near apartment buildings in the city. 108 people were killed and 38 injured. The perpetrator carried out the attacks out of hatred for his ex-wife, ex-mother-in-law and a former lover, who lived in the buildings. He was sentenced to death and executed, along with three others who supplied him with the explosives. |
| 25 | 18 Mar 2001 | Death of John Phillips, American singer, songwriter and guitarist (The Mamas & the Papas). |
| 25 | 21 Mar 2001 | Nintendo's Game Boy Advance handheld video games console was released in Japan. (North America: 11th June, Europe/Australia: 22nd June.) |
| 25 | 22 Mar 2001 | Death of William Hanna, American cartoon animator. Co-founder of Hanna-Barbera (with Joseph Barbera). They created popular characters including Tom and Jerry, Huckleberry Hound, Yogi Bear, the Flintstones, and the Jetsons |
| 25 | 23 Mar 2001 | The Russian space station *Mir* re-entered the Earth's atmosphere after fifteen years in orbit. Most of it burned up on re-entry. The remaining debris landed in the South Pacific. |
| 25 | 24 Mar 2001 | Apple released its Mac OS X operating system (now macOS). |
| 25 | 25 Mar 2001 | Death of Brian Trubshaw, British test pilot. The first British pilot to fly Concorde, in 1969. |
| 25 | 26 Mar 2001 | The UK Post Office was rebranded as Consignia, at a cost of around £2 million. The new name proved extremely unpopular. It was renamed Royal Mail Group in 2002. |
| 20 | 1 Mar 2006 | The Senedd – the National Assembly for Wales's debating chamber – was officially opened by Queen Elizabeth II in Cardiff. |
| 20 | 1 Mar 2006 | The first case of the H5N1 bird flu virus was confirmed in Switzerland – in a dead swan found on Lake Geneva. |
| 20 | 1 Mar 2006 | Death of Peter Osgood, British football player. Best known for his career with Chelsea FC, where he was known as 'The King of Stamford Bridge'. |
| 20 | 1 Mar 2006 | Death of Jack Wild, British stage and film actor and singer. Best known for his role as the Artful Dodger in *Oliver!* |
| 20 | 2 Mar 2006 | Sir Menzies Campbell became leader of Britain's Liberal Democrat Party. |
| 20 | 3 Mar 2006 | Death of Ivor Cutler, Scottish poet, singer, songwriter, and humourist. |
| 20 | 6 Mar 2006 | NTL:Telewest was formed in the UK when the two largest cable operators, NTL and Telewest, merged. It merged with Virgin Mobile in July 2006 and became Virgin Media. |
| 20 | 6 Mar 2006 | Death of Kirby Puckett, American baseball player (Minnesota Twins). |
| 20 | 7 Mar 2006 | The Varanasi bombings, India. The Lashkar-e-Taiba terrorist organisation detonated bombs at a temple and railway station. 28 people were killed and 101 injured. |
| 20 | 7 Mar 2006 | Death of John Junkin, British radio, film and television comedy actor and scriptwriter (*A Hard Day's Night*, *The Plank*, *Confessions of a Driving Instructor*, *The Goodies* [TV], *I'm Sorry I Haven't A Clue* [radio], and more). |

**MARCH 2026**

| Ann. | Date | Event |
|------|------|-------|
| 20 | 7 Mar 2006 | Death of Gordon Parks, American photographer, writer and film director who documented African-American life. Noted for his photo essays for *Life* magazine, where he was the first African American staff photographer. He also directed the film *Shaft*. |
| 20 | 7 Mar 2006 | Death of Ali Farka Touré, Malian singer, guitarist and national hero. One of the most renowned musicians in world music. |
| 20 | 9 Mar 2006 | NASA announced that its *Cassini* space probe had discovered liquid water geysers on Saturn's sixth-largest moon Enceladus. This was the first time that liquid water had been detected outside the Earth's atmosphere. More recent data indicates the presence of a liquid water ocean beneath Enceladus's icy crust. |
| 20 | 9 Mar 2006 | Aníbal Cavaco Silva became President of Portugal (until 2016). |
| 20 | 9 Mar 2006 | Death of John Profumo, British politician. Secretary of State for War (1960–63). He was forced to resign over the Profumo Affair – one of the most infamous sex scandals of the 20th century. |
| 20 | 10 Mar 2006 | NASA's *Mars Reconnaissance Orbiter* spacecraft reached Mars and began orbiting it. At the time of writing it is still operating. |
| 20 | 11 Mar 2006 | Michelle Bachelet became the first female President of Chile (until 2010). She became President again from 2014 to 2018. |
| 20 | 11 Mar 2006 | Death of Slobodan Miloševic, President of the Socialist Republic of Serbia (1989–91), first President of Serbia (1991–97), President of Yugoslavia (1997–2000). He was on trial for war crimes, genocide and crimes against humanity at the time of his death. (Found dead in his cell – heart attack.) |
| 20 | 13 Mar 2006 | Death of Jimmy Johnstone, ('Jinky'), Scottish footballer (Celtic and Scotland). |
| 20 | 14 Mar 2006 | The world première of the computer-generated sports comedy film *Cars*, at the ShoWest Convention (now CinemaCon) in Las Vegas, Nevada, USA. U.S. première: 26th May, released: 9th June. UK: 28th July. |
| 20 | 14 Mar 2006 | Death of Lennart Meri, President of Estonia (1992–2001). |
| 20 | 15 Mar 2006 | The United Nations Human Rights Council was established. It replaced the UN Commission on Human Rights, which was criticised for allowing countries with poor human rights records to become members. |
| 20 | 17 Mar 2006 | Death of Oleg Cassini, American fashion designer. Best known for creating U.S. First Lady Jacqueline Kennedy's iconic wardrobe – 'the Jackie Look'. |
| 20 | 19 Mar 2006 | Belarus presidential election. Incumbent president Alexander Lukashenko won 84.4 percent of the votes and was re-elected. European observers said it failed to meet the requirements of a democratic election. American officials said it was rigged. (Belarus has been called Europe's last dictatorship.) Despite massive public protests and calls for his resignation, Lukashenko remained in office. |
| 20 | 20 Mar 2006 | Cyclone Larry hit Queensland, Australia. It caused A$1.5 billion (£680 million, US$1.1 billion) worth of damage. Up to 90 percent of the country's banana crop was destroyed. |

## MARCH 2026

| Ann. | Date | Event |
|---|---|---|
| 20 | 21 Mar 2006 | Twitter, the online social networking/micro-blogging service, was founded. Its website went live on 15th July. |
| 20 | 21 Mar 2006 | A British court ruled that existing libel laws also applied online – in the first case of its kind. Tracy Williams of Greater Manchester was ordered to pay £17,200 in damages and legal costs after libelling a former parliamentary candidate in a Yahoo! discussion group and on her blog. (Keith-Smith v. Williams.) |
| 20 | 21 Mar 2006 | A study published by the Games for Health Project found that playing casual games, such as puzzle games, could benefit mental and physical health. |
| 20 | 23 Mar 2006 | Death of Desmond Doss, U.S. Army medic. He was awarded the Medal of Honor for saving the lives of his comrades during the Battle of Okinawa. He was the first conscientious objector (of three) to receive the Medal of Honor. He took part in WWII, but refused to carry a weapon into combat or to kill anyone. |
| 20 | 24 Mar 2006 | Death of Lynne Perrie, British film and television actress, singer and entertainer. Best known for her role as Ivy Tilsley in the ITV soap opera *Coronation Street*. |
| 20 | 25 Mar 2006 | The Capitol Hill massacre, Seattle, Washington, USA. A gunman entered an after-party event at a private house, shot and killed six people, wounded two others, and then killed himself. He is thought to have been upset by young people's promiscuity. |
| 20 | 25 Mar 2006 | Death of Richard Fleischer, American film director (*20,000 Leagues Under the Sea, Fantastic Voyage, Soylent Green*). |
| 20 | 26 Mar 2006 | Death of Nikki Sudden, British post-punk/rock singer, songwriter, guitarist and rock critic. |
| 20 | 26 Mar 2006 | Scotland banned smoking in all indoor public places and workplaces. A similar ban came into effect in England and Wales in July 2007. |
| 20 | 27 Mar 2006 | Naypyidaw was named the new capital city of Burma (Myanmar), replacing Yangon. |
| 20 | 28 Mar 2006 | Death of Caspar Weinberger, U.S. Secretary of Defense (1981–87). He resigned over his role in the Iran–Contra Affair. He was pardoned by U.S. President George H. W. Bush shortly before his trial began in 1992. |
| 20 | 30 Mar 2006 | The Terrorism Act 2006 came into effect in the UK. It was introduced following the London bombings on 7th July 2005. |
| 20 | 30 Mar 2006 | Marcos Pontes became the first Brazilian in space. He spent nine days on the International Space Station. |
| 20 | 30 Mar 2006 | Death of John McGahern, Irish novelist and short story writer. Regarded as one of the most important Irish writers of his era. He was named 'the greatest living Irish novelist' shortly before his death. |
| 20 | 31 Mar 2006 | The first Blu-ray player went on sale in Japan – the Samsung BD-P1000. (North America: 25th June. UK: October.) Blu-ray is the high-definition successor to DVD video. |

# MARCH 2026

| Ann. | Date | Event |
|------|------|-------|
| 15 | 11 Mar 2011 | The Tōhoku earthquake and tsunami, Japan.<br>15,897 people were killed, 2,533 went missing and nearly a quarter of a million were made homeless.<br>The earthquake shifted Japan's main island, Honshu, 8 feet (2.4 metres) east. |
| 15 | 11 Mar 2011 | Following the Tōhoku earthquake and tsunami in Japan (see above), three reactors at the Fukushima Daiichi Nuclear Power Plant went into meltdown. It was the second-largest nuclear accident in history, after the Chernobyl disaster in 1986. |
| 15 | 15 Mar 2011 to present | The Syrian Civil War. |
| 15 | 19 Mar 2011 to 31 Oct | NATO-led military intervention in the Libyan Civil War.<br>NATO victory and the overthrow of Muammar Gaddafi's government.<br>Gaddafi was killed on 20th October. |
| 10 | 6 Mar 2016 | Death of Nancy Reagan, American film actress and First Lady of the United States (1981–89). Wife of U.S. President Ronald Reagan. |
| 10 | 8 Mar 2016 | Death of George Martin, British record producer, arranger, composer, musician and audio engineer. Best known for producing the Beatles' records, and sometimes referred to as the 'Fifth Beatle'. |
| 10 | 10 Mar 2016 | Death of Anita Brookner, British novelist and art historian.<br>Best known for her Booker Prize-winning novel *Hotel du Lac*. |
| 10 | 22 Mar 2016 | The Brussels bombings, Belgium.<br>Three suicide bombers belonging to Islamic State detonated bombs at Brussels Airport and the Maalbeek metro station.<br>32 people (plus the three bombers) were killed and more than 300 injured. |
| 10 | 24 Mar 2016 | Death of Johan Cruyff, Dutch football player and manager. |
| 10 | 24 Mar 2016 | Death of Garry Shandling, American television actor, stand-up comedian, screenwriter, producer and director.<br>Best known for *It's Garry Shandling's Show* and *The Larry Sanders Show*. |
| 10 | 29 Mar 2016 | Death of Patty Duke, American stage, film and television actress (*The Miracle Worker*, *The Patty Duke Show*, *Valley of the Dolls*, and more) and mental health advocate. President of the Screen Actors Guild (1985–88). |
| 10 | 31 Mar 2016 | Death of Ronnie Corbett, Scottish film and television comedy actor, comedian, screenwriter and broadcaster (*The Two Ronnies*). |
| 10 | 31 Mar 2016 | Death of Denise Robertson, British writer and television broadcaster.<br>Best known as the agony aunt on the ITV show *This Morning* (1988–2016). |

# APRIL 2026

| Ann. | Date | Event |
|------|------|-------|
| 500 | 21 Apr 1526 | Mughal conquests – the First Battle of Panipat, northern India. Mughal forces invaded the Delhi Sultanate, captured and killed the last Sultan, Ibrahim Lodhi, and annexed the Delhi Sultanate. This led to the establishment of the Mughal Empire in India. |
| 400 | 5 Apr 1626 | Death of Anna Koltovskaya, Tsarina of All Russia (1572–74). Fourth wife of Tsar Ivan IV (Ivan the Terrible). |
| 400 | 5 Apr 1626 ? | Birth of Jan van Kessel the Elder, Flemish artist. Grandson of Jan Brueghel the Elder. Father of Jan van Kessel the Younger. (Baptised on this date. His date of birth is unknown.) |
| 400 | 9 Apr 1626 | Death of Francis Bacon, 1st Viscount St Alban, English philosopher and politician. Attorney General of England and Wales (1613–17), Lord High Chancellor of England (1617–21). He is known as the 'Father of empiricism' and his works influenced the scientific revolution in Europe. |
| 300 | 5 Apr 1726 | Birth of Benjamin Harrison V, American politician. One of the Founding Fathers of the United States. Governor of Virginia (1781–84). Father of U.S. President William Henry Harrison. Great-grandfather of U.S. President Benjamin Harrison. |
| 300 | 9 Apr 1726 | Birth of Saint Gerard Majella, Italian saint. |
| 250 | 6 Apr 1776 | American Revolution: following the British Parliament's order that the American colonies could only trade with Britain and Ireland, the Second Continental Congress opened all American ports to all foreign ships except British ones. |
| 250 | 7 Apr 1776 | American Revolutionary War: the U.S. Navy captured its first British ship, the Royal Navy sloop *HMS Edward*, which was a tender to the frigate *HMS Liverpool*, off Delaware. |
| 250 | 12 Apr 1776 | American Revolution: the Province of North Carolina adopted the Halifax Resolves. It was the first official call for independence in the Thirteen Colonies. |
| 250 | 25 Apr 1776 | Birth of Princess Mary, Duchess of Gloucester and Edinburgh. Daughter of King George III of the United Kingdom. |
| 200 | 1 Apr 1826 | American inventor Samuel Morey was granted a U.S. patent for one of the first internal combustion engines. His engine worked in a different way to modern ones, and was more complex and less efficient. (U.S. Patent 4,378.) |
| 200 | 4 Apr 1826 | Birth of Zénobe Gramme, Belgian electrical engineer. Best known for inventing the Gramme machine, the first successful industrial electric motor. It was also reversible and could function as a dynamo. |
| 200 | 6 Apr 1826 | Birth of Gustave Moreau, French Symbolist artist. |

**APRIL 2026**

| Ann. | Date | Event |
|---|---|---|
| 200 | 10 Apr 1826 | Greek War of Independence – the Third Siege of Missolonghi ended. The Greeks, who had been under siege for a year, ran out of food and staged a mass breakout. Ottoman and Egyptian forces were waiting for them, opened fire, and rushed into the city, killing, raping, and looting everything of value. Thousands of Greeks were killed and very few managed to escape.<br>Europe's public sympathy for the Greeks led to Britain, France and Russia intervening in the war and securing Greece's independence. |
| 200 | 12 Apr 1826 | The première of German Romantic composer Carl Maria von Weber's opera *Oberon*, in London, UK. It was his only English-language opera. |
| 200 | 13 Apr 1826 | Death of Franz Danzi, German cellist, composer and conductor. |
| 175 | 2 Apr 1851 | Rama IV (also known as Mongkut) became King of Siam (now Thailand) (until 1868). His coronation was held on 15th May.<br>He is the king who is featured in the novel and film *Anna and the King of Siam*, and the musical and film *The King and I*. |
| 175 | 20 Apr 1851 to 31 Dec | The Chilean Revolution.<br>Chilean rebels attempted to overthrow the government and repeal the constitution. They were subdued by government forces. |
| 175 | 23 Apr 1851 | Canada issued its first postage stamp – the Three-Pence Beaver. |
| 150 | 3 Apr 1876 | Birth of Tomáš Baťa, Czech shoe manufacturer and businessman. Founder of Bata Shoes. |
| 150 | 4 Apr 1876 | Birth of Maurice de Vlaminck, French artist.<br>One of the principle members of the Fauve movement. |
| 150 | 6 Apr 1876 | The American Chemical Society was founded at New York University. |
| 150 | 14 Apr 1876 | Birth of Cecil Chubb, British barrister. The last private owner of Stonehenge, which he donated to the nation in 1918. |
| 150 | 17 Apr 1876 to 19th | The *Catalpa* rescue, Fremantle, Western Australia.<br>Six Fenian prisoners escaped from prison on the ship *Catalpa*.<br>The ship had been sent to rescue them by another Fenian who had escaped from the prison earlier. They fled to the USA. |
| 150 | 20 Apr 1876 to mid-May | The Great Eastern Crisis – the April Uprising, Bulgaria.<br>Bulgarian rebels staged a revolt against occupying Ottoman forces.<br>The revolt was brutally suppressed, leading to an outcry across Europe. |
| 150 | 24 Apr 1876 | Birth of Erich Raeder, German admiral. High Commander of the German Navy (1935–43). He was sentenced to life imprisonment at the Nuremberg Trials after WWII. (He was released in 1955 because of his failing health.) |
| 125 | 1 Apr 1901 | Birth of Whittaker Chambers, American writer, editor, Communist and Soviet spy. He famously testified against State Department official Alger Hiss in 'the trial of the century' in 1949–50. |
| 125 | 3 Apr 1901 | Death of Richard D'Oyly Carte, British theatrical impresario.<br>He built the Savoy Theatre and the Palace Theatre in London, managed some of the most important theatrical stars of the era, founded a touring opera company, and owned a chain of luxury hotels. |

## APRIL 2026

| Ann. | Date | Event |
|------|------|-------|
| 125 | 5 Apr 1901 | Birth of Melvyn Douglas, American stage, film, radio and television actor. |
| 125 | 11 Apr 1901 | Birth of Adriano Olivetti, Italian engineer and industrialist. Renowned as a manufacturer of typewriters, calculators and computers. Son of Camillo Olivetti, the founder of Olivetti. He significantly expanded the company. |
| 125 | 13 Apr 1901 | Birth of René Pleven, Prime Minister of France (1950–51, 1951–52). |
| 125 | 15 Apr 1901 | Birth of Joe Davis, British snooker and billiards player. He co-founded the World Snooker Championship in 1927, and won the first 15 championships. He was also the first recorded snooker player to score a maximum break (147). |
| 125 | 29 Apr 1901 | Birth of Hirohito (Emperor Shōwa), Emperor of Japan (1926–1989). |
| 100 | 1 Apr 1926 | Birth of Anne McCaffrey, American-born Irish science fiction and fantasy novelist. The first woman to win a Hugo Award and a Nebula Award. (Died 2011.) |
| 100 | 2 Apr 1926 | Birth of Jack Brabham, Australian racing driver. Formula One world champion in 1959, 1960 and 1966. Founder of the Brabham racing team. The only driver to win the Formula One world championship in one of his own cars. (Died 2014.) |
| 100 | 3 Apr 1926 | Birth of Virgil ('Gus') Grissom, American astronaut. One of the original Project Mercury astronauts. The second American to fly into space, and the first to fly into space twice. (Killed in 1967 during a pre-launch test for *Apollo 1*.) |
| 100 | 6 Apr 1926 | United Airlines was founded in the USA (as Varney Air Lines). It became Boeing Air Transport in 1927 and United Air Lines in 1931. |
| 100 | 6 Apr 1926 | Birth of the Reverend Ian Paisley, Baron Bannside, Northern Irish politician and Protestant evangelical minister. First Minister of Northern Ireland (2007–08). Leader of the Democratic Unionist Party (DUP) (1971–2008). (Died 2014.) |
| 100 | 9 Apr 1926 | Birth of Hugh Hefner, American magazine publisher and entrepreneur. Founder of *Playboy* magazine and Playboy Clubs. (Died 2017.) |
| 100 | 9 Apr 1926 | Death of Zip the Pinhead, American freak show performer. Known for his tapered head. |
| 100 | 15 Apr 1926 | The Robertson Aircraft Corporation launched an air mail service between Lambert Field, Missouri and Chicago, Illinois. Its chief pilot was aviation pioneer Charles Lindbergh. The company became part of American Airlines (then known as American Airways) in 1934. |
| 100 | 20 Apr 1926 | A cheque was sent across the Atlantic by radio facsimile for the first time. |
| 100 | 21 Apr 1926 | Birth of Queen Elizabeth II of the United Kingdom. |
| 100 | 24 Apr 1926 | The Treaty of Berlin was signed by Germany and the Soviet Union. They pledged to remain neutral in the event of an attack on the other country by a third party during the next five years. The treaty was renewed in 1931, but relations broke down after Hitler's rise to power in 1933. |

## APRIL 2026

| Ann. | Date | Event |
|------|------|-------|
| 100 | 25 Apr 1926 | Puccini's last opera *Turandot* was performed for the first time, at La Scala in Milan, Italy. The opera was unfinished when Puccini died in 1924. It was completed by Franco Alfano. |
| 100 | 26 Apr 1926 | Karachay Autonomous Oblast and Cherkess Autonomous Oblast were established in the Soviet Union when Karachay–Cherkess Autonomous Oblast was split. During WWII, the Karachay people were exiled to central Asia for allegedly collaborating with the Germans. They were allowed to return in 1957, and the Karachay–Cherkess Autonomous Oblast was re-established. |
| 100 | 28 Apr 1926 | Birth of Harper Lee, American novelist. Best known for *To Kill a Mockingbird*. (Died 2016.) |
| 100 | 30 Apr 1926 | Birth of Cloris Leachman, American film and television actress. (Died 2021.) |
| 90 | 1 Apr 1936 | Birth of Jean-Pascal Delamuraz, President of the Swiss Confederation (1989, 1996). (Died 1998.) |
| 90 | 2 Apr 1936 | Death of Jean-Baptiste Eugène Estienne, French general. One of the founders of modern French artillery and military aviation. Known in France as the 'Father of the Tank'. |
| 90 | 3 Apr 1936 | Death of Bruno Hauptmann, German-born American criminal. (Executed for the kidnap and murder of aviator Charles Lindbergh's baby son.) |
| 90 | 5 Apr 1936 to 6th | The Tupelo–Gainesville Tornado Outbreak. Tupelo, Mississippi, USA was hit by a tornado that killed more than 230 people. Another tornado from the same system hit Gainesville, Georgia, killing more than 200 people. |
| 90 | 6 Apr 1936 | The first instalment of the science fiction film serial *Flash Gordon* was released by Universal Pictures. It ran for thirteen episodes. |
| 90 | 10 Apr 1936 | Birth of John Madden, American football coach (Oakland Raiders 1969–78) and television sports commentator. He is also known for the Madden NFL series of video games. (Died 2021.) |
| 90 | 13 Apr 1936 | British footballer Joe Payne scored a record ten goals in one match, playing for Luton Town against Bristol Rovers. This record still stands in the Football League. |
| 90 | 13 Apr 1936 | Death of Konstantinos Demertzis, Prime Minister of Greece (1935–36). (Heart attack after five months in office.) Succeeded by Ioannis Metaxas. |
| 90 | 17 Apr 1936 | Death of Charles Ruijs de Beerenbrouck, Prime Minister of the Netherlands (1918–25, 1929–33). |
| 90 | 18 Apr 1936 | Death of Milton Brown, 'the Father of Western Swing', American bandleader and singer. (Car accident, aged 32.) |
| 90 | 19 Apr 1936 to 1939 | The Arab Revolt (also known as the Great Uprising) began in Palestine with a general strike that lasted until October. |
| 90 | 19 Apr 1936 | Birth of Wilfried Martens, Prime Minister of Belgium (1979–81, 1981–92). (Died 2013.) |
| 90 | 20 Apr 1936 | Birth of Pauli Ellefsen, Prime Minister of the Faroe Islands (1981–85). (Died 2012.) |

## APRIL 2026

| Ann. | Date | Event |
|---|---|---|
| 90 | 22 Apr 1936 | Birth of Glen Campbell, American Country/Western/folk/pop singer, songwriter, guitarist, actor and television presenter.<br>Best known for the song *Rhinestone Cowboy*. (Died 2017.) |
| 90 | 23 Apr 1936 | Birth of Roy Orbison, American singer, songwriter and musician.<br>Known for his powerful ballads. His songs include *Oh, Pretty Woman*, *Crying, Only the Lonely*, and many more. (Died 1988.) |
| 90 | 24 Apr 1936 | Birth of Jill Ireland, British film and television actress. (Died 1990.) |
| 90 | 25 Apr 1936 | Birth of Henck Arron, first Prime Minister of Suriname (1973–80), Vice President of Suriname (1988–90). (Died 2000.) |
| 90 | 28 Apr 1936 | Birth of Tariq Aziz, Deputy Prime Minister of Iraq (1979–2003), Minister of Foreign Affairs (1983–91). A close advisor of President Saddam Hussein. He was arrested after the 2003 Invasion of Iraq, and later sentenced to death by the Iraqi High Tribunal. Iraqi President Jalal Talabani refused to sign his execution order, and his sentence was commuted to life imprisonment. He died in prison in 2015. |
| 90 | 28 Apr 1936 | Death of Fuad I, King of Egypt (1922–36). Succeeded by his son Farouk I. |
| 90 | 30 Apr 1936 | Death of A. E. Housman, British scholar and poet. |
| 80 | 1 Apr 1946 | The Aleutian Islands earthquake, Alaska, USA. Six people were killed.<br>A tsunami then struck Hawaii, killing a further 159 people. |
| 80 | 1 Apr 1946 | The Malayan Union was formed.<br>In 1948 it was succeeded by the Federation of Malaya. |
| 80 | 1 Apr 1946 | 340,000 coal miners went on strike in the USA, joining the oil, auto, electric, steel workers and meatpackers who had been on strike for several months. In May, 250,000 railway workers also joined the strike.<br>This led to the U.S. Congress passing the Taft–Hartley Act in June 1947, which restricted trade unions' powers and activities. |
| 80 | 1 Apr 1946 | Birth of Ronnie Lane, British rock bassist, singer and songwriter (the Faces/the Small Faces). (Died 1997.) |
| 80 | 1 Apr 1946 | Death of Noah Beery Sr., American stage and film actor.<br>Brother of the actor Wallace Beery. Father of the actor Noah Beery Jr. |
| 80 | 2 Apr 1946 | Birth of Sue Townsend, British writer and humourist.<br>Best known for her *Adrian Mole* series of novels. (Died 2014.) |
| 80 | 3 Apr 1946 | World War II: Lieutenant General Masaharu Homma of the Imperial Japanese Army was executed in the Philippines for war crimes.<br>He commanded the Japanese 14th Army, which invaded the Philippines. He also organised the Bataan Death March, in which 60,000 to 80,000 prisoners of war were forced to march between camps, with thousands dying, or being killed. |
| 80 | 8 Apr 1946 | Électricité de France (EDF), the world's largest utility company, was founded when around 1,700 French energy producers, transporters and distributors were nationalised. |
| 80 | 8 Apr 1946 | Birth of Catfish Hunter, American baseball pitcher (Kansas City/Oakland Athletics, New York Yankees).<br>(Died 1999 – Lou Gehrig's disease, aged 53.) |

## APRIL 2026

| Ann. | Date | Event |
|---|---|---|
| 80 | 10 Apr 1946 | Birth of David Angell, American television producer and screenwriter. Best known for his work on the sitcom *Cheers* and for creating the spin-off sitcom *Frasier*. (Killed in the 9/11 terrorist attacks on the USA in 2001.) |
| 80 | 16 Apr 1946 | The U.S. Army launched its first V-2 rocket from White Sands Missile Range in New Mexico. The rocket has been assembled from parts captured from Germany after WWII. German scientists who had relocated to the USA under Operation Paperclip helped with assembly and testing. More than 75 V-2 rockets were launched from the range between 1946 and 1952, carrying instruments to study the atmosphere and solar radiation. |
| 80 | 17 Apr 1946 | Syria gained its independence from France. |
| 80 | 17 Apr 1946 | Death of Juan Bautista Sacasa, President of Nicaragua (1933–36). |
| 80 | 18 Apr 1946 | The League of Nations was officially dissolved. It transferred the majority of its powers and activities to the United Nations, which was established in October 1945. |
| 80 | 18 Apr 1946 | The International Court of Justice began operating. |
| 80 | 18 Apr 1946 | Nuclear physicists John von Neumann from Hungary and Klaus Fuchs from Germany invented the hydrogen bomb at Los Alamos National Laboratory in New Mexico, USA. (Secret U.S. Patent S-5292X.) |
| 80 | 21 Apr 1946 | Death of John Maynard Keynes, British economist. The most influential economist of the 20th century. His ideas formed the basis of Keynesian economics. |
| 80 | 27 Apr 1946 | The first commercial ship to be equipped with radar, the *SS African Star*, went into service in New York City, USA. It was operated by the American–South African Line. |
| 80 | 29 Apr 1946 | The International Military Tribunal for the Far East was convened to try Japanese war criminals following the end of WWII. Those indicted included former Prime Minister Hideki Tojo and 28 other leaders. |
| 75 | 1 Apr 1951 | Death of Johannes Kielstra, Governor-General of Suriname (1933–44). |
| 75 | 2 Apr 1951 | General Dwight D. Eisenhower (later U.S. President) became NATO's first Supreme Allied Commander. He assumed command of all Allied forces in the Western Mediterranean and Europe. |
| 75 | 4 Apr 1951 | Death of George Albert Smith, American religious leader. President of The Church of Jesus Christ of Latter-day Saints (1945–51). |
| 75 | 5 Apr 1951 | American electrical engineer Julius Rosenberg and his wife Ethel were sentenced to death for passing nuclear secrets to the Soviet Union. They were executed in June 1953. |
| 75 | 7 Apr 1951 | The first USBC Masters ten-pin bowling tournament was held. At that time it was organised by the American Bowling Congress and known as the ABC Masters. |
| 75 | 11 Apr 1951 | Korean War: U.S. President Harry S. Truman relieved General Douglas MacArthur of his command in Korea for insubordination. MacArthur retired from the military on 19th April. In his speech to Congress he said, 'Old soldiers never die, they just fade away.' |

**APRIL 2026**

| Ann. | Date | Event |
| --- | --- | --- |
| 75 | 11 Apr 1951 | The Stone of Scone, which had been stolen from Westminster Abbey in London in December 1950 by Scottish nationalist students, was found on the altar of Arbroath Abbey in Scotland. It was returned to London.<br>There were rumours that the stone returned to London was a copy and the original stayed in Scotland.<br>In November 1996 the stone was officially returned to Scotland on condition that it is loaned to Westminster Abbey for coronations. |
| 75 | 14 Apr 1951 | Death of Ernest Bevin, British politician. Foreign Secretary (1945–51), Minister of Labour and National Service (1940–45).<br>Co-founder and General Secretary of the Transport and General Workers' Union (1922–40). |
| 75 | 16 Apr 1951 | The British submarine *HMS Affray* sank in the English Channel.<br>All 75 crew were killed. |
| 75 | 17 Apr 1951 | The Peak District National Park was established.<br>It was Britain's first national park. |
| 75 | 17 Apr 1951 | The U.S. Senate Special Committee to Investigate Crime in Interstate Commerce (also known as the Kefauver Committee) published its final report. The committee aimed to prove that the Sicilian–Italian Mafia controlled most organised crime in the USA. But it found that people of all nationalities were operating local crime syndicates.<br>The FBI admitted that a national organised crime syndicate did exist, but said it had done little about it.<br>More than 70 state and local crime commissions were established as a result of the committee's findings, and the Racketeer Influenced and Corrupt Organizations Act was passed in 1970. |
| 75 | 17 Apr 1951 | American baseball player Mickey Mantle made his Major League Baseball debut, playing for the New York Yankees. He played until 1968 and became one of the greatest players in baseball history. |
| 75 | 18 Apr 1951 | The European Coal and Steel Community was established when Belgium, France, Italy, Luxembourg, the Netherlands, and West Germany signed the Treaty of Paris.<br>The organisation eventually became the European Union. |
| 75 | 18 Apr 1951 | Death of Óscar Carmona, President of Portugal (1926–51). |
| 75 | 19 Apr 1951 | The first Miss World beauty contest was held, in London. |
| 75 | 20 Apr 1951 | Whirlwind I, the first real-time digital computer began operating.<br>It was the first computer to allow interactive computing via a keyboard and visual display unit. It was built by the Massachusetts Institute of Technology (MIT) for the U.S. Navy, who wanted it to control a flight simulator. It was also connected to a radar system and used for tracking aircraft and warning of air attacks. |
| 75 | 20 Apr 1951 | Birth of Luther Vandross, American soul/R&B singer, songwriter and producer. (Died 2005.) |
| 75 | 22 Apr 1951 to 22 May | Korean War – the Chinese Spring Offensive, 38th Parallel, Korea.<br>United Nations victory – UN forces prevented the Chinese from capturing Seoul, and launched a major counteroffensive in which up to 160,000 Chinese and North Korean forces were killed. |

## APRIL 2026

| Ann. | Date | Event |
|------|------|-------|
| 75 | 22 Apr 1951 to 25th | Korean War – the Chinese Spring Offensive – the Battle of Kapyong, South Korea. UN victory. Australian and Canadian forces fought a famous battle and prevented an entire division of the Chinese People's Volunteer Army from breaking through to the United Nations front. |
| 75 | 23 Apr 1951 | The Associated Press began using the first teletypesetter. It allowed newspapers to automatically set type directly from wire transmissions. |
| 75 | 23 Apr 1951 | Death of Charles G. Dawes, Vice President of the United States (1925–29). Joint winner of the 1925 Nobel Peace Prize for developing the Dawes Plan for WWI reparations. |
| 75 | 26 Apr 1951 | British composer Ralph Vaughan Williams' opera *The Pilgrim's Progress* was performed for the first time, at the Royal Opera House in London. |
| 75 | 29 Apr 1951 | Birth of Dale Earnhardt, American stock car racing driver. The dominant NASCAR driver of the 1980s and 90s. (Died 2001.) |
| 75 | 29 Apr 1951 | Death of Ludwig Wittgenstein, Austrian-born British philosopher. Regarded as the greatest philosopher of the 20th century. |
| 70 | 2 Apr 1956 to 3rd | The April 1956 tornado outbreak, USA. A system of 47 tornadoes hit Kansas, Kentucky, Michigan, Oklahoma, Tennessee and Wisconsin. 40 people were killed, including 20 in the cities of Hudsonville and Standale in Michigan. |
| 70 | 2 Apr 1956 | The first episodes of the television soap operas *As the World Turns* and *The Edge of Night* were broadcast on CBS in the USA. They were the first daytime thirty-minute soaps. |
| 70 | 6 Apr 1956 | The Capitol Records Building (also known as the Capitol Records Tower) opened in Hollywood, Los Angeles, California, USA. The iconic thirteen-storey tower resembles a stack of records on a turntable. |
| 70 | 7 Apr 1956 | Morocco became an independent country when France and Spain relinquished their protectorate. Sultan Mohammed V formed a government. He became King of Morocco in 1957. |
| 70 | 12 Apr 1956 | S. W. R. D. Bandaranaike became Prime Minister of Ceylon (now Sri Lanka). (He was assassinated in September 1959.) |
| 70 | 13 Apr 1956 | Birth of Possum Bourne, New Zealand rally driver. (Died 2003 – car crash, aged 47.) |
| 70 | 14 Apr 1956 | Ampex Corporation demonstrated the world's first commercially successful videotape recorder (the VRX-1000) at the National Association of Radio and Television Broadcasters in Chicago, Illinois, USA. It was first used on the *CBS Evening News* in November 1956 to time delay the New York-based show by three hours for the West Coast. It cost $50,000, which only networks and large TV stations could afford. |
| 70 | 15 Apr 1956 | The first television station in the world to broadcast all of its programming in colour: WNBQ in Chicago, Illinois, USA was launched. (It is now WMAQ-TV – NBC Channel 5.) |
| 70 | 16 Apr 1956 | Birth of David M. Brown, American astronaut. (Killed in the Space Shuttle *Columbia* disaster in February 2003.) |

## APRIL 2026

| Ann. | Date | Event |
|---|---|---|
| 70 | 17 Apr 1956 | Cominform (the Communist Information Bureau) was dissolved as part of the Soviet Union's programme of reconciliation with Yugoslavia. |
| 70 | 17 Apr 1956 | In his 1956 budget, British Chancellor Harold Macmillan announced the introduction of Premium Bonds, which offer monthly cash prizes instead of paying interest. They were designed to encourage more people to save. They went on sale on 1st November 1956. |
| 70 | 18 Apr 1956 | American film actress Grace Kelly married Prince Rainier III of Monaco, and became Princess Grace of Monaco. |
| 70 | 19 Apr 1956 | British Royal Navy Diver Lionel 'Buster' Crabb disappeared in mysterious circumstances during a secret MI6 reconnaissance mission to study the Soviet cruiser *Ordzhonkidze* in Portsmouth Harbour, England. A body, thought to be his, was recovered in June 1957, but it was missing its head and hands. Various theories have been proposed as to how he died. Documents released in 2006 suggest the British government covered up his death. |
| 70 | 21 Apr 1956 | Elvis Presley's song *Heartbreak Hotel* became his first to reach #1 in the U.S. music charts. From 23rd April to 9th May he held his first residency in Las Vegas, but his shows were poorly received by the middle-aged guests. |
| 70 | 26 Apr 1956 | The world's first commercially successful container ship went into service, launching a revolution in transportation. The *SS Ideal X* was a converted WWII oil tanker, which carried 58 containers from Newark, New Jersey to Houston, Texas on its first voyage. (It was not the first container ship. The first was the *Clifford J. Rodgers*, which went into service in 1955.) |
| 70 | 27 Apr 1956 | American heavyweight boxing champion Rocky Marciano retired undefeated: 49 wins and no losses. |
| 70 | 30 Apr 1956 | Death of Alben W. Barkley, Vice-President of the United States (1949–53). |
| 65 | 1 Apr 1961 | American evangelists Jim Bakker and Tammy Faye were married. In 1974 they founded The PTL Club, which became one of the biggest televangelism shows on U.S. television. They divorced in 1992. |
| 65 | 3 Apr 1961 | The British passenger liner *MV Dara*, which was based in the Persian Gulf, sank following a massive explosion. 238 of the 819 people on board were killed. (Cause: most likely an anti-tank mine detonated by terrorists.) |
| 65 | 9 Apr 1961 | The Pacific Electric Railway Company in southern California, USA shut down its passenger service after sixty years. It was once the largest electric streetcar service in the world. Its freight service continued until 1965. |
| 65 | 9 Apr 1961 | Death of Zog I, King of Albania (1928–39), President of Albania (1925–28). |
| 65 | 10 Apr 1961 | South African golfer Gary Player became the first non-American to win the Masters Tournament in Augusta, Georgia. |
| 65 | 11 Apr 1961 | Nazi war criminal Adolf Eichmann went on trial in Jerusalem, Israel. He was convicted on 12th December and executed in June 1962. |
| 65 | 11 Apr 1961 | American folk singer and musician Bob Dylan gave his first major performance, as a support act for John Lee Hooker's two-week residency at Gerde's Folk City in Greenwich Village, New York City. |

**APRIL 2026**

| Ann. | Date | Event |
|---|---|---|
| 65 | 12 Apr 1961 | The first person in space.<br>Soviet cosmonaut Yuri Gagarin became the first person in space and the first to orbit the Earth, in *Vostok I*.<br>He was made a Hero of the Soviet Union. |
| 65 | 17 Apr 1961 to 19th | Cold War: the Bay of Pigs invasion, Cuba.<br>Approximately 1,500 Cuban exiles who opposed Fidel Castro's regime attempted an invasion, financed and directed by the USA.<br>On 21st April, U.S. President John F. Kennedy accepted sole responsibility for the failed invasion. |
| 65 | 17 Apr 1961 | Aklilu Habte-Wold became Prime Minister of Ethiopia (until 1974). |
| 65 | 18 Apr 1961 | The Conference of Nationalist Organisations of the Portuguese Colonies was established in Morocco. It coordinated the liberation movements in African colonies that opposed Portuguese colonial rule. |
| 65 | 21 Apr 1961 to 26th | Algerian War – the Algiers putsch.<br>Four retired generals from the French Army staged a failed coup.<br>It was intended to force the President of France, Charles de Gaulle, not to hand control of French Algeria to the National Liberation Front (FLN).<br>The coup failed. Algeria was granted its independence in March 1962, and was governed by the FLN. |
| 65 | 24 Apr 1961 | The Swedish warship *Vasa* was raised from Stockholm harbour.<br>It sank on its maiden voyage in 1628.<br>The wreck was discovered by an amateur archaeologist in 1956. |
| 65 | 25 Apr 1961 | American engineer Robert Noyce of Fairchild Semiconductor was granted a U.S. patent for the integrated circuit. (U.S. Patent 2,981,877.) |
| 65 | 27 Apr 1961 | Sierra Leone became an independent state within the Commonwealth. |
| 65 | 27 Apr 1961 | NASA launched *Explorer 11*, the first gamma-ray telescope to be launched into space. It operated until November. |
| 65 | 28 Apr 1961 | Death of Tom Connolly, American baseball umpire.<br>National League (1898–1900), American League (1901–31).<br>One of the first two umpires to be elected to the Baseball Hall of Fame. |
| 65 | 29 Apr 1961 | The first episode of the sports anthology TV series *Wide World of Sports* was broadcast on ABC in the USA. It ran until 1998. |
| 65 | 30 Apr 1961 | The Soviet submarine K-19 was commissioned. It was the first Soviet nuclear submarine to be equipped with nuclear ballistic missiles.<br>It remained in service until 1990, but experienced several breakdowns and accidents while in service. |
| 65 | 30 Apr 1961 | The Prime Minister of Cuba, Fidel Castro, was awarded the Lenin Peace Prize by the Soviet Union.<br>The prize was mainly awarded to foreign citizens who were prominent communists and supporters of the Soviet Union. |
| 60 | 1 Apr 1966 to 24th | The first World Festival of Black Arts was held, in Dakar, Senegal.<br>The second Festival was held in Lagos, Nigeria in 1977, and the third in Dakar in 2010. |

**APRIL 2026**

| Ann. | Date | Event |
|------|------|-------|
| 60 | 1 Apr 1966 | Death of Flann O'Brien, Irish novelist, playwright, newspaper columnist and humourist. Noted for his satire.<br>One of the leading Irish writers of the 20th century. |
| 60 | 2 Apr 1966 | Death of C. S. Forester, British historical novelist.<br>Best known for *The African Queen* and for his series of novels featuring the British naval officer Horatio Hornblower during the Napoleonic Wars. |
| 60 | 3 Apr 1966 | The Soviet Union's *Luna 10* became the first spacecraft to orbit the Moon.<br>It operated until 30th May, orbiting the Moon 460 times and returning scientific data, until its batteries were depleted. |
| 60 | 8 Apr 1966 | NASA launched *OAO-1*, the first Orbiting Astronomical Observatory.<br>It was intended to detect X-ray, ultraviolet and gamma ray emissions from various objects in space, but it failed after only three days.<br>*OAO-2* (December 1968 – January 1973) and *OAO-3* (August 1972 – February 1981) were more successful. |
| 60 | 9 Apr 1966 | Emmett Ashford became the first African American umpire in Major League Baseball in the USA. |
| 60 | 10 Apr 1966 | Death of Evelyn Waugh, British satirical novelist, biographer and travel writer (*Decline and Fall, A Handful of Dust, Brideshead Revisited, Sword of Honour*). |
| 60 | 12 Apr 1966 | Death of Chris Soumokil, President of the Republic of South Maluku in Indonesia (1950–66). (Executed.) |
| 60 | 13 Apr 1966 | Death of Abdul Salam Arif, President of Iraq (1963–66). (Plane crash).<br>Succeeded by his brother, Abdul Rahman Arif. |
| 60 | 13 Apr 1966 | Death of Georges Duhamel, French novelist and essayist. |
| 60 | 15 Apr 1966 | Milton Obote became President of Uganda for the first time (until 1971).<br>He was president again from 1980 to 1985. |
| 60 | 18 Apr 1966 | Bill Russell became the first African American to coach a major U.S. sports team: the Boston Celtics NBA basketball team. |
| 60 | 19 Apr 1966 | American athlete Bobbi Gibb became the first woman to run in the Boston Marathon in Massachusetts, USA. Women were not allowed to enter at that time and her application had been refused. But she turned up anyway, sneaked into the mass of entrants at the start, and ran the entire marathon in 3 hours 21 minutes and 40 seconds, beating half the other competitors. She made headline news, and her time was later officially recognised.<br>She was also one of two women who ran the 1967 race, and one of five who ran the 1968 race.<br>Women were not officially sanctioned until the 1972 race. |
| 60 | 21 Apr 1966 | Grounation Day.<br>Emperor Haile Selassie of Ethiopia visited Jamaica.<br>This day is now celebrated annually by the Rastafari movement as one of their most important holy days. |
| 60 | 22 Apr 1966 | The rock song *Wild Thing* by The Troggs was released. |
| 60 | 26 Apr 1966 | The Tashkent earthquake, Uzbekistan.<br>Most of the old city was destroyed and about 300,000 people were left homeless. |

## APRIL 2026

| Ann. | Date | Event |
|------|------|-------|
| 60 | 29 Apr 1966 | Death of William Eccles, British physicist, teacher and radio communications pioneer. |
| 60 | 30 Apr 1966 | The Church of Satan was founded in San Francisco, California, USA. |
| 60 | 30 Apr 1966 | Death of Richard Fariña, American folk singer and novelist. A key figure in the folk music revival of the 1960s. (Motorcycle crash, aged 29.) |
| 50 | 1 Apr 1976 | Apple Computer (now Apple Inc.) was founded in Cupertino, California, USA. |
| 50 | 1 Apr 1976 | Conrail began operating in north-eastern USA, taking over from and consolidating several bankrupt railway companies.<br>It was broken up in 1999 and acquired by CSX Corporation and the Norfolk Southern Railway. |
| 50 | 1 Apr 1976 | Death of Max Ernst, German Surrealist artist, sculptor and poet. |
| 50 | 3 Apr 1976 | The UK won the 1976 Eurovision Song Contest with *Save Your Kisses for Me* by Brotherhood of Man. |
| 50 | 4 Apr 1976 | Prince Norodom Sihanouk, the symbolic (puppet) head of state of the Khmer Republic (Cambodia) was forced out of office.<br>He became the legitimate head of state in June 1993 and was restored as King in September 1993 until his abdication in 2004. |
| 50 | 4 Apr 1976 | Death of Harry Nyquist, Swedish physicist, electrical engineer and inventor. He made major contributions to telecommunications and communications theory. |
| 50 | 5 Apr 1976 | James Callaghan became British Prime Minister (until 1979) following Harold Wilson's resignation. |
| 50 | 5 Apr 1976 | The Tiananmen Incident, Beijing, China.<br>(Not to be confused with the 1989 Tiananmen Square incident.)<br>Thousands of people gathered in the square on a national day of mourning. The government viewed the gathering as a counter-revolutionary threat and forced them to leave. About 4,000 people were arrested. Vice-Premier Deng Xiaoping was accused of organising the event and was dismissed and placed under house arrest.<br>When he became leader of China in 1978, the Central Committee reversed its decision on the event and hailed it as a day of patriotism. |
| 50 | 5 Apr 1976 | Death of Howard Hughes, American business tycoon, record-breaking aviator, Hollywood film producer and philanthropist. One of the world's richest people. Noted for his eccentric/reclusive lifestyle in later years. |
| 50 | 7 Apr 1976 | British politician John Stonehouse, who infamously tried to fake his own death in 1974, resigned from the Labour Party, leaving the government in a minority.<br>After his death in 1988, it was revealed that he had been a Czech spy since 1962. |
| 50 | 7 Apr 1976 | Death of Mary Margaret McBride, 'the First Lady of Radio', American radio presenter and interviewer. |

## APRIL 2026

| Ann. | Date | Event |
|------|------|-------|
| 50 | 9 Apr 1976 | British politician Peter Hain, the President of the Young Liberals, was acquitted of robbing a branch of Barclays Bank. Some sources claim it was a simple case of mistaken identity, while others allege he was framed by the South African state security service for being an anti-apartheid activist. He later joined the Labour Party and became a prominent cabinet minister and Leader of the House of Commons. |
| 50 | 9 Apr 1976 | Death of Phil Ochs, American folk singer, songwriter and musician. Noted for his protest songs. (Suicide, aged 35.) |
| 50 | 13 Apr 1976 | The Lapua Cartridge Factory explosion, Finland. Forty workers were killed and sixty injured and the ammunition factory was completely destroyed. It was the worst industrial accident in Finnish history. (Cause: unknown. Most likely gunpowder had built up in the air due to poor ventilation, and was ignited by a spark from a machine.) |
| 50 | 13 Apr 1976 | Birth of Jonathan Brandis, American film and television actor, screenwriter and film director. Best known for his role as Lucas Wolenczak in the science fiction TV series *seaQuest DSV*. (Died 2003 – suicide.) |
| 50 | 16 Apr 1976 | NASA's *Helios-B* space probe went into orbit around the Sun at a distance of 27 million miles. It was the closest any spacecraft had ever come to the Sun (until the *Parker Solar Probe* in 2018). |
| 50 | 16 Apr 1976 | The Indian government announced a National Population Policy to limit population growth. It proposed raising the age of marriage to 18 for females and 21 for males, raising the level of female education, and offering people financial incentives to become sterilised if they already had two or more children. |
| 50 | 21 Apr 1976 | The first episode of the superhero television series *Wonder Woman* was broadcast on ABC in the USA. It ran for three seasons until 1978, transferring to CBS for the second and third season as *The New Adventures of Wonder Woman*. |
| 50 | 25 Apr 1976 | Death of Sir Carol Reed, British film producer and director. Noted for his suspense/thriller films (*Odd Man Out*, *The Fallen Idol*, *The Third Man*, *Our Man in Havana*) and the musical *Oliver!* |
| 50 | 26 Apr 1976 | Death of Sid James, South African-born British stage, film and television comedy actor. Best known for the *Carry On...* films, *Hancock's Half Hour* and the sitcom *Bless This House*. |
| 50 | 27 Apr 1976 | The Arab Monetary Fund was founded by the Arab League. |
| 40 | 1 Apr 1986 | The novelty pop song *The Chicken Song* by Spitting Image was released. |
| 40 | 2 Apr 1986 | A bomb blew a hole in a TWA jet flying over Greece. This caused rapid decompression and four passengers were killed when they were sucked out of the plane. The remaining 110 passengers and seven crew survived. |
| 40 | 2 Apr 1986 | The IBM PC Convertible was released. It was IBM's first laptop-style computer, and the first IBM computer with a 3½-inch floppy disk drive. |
| 40 | 3 Apr 1986 | Death of Sir Peter Pears, British tenor. |

## APRIL 2026

| Ann. | Date | Event |
|---|---|---|
| 40 | 5 Apr 1986 | Libyan terrorists bombed La Belle Discotheque in Berlin, Germany. The disco was popular with U.S. servicemen. Three people were killed and over 200 injured – many of them U.S. Servicemen. (The USA retaliated by bombing Libya – see 15th April 1986.) |
| 40 | 7 Apr 1986 | British home computer pioneer Sir Clive Sinclair sold his entire computer product range and the Sinclair brand name to Amstrad for £5 million. |
| 40 | 8 Apr 1986 | American actor Clint Eastwood was elected mayor of Carmel, California. |
| 40 | 11 Apr 1986 | Halley's Comet made its closest approach to Earth during its most recent visit. In March 1986 it became the first comet to be studied closely by spacecraft. It will return to the Earth's vicinity in 2061 and 2134. |
| 40 | 11 Apr 1986 | Dodge Morgan became the first American to sail solo non-stop around the world. His time of 150 days was a record for the westward trip, though it has since been broken. |
| 40 | 13 Apr 1986 | The first recorded papal visit to a synagogue. Pope John Paul II visited the Great Synagogue of Rome in Italy. |
| 40 | 14 Apr 1986 | The heaviest hailstones ever recorded, weighing around 2.2 pounds (1 kilogram) each, fell in Gopalganj, Bangladesh. 92 people were killed. |
| 40 | 14 Apr 1986 | Death of Simone de Beauvoir, French writer, feminist and philosopher. |
| 40 | 15 Apr 1986 | Operation El Dorado Canyon. Following the Libyan bombing of a German discotheque (see 5th April 1986), the USA launched bombing raids on Tripoli and Benghazi in Libya, killing 60 people. Libya responded by blowing up a Pan Am passenger jet over Lockerbie, Scotland in 1988. |
| 40 | 15 Apr 1986 | Death of Jean Genet, French novelist, playwright and political activist. |
| 40 | 17 Apr 1986 | The Hindawi Affair. Jordanian terrorist Nezar Hindawi attempted to place a bomb on an El Al plane at Heathrow Airport in London by concealing it in his pregnant Irish fiancée's hand luggage. In October he was sentenced to 45 years in prison – the longest sentence ever handed down by a British court. The UK also broke off diplomatic relations with Syria, claiming that Syrian officials had helped him. |
| 40 | 17 Apr 1986 | The 335 Years' War between the Netherlands and the Isles of Scilly in the UK ended with the signing of a peace treaty. The war had been long forgotten and many people regarded it as a myth until historical records were unearthed that showed they were technically still at war |
| 40 | 17 Apr 1986 | British television journalist John McCarthy was kidnapped in Beirut, Lebanon by the militant group Islamic Jihad. (Released August 1991.) |
| 40 | 17 Apr 1986 | Death of Marcel Dassault, French aircraft designer and industrialist. Noted for his military aircraft. |
| 40 | 18 Apr 1986 | NASA crisis: the first satellite launch after the space shuttle *Challenger* disaster (a classified spy satellite) failed when the Titan rocket carrying it exploded seconds after launch. A second satellite launch on 3rd May (a GOES-G weather satellite) also failed. The Delta rocket suffered an electrical fault 71 seconds after launch and was destroyed remotely. |

## APRIL 2026

| Ann. | Date | Event |
|---|---|---|
| 40 | 20 Apr 1986 | Russian-born American piano virtuoso Vladimir Horowitz performed in his native Russia for the first time in 61 years, giving a concert at the Moscow Conservatory. It was one of the most widely publicised concerts of the 20th century and was seen by millions on television. |
| 40 | 23 Apr 1986 | Death of Harold Arlen, American composer of popular music, especially for Broadway musicals and Hollywood films, including *The Wizard of Oz*. |
| 40 | 23 Apr 1986 | Death of Jim Laker, British cricketer. |
| 40 | 23 Apr 1986 | Death of Otto Preminger, Austrian-born American film director and producer. |
| 40 | 24 Apr 1986 | Death of Wallis Simpson, Duchess of Windsor. American wife of Prince Edward, Duke of Windsor (formerly King Edward VIII). He abdicated in order to marry her. |
| 40 | 25 Apr 1986 | The Coronation of King Mswati III of Swaziland. |
| 40 | 26 Apr 1986 | The Chernobyl disaster, Ukraine, Soviet Union. The world's worst nuclear power plant accident. 31 people were killed in the explosion and fire, and leaked radiation spread across the western Soviet Union and Europe. |
| 40 | 26 Apr 1986 | Death of Broderick Crawford, American actor. |
| 40 | 27 Apr 1986 | Death of J. Allen Hynek, American astronomer, astrophysicist, educator and ufologist. Best known for developing the 'Close Encounter' classification system for UFO/extraterrestrial encounters. He was also a scientific adviser to the U.S. Air Force for three UFO studies: Project Sign, Project Grudge and Project Blue Book. |
| 40 | 29 Apr 1986 | The Los Angeles Public Library (Central Library) in California, USA burned down in an arson attack. About 400,000 books were destroyed, along with countless irreplaceable documents, newspaper archives, maps, artworks and photos. It reopened in 1993 after substantial renovations. |
| 30 | 1 Apr 1996 | Halifax Regional Municipality was created in Nova Scotia, Canada. |
| 30 | 1 Apr 1996 | BSE ('mad cow disease'): The British government announced that it would begin slaughtering all cattle over the age of 30 months in order to eradicate the disease. Their carcasses would be destroyed. Initially 40,000 cattle were scheduled to be destroyed, but this was later increased to 80,000. |
| 30 | 1 Apr 1996 to Feb 1997 | Bulgaria was hit by a severe financial crisis. Banks closed, the interest rate rose multiple times, and inflation reached 2,000 percent at its peak. The national currency, the levy, collapsed on 9th May. The International Monetary Fund (IMF) and a new government managed to stabilise the economy and end the crisis. |
| 30 | 3 Apr 1996 | The 'Unabomber', Ted Kacynski, was arrested at a remote cabin in Montana, USA. He had waged a seventeen-year bombing campaign in the USA, attempting to bring about a revolution against industrialism. The cabin contained bomb-making components, a live bomb, and thousands of pages of a handwritten journal that documented his campaign. He refused to be examined by a psychiatrist, so he could not be declared insane. In January 1998 he pleaded guilty to all charges, thus avoiding the death penalty. He was sentenced to life imprisonment. |

## APRIL 2026

| Ann. | Date | Event |
|---|---|---|
| 30 | 3 Apr 1996 | A U.S. Air Force plane crashed in Croatia while on a trade mission, killing all 35 people on board, including U.S. Secretary of Commerce Ron Brown. |
| 30 | 3 Apr 1996 | Nineteen-year-old American student Jennifer Ringley launched Jenni-Cam, a website that documented her life by taking live photos of her room every three minutes and posting them online. It became one of the most popular internet sites, receiving over 4 million views per day. It remained online until 2003. |
| 30 | 3 Apr 1996 | Death of Carl Stokes, American politician. The first African American mayor of a major U.S. city (Cleveland, Ohio 1967–71). |
| 30 | 4 Apr 1996 | Mathieu Kérékou became President of Benin (until 2006). He was also President from 1972 to 1991 after seizing power in a military coup. |
| 30 | 4 Apr 1996 | Death of Barney Ewell, American athlete. One of the world's leading sprinters of the 1940s. Gold medallist at the 1948 Olympics (4 x 100 m relay). |
| 30 | 6 Apr 1996 | Death of Greer Garson, British-born American stage and film actress. One of the most popular Hollywood stars of the 1940s (*Pride and Prejudice, Blossoms in the Dust, Random Harvest, Madame Curie, Mrs. Miniver*). |
| 30 | 8 Apr 1996 | Death of Ben Johnson, American film actor, stuntman and world rodeo champion. Noted for his many Westerns and for his horsemanship skills. His films include *Shane, One-Eyed Jacks, The Wild Bunch* and *The Last Picture Show*. |
| 30 | 9 Apr 1996 | Death of Richard Condon, American novelist. Known for his political thrillers. Best known for *The Manchurian Candidate, Winter Kills* and *Prizzi's Honor*. |
| 30 | 9 Apr 1996 | Death of James Rouse, American real estate developer, urban planner and philanthropist. He pioneered the enclosed shopping mall and created planned communities. |
| 30 | 10 Apr 1996 | U.S. President Bill Clinton vetoed a bill that would have outlawed late abortions. He said the procedure was rarely used, and only in cases where the mother's health was in jeopardy, so its use was justified. |
| 30 | 11 Apr 1996 | The Düsseldorf Airport fire, Germany. A fire in the passenger terminal killed seventeen people and injured more than sixty. (Cause: welding work on an elevated access road above the terminal resulted in molten metal dropping onto polystyrene insulation in the terminal's roof, setting it alight.) |
| 30 | 11 Apr 1996 to 27th | The South Lebanon conflict – Operation Grapes of Wrath. Israel carried out sixteen days of air strikes on targets in the Lebanese capital, Beirut. It ended with a ceasefire agreement that banned attacks on civilians. Much of Lebanon's infrastructure had already been destroyed. |
| 30 | 11 Apr 1996 | Barclays Bank revealed that a terrorist known as 'Mardi Gra' had been targeting its branches in London, UK since December 1994. He had sent more than 25 homemade bombs, some of which had exploded, causing several injuries. The bombing continued until 1998, and he also began targeting Sainsbury's supermarkets. Edgar Pearce was arrested in April 1998, convicted in April 1999, and sentenced to 21 years in prison. |

## APRIL 2026

| Ann. | Date | Event |
|------|------|-------|
| 30 | 11 Apr 1996 | Death of Jessica Dubroff, seven-year-old American trainee pilot. Killed in a plane crash in Wyoming while attempting to become the youngest person to fly a light aircraft across the USA. Her father and her flight instructor were also killed. Investigators blamed her flight instructor for the crash. |
| 30 | 12 Apr 1996 | Yahoo! went public, making its Initial Public Offering (IPO). |
| 30 | 16 Apr 1996 | France Télécom launched its Wanadoo internet service. It took over the British service Freeserve in 2000 and was rebranded as Orange in 2006. |
| 30 | 18 Apr 1996 | The Europa Hotel shooting, Cairo, Egypt. Four terrorists from the Egyptian Sunni jihadist group opened fire on a group of 88 Greek tourists outside the hotel. Eighteen people were killed. The terrorist group later said they thought the tourists were Israelis. |
| 30 | 18 Apr 1996 | The First Qana Massacre, southern Lebanon. The Israeli Defence Force shelled a United Nations compound. 106 Lebanese civilians were killed. |
| 30 | 18 Apr 1996 | Death of Bernard Edwards, American bass guitarist and songwriter (Chic and other bands/artists) and record producer (Diana Ross, Robert Palmer, Sister Sledge, Rod Stewart and more). |
| 30 | 20 Apr 1996 | Death of Christopher Robin Milne, British bookseller and writer. Son of the author A. A. Milne. The character Christopher Robin in his father's *Winnie-the-Pooh* stories is based on him. |
| 30 | 21 Apr 1996 | Death of Dzhokhar Dudaev, first President of Chechnya (1991–96). His declaration of independence from the Soviet Union led to the First Chechen War. (Killed in a missile attack.) |
| 30 | 21 Apr 1996 | Death of Jimmy Snyder, ('Jimmy the Greek'), American betting analyst, bookmaker and sports commentator. He was fired by CBS in 1988 for making a racist comment. |
| 30 | 22 Apr 1996 | Death of Erma Bombeck, American humourist, columnist and writer. Noted for her self-deprecating humour and tales of suburban family life. |
| 30 | 23 Apr 1996 to 26th | Former U.S. First Lady Jacqueline Kennedy Onassis's possessions were auctioned by Sotheby's in New York City, USA. Prices wildly exceeded expectations, with the 5,000+ items selling for a total of $34.5 million. (The highest pre-auction estimate was $4.6 million.) |
| 30 | 23 Apr 1996 | Death of P. L. Travers, Australian-British children's writer. Best known for creating the character Mary Poppins (later adapted into a Disney film – that she hated). |
| 30 | 24 Apr 1996 | The Antiterrorism and Effective Death Penalty Act was signed into law in the USA. |
| 30 | 24 Apr 1996 to Feb 2004 | Shoko Asahara, the leader of the Japanese religious cult Aum Shinrikyo, went on trial for the sarin gas attack on the Tokyo subway in March 1995, and for other crimes. The marathon trial lasted for almost eight years. In February 2004 he was convicted and sentenced to death. He was executed in 2018, along with six other members of the cult. |

## APRIL 2026

| Ann. | Date | Event |
|---|---|---|
| 30 | 24 Apr 1996 | The Palestine Liberation Organisation agreed to revoke the clauses in its charter that called for the destruction of Israel.<br>At the time of writing (2022), the clauses have still not been revoked. |
| 30 | 25 Apr 1996 | Death of Saul Bass, American graphics designer and filmmaker.<br>Known for his film title sequences (*The Man with the Golden Arm*, *North by Northwest*, *Psycho* and more), film posters, and corporate logos (AT&T, Continental Airlines, United Airlines and more). |
| 30 | 26 Apr 1996 | Death of Stirling Silliphant, American film and television screenwriter (*Alfred Hitchcock Presents*, *Route 66*, *The Naked City*, *In the Heat of the Night*, *The Poseidon Adventure*, *The Towering Inferno*). |
| 30 | 27 Apr 1996 | Death of William Colby, American Director of the CIA (1973–76). (Drowned in a boating accident.)<br>His body was found on a riverbank in Maryland on 6th May. |
| 30 | 28 Apr 1996 to 29th | The Port Arthur massacre, Tasmania, Australia.<br>A psychologically disturbed local resident (Martin Bryant) killed 35 people and wounded eighteen in a shooting spree. |
| 30 | 28 Apr 1996 | The Whitewater scandal: U.S. President Bill Clinton gave a four-hour videotaped testimony as a defence witness in the trial of his former business partners, James and Susan McDougal, and the former Governor of Arkansas, Jim Guy Tucker. |
| 30 | 29 Apr 1996 | The musical *Rent* by Jonathan Larson opened on Broadway.<br>(See also: 25th January 1996.) |
| 30 | 30 Apr 1996 | The controversial 'fat cat' chief executive of British Gas, Cedric Brown, took early retirement. He was known for his massive salary, huge pay rises, and lavish lifestyle, despite British Gas making huge losses<br>He was portrayed in the media as 'Cedric the Pig'.<br>He received a huge pension and was allowed to keep his office, secretary and chauffeur-driven Jaguar, and remained a consultant for the company.<br>He was also appointed President of the Institution of Gas Engineers, which involved travel to overseas conferences. |
| 30 | 30 Apr 1996 | Death of Julio César Méndez Montenegro, President of Guatemala (1966–70). |
| 25 | 1 Apr 2001 | The Hainan Island incident, China.<br>A U.S. Navy signals intelligence plane collided with a Chinese Navy fighter plane, killing the Chinese pilot. Chinese authorities detained and interrogated the 24 crew members of the U.S. plane after it made an emergency landing. This led to a diplomatic incident between the two countries. It was resolved when the USA sent China a letter of apology for the death of the pilot and for entering Chinese airspace. |
| 25 | 1 Apr 2001 | The former President of Yugoslavia, Slobodan Miloševic, was arrested in Belgrade on charges of corruption, embezzlement and genocide<br>He died in prison in The Hague, Netherlands in 2006 during his trial. |
| 25 | 1 Apr 2001 | Same-sex marriage was legalised in the Netherlands.<br>It was the first country to legalise it.<br>The first four same-sex marriages took place that day. |

## APRIL 2026

| Ann. | Date | Event |
|---|---|---|
| 25 | 6 Apr 2001 | Death of Charles Pettigrew, American soul singer and songwriter (Charles & Eddie). Best known for the song *Would I Lie to You?* (Cancer, aged 37.) |
| 25 | 7 Apr 2001 | NASA launched its *Mars Odyssey* spacecraft to search for evidence of water and volcanic activity on Mars.<br>It went into orbit around Mars on 24th October and remains operational (though it will run out of propellant in 2025). It is the longest-surviving continually active spacecraft orbiting another planet.<br>It successfully mapped the distribution of water below the surface and discovered a vast amount of ice below the equatorial regions. |
| 25 | 7 Apr 2001 | Death of David Graf, American actor. Best known for his role as Officer Eugene Tackleberry in the *Police Academy* series of films.<br>(Heart attack, aged 50.) |
| 25 | 9 Apr 2001 | American Airlines acquired the assets of the bankrupt Trans World Airlines (TWA), and became the USA's largest airline. |
| 25 | 9 Apr 2001 | Death of Willie 'Pops' Stargell, American baseball player and humanitarian. |
| 25 | 10 Apr 2001 | Death of Nyree Dawn Porter, New Zealand-born British stage, film and television actress. Best known for her role as Irene in the TV drama series *The Forsyte Saga*. |
| 25 | 11 Apr 2001 | Death of Robert Moon, American postal inspector who invented the ZIP code. |
| 25 | 11 Apr 2001 | Death of Sir Harry Secombe, Welsh comedian, actor, writer, singer and TV presenter. One of the stars of the 1950s radio series *The Goon Show*. |
| 25 | 12 Apr 2001 | Death of Harvey Ball, American commercial artist who created the 'smiley' in 1963. |
| 25 | 15 Apr 2001 | The Real IRA detonated a small bomb outside a Royal Mail sorting office in Hendon, north London. No one was injured.<br>They detonated a second bomb outside the same building on 6th May.<br>This was the penultimate attack that occurred after the Good Friday Agreement was signed in 1999.<br>The final attack was the Ealing bombing on 3rd August 2001. |
| 25 | 15 Apr 2001 | Death of Joey Ramone, American punk/rock singer and musician (The Ramones). (Cancer, aged 49.) |
| 25 | 19 Apr 2001 | Mel Brooks's musical *The Producers* opened on Broadway. |
| 25 | 22 Apr 2001 | Chris Hadfield became the first Canadian astronaut to perform a spacewalk. He helped install the *Canadarm2* robotic arm (the Space Station Remote Manipulator System) outside the *International Space Station*. |
| 25 | 22 Apr 2001 | The world première of the computer-animated comedy film *Shrek*, in Westwood, California, USA. Released USA: 18th May. UK: 29th June. |
| 25 | 24 Apr 2001 | The U.S. unmanned aerial vehicle (UAV) *Global Hawk* made the first non-stop autonomous unmanned flight across the Pacific. It flew from Edwards Air Force Base, USA to the RAAF Base in Edinburgh, South Australia. |

**APRIL 2026**

| Ann. | Date | Event |
|------|------|-------|
| 25 | 25 Apr 2001 to 1 May | EDSA III (also called the May 1 riots), Philippines. Public protests were held following the arrest of former President Joseph Estrada, who had been deposed in January. The protests turned into an uprising and the presidential palace was attacked. The new president, Gloria Macapagal Arroyo, declared a state of rebellion, the protestors were violently dispersed, and the leaders of the opposition were arrested. |
| 25 | 25 Apr 2001 | Death of Michele Alboreto, Italian racing driver. Killed while testing an Audi R8 sports car in Germany, aged 44. |
| 25 | 28 Apr 2001 | American businessman Dennis Tito became the world's first space tourist. He travelled on a Russian *Soyuz* spacecraft for a seven-day visit to the International Space Station. He paid $20 million (£12.5 million). |
| 20 | 1 Apr 2006 | The Serious Organised Crime Agency (SOCA) was formed in the UK. It was replaced by the National Crime Agency in 2013. |
| 20 | 2 Apr 2006 | Tornado outbreak, central USA. 66 tornadoes were confirmed across seven states. At least 28 people were killed. On 6th to 8th April a further 73 tornadoes were confirmed across thirteen central and southern states, especially Tennessee. Ten people were killed. |
| 20 | 2 Apr 2006 | Gnarls Barkley's debut single *Crazy* became the first song to reach #1 in the UK Singles Chart based solely on download sales. |
| 20 | 5 Apr 2006 | Death of Gene Pitney, American pop/rock and roll singer, songwriter and musician. |
| 20 | 6 Apr 2006 | The first case of H5N1 avian flu (bird flu) in the UK was confirmed following blood tests on a dead swan found in Cellardyke, Fife, Scotland. |
| 20 | 8 Apr 2006 | The Shedden massacre, Ontario, Canada. Eight men were shot dead in a field by members of the Bandidos motorcycle gang. Their bodies were found by a farmer. In October 2009 six members of the gang were convicted of first-degree murder and manslaughter. |
| 20 | 11 Apr 2006 | Death of June Pointer, American pop/R&B singer (The Pointer Sisters). |
| 20 | 13 Apr 2006 | Death of Dame Muriel Spark, Scottish novelist, short story writer, poet and essayist. Best known for her novel *The Prime of Miss Jean Brodie*. |
| 20 | 14 Apr 2006 | The Prime Minister of Israel, Ariel Sharon, was declared permanently incapacitated. He had suffered a stroke in January and remained in a coma. He was officially replaced by Ehud Olmert, who had been acting Prime Minister since 4th January. He remained in a persistent vegetative state until his death in 2014. |
| 20 | 18 Apr 2006 | The first HD DVD players were launched in the USA by Toshiba (the HD-A1 and HD-XA1). HD DVD was abandoned in February 2008 after losing a format war to its rival Blu-ray. The first Blu-ray Disc player went on sale in the USA on 4th December 2006. |
| 20 | 19 Apr 2006 | Death of Scott Crossfield, American naval officer and test pilot. The first person to fly at Mach 2 (twice the speed of sound). He also helped design the full-pressure flight suit, which was later used by NASA astronauts. |

## APRIL 2026

| Ann. | Date | Event |
|------|------|-------|
| 20 | 20 Apr 2006 | Scientists studying data returned by the European Space Agency's *Mars Express* spacecraft proposed dividing the history of Mars into three main geological ages based on its mineral distribution: the Phyllosian era (4.5 – 4.2 billion years ago), the Theiikian era (4.2 – 3.8 billion years ago) and the Siderikian era (3.8 billion years ago – present).<br>Of these, only the Phyllosian era could have supported life. |
| 20 | 20 Apr 2006 | The U.S. première of the psychological horror film *Silent Hill*.<br>Released in the UK and USA on 21st April.<br>It was based on Konami's 1999 video game of the same name. |
| 20 | 25 Apr 2006 | A team of IBM researchers studying so-called 'junk DNA' in the human genome (sections that do not encode protein sequences) announced that, contrary to expectations, they had found similar patterns in junk DNA and the parts of DNA that give rise to proteins. This suggested that some 'junk DNA' might actually have an important biological role. |
| 15 | 6 Apr 2011 | Portugal became the third European country (after Greece and Ireland) to request a bailout (loan) from the International Monetary Fund because of its financial crisis. Its request for a €78 billion bailout package was approved on 16th May, and it received the money in June.<br>It had fully recovered by June 2014, and made its final repayment to the IMF in November. |
| 15 | 18 Apr 2011 | The U.S. credit-rating agency Standard & Poor's (S&P) downgraded the USA's long-term fiscal health outlook from 'stable' to 'negative' for the first time in its history.<br>On 5th August, S&P downgraded the USA's credit rating from AAA (outstanding) to AA+ (excellent).<br>In 2013, the U.S. government filed a $5 billion fraud lawsuit against S&P, which the company said was in retaliation for the downgrading. |
| 15 | 25 Apr 2011 to 28th | The 2011 Super Outbreak, Southern, Midwestern and Eastern USA.<br>360 tornadoes hit 21 U.S. states, including 216 tornadoes on 27th April.<br>348 people were killed, including 238 in Alabama. |
| 15 | 27 Apr 2011 | U.S. President Barack Obama produced a detailed Hawaii birth certificate to prove he had been born there. This was in response to persistent rumours spread by his critics that he had not been born in the USA, so he was not eligible to be President. |
| 15 | 29 Apr 2011 | Prince William and Catherine (Kate) Middleton were married at Westminster Abbey in London.<br>They were given the titles the Duke and Duchess of Cambridge. |
| 10 | 1 Apr 2016 to 5th | The Nagorno–Karabakh conflict (also called the Four-Day War or the April War) between Azerbaijan and Armenia.<br>Result: inconclusive. Azerbaijan claimed victory and captured some territory, while Armenia claimed to have successfully repelled the Azerbaijani offensive. |

## APRIL 2026

| Ann. | Date | Event |
|------|------|-------|
| 10 | 3 Apr 2016 | The *Panama Papers* were published.<br>The 11.5 million leaked documents revealed personal financial details about the owners, directors and shareholders of 214,488 offshore companies. Many of the companies had been used for fraud, tax evasion, and avoiding international sanctions.<br>Five heads of state, and many senior politicians, leading businessmen, and celebrities were named, causing them major embarrassment.<br>At least 140 politicians from more than 50 countries were implicated in tax evasion schemes. |
| 10 | 6 Apr 2016 | Death of Merle Haggard, American country music singer, songwriter, guitarist and fiddle player. |
| 10 | 10 Apr 2016 | The Paravur temple fire, Kerala, India.<br>Firework celebrations went badly wrong when one of the fireworks ignited others that were stored for a later display and caused an explosion. 111 people were killed and 350 injured. |
| 10 | 19 Apr 2016 | Death of Patricio Aylwin, President of Chile (1990–94). |
| 10 | 20 Apr 2016 | Death of Victoria Wood, British comedian, actress, singer and songwriter. She won the television talent show *New Faces* and became well known for the sketch show *Victoria Wood as Seen on TV*, the sitcom *Dinnerladies* and the TV film *Pat and Margaret*. |
| 10 | 21 Apr 2016 | Death of Prince, American pop/funk/hip hop singer, songwriter, musician and record producer. A pioneer of the Minneapolis sound.<br>His hit songs include *Purple Rain, When Doves Cry, 1999, Little Red Corvette, Let's Go Crazy, Raspberry Beret, Kiss, U Got the Look*, and many more. |
| 10 | 22 Apr 2016 | The Paris Agreement on Climate Change (also known as the Paris Climate Accords) was signed. It came into effect on 4th November 2016. |

# MAY 2026

| Ann. | Date | Event |
|------|------|-------|
| 1500 | 18 May 526 | Death of Pope John I (523–526). Succeeded by Felix IV. |
| 1500 | 20 May 526 to 29th | Antioch earthquake, Syria.<br>Around 250,000 people were killed, especially in the city of Antioch where a fire destroyed most of the buildings that had been left standing.<br>The ruins of the city are near the modern city of Antakya in Turkey.<br>The exact date of the earthquake is uncertain. |
| 1400 | 22 May 626 | Birth of Itzam K'an Ahk I, King of Piedras Negras, a Mayan settlement in Guatemala (639–686). |
| 1100 | 15 May 926 | Death of Emperor Zhuangzong of Later Tang, China (923–926).<br>Killed in a mutiny. |
| 700 | 1 May 1326 | Birth of Rinchinbal Khan, Emperor Ningzong of Yuan, China (1332 – he died after two months). |
| 600 | 16 May 1426 | Mohnyin Thado became King of Ava (now in Myanmar) (until 1439). |
| 500 | 19 May 1526 | Death of Emperor Go-Kashiwabara of Japan (1500–26).<br>Succeeded by Emperor Go-Nara. |
| 500 | 22 May 1526 | The League of Cognac was formed by Pope Clement VII, France, Venice, England, Milan and Florence.<br>This led to the War of the League of Cognac (1526–30) against the Hapsburg dominions (mainly the Holy Roman Empire and Spain).<br>Hapsburg victory. |
| 400 | 4 May 1626 | Dutch explorer Peter Minuit from the Dutch West India Company arrived in New Netherland on the east coast of what is now the USA to take over the role of Director.<br>He negotiated the purchase of Manhattan Island from the Lenape Native Americans for $24 worth of cloth and buttons (equivalent to $1,150 today).<br>Manhattan became the Dutch city of New Amsterdam, and was later incorporated into New York City. |
| 400 | 4 May 1626 | Death of Arthur Lake, Bishop of Bath and Wells (1616–26).<br>Thought to be one of the translators of the King James Version of the Bible. |
| 400 | 27 May 1626 | Birth of William II, Prince of Orange (1647–50). Father of King William III of England, Ireland and Scotland (William of Orange). |
| 400 | 28 May 1626 | Death of Thomas Howard, 1st Earl of Suffolk. British admiral, politician and nobleman. Lord High Treasurer (1614–18). |
| 300 | 20 May 1726 | Birth of Francis Cotes, British artist. A pioneer of English pastel painting.<br>A founding member of the Royal Academy. |
| 300 | 25 May 1726 ? | The world's first Circulating Library (lending library) was launched by Scottish poet and bookseller Allan Ramsay at his bookshop in Edinburgh, Scotland. He rented the books from his shop to his customers.<br>Lending libraries soon became popular – several opened in England in 1728.<br>(The date is uncertain. Sources give various dates between 1725 and 1728.) |

## MAY 2026

| Ann. | Date | Event |
|------|------|-------|
| 250 | 1 May 1776 | The Illuminati (officially the Bavarian Illuminati), a secret society, was founded in Bavaria, Germany. Its purpose was to oppose superstition, religious influence on public life, the government's abuse of power, and the deliberate presentation of information in an obscure manner to prevent understanding and inquiry.<br>The society was banned in 1784, but continued to operate underground. Other secret groups have used the same name, and are the subject of conspiracy theories. |
| 250 | 4 May 1776 | American Revolution: Rhode Island became the first of the Thirteen Colonies to renounce its allegiance to the British Crown and declare independence. |
| 250 | 15 May 1776 | American Revolution: the Fifth Virginia Convention declared that the government of Virginia was totally dissolved and that Virginia was an independent state. It instructed Virginia's delegates to the Second Continental Congress to declare independence from Great Britain. |
| 250 | 19 May 1776 | American Revolutionary War – the Battle of the Cedars, Quebec, Canada. British and Iroquois victory. |
| 200 | 3 May 1826 | Birth of Charles XV, King of Sweden and Norway (1859–72). |
| 200 | 4 May 1826 | Birth of Frederick Church, American artist. Noted for his large landscapes and realistic detail. One of the most famous U.S. artists of his era. |
| 200 | 5 May 1826 | Birth of Eugénie de Montijo, Empress consort of the French (1853–70). Wife of Emperor Napoleon III. |
| 200 | 7 May 1826 | Birth of Varina Davis, First Lady of the Confederate States of America (1862–65). Wife of the Confederate President Jefferson Davis. |
| 200 | 22 May 1826 | Birth of George Parr, ('the Lion of the North'), British cricketer. Captain of the first England touring team. The world's best cricketer of his era. |
| 200 | 24 May 1826 | Death of Friedrich Ernst Fesca, German violinist and composer. |
| 200 | 25 May 1826 | Birth of Danilo I, Prince of Montenegro (1852–60). |
| 200 | 29 May 1826 | Birth of Ebenezer Butterick, American tailor who invented tissue paper dress patterns in multiple sizes with his wife Ellen.<br>Their invention revolutionised home dressmaking. |
| 175 | 1 May 1851 to 15 Oct | The Great Exhibition was held in Hyde Park, London, UK.<br>Many historians regard it as the first World's Fair. More than 10,000 exhibitors showcased technology from around the world.<br>The event was held in The Crystal Palace, which was dismantled and rebuilt in south London after the exhibition. It burned down in 1936. |
| 175 | 3 May 1851 to 4th | The San Francisco fire of 1851, California, USA.<br>Three-quarters of the city was destroyed – around 2,000 buildings.<br>The fire broke out in a storeroom above a hotel, and may have been lit by an arsonist. It was spread by gale-force winds. At least nine people were killed. This was the sixth of seven fires that affected San Francisco between December 1849 and June 1851. |

**MAY 2026**

| Ann. | Date | Event |
|---|---|---|
| 175 | 20 May 1851 | Birth of Emile Berliner, German-American inventor of the gramophone and gramophone records. |
| 175 | 21 May 1851 | Slavery was abolished in Colombia (with effect from 1st January 1852). Slave owners were compensated with government bonds. |
| 150 | 6 May 1876 | Thomas Gainsborough's painting of the Duchess of Devonshire was stolen from a gallery in London, three weeks after the gallery's owner had paid 10,000 guineas for it. It was the highest price ever paid for a painting at that time, and the theft attracted huge press attention. It was recovered by Pinkerton's detective agency in Chicago, Illinois, USA in 1901, returned to the UK, and sold to the American financier J. P. Morgan. It was purchased by the 11th Duke of Devonshire in 1994 and returned to its original home in Chatsworth House. |
| 150 | 8 May 1876 | Death of Truganini, commonly regarded as the last full-blooded Aboriginal Tasmanian. (However, at least three others are known to have outlived her.) |
| 150 | 10 May 1876 to 10 Nov | The Centennial International Exposition was held in Philadelphia, Pennsylvania, USA. It celebrated the 100th anniversary of the signing of the Declaration of Independence. It was the first World's Fair to be held in the USA. |
| 150 | 25 May 1876 | Scottish-born American inventor Alexander Graham Bell gave the first public demonstration of the telephone, at the American Academy of Arts and Sciences in Boston, Massachusetts. |
| 150 | 26 May 1876 | Birth of Jack Root, American boxer. Regarded as the first world light-heavyweight champion (1903). (Historians have found records of an August 1899 match won by Joe Choynski that could be regarded as the first light-heavyweight championship.) |
| 150 | 30 May 1876 | The Turkish coup. The Sultan of the Ottoman Empire, Abdulaziz, was overthrown by his nephew, Murad V, who was himself deposed on 31st August. |
| 150 | 30 May 1876 | American inventor Thomas Edison was granted three U.S. patents for his 'Improvements in Duplex Telegraphs'. They enabled outgoing telegraph signals to be sent over the same wire as incoming signals. (U.S. Patents 178,221 – 178,223.) |
| 125 | 1 May 1901 to 2 Nov | The Pan-American Exposition, a World's Fair, was held in Buffalo, New York, USA. U.S. President William McKinley was assassinated at the exposition in September. |
| 125 | 3 May 1901 | The Great Fire of 1901, Jacksonville, Florida, USA. Sparks from a chimney set fire to moss that had been laid out to dry. The wind carried the flames and set fire to buildings, and the fire spread rapidly. 2,368 buildings were destroyed and seven people were killed. It was the third-largest urban fire in U.S history. |
| 125 | 7 May 1901 | Birth of Gary Cooper, American film actor (*The Virginian*, *A Farewell to Arms*, *Mr. Deeds Goes to Town*, *For Whom the Bell Tolls*, *High Noon*, and more). |

## MAY 2026

| Ann. | Date | Event |
|------|------|-------|
| 125 | 9 May 1901 | The Parliament of Australia was founded. |
| 125 | 11 May 1901 | Birth of Rose Ausländer, Austro-Hungarian-born German-American poet. |
| 125 | 17 May 1901 | Birth of Werner Egk, German composer. |
| 125 | 18 May 1901 | Birth of Vincent du Vigneaud, American biochemist.<br>Noted for synthesising the hormones oxytocin and vasopressin. Winner of the 1955 Nobel Prize in Chemistry for his work on sulphur compounds. |
| 125 | 19 May 1901 | Death of Marthinus Wessel Pretorius, first President of the South African Republic (1866–71). |
| 125 | 20 May 1901 | Birth of Max Euwe, Dutch chess player. World Chess Champion 1935–37. President of the World Chess Federation (FIDE) 1970–78. |
| 125 | 21 May 1901 | Connecticut became the first U.S. state to introduce speed limits for motor vehicles: 12 mph in cities and 15 mph on rural roads. |
| 125 | 22 May 1901 | Death of Gaetano Bresci, Italian anarchist who assassinated King Umberto I in 1900. (Died in prison, aged 31. Some historians believe he hanged himself, while others say he was murdered.) |
| 125 | 27 May 1901 | The Edison Storage Battery Company was founded in New Jersey, USA. It was acquired by the Exide Battery Corporation in 1972. |
| 100 | 1 May 1926 | The Ford Motor Company became one of the first companies in the USA to adopt a five-day, forty-hour week for its factory workers. Its office workers also began working five-day, forty-hour weeks from August. |
| 100 | 2 May 1926 to 4 May 1927 | The Nicaraguan Civil War.<br>U.S. Marines intervened in January 1927 and remained in the country until 1933. |
| 100 | 3 May 1926 | Death of Victor, Prince Napoléon, pretender to the French throne (1879–1926) as Napoleon V. |
| 100 | 4 May 1926 to 12th | The United Kingdom general strike.<br>The Trade Union Congress (TUC) called a general strike in support of 1.2 million coal miners, whose pay and hours had been cut because of falling demand for coal. 1.7 million workers took part in the strike, but middle-class volunteers covered their absence to maintain essential services.<br>The strike had little effect, and the TUC ended it after nine days. |
| 100 | 7 May 1926 to 9th | The Great Syrian Revolt: French forces shelled the city of Damascus, killing 500 civilians and 100 rebels, and destroying the old city. |
| 100 | 8 May 1926 | Birth of Don Rickles, American stand-up comedian and film and television actor. (Died 2017.) |
| 100 | 9 May 1926 | American naval officer and explorer Admiral Richard E. Byrd and Chief Aviation Pilot Floyd Bennett claimed to have flown over the North Pole on this date. Byrd became a national hero afterwards, and they were both awarded the Medal of Honor.<br>However, their claim to have reached the pole has since been disputed, as they were not in the air long enough to complete the entire journey.<br>Many historians believe they flew eighty percent of the way to the pole, but turned back because of an oil leak, and falsified their records to make it look as if they had succeeded. (See also: 12th May 1926.) |

**MAY 2026**

| Ann. | Date | Event |
|------|------|-------|
| 100 | 10 May 1926 | Birth of Hugo Banzer, President of Bolivia (1971–78, 1997–2001). (Died 2002.) |
| 100 | 12 May 1926 | The May Coup, Poland. President Stanislaw Wojciechowski and Prime Minister Wincenty Witos were overthrown and a new government was installed. Kazimierz Bartel became Prime Minister on 15th May and Ignacy Moscicki became President on 4th June. |
| 100 | 12 May 1926 | The first undisputed flight over the North Pole was made by Norwegian explorer Roald Amundsen and fifteen others in the airship *Norge*. (Three earlier claims in 1908, 1909 and 9th May 1926 are all disputed.) |
| 100 | 12 May 1926 | Russian composer Dmitri Shostakovich's *Symphony No. 1* was performed for the first time, in Saint Petersburg. He completed it at the age of 19, as his graduation piece at the Saint Petersburg Conservatory. |
| 100 | 14 May 1926 | Birth of Eric Morecambe, British comedian (Morecambe and Wise). (Died 1984.) |
| 100 | 15 May 1926 | Birth of Anthony Shaffer and Peter Shaffer, British playwrights, screenwriters and novelists. (Anthony died in 2001, Peter died in 2016.) |
| 100 | 16 May 1926 | Death of Mehmed VI, last Sultan of the Ottoman Empire (1918–22). |
| 100 | 18 May 1926 | American Christian evangelist Aimee Semple McPherson disappeared after swimming at Venice Beach in California. Searches failed to find her, but she turned up in Mexico five weeks later. She claimed she had been kidnapped, but many suspected it was a hoax. The story caused a media sensation, and there was a major court case with numerous theories, witnesses and alleged kidnappers – but little evidence. |
| 100 | 19 May 1926 | American inventor Thomas Edison spoke on the radio for the first time, at a dinner for the National Electric Light Association in Atlantic City, New Jersey, USA. |
| 100 | 20 May 1926 | The Air Commerce Act came into effect in the USA. It regulated civil aviation, introduced safety standards, tested and licensed planes and pilots, and investigated accidents. |
| 100 | 20 May 1926 | The Railway Labor Act was signed into law in the USA. It was established to prevent strikes in the railway and airline industries, and declared that labour disputes should be solved through bargaining, arbitration and mediation. |
| 100 | 20 May 1926 | American inventor Thomas Edison said Americans were not interested in talking films, and preferred the restful quiet of silent films. |
| 100 | 23 May 1926 | Birth of Joe Slovo, Lithuanian-born South African politician and anti-apartheid activist. Commander of the African National Congress's military wing, Umkhonto we Sizwe. (Died 1995.) |
| 100 | 25 May 1926 | Death of Symon Petliura, Ukrainian nationalist leader. (Assassinated in Paris, France by a Russian anarchist.) |
| 100 | 26 May 1926 | Birth of Miles Davis, American jazz trumpeter, bandleader and composer. (Died 1991.) |

## MAY 2026

| Ann. | Date | Event |
|---|---|---|
| 100 | 27 May 1926 | The Rif War in Morocco ended and the Republic of the Rif was dissolved. |
| 100 | 28 May 1926 | Military coup in Portugal (also known as the 28 May Revolution) led by General Gomes da Costa. The unstable First Republic was ended and a military dictatorship was established. |
| 100 | 28 May 1926 | The United States Customs Court was established.<br>It adjudicates civil actions in U.S. customs and international trade cases. It replaced the Board of General Appraisers, which was established in 1890. It was replaced by the U.S. Court of International Trade in 1980. |
| 100 | 29 May 1926 | Birth of Katie Boyle, Italian-born British television personality. (Died 2018.) |
| 100 | 31 May 1926 to 30 Nov | The Sesquicentennial Exposition, a World's Fair, was held in Philadelphia, Pennsylvania, USA. It celebrated the 150th anniversary of the signing of the U.S. Declaration of Independence. |
| 90 | 2 May 1936 | Second Italo–Ethiopian War: Ethiopian emperor Haile Selassie left the country and went into exile in Djibouti following Ethiopia's invasion by Italy. He returned in 1941. (See also: 7th May 1936.) |
| 90 | 2 May 1936 | Russian composer Sergei Prokofiev's symphonic fairy tale *Peter and Wolf* was performed for the first time, in Moscow. |
| 90 | 3 May 1936 | American baseball star Joe DiMaggio made his Major League Baseball debut with the New York Yankees. |
| 90 | 7 May 1936 | Second Italo–Ethiopian War: Italy annexed Ethiopia after capturing the capital, Addis Ababa, on 5th May.<br>On 9th May, Italy established Italian East Africa. |
| 90 | 7 May 1936 | British aviator Amy Johnson made the fastest-ever solo flight from England to Cape Town, South Africa.<br>She broke the record that was first set by her husband, James Mollison. |
| 90 | 9 May 1936 | The first episode of the radio quiz show *Professor Quiz* was broadcast on CBS in Washington, D.C., USA. It was the first true quiz show on radio.<br>It was expanded to the full CBS network on 18th September.<br>It transferred to ABC in 1946 and continued until 1948. |
| 90 | 9 May 1936 | Birth of Albert Finney, British stage, film and television actor (*Saturday Night and Sunday Morning, Tom Jones, Scrooge, Annie, Erin Brockovich, The Bourne Ultimatum, The Bourne Legacy, Skyfall*). (Died 2019.) |
| 90 | 10 May 1936 | Manuel Azaña became President of Spain (until 1939 when he fled to France at the end of the Spanish Civil War). |
| 90 | 12 May 1936 | American educators and efficiency experts August Dvorak and William Dealey were granted a U.S. patent for the Dvorak simplified keyboard layout. It claims to reduce finger movement, increase typing rate, and reduce errors compared with the standard QWERTY layout. (U.S. Patent 2,040,248.) |
| 90 | 12 May 1936 | Birth of Guillermo Endara, President of Panama (1989–94). (Died 2009.) |

## MAY 2026

| Ann. | Date | Event |
|------|------|-------|
| 90 | 12 May 1936 | Birth of Tom Snyder, American radio and television news anchorman and talk-show host. Best known for NBC's *The Tomorrow Show* and CBS's *The Late Late Show*. (Died 2007.) |
| 90 | 14 May 1936 | Birth of Bobby Darin, American big band/rock and roll/pop singer and songwriter. (Died 1973.) |
| 90 | 14 May 1936 | Death of Edmund Allenby, 1st Viscount Allenby, British field marshal and diplomat. Best known for directing the Palestine Campaign in WWI. |
| 90 | 15 May 1936 | Birth of Paul Zindel, American playwright and novelist. (Died 2003.) |
| 90 | 16 May 1936 | Daphne Kearley, aged 19, became Britain's first air hostess. She served passengers on Air Dispatch flights between Croydon and Paris, France. She was previously a secretary at the company. |
| 90 | 16 May 1936 | Birth of Roy Hudd, British comedian, radio presenter, stage and television actor, and writer. Known for his satirical radio series *The News Huddlines*. He was also a noted authority on British music hall. (Died 2020.) |
| 90 | 17 May 1936 | Birth of Dennis Hopper, American film and television actor, director, photographer and artist (*Rebel Without a Cause, Giant, Easy Rider, Cool Hand Luke, Blue Velvet, Hoosiers*, and more). (Died 2010.) |
| 90 | 18 May 1936 | Japanese prostitute Sada Abe strangled her lover and cut off his genitals, which she carried around with her until she was arrested three days later (on 21st May). This became one of Japan's most notorious scandals. |
| 90 | 22 May 1936 | Aer Lingus, Ireland's national airline, began operating. |
| 90 | 22 May 1936 | Birth of M. Scott Peck, American psychiatrist and writer. Best known for his book *The Road Less Traveled*. (Died 2005.) |
| 90 | 25 May 1936 to Apr 1937 | The Remington Rand strike, USA. The owners of the Remington Rand typewriter company refused to bargain with workers who had organised themselves into a union. They went out of their way to antagonise union members, leading to a violent strike, notable for its beatings, bombings, shootings and rioting. |
| 90 | 27 May 1936 | The British ocean liner *RMS Queen Mary* began her maiden voyage, from Southampton to New York, USA. |
| 80 | 1 May 1946 to Aug 1949 | The Pilbara strike, Western Australia. 800 Indigenous Australians held a three-year strike over their human rights, wages and working conditions. The landmark strike was one of the longest in Australian history. Many Aboriginal workers refused to work for white landowners afterwards, and pooled their funds to establish farming cooperatives. |
| 80 | 2 May 1946 to 4th | The Battle of Alcatraz. Alcatraz federal prison in San Francisco Bay, California, USA was taken over by prisoners after a failed escape attempt. A violent battle ensued. |
| 80 | 2 May 1946 | Birth of Lesley Gore, American pop singer, songwriter and actress. Best known for her hit song *It's My Party*. (Died 2015.) |
| 80 | 7 May 1946 | Sony, the Japanese consumer electronics company, was founded (as the Tokyo Telecommunications Engineering Corporation). |

## MAY 2026

| Ann. | Date | Event |
|------|------|-------|
| 80 | 8 May 1946 | Two schoolgirls blew up a Soviet war memorial in Tallinn, Estonia to avenge the Soviet destruction of Estonian war memorials. They were arrested and sent to a forced labour camp. The memorial was replaced in September 1947 with a new memorial: the Bronze Soldier of Tallinn. |
| 80 | 9 May 1946 | King Victor Emmanuel III of Italy abdicated and was succeeded by his son, Umberto II.<br>(Italy became a republic in June, and the new king was banished from Italy.) |
| 80 | 9 May 1946 | The first episode of the television variety show *Hour Glass* was broadcast on NBC in the USA. It was the first regularly scheduled variety show on U.S. network TV. It ran for ten months. |
| 80 | 11 May 1946 | The first CARE packages for Europe arrived in Le Havre, France to help people who were starving after WWII.<br>The first CARE packages were actually surplus U.S. Army rations.<br>CARE is a humanitarian aid organisation: the Cooperative for Assistance and Relief Everywhere. |
| 80 | 13 May 1946 | Birth of Tim Pigott-Smith, British film and television actor and writer.<br>Best known for his role as Ronald Merrick in the TV drama series *The Jewel in the Crown*. He also had several notable film and TV roles.<br>(Died 2017.) |
| 80 | 13 May 1946 | The first trial of staff from the Mauthausen concentration camp in Austria ended. All 61 defendants were convicted, with 58 sentenced to death and the others to life imprisonment.<br>Nine of those sentenced to death later had their sentences commuted to life imprisonment. The others were executed in May 1947. |
| 80 | 16 May 1946 | The musical *Annie Get Your Gun* opened on Broadway. |
| 80 | 17 May 1946 | William H. Hastie became the first African American Governor of the U.S. Virgin Islands. |
| 80 | 19 May 1946 | Birth of André the Giant, French professional wrestler and actor.<br>(Died 1993.) |
| 80 | 19 May 1946 | Death of Booth Tarkington, American novelist and playwright.<br>Known as America's greatest living author during the 1910s and 20s.<br>Best known for his novels *The Magnificent Ambersons* and *Alice Adams*. |
| 80 | 20 May 1946 | Birth of Bobby Murcer, American baseball player (New York Yankees) and broadcaster. (Died 2008.) |
| 80 | 21 May 1946 | Birth of Allan McKeown, British stage and television producer.<br>One of the first independent TV producers in the UK.<br>Co-founder of WitzEnd. He worked for all of the TV networks in the USA.<br>Husband of the actress, comedian and singer Tracey Ullman. (Died 2013.) |
| 80 | 22 May 1946 | The first U.S. rocket to reach space (a WAC Corporal) was launched at White Sands Missile Range in New Mexico.<br>(A German V-2 was the first rocket to reach space, in June 1944.) |
| 80 | 22 May 1946 | National railroad strike, USA. Part of a wave of strikes that affected several major industries in 1945–46, including coal, steel and mining.<br>U.S. President Harry S. Truman seized the railroads and put the U.S. Army in charge of them. The strike was settled within 48 hours. |

**MAY 2026**

| Ann. | Date | Event |
|------|------|-------|
| 80 | 22 May 1946 | Birth of George Best, Northern Irish footballer. European Footballer of the Year (1968). Also known for his long battle with alcoholism, which eventually led to his death in 2005. |
| 80 | 22 May 1946 | Birth of Howard Kendall, British football player and manager. (Died 2015.) |
| 80 | 23 May 1946 | British playwright Terrance Rattigan's play *The Winslow Boy* opened in London. It was adapted into a film in 1943 and 1999. |
| 80 | 25 May 1946 | Transjordan gained its independence when the United Nations approved the end of the British Mandate. Abdullah I became its first King. Tranjordan was renamed Jordan in 1948. |
| 80 | 25 May 1946 | Death of Patty Smith Hill, American kindergarten teacher who co-wrote the song *Good Morning to All* with her sister Mildred Hill. The song is traditionally recognised as the basis for the song *Happy Birthday to You*, but this is disputed. Some claim the melody came from an existing song. |
| 80 | 26 May 1946 | Birth of Mick Ronson, British rock guitarist, songwriter, arranger and record producer. Best known for his work with David Bowie. (Died 1993). |
| 80 | 27 May 1946 | Birth of Lewis Collins, British stage, film and television actor. Best known for his role as Bodie in the crime drama TV series *The Professionals*. (Died 2013.) |
| 80 | 27 May 1946 | Birth of Niels-Henning Ørsted Pedersen, Danish jazz double bassist and composer. (Died 2005.) |
| 80 | 28 May 1946 | Manuel Roxas became President of the Philippines (until 1948). |
| 80 | 28 May 1946 | Scientists working on the Manhattan Project in the USA filed a secret patent for their invention of the hydrogen bomb (H-bomb). Secret patents cannot be granted until such time as they become non-secret. (One of the scientists, Klaus Fuchs, later leaked the design to the Soviet Union.) |
| 75 | 3 May 1951 | The Festival of Britain and the Royal Festival Hall in London were opened. |
| 75 | 3 May 1951 | The first officially recognised Holocaust Remembrance Day was marked in Israel. The day is now marked annually in March or April each year. |
| 75 | 9 May 1951 | The Lake District National Park was established in England. It was Britain's second national park. |
| 75 | 14 May 1951 | The Talyllyn Railway in Wales reopened after ceasing operations in October 1950. It was the first railway in the world to be preserved as a heritage railway operated by volunteers. |
| 75 | 19 May 1951 | Birth of Joey Ramone, American punk rock singer (The Ramones). (Died 2001.) |
| 75 | 20 May 1951 to 1 Jul | Korean War: the United Nations counter-offensive of May – June 1951. The UN launched the final large-scale offensive of the war, and recaptured most of the territory it had lost in the Chinese spring offensive. A military stalemate followed that lasted until the end of the war in July 1953. |
| 75 | 23 May 1951 | China annexed Tibet after pressuring Tibetan negotiators to sign the Seventeen Point Agreement – which many argue they had no real authority to sign and is therefore invalid. The Tibetan government remained in place, but was dissolved in 1959 following an uprising that forced the Dalai Lama into exile. Tibet Autonomous Region was established in 1965. |

## MAY 2026

| Ann. | Date | Event |
|------|------|-------|
| 75 | 25 May 1951 | British spies Guy Burgess and Donald Maclean fled to Moscow, Soviet Union. They were members of the infamous Cambridge spy ring. Their whereabouts remained unknown until 1956. (See also: 11th May 1956.) |
| 75 | 25 May 1951 | U.S. baseball star Willie Mays made his Major League debut with the New York Giants. |
| 75 | 26 May 1951 | Birth of Sally Ride, American astronaut, physicist and engineer. The first American woman in space. (Died 2012.) |
| 75 | 26 May 1951 | Death of Lincoln Ellsworth, American polar explorer. He accompanied the Norwegian explorer Roald Amundsen on one of the first flights over the North Pole, and discovered the Ellsworth Mountains in Antarctica. |
| 75 | 28 May 1951 | The first episode of the radio comedy series *The Goon Show* was broadcast in the UK. It ran until 1960. (The first series was called *Crazy People*). |
| 75 | 29 May 1951 | U.S. Navy pilot Charles F. Blair made the first solo flight over the North Pole. He flew from Bardufoss in Norway to Fairbanks in Alaska, USA – 3,260 miles, non-stop. |
| 75 | 29 May 1951 | Death of Fanny Brice, American singer, comedian, and stage and film actress. Best known for the radio comedy series *The Baby Snooks Show*. The musical *Funny Girl* is based on her life and career. |
| 70 | 1 May 1956 | A public polio immunisation programme began in Britain, using the vaccine developed in the USA by Dr Jonas Salk. |
| 70 | 1 May 1956 | Minamata disease was discovered in Japan. It affects the central nervous system and is caused by mercury poisoning. The mass outbreak in Japan was found to be caused by waste water from a chemical plant entering the sea and contaminating fish, which were eaten by the local population. 1,784 people are known to have died from the disease, and over 10,000 received financial compensation from the chemical company Chisso. |
| 70 | 3 May 1956 | The first World Judo Championships were held, in Tokyo, Japan. |
| 70 | 6 May 1956 | American athlete Jim Bailey became the first person to break the four-minute mile in the USA (3:58.6). Fellow athlete John Landy came second in the race and also broke the four-minute barrier. The first person to break four minutes was British athlete Roger Bannister exactly two years earlier, on 6th May 1954. |
| 70 | 7 May 1956 | The British Minister for Health, Robin Turton, rejected calls for a national publicity campaign to warn of the dangers of smoking. He said the link between smoking and lung cancer had not yet been proven, but he agreed to review the situation in the future. The link was proven in the UK in 1962 and in the USA in 1964. TV advertisements for cigarettes were banned in the UK from 1965. |
| 70 | 8 May 1956 | John Osborne's play *Look Back in Anger* was performed for the first time, at the Royal Court Theatre in London. |
| 70 | 9 May 1956 | The first successful ascent of Manaslu in the Himalayas (the world's eighth-highest mountain) by a Japanese team led by Yuko Maki. |

**MAY 2026**

| Ann. | Date | Event |
|------|------|-------|
| 70 | 10 May 1956 | Birth of Vladislav Listyev, Russian investigative journalist, television host and network executive. Head of ORT TV (now Channel One). (Shot dead in 1995, possibly by a group of corrupt advertising agencies that objected to his ban on advertising. The case remains unsolved.) |
| 70 | 16 May 1956 | Death of H. B. Reese, American confectioner. Founder of the H. B. Reese Candy Company. Creator of Reese's Peanut Butter Cups. |
| 70 | 17 May 1956 | Birth of Bob Saget, American stand-up comedian, actor, and television host. (Died 2022.) |
| 70 | 18 May 1956 | The first successful ascent of Lhotse I in the Himalayas (the world's fourth-highest mountain) by Swiss climbers Fritz Luchsinger and Ernst Reiss. |
| 70 | 20 May 1956 | Operation Redwing: the USA carried out its first airborne explosion of a hydrogen bomb, in a test over Bikini Atoll in the Pacific Ocean. (Operation Redwing was a series of seventeen nuclear test explosions carried out between May and July 1956. This was the second explosion, codenamed Cherokee.) |
| 70 | 20 May 1956 | Death of Sir Max Beerbohm, British caricaturist, writer, essayist and drama critic. Best known for his novel *Zuleika Dobson*. |
| 70 | 24 May 1956 | The first Eurovision Song Contest was held in Lugano, Switzerland. It was won by Switzerland. |
| 70 | 25 May 1956 | Birth of Sugar Minott, Jamaican reggae/dancehall singer, record producer and record label executive. He also nurtured and promoted young talent. (Died 2010.) |
| 65 | 1 May 1961 | Cuban leader Fidel Castro declared the country a socialist state and abolished multi-party elections. |
| 65 | 1 May 1961 | The first major airline hijacking in the USA. A National Airlines flight between Marathon and Key West, Florida was hijacked by an armed man who forced the pilot to fly him to Cuba. |
| 65 | 1 May 1961 | The first episode of the anime television series *Instant History* was broadcast on Fuji Television in Japan. It was the world's first anime TV series. It ran until February 1962, and then became *Otogi Manga Calendar*, which ran until 1964. |
| 65 | 1 May 1961 | Betting away from racecourses was legalised in the UK and the first betting shops opened. |
| 65 | 4 May 1961 | A thirteen-member civil rights group known as the Freedom Riders set off from Washington D.C., USA, heading for New Orleans, Louisiana, with the aim of challenging racial segregation on buses. During their journey they were attacked, beaten, arrested, and sparked a riot. |
| 65 | 5 May 1961 | Alan Shepard became the first American to travel into space. He made a fifteen-minute sub-orbital flight aboard *Freedom 7*. |
| 65 | 9 May 1961 | The chairman of the Federal Communications Commission in the USA, Newton N. Minow gave a speech entitled *Television and the Public Interest*. He condemned television schedules as 'a vast wasteland'. His speech became known as the 'Wasteland Speech'. |

**MAY 2026**

| Ann. | Date | Event |
|---|---|---|
| 65 | 12 May 1961 | Vietnam War: During his two-week tour of Asian countries, U.S. Vice President Lyndon B. Johnson visited South Vietnam and met the South Vietnamese President, Ngo Dinh Diem. |
| 65 | 13 May 1961 | Death of Gary Cooper, American film actor (*High Noon*, *The Virginian*, *For Whom the Bell Tolls*, and more). |
| 65 | 16 May 1961 | The May 16 Coup, South Korea. The military overthrew the government and dissolved the National Assembly. The Supreme Council for National Reconstruction was established as a replacement government. Its chairman, Park Chung-hee, took office as President in December 1963. |
| 65 | 18 May 1961 | The first community nuclear fallout shelter in the USA was dedicated: the Highlands Community Fallout Shelter in Boise, Idaho. It could hold 1,000 people. Family membership cost $100. |
| 65 | 19 May 1961 | The Soviet space probe *Venera 1* became the first man-made object to fly past another planet. It passed within 62,000 miles (100,000 km) of Venus, but did not return any data as contact had been lost a month earlier. |
| 65 | 25 May 1961 | U.S. President John F. Kennedy gave his famous 'Man on the Moon' speech. He urged Congress and America to commit itself to landing a man on the Moon and returning him safely to Earth before the end of the decade. |
| 65 | 28 May 1961 | Amnesty International was founded in London, UK. |
| 65 | 30 May 1961 | Death of Rafael Trujillo, President of the Dominican Republic (1930–38, 1942–52), and dictator (1930–61). His regime was noted for its oppression, human rights violations, and state terrorism, but brought the country great prosperity and stability. (Assassinated.) |
| 65 | 31 May 1961 | South Africa withdrew from the British Commonwealth and became an independent republic. (It re-joined the Commonwealth in 1994.) |
| 65 | 31 May 1961 | Michael Ramsay became Archbishop of Canterbury (until 1974). |
| 60 | 1 May 1966 | British rock band the Beatles played their last concert in the UK at the Empire Pool (now Wembley Arena) in London. (Their last performance in the UK was on the roof of Apple Corps' headquarters in January 1969.) |
| 60 | 3 May 1966 | The game *Twister* was featured on *The Tonight Show* in the USA. Host Johnny Carson played it with actress and socialite Eva Gabor. It became an immediate success with people queuing up to buy it the next day. The manufacturer, Milton Bradley, had been considering withdrawing it as they thought it was too risqué. |
| 60 | 6 May 1966 | The Moors Murderers, Ian Brady and Myra Hindley, were sentenced to life imprisonment in the UK. Brady was convicted of three murders and Hindley of two, though they later confessed to a total of five. Their victims were aged between 10 and 17. |
| 60 | 7 May 1966 | The Rolling Stones' rock song *Paint it Black* was released in the USA. (UK: 13th May.) |
| 60 | 8 May 1966 | American civil rights activist Stokely Carmichael was elected chairman of the Student Nonviolent Coordinating Committee. |

# MAY 2026

| Ann. | Date | Event |
|------|------|-------|
| 60 | 12 May 1966 | Busch Memorial Stadium in St. Louis, Missouri, USA officially opened.<br>It was the home of the St. Louis Cardinals baseball team (1966–2005) and the Cardinals football team (1966–87).<br>It was demolished in 2005 and replaced by the new Busch Stadium, which opened on 4th April 2006. |
| 60 | 14 May 1966 to 24 Jun | Vietnam War: 1 million students at colleges and universities in the USA sat the draft deferment examination, answering 150 questions in three hours. The students aimed to achieve a high enough score to avoid being drafted into the U.S. Military during the war. |
| 60 | 16 May 1966 to 6 Oct 1976 | Mao Zedong, Chairman of the Communist Party of China, issued the May 16 Notice. This signalled the beginning of the Cultural Revolution, which officially began on 1st August. |
| 60 | 16 May 1966 to 1 Jul | Britain's National Union of Seamen went on strike over pay and long working hours. The strike caused significant disruption to British shipping and the government declared a state of emergency on 23rd May – though the emergency powers were never used. |
| 60 | 16 May 1966 | The Beach Boys' album *Pet Sounds* was released. |
| 60 | 16 May 1966 | Bob Dylan's album *Blonde on Blonde* was released. |
| 60 | 17 May 1966 | Death of Randy Turpin, British world middleweight boxing champion in 1951. (Suicide, aged 37.) |
| 60 | 21 May 1966 | The newly established Ulster Volunteer Force (UVF) declared war on the Irish Republican Army (IRA) in Northern Ireland and announced that any known IRA members would be immediately executed. |
| 60 | 26 May 1966 | British Guiana gained its independence from the UK and became Guyana. |
| 60 | 28 May 1966 | Russian composer Dmitri Shostakovich's *String Quartet No. 11* was performed for the first time, in Saint Petersburg. |
| 60 | 30 May 1966 | NASA launched its *Surveyor 1* spacecraft on a mission to the Moon to collect data for the *Apollo* missions. On 2nd June it became the first U.S. spacecraft to soft-land on another extraterrestrial body. |
| 60 | 30 May 1966 | British racing driver Graham Hill won the 1966 Indianapolis 500.<br>He is the only driver in history to win the 'triple crown of motor racing' – the Formula One World Championship (1962 and 1968), the 24 Hours of Le Mans (1972), and the Indianapolis 500 (1966).<br>(The triple crown has since been redefined to include the Monaco Grand Prix instead of the Formula One World Championship, but he is still the only driver to win all three.) |
| 60 | 30 May 1966 | British rock band the Beatles released the song *Paperback Writer*.<br>The B-side of the single was the song *Rain*, which was the first record to feature backward vocals. |
| 50 | 6 May 1976 | The Friuli earthquake, north-east Italy.<br>939 people were killed, 2,400 injured and over 150,000 left homeless.<br>77 villages were affected. The worst-hit was the town of Gemona del Friuli. |
| 50 | 7 May 1976 | The Honda Accord motorcar was launched. |

## MAY 2026

| Ann. | Date | Event |
|---|---|---|
| 50 | 8 May 1976 | The roller coaster *The New Revolution* (then known as the *Great American Revolution*) opened at Six Flags Magic Mountain in Valencia, California, USA. It was the first modern roller coaster to feature a vertical loop.<br>(The roller coaster *Corkscrew* opened at Cedar Point in Sandusky, Ohio a week later. It features three inversions: a vertical loop and two corkscrews. Both roller coasters are still in operation at the time of writing.) |
| 50 | 9 May 1976 | Death of Ulrike Meinhof, German left-wing militant.<br>Co-founder of the Red Army Faction (the Baader–Meinhof Gang).<br>(Found hanged in her prison cell, aged 41.) |
| 50 | 12 May 1976 | The oil tanker *Urquiola* ran aground on uncharted rocks as it approached La Coruña in Spain. It was towed out to sea in case it exploded, but it ran aground again, causing further ruptures, and most of the crew were evacuated. On 14th May the tide drove it onto Yacentes bank and it exploded, killing the captain, and spilling 100,000 tons of crude oil, which polluted the Spanish coastline.<br>It was one of the worst oil spill disasters in history. |
| 50 | 14 May 1976 | Death of Keith Relf, British blues/rock singer and harmonica player (The Yardbirds). |
| 50 | 20 May 1976 | Death of Syd Howe, Canadian ice hockey player. |
| 50 | 21 May 1976 | The Yuba City bus disaster, Martinez, California, USA.<br>A school bus crashed through a bridge rail, fell 21 feet (6.6 metres), and landed on its roof after its brakes failed. 29 people were killed, including 28 students who were members of the Yuba City High School choir. It remains the deadliest school bus disaster in U.S. history. |
| 50 | 24 May 1976 | The Judgement of Paris took place in France. This was a famous wine-tasting event in which Californian wines beat French wines in a blind tasting. The results shocked the wine world.<br>The event was repeated thirty years later in May 2006 using wines from the same vintage to see how well they had aged. Once again, the Californian wines beat the French ones in the majority of categories. |
| 50 | 26 May 1976 | Death of Martin Heidegger, German philosopher. |
| 50 | 28 May 1976 | The Peaceful Nuclear Explosions (PNE) Treaty was signed by the USA and the Soviet Union. It limited underground nuclear explosions to a maximum yield of 150 kilotons. (It came into effect in December 1990.) |
| 40 | 1 May 1986 | Death of Hylda Baker, British stage and television comedy actress.<br>Best known for her role in the TV comedy series *Nearest and Dearest*. |
| 40 | 2 May 1986 to 13 Oct | Expo 86: the 1986 World Exposition was held in Vancouver, Canada. |
| 40 | 3 May 1986 | Air Lanka Flight 512 exploded at Bandaranaike International Airport in Colombo, Sri Lanka. 21 people were killed and 41 injured.<br>(Cause: a bomb planted by Tamil Tiger terrorists who aimed to sabotage peace talks between the Tamil Tigers and the government.) |
| 40 | 4 May 1986 | The head of state of Afghanistan, Barbrak Karmal, was forced out of office by the Soviet Union and exiled in Moscow.<br>He was succeeded by Mohammad Najibullah. |

**MAY 2026**

| Ann. | Date | Event |
|------|------|-------|
| 40 | 7 May 1986 | Canadian mountaineer Patrick Morrow became the first person to climb all of the Seven Summits (the highest peaks on each of the seven continents). |
| 40 | 8 May 1986 | Óscar Arias became President of Costa Rica (until 1990). He was president again from 2006 to 2010. |
| 40 | 8 May 1986 | Death of Emanuel ('Manny') Shinwell, Baron Shinwell of Easington, British politician and trade union official. |
| 40 | 9 May 1986 | Death of Tenzing Norgay, (Sherpa Tenzing), Tibetan/Nepalese mountaineer. He and Sir Edmund Hillary of New Zealand were the first people to reach the summit of Mount Everest in 1953. |
| 40 | 12 May 1986 | The U.S. and World première of the action-drama film *Top Gun*, in New York City, USA and Mexico. Released: 16th May. UK: 3rd October. |
| 40 | 14 May 1986 | *The Pride of Baltimore*, a reproduction of a 19th century Baltimore clipper topsail schooner, sank in a storm near Puerto Rico. Four of its twelve crew were killed. The ship had been commissioned by the citizens of Baltimore, Maryland, USA as a goodwill ambassador for the city and state. It was replaced by *The Pride of Baltimore II* in 1988. |
| 40 | 15 May 1986 | Following the Space Shuttle *Challenger* disaster in January, the U.S. government's Committee on Science and Technology published the *Strategy for Safely Returning the Space Shuttle to Flight Status*. |
| 40 | 16 May 1986 | The former President of Argentina, General Leopoldo Galtieri, was sentenced to twelve years in prison for military misconduct, for launching, mismanaging and losing the Falklands War against Britain. He was pardoned by President Carlos Menem in 1989, and released. |
| 40 | 16 May 1986 | In the American television series *Dallas*, the character Bobby Ewing 'returned from the dead' when he appeared in a shower scene at the end of the season finale. He had been killed off in a car accident at the end of the previous season. The first episode of the next season explained that his death had occurred in Pamela Barnes Ewing's dream. |
| 40 | 19 May 1986 | South African troops attacked African National Congress (ANC) camps in Zambia, Zimbabwe and Botswana, ending diplomatic efforts to end apartheid. |
| 40 | 19 May 1986 | The Firearm Owners Protection Act was signed into law in the USA. |
| 40 | 24 May 1986 | Margaret Thatcher became the first British Prime Minister to visit Israel. |
| 40 | 25 May 1986 | Hands Across America: Approximately seven million people joined hands to form a line that stretched right across the USA. The event was held to raise money to fight poverty, hunger and homelessness. |
| 40 | 25 May 1986 | The overloaded ferry *MV Shamia* sank on the Maghna River in Bangladesh during stormy weather. 600 people were killed. The boat was packed with people returning home from Ramadan celebrations and was carrying up to 1,500 people, though it was only designed to carry 500. It was one of the worst maritime disasters in history. |
| 40 | 25 May 1986 | Death of Chester Bowles, American politician. Governor of Connecticut (1949–51), U.S. Ambassador to India (1951–53, 1963–69), Under Secretary of State (1961). |

## MAY 2026

| Ann. | Date | Event |
|------|------|-------|
| 30 | 3 May 1996 | The 1980 Geneva Protocol on Mines, Booby-Traps and Other Devices was amended to regulate (but not ban) the use of land mines.<br>Signatories agreed to phase out the use of land mines over the next decade. |
| 30 | 3 May 1996 | The science fiction action film *Barb Wire* was released. |
| 30 | 5 May 1996 | Death of Beryl Burton, British racing cyclist who dominated British women's cycling from the late 1950s to the early 1980s.<br>She regularly beat male competitors. |
| 30 | 7 May 1996 | The first international war crimes tribunal for crimes committed during the war in the former Yugoslavia opened in The Hague, Netherlands. |
| 30 | 8 May 1996 | The U.S. première of the epic disaster film *Twister*.<br>Released: 10th May. UK: 26th July. |
| 30 | 8 May 1996 | Death of Dominguín, Spanish matador and socialite.<br>One of the most famous bullfighters of the mid-20th century. |
| 30 | 10 May 1996 | Eight climbers were killed in a 'rogue storm' blizzard near the summit of Mount Everest – the deadliest day in the mountain's history (until 2014). |
| 30 | 11 May 1996 | ValuJet Airlines Flight 592 crashed into the Florida Everglades in the USA shortly after taking off from Miami. All 110 people on board were killed. (Cause: a fire in the cargo compartment caused by improperly stored hazardous chemicals.)<br>The incident caused lasting damage to ValuJet, and it was rebranded as AirTran Airlines in 1997 after purchasing a smaller company of that name. It was acquired by Southwest Airlines in 2011. |
| 30 | 11 May 1996 | Death of Nnamdi Azikiwe, first President of Nigeria (1963–66). |
| 30 | 13 May 1996 | A powerful tornado hit Bangladesh. 600 people were killed and more than 37,000 injured. More than 36,000 houses were damaged or destroyed, and 100,000 people were made homeless. |
| 30 | 16 May 1996 | Death of Michael Boorda, U.S. Navy admiral. Chief of Naval Operations (1994–96). (Committed suicide, aged 56, after journalists questioned his right to wear service decorations bearing the 'V' for valour marking, which were only appropriate if he had personally served in combat.) |
| 30 | 17 May 1996 | Megan's Law came into effect in the USA. The public must be notified if dangerous sex offenders are released into their community. |
| 30 | 20 May 1996 | Oil-for-food programme: the United Nations agreed to allow Iraq to sell up to $2 billion worth of oil to buy humanitarian supplies. |
| 30 | 20 May 1996 | The U.S. Supreme Court struck down a Colorado measure that excluded homosexuals and bisexuals from equal protection laws. (Romer v. Evans.) |
| 30 | 20 May 1996 | The U.S. première of the action spy film *Mission: Impossible*.<br>Released: 22nd May. UK: 5th July. |
| 30 | 20 May 1996 | Death of Jon Pertwee, British stage, film, radio and television actor.<br>Best known for his TV roles as *Doctor Who* and *Worzel Gummidge*. |
| 30 | 21 May 1996 | A heavily overcrowded ferry, the *MV Bukoba*, capsized and sank on Lake Victoria in Tanzania, killing hundreds of people. |

**MAY 2026**

| Ann. | Date | Event |
|------|------|-------|
| 30 | 21 May 1996 | BSE ('mad cow disease'): the British government adopted a policy of non-cooperation with the European Union after it refused to ease a ban on British beef. |
| 30 | 21 May 1996 | Death of Lash LaRue, American film actor. Known for his many Westerns of the 1940s and 50s, and for his exceptional bullwhip skills. |
| 30 | 23 May 1996 | Death of Patrick Cargill, British stage, film and television actor. Noted for his farces, impeccable timing, and distinguished appearance. Best known for the TV sitcom *Father, Dear Father*. |
| 30 | 26 May 1996 | Whitewater scandal: U.S. President Bill Clinton's former business partners in the Whitewater Development Corporation, James and Susan McDougal, and the Governor of Arkansas Jim Guy Tucker, were convicted of fraud and conspiracy. Tucker received a suspended sentence due to his liver disease and resigned as Governor on 15th July. Susan McDougal was sentenced to two years in prison. James McDougal was sentenced to three years and died in prison in March 1998. |
| 30 | 29 May 1996 | Death of Jeremy Sinden, British stage, film and television actor. Son of the actor Donald Sinden. (Lung cancer, aged 45. His best friend, the actor Simon Cadell, also died of lung cancer a few weeks earlier – see 6th March 1996.) |
| 30 | 30 May 1996 | The Duke and Duchess of York (Prince Andrew and Sarah Ferguson) were divorced after ten years of marriage. |
| 30 | 31 May 1996 | Death of Timothy Leary, American psychologist and writer. A leading advocate of LSD and other psychedelic drugs. |
| 25 | 1 May 2001 | Former Ku Klux Klansman Thomas Blanton Jr. was convicted of bombing a church in Birmingham, Alabama, USA in 1963, killing four black girls. It is regarded as one of the most horrific acts of the civil rights era. He was the second of four to be convicted. He received four life sentences. |
| 25 | 1 May 2001 | Chandra Levy, an intern at the Federal Bureau of Prisons in Washington, D.C., USA, disappeared. Her remains were found in a remote area of Rock Creek Park in May 2002. The circumstances of her death remained unclear until November 2010 when an illegal immigrant from El Salvador, convicted of assaulting other women, was convicted of tying her up and leaving her to die. He was sentenced to 60 years in prison. |
| 25 | 2 May 2001 | Death of Ted Rogers, British comedian and entertainer. Best known for hosting the television game show *3-2-1*. |
| 25 | 3 May 2001 | The USA lost its seat on the United Nations Human Rights Commission for the first time since the commission was founded in 1947. It regained its seat the following year. The commission was replaced by the United Nations Human Rights Council in 2006. |
| 25 | 4 May 2001 | Death of Bonny Lee Bakley, wife of the American actor Robert Blake. (Shot in the head while sitting in their car in Los Angeles. Robert Blake was acquitted of her murder, but was later found liable in a civil case.) |
| 25 | 5 May 2001 | Death of Clifton Hillegass, American publisher who created CliffsNotes – a popular series of literary study guides. |

**MAY 2026**

| Ann. | Date | Event |
|------|------|-------|
| 25 | 6 May 2001 | Pope John Paul II became the first pontiff in history to enter a mosque. He visited the Umayyad Mosque in Damascus during his visit to Syria. He prayed there and gave an address promoting peace between Muslims and Christians. |
| 25 | 7 May 2001 | British 'Great Train Robber' Ronnie Biggs returned to Britain from Brazil, where he had lived as a fugitive for 36 years. He was immediately arrested and returned to prison to complete his sentence. |
| 25 | 9 May 2001 | The Accra Sports Stadium disaster, Ghana. 127 football fans were killed in a stampede after police fired tear gas and rubber bullets into the crowd near the end of the match. The police were blamed for overreacting to moderate crowd violence. Medical staff had already left the stadium as the match was nearly over. |
| 25 | 11 May 2001 | Death of Douglas Adams, British comic writer and dramatist. Best known for the radio/TV/novel series and film *The Hitchhiker's Guide to the Galaxy*. |
| 25 | 12 May 2001 | Death of Perry Como, American singer and entertainer. |
| 25 | 12 May 2001 | Death of Alexei Tupolev, Russian aircraft designer. He led the development of the Tupolev Tu-144 supersonic passenger jet and the Buran space shuttle. |
| 25 | 14 May 2001 | The U.S. Supreme Court ruled that the use of marijuana for medical purposes was illegal. (United States v. Oakland Cannabis Buyers' Cooperative.) The use of marijuana remains a federal offence, though several states have legalised its use for personal/recreational purposes. |
| 25 | 15 May 2001 | The British High Court abolished price-fixing on non-prescription drugs. Supermarkets immediately slashed the price of over-the-counter medicines. |
| 25 | 16 May 2001 | Britain's Deputy Prime Minister, John Prescott, punched a man who threw an egg at him while he was campaigning in Rhyl, north Wales. |
| 25 | 16 May 2001 | The Duchess of York's former personal dresser, Jane Andrews, was sentenced to life imprisonment for murdering her boyfriend. He had told her he did not want to marry her. (She was released in 2015.) |
| 25 | 17 May 2001 | Death of Frank G. Slaughter, American novelist. |
| 25 | 19 May 2001 | Apple opened its first two retail stores in the USA, at Tysons Corner Center in Virginia, and Glendale Galleria in California. |
| 25 | 21 May 2001 | France passed the Taubira law, which recognised the Atlantic slave trade and slavery as crimes against humanity. The driving force behind the law was French politician Christiane Taubira. |
| 25 | 21 May 2001 | The U.S. première of the romantic war drama film *Pearl Harbor*. Released: 25th May. UK: 1st June. |
| 25 | 24 May 2001 | The Versailles Wedding Hall disaster, Jerusalem, Israel. The third floor of the building collapsed due to structural failure and a flawed design. 23 people were killed and 380 injured. The owners, who had recently removed structural partitions from the floor below, were convicted of causing death by negligence, as were the building's designer and three engineers. The hall was later demolished. |

**MAY 2026**

| Ann. | Date | Event |
|------|------|-------|
| 25 | 25 May 2001 | American mountaineer Erik Weihenmayer became the first blind person to reach the summit of Mount Everest. |
| 25 | 26 May 2001 to 28th | The Oldham riots in the UK, between white youths and Asians. This was the first in a series of race riots in northern England in 2001. Other riots followed in Bradford, Leeds, and Burnley. |
| 25 | 28 May 2001 | The body of British racing driver Donald Campbell was recovered from the bottom of Coniston Water in Cumbria. (He was killed there when his speedboat crashed and sank during a record attempt in January 1967.) |
| 25 | 29 May 2001 | A jury in New York, USA convicted four followers of the terrorist Osama bin Laden of the 1998 bombing to two U.S. embassies in Africa, which killed 224 people. They were sentenced to life imprisonment. It was the first conviction in relation to Osama bin Laden's terrorist activities. |
| 25 | 30 May 2001 | Former French Foreign Minister Roland Dumas was sentenced to six months in prison for illegally receiving funds from the oil company Elf Aquitaine. It was one of the biggest political scandals in recent French history. He was cleared in 2003. Attempts to prosecute other politicians implicated in the scandal, including French President Jacques Chirac, also failed. |
| 25 | 31 May 2001 | Microsoft's Office XP office suite was released. |
| 20 | 1 May 2006 | BSE ('mad cow disease'): the European Union lifted its ten-year ban on the export of British beef. |
| 20 | 1 May 2006 to 14th | The Puerto Rico budget crisis. The Puerto Rican government ran out of money after political parties involved in a power struggle failed to agree a budget. Government agencies and schools were shut down, leaving nearly 100,000 people temporarily unemployed. |
| 20 | 1 May 2006 | The Great American Boycott. U.S. immigrants boycotted schools and businesses for a day in an attempt to show how much those businesses depended on illegal immigrants to operate, and to protest against pending immigration laws. Commentators noted little or no effect on the businesses, which continued to operate as normal. |
| 20 | 3 May 2006 | Death of Karel Appel, Dutch artist, sculptor and poet. Noted for his colourful semi-abstract works. Co-founder of the CoBrA group of Expressionists, noted for the spontaneity and impulsiveness of their work. |
| 20 | 5 May 2006 | The Walt Disney Company acquired Pixar Animation Studios. Steve Jobs became Disney's largest individual shareholder and joined its board of directors. |
| 20 | 7 May 2006 | The first Ultra-Mobile Personal Computer (UMPC) went on sale – the Samsung Q1. |
| 20 | 8 May 2006 | The British High Court ruled in favour of Apple Computer in their long-running dispute with Apple Corps. Apple Corps, founded by the Beatles to promote, manage and distribute their music and merchandise, alleged that the iTunes Music Store and the iPod media player violated an earlier agreement that prohibited Apple Computer from distributing music. (Apple Corps v. Apple Computer.) |

## MAY 2026

| Ann. | Date | Event |
|---|---|---|
| 20 | 8 May 2006 | Researchers from St. Andrews University in Scotland announced that dolphins had names for themselves and each other. They call to each other and refer to other dolphins in the same way that humans use names, using their distinctive whistles. The researchers' paper was published in the *Proceedings of the National Academy of Sciences*. |
| 20 | 8 May 2006 | Death of Iain Macmillan, British photographer. Best known for the cover image for the Beatles' album *Abbey Road*. |
| 20 | 11 May 2006 | Death of Floyd Patterson, American world heavyweight boxing champion and Olympic gold medallist (middleweight, 1952). |
| 20 | 12 May 2006 to 17th | A wave of organised gang violence broke out in São Paulo, Brazil – the worst in Brazil's history. Gang members attacked and killed 30 – 40 police officers, and the police then hunted down and shot gang members. At least 133 people were killed: 30 police officers, 3 municipal guards, 79 gang members and 21 civilians. |
| 20 | 12 May 2006 | The Iranian cockroach newspaper cartoon controversy. A cartoon featuring a cockroach was published in the Iranian state newspaper *Iran*. It was interpreted as an insult to Iranian Azerbaijanis, and there were massive protests in Azerbaijani-populated cities, many of which turned violent. Security forces arrested hundreds (some sources say thousands) of people and several people were killed. The newspaper was shut down for several months and the artist who drew the cartoon and the newspaper's editor-in-chief were both arrested |
| 20 | 14 May 2006 | Death of Stanley Kunitz, American poet. U.S. Poet Laureate (1974 and 2000). |
| 20 | 17 May 2006 | The world première of the mystery thriller film *The Da Vinci Code*, at various locations. Released: 19th May. |
| 20 | 17 May 2006 | Death of Nichola Goddard, the first female Canadian soldier killed in combat. |
| 20 | 18 May 2006 | The Nepalese government passed the May 18 Act, which overwrote the constitution. It stripped the King of many of his powers and declared Nepal a secular country. The monarchy was abolished in 2008. |
| 20 | 19 May 2006 | Death of Freddie Garrity, British singer (Freddie and the Dreamers), children's television presenter and actor. |
| 20 | 21 May 2006 | In a referendum, the citizens of Montenegro voted in favour of independence from the union of Serbia and Montenegro. It declared its independence on 3rd June. |
| 20 | 22 May 2006 | The data storage company Seagate Technology acquired the American hard disk drive manufacturer Maxtor. |
| 20 | 22 May 2006 | The European satellite television company Sky launched Sky HD (now Sky+ HD), its high-definition television service. It was replaced by Sky Q in 2016. |
| 20 | 24 May 2006 | The limited U.S. release of the documentary film *An Inconvenient Truth*, in which former U.S. Vice President Al Gore discusses the evidence for global warming. Full U.S. release: 30th June. UK: 15th September. |

## MAY 2026

| Ann. | Date | Event |
|------|------|-------|
| 20 | 25 May 2006 | Kenneth Lay, the former chairman of the American energy company Enron, was convicted of fraud and corruption. He faced 45 years in prison but died in July 2006, before he was sentenced.<br>Former CEO Jeffrey Skilling was convicted of conspiracy, insider trading, false accounting and securities fraud on the same day.<br>In October 2006, Skilling was sentenced to 24 years in prison (later reduced to 14 years) and fined $45 million. He was released in 2019. |
| 20 | 25 May 2006 | Death of Desmond Dekker, Jamaican reggae/ska/rock steady singer, songwriter and musician. Best known for his hit song *The Israelites*. |
| 20 | 27 May 2006 | The Java earthquake, Indonesia.<br>More than 5,700 people were killed and over 37,000 injured. |
| 20 | 30 May 2006 | A court in Maryland, USA convicted John Allen Muhammad of six counts of first-degree murder for the Washington D.C. Beltway sniper attacks in 2002, in which ten people were killed. He was executed in 2009. |
| 15 | 2 May 2011 | Death of Osama bin Laden, Saudi Arabian-born terrorist.<br>Founder of Al-Qaeda. Thought to have masterminded the 9/11 attacks on the USA. (Shot dead by U.S. forces in Pakistan.) |
| 15 | 12 May 2011 | Retired Ukrainian-born American car factory worker John Demjanjuk was convicted by a German court of being an accessory to the murders of 28,000 people at the Sobibor extermination camp during WWII.<br>He was sentenced to five years in prison, released pending an appeal, and died in a German nursing home in 2012.<br>He had previously been convicted of being 'Ivan the Terrible', a notorious camp guard at the Treblinka extermination camp, and had been sentenced to death. His conviction in that case was eventually overturned when new evidence cast doubt on his identity. |
| 15 | 22 May 2011 | The Joplin tornado, Missouri, USA.<br>One of the deadliest tornadoes in U.S. history struck the city.<br>158 people were killed. It caused $2.8 billion worth of damage, making it the costliest tornado strike in U.S. history. |
| 15 | 30 May 2011 | Following the Fukushima nuclear disaster in Japan in March, Germany announced that it was phasing out nuclear power. It would permanently shut down all of its nuclear power stations by December 2022. |
| 10 | 6 May 2016 | Death of Reg Grundy, Australian television producer and businessman.<br>He produced numerous Australian game shows, soap operas and drama serials, including *Neighbours*, *The Young Doctors*, and *Sons and Daughters*. |
| 10 | 27 May 2016 | Barack Obama became the first U.S. President to visit Hiroshima in Japan. In August 1945 it became the first city in the world to be attacked by a nuclear weapon. |
| 10 | 31 May 2016 | Death of Carla Lane, British television screenwriter.<br>Best known for creating the sitcoms *The Liver Birds*, *Butterflies*, and *Bread*. |

## JUNE 2026

| Ann. | Date | Event |
|------|------|-------|
| 1800 | 29 Jun 226 | Death of Cao Pi, also known as Emperor Wen of Wei (220–226), Chinese emperor. Succeeded by his son, Cao Rui (as Emperor Ming). |
| 1400 | 29 Jun 626 to Jul | The Byzantine–Sasanian War of 602–628/the Avar–Byzantine Wars – the Siege of Constantinople (now Istanbul, Turkey). Byzantine victory. |
| 1100 | 2 Jun 926 | Birth of Emperor Murakami, Emperor of Japan (946–967). |
| 800 | 21 Jun 1226 | Birth of Bolesław V the Chaste, High Duke (ruler) of Poland (1243–79). |
| 750 | 15 Jun 1276 | Emperor Duanzong became Emperor of the Song Dynasty in China and Hong Kong (until 1278). |
| 750 | 22 Jun 1276 | Death of Pope Innocent V (January – June 1276). Succeeded by Adrian V on 11th July (but he also died a month later). |
| 700 | 3 Jun 1326 | The Treaty of Novgorod was signed by Norway and the Novgorod Republic. It defined the border between northern Norway and Russia. |
| 700 | 29 Jun 1326 | Birth of Murad I, Sultan of the Ottoman Empire (1362–89). |
| 300 | 3 Jun 1726 | Birth of James Hutton, Scottish geologist. The father of modern geology. |
| 300 | 11 Jun 1726 | Birth of María Teresa Rafaela of Spain, Dauphine of France (1745–46 – died). Wife of Louis, Dauphin of France. Daughter of King Philip V of Spain. |
| 300 | 14 Jun 1726 (OS) | Birth of Thomas Pennant, Welsh naturalist, historian and traveller. He wrote several notable books on natural history, geology and geographical expeditions. |
| 300 | 18 Jun 1726 | Death of Michel Richard Delalande, French Baroque organist and composer. |
| 300 | 26 Jun 1726 | Birth of Victor Amadeus III, King of Sardinia and Duke of Savoy (1773–96). |
| 250 | 8 Jun 1776 | American Revolutionary War – the Battle of Trois-Rivières, Quebec, Canada. British victory. |
| 250 | 10 Jun 1776 | Death of Hsinbyushin, King of Burma (1763–76). Succeeded by his son, Singu Min. |
| 250 | 11 Jun 1776 | American Revolution: the Second Continental Congress appointed the Committee of Five (John Adams, Benjamin Franklin, Thomas Jefferson, Robert R. Livingston and Roger Sherman) to create the first draft of the Declaration of Independence. |
| 250 | 11 Jun 1776 | Birth of John Constable, British landscape artist. |
| 250 | 12 Jun 1776 | The Virginia Declaration of Rights was adopted. It declared the inherent rights of Virginians (and all mankind). It influenced the U.S. Declaration of Independence and was a model for the U.S. Bill of Rights. |
| 250 | 15 Jun 1776 | Delaware Separation Day: the Colonial Assembly of Delaware declared itself separated from the British Crown and Pennsylvania. Delaware became the first state admitted to the USA in 1787. |
| 250 | 28 Jun 1776 | American Revolutionary War – the Battle of Sullivan's Island, South Carolina. American victory. |
| 250 | 28 Jun 1776 | American Revolutionary War: Continental Army soldier Thomas Hickey became the first person to be executed by the Army for mutiny, sedition and treachery. He was involved in a plot to assassinate George Washington. |

**JUNE 2026**

| Ann. | Date | Event |
|---|---|---|
| 200 | 1 Jun 1826 | Birth of Carl Bechstein, German piano maker. |
| 200 | 5 Jun 1826 | Death Carl Maria von Weber, German Romantic composer, conductor, pianist and guitarist. Best known for his operas, particularly *Oberon*. |
| 200 | 7 Jun 1826 | Death of Joseph von Fraunhofer, German physicist, lens manufacturer and astronomer. Inventor of the spectroscope and diffraction grating. He discovered dark absorption lines (Fraunhofer lines) in the Sun's spectrum. The Fraunhofer Society in Germany is named in his honour. |
| 200 | 15 Jun 1826 | The Auspicious Incident, Ottoman Empire (now Turkey). Sultan Mahmud II forcibly disbanded the Janissary corps and replaced it with a modern military force. Most of the 135,000 Janissaries revolted. The revolt was suppressed by Ottoman government forces, and many of the Janissaries were killed. After the revolt, the surviving Janissaries were executed, imprisoned or exiled. |
| 200 | 21 Jun 1826 to 28 Aug | The Greek War of Independence – the Ottoman–Egyptian invasion of Mani (now Laconia, Greece). Greek victory: the invaders were successfully repelled in three battles, and forced to retreat. |
| 200 | 22 Jun 1826 to 15 Jul | The Congress of Panama was held. It was the first Pan-American conference. It was organised by Simón Bolívar, who proposed creating a league of American republics. The conference signed The Treaty of Union, League, and Perpetual Confederation, but only Gran Colombia ratified it, and the proposed league never materialised. |
| 175 | 2 Jun 1851 | Prohibition: Maine passed the Maine Law (also known as the Maine Liquor Law) and became the first U.S. state to outlaw the sale of alcoholic beverages. By 1855 twelve other states had also introduced total prohibition. They were known as the 'dry' states. |
| 175 | 9 Jun 1851 | Birth of Charles Joseph Bonaparte, U.S. Attorney General (1906–09), Secretary of the Navy (1905–06). |
| 175 | 12 Jun 1851 | Birth of Oliver Lodge, British physicist, inventor, writer and academic. He made significant improvements to the components for radio, and held several key patents. He was also the Principal of the University of Birmingham (1900–20). |
| 175 | 15 Jun 1851 | American dairyman Jacob Fussell established the first ice cream factory in the USA, in Seven Valleys, Pennsylvania. The products were shipped by train to Baltimore, Maryland, where they were sold. He moved the factory to Baltimore two years later, and opened factories in several other cities. |
| 150 | 4 Jun 1876 | The express train *Transcontinental Express* arrived in San Francisco, California, USA after travelling along the First Transcontinental Railroad from New York City in 83 hours and 39 minutes (about 3½ days). The record time was widely reported in the press. |
| 150 | 4 Jun 1876 | Death of Abdülaziz, Sultan of the Ottoman Empire (1861–76 – overthrown). (Found dead in mysterious circumstances, aged 46.) |
| 150 | 8 Jun 1876 | Death of George Sand, French novelist. One of the most popular writers in Europe during her lifetime. |
| 150 | 17 Jun 1876 | The Great Sioux War of 1876 – the Battle of the Rosebud, Montana. Lakota/Cheyenne victory. The Native Americans were led by Crazy Horse. |

## JUNE 2026

| Ann. | Date | Event |
|------|------|-------|
| 150 | 18 Jun 1876 to 19 Feb 1878 | The Great Eastern Crisis: the Montenegrin–Ottoman War of 1876–1878. Montenegrin victory. Montenegro doubled the size of its territory and secured its independence from the Ottoman Empire. |
| 150 | 19 Jun 1876 | Birth of Nigel Gresley, British railway engineer. He designed some of the best-known steam locomotives in Britain, including the *Flying Scotsman* and the *Mallard*. |
| 150 | 21 Jun 1876 | Death of Antonio López de Santa Anna, President of Mexico (1847, 1853–55 – overthrown). |
| 150 | 23 Jun 1876 | Birth of Irvin S. Cobb, American writer, journalist and humourist. The highest-paid reporter in the USA in the early 1900s. |
| 150 | 25 Jun 1876 to 26th | Custer's Last Stand. The Great Sioux War of 1876 – the Battle of the Little Bighorn. Lakota/Northern Cheyenne/Arapaho victory. The commander of the U.S. Army's 7th Cavalry, George Armstrong Custer, and 267 of his cavalrymen and scouts were killed. |
| 150 | 25 Jun 1876 | Death of George Armstrong Custer, American general. A cavalry commander in the American Civil War and the American Indian Wars. (Killed in the Battle of the Little Bighorn, aged 36.) |
| 150 | 30 Jun 1876 to 3 Mar 1878 | The Great Eastern Crisis – the Serbian–Ottoman Wars of 1876–78. Serbian victory: Serbia gained its independence from the Ottoman Empire. |
| 125 | 1 Jun 1901 | Birth of John Van Druten, British-born American playwright and theatrical director. One of the most successful playwrights of the 1930s and 40s. |
| 125 | 3 Jun 1901 | Birth of Maurice Evans, British stage, film and television actor. Noted for his Shakespearean roles. Best known for playing Dr Zaius in the film *Planet of the Apes* (1968) and Samantha's father Maurice in the TV sitcom *Bewitched*. |
| 125 | 5 Jun 1901 | Birth of Jan Struther (pen name of Joyce Maxtone Graham), British novelist and hymn writer. Best known for her novel *Mrs Miniver* (adapted into a film in 1942), and her hymn *Lord of all Hopefulness*. |
| 125 | 6 Jun 1901 | Birth of Sukarno, first President of Indonesia (1945–67). |
| 125 | 10 Jun 1901 | Birth of Frederick Loewe, German-born American composer. Best known for his collaborations with the lyricist Alan Jay Lerner on Broadway musicals including *Brigadoon*, *Paint Your Wagon*, *My Fair Lady* and *Camelot*. |
| 125 | 11 Jun 1901 | The Cook Islands became part of the Colony of New Zealand. In 1965 the Islands became self-governing in free association with New Zealand. |
| 125 | 12 Jun 1901 | Cuba incorporated the Platt Amendment into its constitution, and effectively became a United States protectorate. |
| 125 | 13 Jun 1901 | Birth of Tage Erlander, Prime Minister of Sweden (1946–69). Sweden's longest-serving Prime Minister. |
| 125 | 18 Jun 1901 | Birth of Grand Duchess Anastasia Nikolaevna of Russia. Youngest daughter of Tsar Nicholas II. (Killed by Bolsheviks in 1918, aged 17, along with the rest of her family.) |

## JUNE 2026

| Ann. | Date | Event |
|------|------|-------|
| 125 | 24 Jun 1901 | Spanish artist Pablo Picasso held his first major solo exhibition, in Paris, France. He was 19 years old. |
| 125 | 29 Jun 1901 | Birth of Nelson Eddy, American singer and actor. The highest paid singer in the world. A star of Hollywood musicals, operas, stage, radio and television, as well as having a successful recording career.<br>He appeared in several films alongside Jeanette MacDonald, with whom he had a long-running personal relationship. |
| 100 | 1 Jun 1926 | Ignacy Mościcki became President of Poland (until 1939).<br>He was the serving president when Germany invaded Poland at the outbreak of WWII. He remained in office until September 1939 when he was interned in Romania and forced to resign. |
| 100 | 1 Jun 1926 | Birth of Andy Griffith, American actor, comedian and singer.<br>Best known for his roles as Andy Taylor in the TV sitcom *The Andy Griffith Show* and Ben Matlock in the legal drama series *Matlock*. (Died 2012.) |
| 100 | 1 Jun 1926 | Birth of Marilyn Monroe, American film actress, model, singer and sex symbol (*Gentlemen Prefer Blondes*, *How to Marry a Millionaire*, *There's No Business Like Show Business*, *The Seven Year Itch*, *Bus Stop*, *Some Like It Hot*, *The Misfits*). (Died 1962.) |
| 100 | 3 Jun 1926 | Birth of Allen Ginsberg, American poet. One of the leading figures of the Beat movement. Best known for his poem *Howl*. (Died 1997.) |
| 100 | 4 Jun 1926 | Birth of Robert Earl Hughes, American entertainer and sideshow performer. During his lifetime he was the heaviest person ever recorded (1,071 pounds/76 stones 7 pounds/486 kg). He remains the heaviest recorded person who could walk unassisted. (Died 1958, aged 32.) |
| 100 | 4 Jun 1926 | Death of Fred Spofforth, 'the Demon Bowler', Australian-born British cricket player (New South Wales, Victoria, Derbyshire, Australia). |
| 100 | 5 Jun 1926 | The Treaty of Ankara was signed by Turkey, Iraq and the UK.<br>It settled a border dispute between Turkey and Iraq, solved the 'Mosul question', and helped improve relations between the two countries. |
| 100 | 10 Jun 1926 | Birth of Lionel Jeffries, British film actor, screenwriter and director. (Died 2010.) |
| 100 | 10 Jun 1926 | Death of Antoni Gaudí, Spanish architect. Known for his unique Modernist style. His most famous works include the Basílica de la Sagrada Família in Barcelona. |
| 100 | 14 Jun 1926 | Brazil withdrew from the League of Nations in protest at plans to admit Germany. (Germany joined the League of Nations on 8th September, and Spain immediately withdrew as well.) |
| 100 | 18 Jun 1926 | The first election in India in which Sikh women were allowed to stand for public office. |
| 100 | 18 Jun 1926 | Death of Olga Constantinovna of Russia, Queen consort of the Hellenes (1867–1913). Wife of King George I of Greece. |
| 100 | 19 Jun 1926 | NBC, the American radio and television network, was founded.<br>It launched its radio service on 15th November 1926 and its television service in 1939. |

**JUNE 2026**

| Ann. | Date | Event |
|------|------|-------|
| 100 | 20 Jun 1926 | A wireless car phone was demonstrated at the Berlin motor show in Germany by its inventor, Mr Schaetzle.<br>(The first car phones went into service in St. Louis, Missouri, USA in June 1946.) |
| 100 | 23 Jun 1926 | The first SATs (Scholastic Aptitude Tests) were administered by the College Board in the USA.<br>More than 8,000 students sat the test at over 300 test centres. |
| 100 | 23 Jun 1926 | Mercedes-Benz, the German luxury and commercial vehicle manufacturer, was founded when the Benz and Daimler companies merged. |
| 100 | 29 Jun 1926 | Arthur Meighen became Prime Minister of Canada for the second time (for three months). |
| 100 | 29 Jun 1926 | Birth of Jaber Al-Ahmad Al-Sabah, Emir of Kuwait (1977–2006). |
| 90 | 3 Jun 1936 | Birth of Larry McMurtry, American novelist and screenwriter.<br>Known for his Westerns and stories set in contemporary Texas. His novels include *Lonesome Dove*, *The Last Picture Show* and *Terms of Endearment*.<br>He also co-wrote the screenplay for the film *Brokeback Mountain*.<br>(Died 2021.) |
| 90 | 5 Jun 1936 | Birth of Levi Stubbs, American R&B/soul singer (The Four Tops). (Died 2008.) |
| 90 | 7 Jun 1936 | The Steel Workers Organizing Committee (a trade union) was established in Pittsburgh, Pennsylvania, USA. (It was disbanded in 1942 and became the United Steel Workers of America.) |
| 90 | 11 Jun 1936 | The Orthodox Presbyterian Church was founded (as the Presbyterian Church of America) after splitting from the Presbyterian Church in the United States of America. |
| 90 | 11 Jun 1936 to 4 Jul | The International Surrealist Exhibition was held in London, UK. |
| 90 | 11 Jun 1936 | Death of Robert E. Howard, American pulp fiction novelist, short story writer and poet. Best known as the creator of Conan the Barbarian. |
| 90 | 14 Jun 1936 | Death of G. K. Chesterton, British novelist, short story writer, journalist, essayist, poet, social/literary critic and theologian.<br>Known for his stories about the priest-detective Father Brown. |
| 90 | 15 Jun 1936 | The Vickers Wellington long-range bomber made its first flight.<br>It was in service from 1938 until 1953, and was used by the Royal Air Force, the Royal Navy's Fleet Air Arm, the Royal Australian Air Force, and the Royal Canadian Air Force. |
| 90 | 18 Jun 1936 | The first bicycle traffic court in the USA was established, in Racine, Wisconsin. |
| 90 | 18 Jun 1936 | Birth of Denny Hulme, New Zealand racing driver.<br>Winner of the 1967 Formula One World Championship. (Died 1992.) |
| 90 | 18 Jun 1936 | Death of Maxim Gorky, Russian writer, dramatist and political activist. |
| 90 | 26 Jun 1936 | The first practical helicopter, the Focke-Wulf Fw 61, made its first successful test flight in Bremen, Germany.<br>(The first successful helicopter flight was made by the Breguet-Dorand 'Gyroplane' in France exactly a year earlier, on 26th June 1935.) |

## JUNE 2026

| Ann. | Date | Event |
|---|---|---|
| 90 | 30 Jun 1936 | Emperor Haile Selassie of Abyssinia (now Ethiopia) addressed the League of Nations and gave an impassioned speech appealing for help following Italy's annexation of his country. (His appeal largely failed.) |
| 90 | 30 Jun 1936 | Margaret Mitchell's novel *Gone with the Wind* was published. |
| 80 | 1 Jun 1946 | Television licences were introduced in Britain. (The licences were actually combined radio and television licences.) |
| 80 | 1 Jun 1946 | Death of Ion Antonescu, Romanian dictator (1940–44). (Executed for war crimes.) |
| 80 | 2 Jun 1946 | Republic Day in Italy. In a referendum the people of Italy voted to abolish the monarchy and become a republic. The monarchy was abolished on 12th June, and King Umberto II was forced into exile. |
| 80 | 2 Jun 1946 | Birth of Peter Sutcliffe, ('the Yorkshire Ripper'), British serial killer. He was convicted of killing thirteen women and attempting to kill seven others. (Died 2020.) |
| 80 | 3 Jun 1946 | Death of Mikhail Kalinin, Leader of Soviet Russia and the Soviet Union (1919–46). |
| 80 | 4 Jun 1946 | Juan Perón became President of Argentina (until 1955). He was President again from 1973 to 1974. |
| 80 | 6 Jun 1946 | The National Basketball Association (NBA) was founded in the USA (as the Basketball Association of America). |
| 80 | 6 Jun 1946 | Death of Gerhart Hauptmann, German Naturalist playwright and novelist. Winner of the 1912 Nobel Prize in Literature. |
| 80 | 7 Jun 1946 | BBC Television began broadcasting in the UK after a seven-year break because of WWII. |
| 80 | 8 Jun 1946 | World War II – the London Victory Celebrations. Allied forces paraded through London, UK and there was a fireworks display in the evening. There was a political controversy over the lack of Polish representation in the parade. The Soviet Union and Yugoslavia also declined to take part. |
| 80 | 9 Jun 1946 | The first episode of the television travel show *Geographically Speaking* was broadcast on NBC in the USA. It ran weekly until December. No episodes survive. From 27th October it was sponsored by the pharmaceutical company Bristol–Myers (now Bristol–Myers Squibb), becoming one of the first sponsored television shows in the USA. |
| 80 | 9 Jun 1946 | Death of Rama VIII (also known as Ananda Mahidol), King of Siam/Thailand (1935–46). (Shot dead in his bedroom – probably murdered.) Succeeded by Bhumibol Adulyadej (Rama IX). |
| 80 | 10 Jun 1946 | Death of Jack Johnson, the first African American world heavyweight boxing champion. (Car crash.) |
| 80 | 13 Jun 1946 | Death of Edward Bowes, American radio presenter. Best known for hosting the talent show *Major Bowes Amateur Hour*. |

**JUNE 2026**

| Ann. | Date | Event |
|------|------|-------|
| 80 | 14 Jun 1946 | The Canadian Library Association was established. |
| 80 | 14 Jun 1946 | The USA presented the *Baruch Plan* at the first meeting of the United Nations Atomic Energy Commission. The plan called for the establishment of an international organisation to control atomic weapons. It was rejected by the Soviet Union, which said the USA would use the organisation to preserve its own monopoly on nuclear weapons. This led to the beginning of the Cold War arms race. |
| 80 | 14 Jun 1946 | Death of John Logie Baird, Scottish engineer who pioneered the invention and development of television. |
| 80 | 15 Jun 1946 | Birth of Demis Roussos, Egyptian-born Greek pop/soft rock/progressive rock singer, songwriter and musician. Known as a member of the band Aphrodite's Child and for his successful solo career. (Died 2015.) |
| 80 | 17 Jun 1946 | The first mobile phone service in the USA was inaugurated in St. Louis, Missouri. SW Bell's service used radio telephones installed in cars, allowing them to connect to the landline network. The equipment weighed around 80 pounds (36 kg). |
| 80 | 18 Jun 1946 | Indian independence activist Dr Ram Manohar Lohia launched a Civil Disobedience Movement to protest against Portuguese rule in Goa. |
| 80 | 23 Jun 1946 | The Vancouver Island earthquake, Canada. One of the largest earthquakes in Canadian history. It occurred in a sparsely populated area and only two people were killed. |
| 80 | 24 Jun 1946 | Birth of Ellison Onizuka, American astronaut and engineer. (Killed in the 1986 Space Shuttle *Challenger* disaster.) |
| 80 | 26 Jun 1946 | Field Marshal Bernard Montgomery became Chief of the General Staff (Head of the British Army). |
| 80 | 28 Jun 1946 | Enrico de Nicola became Head of State of the Provisional Government of Italy. He became the first President of Italy on 1st January 1948. |
| 80 | 28 Jun 1946 | Birth of Robert Asprin, American humorous science fiction and fantasy writer. Best known for his *MythAdventures* and *Phule's Company* series of novels. (Died 2008.) |
| 80 | 28 Jun 1946 | Birth of Gilda Radner, American comedian and actress. Best known for her appearances on the television series *Saturday Night Live*. Wife of Gene Wilder. (Died 1989.) |
| 80 | 29 Jun 1946 to 1 Jul | Operation Agatha (also known as Black Sabbath or Black Saturday), Mandatory Palestine. Thousands of British soldiers and police launched an operation to end the state of anarchy, arrest Zionist underground members, and prevent terrorism. They blocked roads, halted trains, and searched 27 Jewish settlements. 2,718 people were arrested and fifteen arms caches were seized. |
| 75 | 1 Jun 1951 | The International Cheese Treaty was signed in Stresa, Italy. It formalised the naming, denominations, origins and uses of cheeses. |
| 75 | 6 Jun 1951 to 17th | The first Berlin International Film Festival was held in West Germany. |

## JUNE 2026

| Ann. | Date | Event |
|---|---|---|
| 75 | 7 Jun 1951 | The American Telephone and Telegraph Company (AT&T) and International Telephone and Telegraph (ITT) signed a cross-licensing patent agreement. This led to the standardisation of the U.S. telephone industry, with interchangeable telephone hardware being used throughout the country. |
| 75 | 13 Jun 1951 | Death of Ben Chifley, Prime Minister of Australia (1945–49). |
| 75 | 14 Jun 1951 | UNIVAC I, the first commercial computer built in the USA for business/administrative use (rather than scientific/military use) was officially dedicated at the U.S. Census Bureau. |
| 75 | 25 Jun 1951 | The U.S. television network CBS became the first in the world to begin broadcasting in colour.<br>Colour broadcasting was abandoned after a few months because of the Korean War, and the colour system CBS used was scrapped.<br>The USA adopted the NTSC colour system instead in 1953. |
| 75 | 28 Jun 1951 | The first episode of the television series *The Amos 'n Andy Show* was broadcast in the USA. It was the first show to have an all-black cast.<br>It ran until 1953. It was adapted from the radio series that began in 1928. |
| 70 | 1 Jun 1956 | The first international flight took off from Atlanta Municipal Airport (now Hartsfield–Jackson Atlanta International Airport) in Georgia, USA.<br>The first scheduled international flights began in 1964.<br>Atlanta is now the world's busiest airport. |
| 70 | 3 Jun 1956 | British Rail renamed its Third Class service as Second Class.<br>Second Class had been abolished in 1875, leaving First Class and Third Class. Second Class was renamed Standard Class in 1987. |
| 70 | 4 Jun 1956 | Gene Vincent's rockabilly song *Be-Bop-A-Lula* was released. |
| 70 | 4 Jun 1956 | The Montgomery bus boycott, Alabama, USA.<br>In a landmark civil rights decision, a U.S. District Court in Alabama ruled that racial segregation on buses was unconstitutional. (Browder v. Gayle.)<br>The state lodged an appeal, so the boycott continued.<br>The U.S. Supreme Court upheld the district court's decision in November, and the boycott ended in December. |
| 70 | 5 Jun 1956 | Elvis Presley performed his new single, *Hound Dog*, on *The Milton Berle Show* in the USA. TV audiences were shocked by his suggestive hip movements and he was attacked by the media for the first time in his career. |
| 70 | 11 Jun 1956 to 16th | The Gal Oya riots, Sri Lanka.<br>Sinhalese mobs attacked minority Tamil civilians, killing 150 people. |
| 70 | 13 Jun 1956 | The first European Cup final was played, in Paris, France.<br>Real Madrid (Spain) beat Stade de Reims (France) 4–3.<br>The European Cup is now known as the UEFA Champions League. |
| 70 | 13 Jun 1956 | The U.S. première of the science fiction film *Earth vs. the Flying Saucers*.<br>Released: 1st July. |
| 70 | 16 Jun 1956 | British poet Ted Hughes married American poet and writer Sylvia Plath. |

## JUNE 2026

| Ann. | Date | Event |
|------|------|-------|
| 70 | 13 Jun 1956 to 17 Aug | The Dartmouth Workshop (the Dartmouth Summer Research Project on Artificial Intelligence) was held at Dartmouth College in New Hampshire, USA. It is considered to be the founding event of the field of artificial intelligence. |
| 70 | 19 Jun 1956 | Death of Thomas J. Watson, American businessman. Chairman and CEO of IBM who built the company into the world's largest manufacturer of data-processing equipment. Named 'the world's greatest salesman'. |
| 70 | 22 Jun 1956 | Death of Walter de la Mare, British children's writer, novelist, short story writer and poet. Noted for his novel *Memoirs of a Midget* and his poem *The Listeners*. |
| 70 | 23 Jun 1956 | The French National Assembly passed the Loi Cadre Defferre. It transferred a number of powers to elected governments in the French African colonies and established universal suffrage. All French African colonies held elections under the new system within two years. |
| 70 | 23 Jun 1956 | Gamal Abdel Nasser became President of Egypt (until 1970). |
| 70 | 23 Jun 1956 | Women in Egypt were granted the right to vote. |
| 70 | 25 Jun 1956 | Birth of Boris Trajkovski, President of the Republic of Macedonia (1999–2004). (Killed in a plane crash in 2004.) |
| 70 | 28 Jun 1956 to 30th | The Poznan protests, Poland. 100,000 workers gathered in the city centre to demand better pay and to protest against the authoritarian communist government. Government forces (including 400 tanks and 10,000 soldiers) suppressed the uprising, killing about 100 people and injuring about 600. |
| 70 | 28 Jun 1956 | The first privately owned nuclear reactor began operating at the Illinois Institute of Technology in Chicago, USA. |
| 70 | 29 Jun 1956 | The Federal Aid Highway Act came into effect in the USA. It authorised the construction of the Interstate Highway System – the largest public works project in U.S. history at that time. Construction was meant to take 10 – 12 years but it actually took 35 years. The system was declared complete in October 1992. |
| 70 | 29 Jun 1956 | American actress and model Marilyn Monroe married the playwright Arthur Miller. They were divorced in 1961. |
| 70 | 30 Jun 1956 | Grand Canyon mid-air collision I, Arizona, USA. United Airlines Flight 718 and TWA Flight 2 collided in uncontrolled airspace. All 128 passengers and crew on both planes were killed. This led to major reforms in air traffic control. (See also: 18th June 1986.) |
| 65 | 1 Jun 1961 | The Canadian Imperial Bank of Commerce was formed when the Canadian Bank of Commerce and the Imperial Bank of Canada merged. It was the biggest bank merger in Canadian history. |
| 65 | 1 Jun 1961 | FM stereo radio broadcasting began in the USA. The first station to broadcast in stereo was WGFM (now WRVE) in Schenectady, New York, which switched to stereo on the stroke of midnight. WEFM in Chicago also began broadcasting in stereo from midnight – though it was an hour behind WGFM because it was in a different time zone. |
| 65 | 2 Jun 1961 | Death of George S. Kaufman, American playwright, director and producer. |

## JUNE 2026

| Ann. | Date | Event |
|---|---|---|
| 65 | 4 Jun 1961 to 9 Nov | Cold War: the Berlin Crisis of 1961. The Soviet Union demanded the withdrawal of all armed forces from Berlin, including Western forces in West Berlin. This led to Berlin being partitioned into East Berlin and West Berlin, and the erection of the Berlin Wall on 13th August. |
| 65 | 5 Jun 1961 | Birth of Mary Kay Bergman, American voice actress. Best known for the television series *South Park* and *The Fairly OddParents*. (Died 1999 – suicide, aged 38.) |
| 65 | 6 Jun 1961 | Death of Carl Jung, Swiss psychiatrist and psychologist. Founder of analytical psychology. |
| 65 | 9 Jun 1961 | Death of Camille Guérin, French bacteriologist and immunologist. Co-developer of the BCG vaccine against tuberculosis. |
| 65 | 16 Jun 1961 | Soviet ballet dancer Rudolf Nureyev defected to the West while on tour with the Kirov Ballet in Paris, France. |
| 65 | 19 Jun 1961 | Kuwait gained its full independence from the UK. |
| 65 | 19 Jun 1961 | The U.S. Supreme Court ruled that people entering public office in the USA did not need to pass any kind of religious test or profess a belief in God. (Torcaso v. Watkins.) This reversed a clause in the Constitution of Maryland that required a declaration of belief in the existence of God. |
| 65 | 21 Jun 1961 | The first full-scale seawater desalination plant in the USA was officially opened in Freeport, Texas by U.S. President John F. Kennedy. The plant actually began producing fresh water on 8th May. |
| 65 | 22 Jun 1961 | The first Japanese anime film to be released in the USA: *Magic Boy*. |
| 65 | 23 Jun 1961 | The Antarctic Treaty came into effect. It established Antarctica as a scientific preserve and banned military activity. |
| 65 | 29 Jun 1961 | The U.S. Navy launched its *Transit 4A* satellite – part of the Transit satellite navigation system. *Transit 4A* was the first satellite with a radio-active power source – a SNAP-3 radioisotope thermoelectric generator (a type of nuclear battery). |
| 65 | 30 Jun 1961 | Death of Lee De Forest, American inventor. Best known for the Audion vacuum tube or 'valve' that amplifies weak electrical signals. It was a key component of television, radio, telephone, radar and computer systems before the invention of the transistor. |
| 60 | 1 Jun 1966 | Léopoldville, the capital of the Democratic Republic of the Congo, was renamed Kinshasa. |
| 60 | 1 Jun 1966 | Death of Papa Jack Laine, American marching band/jazz drummer, bandleader and educator. He trained many successful jazz musicians, including the members of the Original Dixieland Jass Band. |
| 60 | 2 Jun 1966 | NASA's space probe *Surveyor 1* landed on the Moon to collect data for the Apollo programme. It was the first U.S. craft to soft-land on another extraterrestrial body. (The Soviet Union's *Luna 9* achieved this four months earlier on 3rd February.) |

**JUNE 2026**

| Ann. | Date | Event |
|------|------|-------|
| 60 | 2 Jun 1966 | Death of Évariste Kimba, Prime Minister of the Democratic Republic of the Congo (October – November 1965). (Executed for treason, aged 39, along with three other former ministers, after being accused of plotting a coup.) |
| 60 | 4 Jun 1966 | American singer Janis Joplin joined the psychedelic rock band Big Brother and the Holding Company. Her first live performance with them was on 10th June at the Avalon Ballroom in San Francisco, California. |
| 60 | 7 Jun 1966 | American civil rights activist James Meredith was shot and wounded while leading a private 220-mile 'March Against Fear' from Memphis, Tennessee to Jackson, Mississippi. 15,000 people joined the march as a result. and completed it on 26th June, by which time he had recovered enough to join them. In 1962 he became the first African American student to enrol at the University of Mississippi, after being refused entry twice. |
| 60 | 7 Jun 1966 | Death of Jean Arp, German/French avant-garde sculptor, artist and poet. |
| 60 | 8 Jun 1966 | The Topeka tornado, Kansas, USA. The state capital of Kansas was devastated by the powerful tornado. It caused more than $100 million in damage, making it one of the costliest tornadoes in U.S. history. 16 people were killed, 450 injured, and thousands of homes damaged or destroyed. |
| 60 | 13 Jun 1966 | In a landmark case, the U.S. Supreme Court ruled that police must inform suspects of their constitutional rights (commonly known as the Miranda rights) before questioning them. (Miranda v. Arizona.) |
| 60 | 14 Jun 1966 | The Catholic Church's list of banned books (the *Index Librorum Prohibitorum*) was abolished by Pope Paul VI. The first version of the list was compiled by Pope Paul IV in 1559. |
| 60 | 15 Jun 1966 to 18th | The world's first hovercraft show (hovershow) was held at Browndown near Gosport in Hampshire, UK. The show was intended to promote export sales of hovercraft. On the first day of the show the Ministry of Defence announced that they had placed a £1 million order. |
| 60 | 15 Jun 1966 | The Beatles' album *Yesterday and Today* was released in North America. |
| 60 | 16 Jun 1966 | The Black Power movement was established in the USA by civil rights activist Stokely Carmichael. It operated until the 1980s. |
| 60 | 19 Jun 1966 | Death of Ed Wynn, (the 'Perfect Fool'), American stage, film, radio and television comedian, actor, writer and producer. Known for his giggly voice and exaggerated mannerisms, props, costumes and sight gags. He later turned to serious acting. |
| 60 | 20 Jun 1966 | Death of Georges Lemaître, Belgian cosmologist, theoretical physicist, astrophysicist and Catholic priest. He determined that the recession of galaxies is caused by the expansion of the universe, and that they are moving away at speeds proportional to their distance (known as the Hubble-Lemaître law). He also proposed a version of the Big Bang theory of the origin of the universe. |
| 60 | 21 Jun 1966 | France announced that it was withdrawing all of its forces from NATO's military command structure. It ordered non-French NATO forces to leave France by the end of 1967. (It returned as a full member in 2009.) |

## JUNE 2026

| Ann. | Date | Event |
|------|------|-------|
| 60 | 21 Jun 1966 | The U.S. première of the drama film *Who's Afraid of Virginia Woolf?* Released: 22nd June. UK: 12th March 1967. |
| 60 | 27 Jun 1966 | The first episode of the Gothic fantasy/science fiction television soap opera *Dark Shadows* was broadcast on ABC in the USA. It ran for five years and now has an intense cult following. |
| 60 | 29 Jun 1966 | Vietnam War: U.S. planes bombed fuel and oil facilities in North Vietnam's largest cities, Hanoi and Haiphong, for the first time. This led to an escalation of the war, but it failed to have a significant impact or affect the course of the war. |
| 60 | 30 Jun 1966 | The National Organization for Women was founded in the USA. |
| 60 | 30 Jun 1966 | Death of Giuseppe ('Nino') Farina, Italian racing driver. The first ever Formula One World Champion (1950). (Car crash, aged 59.) |
| 50 | 1 Jun 1976 | The Third Cod War ended. Icelandic victory. Iceland expanded its exclusive fishing zone to 200 nautical miles. Britain was granted a temporary licence to fish in the waters but the size of its catch was limited. Thousands of British fishermen lost their jobs and the northern fishing ports suffered economic decline. |
| 50 | 2 Jun 1976 | Death of Juan José Torres, President of Bolivia (1970–71). (Kidnapped and assassinated during Operation Condor.) |
| 50 | 5 Jun 1976 | The Teton Dam in Idaho, USA collapsed as it was being filled for the first time. Eleven people were killed. It was never rebuilt. |
| 50 | 6 Jun 1976 | Death of J. Paul Getty, American industrialist and art collector. Founder of the Getty Oil Company and the J. Paul Getty Museum. He was the richest man in the world, but he had a reputation as a miser and eccentric. |
| 50 | 9 Jun 1976 | Death of Dame Sybil Thorndike, British stage actress. Particularly noted for her Shakespearean roles. |
| 50 | 10 Jun 1976 | Death of Adolph Zukor, Hungarian-born American film studio entrepreneur. Co-founder and chairman of Paramount Pictures. |
| 50 | 11 Jun 1976 to 16th | Angolan Civil War – the Luanda Trial. Thirteen mercenaries from the UK, USA and Ireland were convicted of fighting for the National Liberation Front of Angola (FNLA). Four were executed (on 10th July), and the others received prison sentences of between 16 and 30 years. The U.S. prisoners were released in 1982, and the British in 1984. |
| 50 | 14 Jun 1976 | The first episode of the amateur talent television show *The Gong Show* was broadcast on NBC in the USA. It ran until 1989, and was revived in 2017–18. |
| 50 | 16 Jun 1976 | The Soweto uprising, South Africa. Up to 20,000 black high school students held a protest rally in the streets of Soweto following the Afrikaans Medium Decree, which ruled that black schools must teach subjects in Afrikaans as well as English. (Afrikaans was closely associated with apartheid and its popularity was in decline.) Police opened fire on the protesters, killing between 176 and 700 of them (the official figure was 23). Over 1,000 were injured. |

## JUNE 2026

| Ann. | Date | Event |
|---|---|---|
| 50 | 16 Jun 1976 | Death of Francis E. Meloy Jr., American diplomat.<br>U.S. Ambassador to Lebanon. (Assassinated in Beirut.)<br>On 20th June about 300 Americans and Britons were evacuated from the war-torn city by the U.S. Military. |
| 50 | 19 Jun 1976 | NASA's *Viking 1* spacecraft went into orbit around Mars.<br>It dropped a lander onto the surface on 20th July, which transmitted the first image from the surface of Mars and continued operating for six years. |
| 50 | 19 Jun 1976 | King Carl XVI Gustaf of Sweden married Silvia Sommerlath, and she became Queen Silvia of Sweden.<br>She is the longest-serving queen in Swedish history. |
| 50 | 23 Jun 1976 to 27 Aug | The 1976 British Isles heat wave.<br>One of the hottest and driest summers on record caused a drought, some rivers completely dried up, and reservoirs fell to extremely low levels. Domestic water supplies were rationed and public standpipes were installed in the streets in some areas. Denis Howell was appointed Minister for Drought in August, and thunderstorms began within days, ending the drought. September and October both saw very heavy rainfall. |
| 50 | 25 Jun 1976 | The Governor of the U.S. state of Missouri, Kit Bond, rescinded the 1838 Extermination Order which called for Mormons to be exterminated or driven from the state.<br>There is no record of anyone having been killed directly, though some are thought to have perished from hardship or exposure as a result of a forced migration to Illinois during wintry conditions. |
| 50 | 25 Jun 1976 | Death of Johnny Mercer, American singer, songwriter and composer who contributed to many Broadway musicals and Hollywood movies.<br>Co-founder of Capitol Records. |
| 50 | 26 Jun 1976 | The CN Tower in Toronto, Canada opened to the public.<br>(The official opening was on 1st October.)<br>It was the world's tallest free-standing building until it was surpassed by the Burj Khalifa in Dubai in 2010. |
| 50 | 27 Jun 1976 to Nov | The first known outbreak of the Ebola virus occurred in Sudan.<br>The first known victim was a storekeeper at a cotton factory in Nzaram, who died on 6th July.<br>284 people became infected in the first outbreak, and 151 died.<br>A second outbreak occurred in Zaire (now the Democratic Republic of the Congo) in August. |
| 50 | 27 Jun 1976 | Air France Flight 139 (Tel Aviv, Israel to Paris, France) was hijacked by Palestinian terrorists after a stopover in Athens, Greece. It was forced to fly to Entebbe, Uganda, where the passengers and crew were held hostage in the airport terminal.<br>Israeli commandos stormed the airport on 4th July (Operation Entebbe). 148 hostages had been released prior to the operation and 102 were rescued during it. Seven hijackers, three hostages and 45 Ugandan soldiers were killed and up to 30 aircraft destroyed. |
| 50 | 28 Jun 1976 | The first women enrolled in the U.S. Air Force Academy. |
| 50 | 29 Jun 1976 | The Seychelles gained its independence from the UK. |

## JUNE 2026

| Ann. | Date | Event |
|------|------|-------|
| 40 | 2 Jun 1986 | Live national television coverage of the U.S. Senate began. |
| 40 | 3 Jun 1986 | The U.S. state of California passed Proposition 51 (the Deep Pockets Law). It limited the liability of the government, manufacturers and other wealthy defendants. Before the law was passed, victims often sought 100 percent of damage claims from those indirectly responsible, because they could afford to pay substantial amounts, whereas those directly responsible could not. (For example, shooting victims would seek compensation from gun manufacturers rather than those who shot them.) |
| 40 | 3 Jun 1986 | Death of Dame Anna Neagle, British stage and film actress, singer and dancer. |
| 40 | 4 Jun 1986 | American intelligence analyst Jonathan Pollard pleaded guilty to selling classified U.S. military information to Israel.<br>He was sentenced to life imprisonment in March 1987.<br>(He was released in 2015 and later moved to Israel.) |
| 40 | 5 Jun 1986 | Former U.S. intelligence specialist Ronald Pelton was convicted of selling secrets to the Soviet Union. He did not pass any documents over, but apparently used his photographic memory to remember information that he later gave to the Soviets verbally.<br>In December 1986 he was sentenced to three concurrent life prison terms.<br>(He was released in 2015.) |
| 40 | 5 Jun 1986 | Excedrin deaths in the USA.<br>Bruce Nickell from Auburn, Washington collapsed and died after taking four extra-strength Excedrin capsules.<br>On 11th June, local bank manager Sue Snow died after taking two capsules.<br>Investigations found they had both died from cyanide poisoning, and the product was withdrawn from sale.<br>After further investigations, Stella Nickell, Bruce's wife, was arrested.<br>She was convicted of five counts of product tampering in May 1988, and was sentenced to 90 years in prison. |
| 40 | 9 Jun 1986 | The Rogers Commission published its report on the space shuttle *Challenger* disaster. It documented the technical and managerial factors that led to the catastrophic accident. |
| 40 | 9 Jun 1986 | The Pittsburgh Supercomputing Center opened in Pennsylvania, USA. |
| 40 | 10 Jun 1986 | IRA member Patrick Magee was found guilty of planting the bomb that exploded at the Grand Hotel, Brighton, UK during the 1984 Conservative Party conference. Five people were killed in the explosion.<br>He was sentenced to life imprisonment, and released in 1999. |
| 40 | 11 Jun 1986 | The comedy film *Ferris Bueller's Day Off* was released in the USA.<br>UK: 20th February 1987. |
| 40 | 11 Jun 1986 | The pop song *Papa Don't Preach* by Madonna was released. |
| 40 | 12 Jun 1986 | South Africa declared a national state of emergency following a wave of social and political unrest. News coverage was restricted, filming was banned in areas where there was unrest, security forces were given almost unlimited power, curfews were imposed and some gatherings were banned. (See also: 11th December 1986.) |

## JUNE 2026

| Ann. | Date | Event |
|---|---|---|
| 40 | 12 Jun 1986 | British politician Derek Hatton, the controversial deputy leader of Liverpool Council, was expelled from the Labour Party for belonging to the left-wing Militant Tendency. |
| 40 | 13 Jun 1986 | Death of Benny Goodman, (the 'King of swing'), American jazz clarinet player and bandleader. |
| 40 | 14 Jun 1986 | Death of Jorge Luis Borges, Argentine poet and writer. |
| 40 | 14 Jun 1986 | Death of Alan Jay Lerner, American lyricist. Best known for his collaborations with the composer Frederick Loewe on hit musicals such as *Paint Your Wagon*, *My Fair Lady*, *Camelot* and others. |
| 40 | 16 Jun 1986 to 20th | Apartheid: the United Nations World Conference on Sanctions against Racist South Africa was held. |
| 40 | 17 Jun 1986 | Death of Kate Smith, (the 'first lady of radio'), American singer. Best known for the song *God Bless America*. |
| 40 | 18 Jun 1986 | The Grand Canyon mid-air collision II, Arizona, USA. A small passenger plane and a helicopter, both carrying tourists on sight-seeing trips, collided above the canyon. All 25 people on both aircraft were killed. (Cause: the two pilots failed to see each other.) Fixed-wing aircraft and helicopters now fly separate routes over the canyon. |
| 40 | 19 Jun 1986 | Richard Miller became the first FBI agent to be convicted of espionage. He was sentenced to life imprisonment in July. His conviction was over-turned in 1989, but he was re-convicted in October 1990 and sentenced to twenty years – later reduced to thirteen years. He was released in 1994. He was described by a colleague as 'one of the dumbest, most unkempt, most unpopular misfits the agency had ever hired'. |
| 40 | 19 Jun 1986 | Death of Coluche, French comedian and actor. He also founded the charity Les Restaurants du Coeur (Restaurants of Love) that distributes food to people in need. (Motorcycle crash, aged 41.) |
| 40 | 22 Jun 1986 | The 'Hand of God' goal: Argentine football player Diego Maradona scored a goal against England using his hand in the quarter-final of the 1986 FIFA World Cup in Mexico City. The referee mistakenly thought he had used his head, and allowed the goal. England were knocked out of the World Cup as a result, and Argentina went on to win it. |
| 40 | 27 Jun 1986 | The International Court of Justice found the USA guilty of violating international law for supporting the Contra rebels in Nicaragua. |
| 40 | 27 Jun 1986 | Death of George Nepia, New Zealand rugby player. Regarded as one of the finest rugby players in history. |
| 40 | 29 Jun 1986 | British entrepreneur Richard Branson broke the record for the fastest crossing of the Atlantic Ocean in a powerboat. |
| 40 | 30 Jun 1986 | The U.S. Supreme Court ruled that states could declare sexual acts between same-sex adults illegal. (Bowers v. Hardwick.) The decision was overturned in 2003 when same-sex sexual activity between consenting adults became legal in every U.S. state and territory. (Lawrence v. Texas.) |
| 40 | 30 Jun 1986 | Madonna's album *True Blue* was released. |

## JUNE 2026

| Ann. | Date | Event |
|---|---|---|
| 30 | 1 Jun 1996 | Death of Neelam Sanjiva Reddy, President of India (1977–82). |
| 30 | 2 Jun 1996 | Death of John Alton, Hungarian-born American cinematographer who helped to create the look of film noir. Best known for *An American in Paris*. |
| 30 | 2 Jun 1996 | Death of Ray Combs, American television game show host and stand-up comedian. Best known for hosting *Family Feud*. (Suicide, aged 40.) |
| 30 | 3 Jun 1996 | Death of Peter Bird, British ocean rower. The first person to row non-stop across the Pacific (1983). He set off from San Francisco, California, USA, and had to be rescued when he reached the Great Barrier Reef off Australia 294 days later. Guinness World Records recognised it as the first successful non-stop row across the Pacific.<br>(He died when his boat capsized while he was attempting to row across the Northern Pacific Ocean, aged 49.) |
| 30 | 3 Jun 1996 | Death of Tito Okello, President of Uganda (1985–86). |
| 30 | 4 Jun 1996 | The first test flight of the European Space Agency's Ariane 5 rocket ended in failure when it veered off course shortly after launch and was commanded to self-destruct. Its payload of four satellites, worth around £225 million ($370 million), was lost. (Cause: software error.) |
| 30 | 4 Jun 1996 | The Second Severn Crossing was officially opened. The bridge spans the River Severn and links England and Wales via the M4 motorway. |
| 30 | 7 Jun 1996 | Death of Percy Edwards, British animal imitator and radio and television entertainer. |
| 30 | 7 Jun 1996 | Death of Max Factor Jr., American cosmetician and businessman.<br>He developed Pan-Cake make-up for film studios and co-founded Max Factor Cosmetics with his father, Max Factor Sr. |
| 30 | 7 Jun 1996 | Death of Glyn Worsnip, British radio and television broadcaster<br>Best known for his appearances on the TV series *That's Life!* and *Nationwide*. (Multiple System Atrophy, aged 57.) |
| 30 | 10 Jun 1996 | All-party peace negotiations (the Stormont talks) were held in Northern Ireland. Representatives from nine political parties attended.<br>Sinn Féin was refused entry. |
| 30 | 11 Jun 1996 | U.S. Senate Majority Leader Bob Dole resigned his seat to challenge Bill Clinton in the 1996 U.S. presidential election. (Clinton won.) |
| 30 | 11 Jun 1996 | Death of Brigitte Helm, German film actress. Best known for her dual roles as Maria and the robot in Fritz Lang's *Metropolis*. |
| 30 | 12 Jun 1996 | Part of the U.S. Communications Decency Act dealing with indecency was blocked by a federal court in Philadelphia, Pennsylvania as it infringed the right of free speech.<br>The decision was later upheld by the U.S. Supreme Court. |
| 30 | 13 Jun 1996 | BSE ('mad cow disease'): French scientists announced that macaque monkeys that had been injected with BSE-infected brain matter from cattle had developed brain lesions identical to those found in victims of Creutzfeldt–Jakob Disease (CJD).<br>This was the first time that a link between BSE and CJD had been proven, though it had already been suspected. |

**JUNE 2026**

| Ann. | Date | Event |
|------|------|-------|
| 30 | 13 Jun 1996 | Members of the Montana Freemen, a militia group, surrendered to the FBI after an 81-day siege at their remote ranch.<br>Eight members were later convicted of various offences including fraud, conspiracy, falsifying tax returns, handling stolen property, and armed robbery. They were given prison sentences. |
| 30 | 15 Jun 1996 | The centre of Manchester, England was devastated by an IRA bomb.<br>200 people were injured and the city centre had to be redeveloped because of the immense amount of damage. |
| 30 | 15 Jun 1996 | Death of Ella Fitzgerald, American jazz singer. |
| 30 | 16 Jun 1996 | Russia held its first post-independence presidential election.<br>Boris Yeltsin was declared the winner after a second round of voting on 3rd July and was inaugurated on 9th August.<br>(There were many claims that the election had been rigged in his favour.) |
| 30 | 16 Jun 1996 | Death of Mel Allen, American radio and television sportscaster.<br>Best known for his play-by-play announcements for the New York Yankees baseball team. |
| 30 | 18 Jun 1996 | Benjamin Netanyahu became Prime Minister of Israel (until 1999).<br>He was also Prime Minister from 2009 to 2021. |
| 30 | 20 Jun 1996 | Scientists announced that they had discovered a vast freshwater lake (Lake Vostok) 2½ miles beneath the ice in Antarctica. |
| 30 | 21 Jun 1996 | BSE ('mad cow disease'): European heads of government announced that they had reached an agreement on the phased lifting of the ban on British beef. French farmers immediately blockaded two channel ports.<br>(The ban was not fully lifted until November 1998.) |
| 30 | 22 Jun 1996 | The first-person shooter video game *Quake* was released.<br>It was the successor to *Doom*. |
| 30 | 23 Jun 1996 | The Nintendo 64 video games console was released in Japan.<br>(USA: 29th September 1996. Europe: 1st March 1997.) |
| 30 | 23 Jun 1996 | Death of Andreas Papandreou, Prime Minister of Greece (1981–89, 1993–96). |
| 30 | 25 Jun 1996 | The Khobar Towers bombing, Saudi Arabia.<br>Terrorists detonated a truck bomb outside a housing complex used by foreign military personnel. Twenty people were killed – nineteen of them U.S. servicemen. Nearly 500 were injured.<br>There were claims that Al-Qaeda was behind the bombing, but the Saudis suspected Iranian-backed Shiite militants. In 2006 a U.S. federal judge ruled that Iran and Hezbollah were responsible. |
| 30 | 25 Jun 1996 | The U.S. première of the science fiction action film *Independence Day*.<br>Released: 3rd July. UK première: 4th July, released: 9th August. |
| 30 | 26 Jun 1996 | Attempted military coup in Iraq, organised by the Iraqi National Accord with help from the American CIA and British MI6.<br>The coup failed when it was infiltrated by President Saddam Hussein's security service.<br>Hundreds of Iraqi military officers were arrested and up to 80 (some sources say 120) were tortured and executed. |

**JUNE 2026**

| Ann. | Date | Event |
|------|------|-------|
| 30 | 26 Jun 1996 | Death of Veronica Guerin, Irish journalist.<br>(Shot dead by drug dealers in Dublin, aged 36.) |
| 30 | 27 Jun 1996 | The U.S. première of the science fiction comedy film *The Nutty Professor*.<br>Released: 28th June. UK: 4th October. |
| 30 | 27 Jun 1996 | Death of Albert R. ('Cubby') Broccoli, American film producer.<br>Best known for producing the *James Bond* films. |
| 25 | 1 Jun 2001 | Crown Prince Dipendra, the heir to the Nepalese throne, massacred eight members of the royal family including the King and Queen.<br>He then shot himself and died three days later.<br>Gyanendra, the last King of Nepal, ascended the throne on 4th June.<br>The monarchy was abolished in 2008. |
| 25 | 1 Jun 2001 | The Dolphinarium discotheque massacre, Tel Aviv, Israel.<br>A Palestinian suicide bomber blew himself up outside the club as patrons were queuing to enter. 21 people were killed (plus the bomber) and more than a hundred were injured. Most of the victims were teenagers who had recently immigrated from the former Soviet Union with their families. |
| 25 | 1 Jun 2001 | Death of Hank Ketcham, American cartoonist who created the *Dennis the Menace* comic strip (the U.S. version not the British version that appears in *The Beano* comic). |
| 25 | 2 Jun 2001 | Death of Imogene Coca, American stage, film and television actress and comedian. Best known for the 1950s TV variety series *Your Show of Shows*. |
| 25 | 3 Jun 2001 | Death of Anthony Quinn, Mexican-born American actor (*Zorba the Greek*, *Lust for Life*, *The Guns of Navarone*, *Lawrence of Arabia*). |
| 25 | 4 Jun 2001<br>to 18th | Tropical Storm Allison hit Texas, Louisiana, Mississippi, Florida and most of the eastern USA, causing massive damage and flooding.<br>41 people were killed.<br>Allison is the only non-hurricane-strength storm to have its name retired. |
| 25 | 5 Jun 2001<br>to 6th | The Harehills riot, Leeds, UK.<br>Following the wrongful arrest of an Asian man, more than 100 Asian, white and black youths were involved in a six-hour riot against police.<br>This was one of a series of race riots in northern England in 2001. |
| 25 | 7 Jun 2001 | Death of Víctor Paz Estenssoro, President of Bolivia (1952–56, 1960–64, 1985–89). |
| 25 | 8 Jun 2001 | The Osaka school massacre, Japan.<br>An ex-convict entered Ikeda Elementary School, stabbed eight students to death and wounded fifteen others. The perpetrator, Mamoru Takuma, was sentenced to death in August 2003 and executed in September 2004. |
| 25 | 8 Jun 2001 | The science fiction comedy film *Evolution* was released in the USA.<br>UK: 22nd June. |
| 25 | 10 Jun 2001 | Lebanon's first female saint, Saint Rafqa, was canonised by Pope John Paul II. |
| 25 | 10 Jun 2001 | Death of Princess Leila of Iran.<br>Youngest daughter of the Shah of Iran, Mohammad Reza Pahlavi.<br>(Anorexia and prescription drug overdose, aged 31.) |

**JUNE 2026**

| Ann. | Date | Event |
|------|------|-------|
| 25 | 11 Jun 2001 | Nintendo's Game Boy Advance portable video game system was launched in the USA. (Japan: 21st March, Europe: 22nd June.) |
| 25 | 11 Jun 2001 | The U.S. première of the action-adventure film *Lara Croft: Tomb Raider*. Released: 15th June. UK première: 4th July, released: 6th July. |
| 25 | 11 Jun 2001 | Death of Timothy McVeigh, American terrorist convicted of the Oklahoma City bombing in April 1995 which killed 168 people. (Executed.) |
| 25 | 15 Jun 2001 | The Shanghai Cooperation Organisation was established by China, Kazakhstan, Kyrgyzstan, Russia, Tajikistan and Uzbekistan. It is the world's largest political, economic and security alliance. |
| 25 | 16 Jun 2001 | The Leaning Tower of Pisa in Italy re-opened for the first time since 1990 following remedial work to prevent it from falling. It reopened to tourists in December. |
| 25 | 16 Jun 2001 | U.S. President George W. Bush and Russian President Vladimir Putin met for the first time, at Brdo Castle near Kranj, Slovenia. |
| 25 | 17 Jun 2001 | Death of Thomas Winning, Scottish cardinal. Archbishop of Glasgow (1974–2001). The leader of the Roman Catholic Church in Scotland. |
| 25 | 18 Jun 2001 | The U.S. première of the action film *The Fast and the Furious*. Released 22nd June. UK: 14th September. At the time of writing, eight sequels have been released, and two more are planned. |
| 25 | 20 Jun 2001 | American mother Andrea Yates drowned her five children in the bath at their home in Houston, Texas. At her trial in 2002 she was convicted of murder and sentenced to life in prison. The verdict was overturned on appeal after it was discovered that one of the expert witnesses had given a false testimony. At her retrial in 2006 she was found not guilty by reason of insanity, and was detained in a mental health facility. |
| 25 | 20 Jun 2001 | Pervez Musharraf became President of Pakistan (until 2008 when he resigned to avoid impeachment). |
| 25 | 21 Jun 2001 | Death of John Lee Hooker, American blues singer and guitarist. |
| 25 | 21 Jun 2001 | Death of Carroll O'Connor, American film and television actor. Best known for his role as Archie Bunker in the sitcoms *All in the Family* and *Archie Bunker's Place*. He was also known for his roles in the TV drama series *In the Heat of the Night* and the sitcom *Mad About You*. |
| 25 | 22 Jun 2001 | Two British schoolboys who murdered two-year-old James Bulger in Liverpool in 1993 were released from secure custody after eight years. They were given new identities and moved to secret locations. |
| 25 | 23 Jun 2001 | The Southern Peru earthquake. At least 74 people were killed and more than 2,600 injured. 17,500 homes were destroyed and 35,000 damaged, and numerous historic buildings were damaged or destroyed. |
| 25 | 23 Jun 2001 to 24th | The Burnley race riot, UK. The riot was the culmination of years of racial tension fuelled by far-right activists from the British National Party and the National Front. It was one of a series of race riots in northern England in 2001. |

## JUNE 2026

| Ann. | Date | Event |
|---|---|---|
| 25 | 26 Jun 2001 | .biz internet domain names were introduced.<br>.biz was created for businesses, and was intended to relieve the demand for .com domain names and provide an alternative for businesses whose domain name had already been taken. |
| 25 | 26 Jun 2001 | The U.S. première of the science fiction action film *A.I. Artificial Intelligence*. Released: 29th June. UK: 21st September. |
| 25 | 27 Jun 2001 | Death of Tove Jansson, Finnish artist and writer.<br>Best known as the creator of the Moomins. |
| 25 | 27 Jun 2001 | Death of Jack Lemmon, American actor (*Some Like it Hot, The Odd Couple, Days of Wine and Roses*, and many more). |
| 25 | 27 Jun 2001 | Death of Joan Sims, British actress.<br>Best known for her roles in the *Carry On...* comedy films. |
| 25 | 28 Jun 2001 | The U.S. Court of Appeals ruled that Microsoft had violated the Antitrust Act and illegally maintained its monopoly in the personal computer and web browser markets. (United States v. Microsoft Corporation.)<br>On 2nd November, Microsoft reached a settlement with the Department of Justice in which it agreed to license Windows uniformly among its distributors, provide third-party software developers access to its application programming interfaces (APIs), and refrain from entering into partnerships that prevented or prohibited users from installing other companies' software products. The agreement would remain in effect for five years. The settlement was approved by the Court of Appeals in June 2004. It expired in November 2009.<br>Critics said the settlement was merely a slap on the wrist for Microsoft. |
| 25 | 30 Jun 2001 | Death of Chet Atkins, American country and western guitarist, record producer and executive.<br>He is credited with creating the 'Nashville' sound. |
| 20 | 3 Jun 2006 and 5th | Montenegro declared its independence from the State union of Serbia and Montenegro.<br>On 5th June Serbia also declared its independence, and the union was dissolved. Both countries were immediately recognised as independent nations by the international community. |
| 20 | 6 Jun 2006 | Death of Billy Preston, American R&B/rock/soul/funk/gospel keyboard player, singer and songwriter. He worked with Little Richard, Syreeta, Sam Cooke, the Beatles, Sly & the Family Stone, the Rolling Stones, Ray Charles and Eric Clapton, and was also a successful solo artist. |
| 20 | 7 Jun 2006 | Death of Abu Musab al-Zarqawi, Jordanian-born Iraqi militant.<br>An associate of Osama bin Laden. He is thought to have masterminded numerous terrorist acts in Iraq and Jordan. (Killed by a U.S. air strike.) |
| 20 | 11 Jun 2006 | Death of Major Bruce Shand, British Army officer.<br>Father of Camilla, Duchess of Cornwall. |
| 20 | 12 Jun 2006 | Death of Anna Lee Aldred, American jockey and rodeo rider.<br>The first woman in the USA to receive a jockey's license. |
| 20 | 12 Jun 2006 | Death of Kenneth Roy Thomson, 2nd Baron Thomson of Fleet, Canadian media magnate and art collector. The richest person in Canada. |

## JUNE 2026

| Ann. | Date | Event |
|---|---|---|
| 20 | 13 Jun 2006 | Death of Charles Haughey, Taoiseach (Prime Minister) of Ireland (1979–81, 1982, 1987–92). |
| 20 | 14 Jun 2006 | Death of Monty Berman, British film and television producer and cinematographer. Best known for producing popular TV action series for ITC (*The Saint, The Baron, The Champions, Department S, Jason King, Randall and Hopkirk (Deceased), The Adventurer*). |
| 20 | 15 Jun 2006 | Microsoft chairman Bill Gates announced that he would be transitioning out of his role with the company over the next two years. He would dedicate his time to philanthropic work with the Bill and Melinda Gates Foundation. |
| 20 | 18 Jun 2006 | Kazakhstan's first satellite *KazSat-1* was launched. The communications satellite was designed to operate for up to twelve years, but control was lost in July 2008. |
| 20 | 18 Jun 2006 | American bishop Katharine Jefferts Schori became the first woman to be elected as a primate in the Anglican Communion. She became the Presiding Bishop and Primate of the Episcopal Church from 1st November 2006 until 1st November 2015. |
| 20 | 20 Jun 2006 | The Blu-ray high-definition digital video disc system was launched worldwide, beginning a format war with the rival HD DVD system. Blu-ray won the war, and the HD DVD format was discontinued in March 2008. |
| 20 | 22 Jun 2006 | Death of Moose, American dog actor. Best known for his role as Eddie in the TV series *Frasier*. He also appeared in the film *My Dog Skip* with his son Enzo (who was bred to look exactly like him). |
| 20 | 23 Jun 2006 | Death of Aaron Spelling, American television and film producer (*Charlie's Angels, T. J. Hooker, The Love Boat, Fantasy Island, Hart to Hart, Beverly Hills 90210, Charmed*, and many more). |
| 20 | 28 Jun 2006 | Death of Peter Rawlinson, Baron Rawlinson of Ewell, British barrister and politician. Solicitor General (1962–64). Attorney General for England and Wales (1970–74) and for Northern Ireland (1972–74). |
| 20 | 29 Jun 2006 | The U.S. Supreme Court ruled that President George W. Bush's plan to try Guantanamo Bay detainees in military tribunals violated the Uniform Code of Military Justice and the Geneva Convention. (Hamdan v. Rumsfeld.) |
| 20 | 29 Jun 2006 | Death of Lloyd Richards, Canadian-born American theatre director, actor and educator who mentored many young playwrights. Dean of the Yale School of Drama. The first African American to direct a Broadway play (*A Raisin in the Sun*). |
| 20 | 30 Jun 2006 | The USA removed Libya from its list of terrorist states. |
| 15 | 21 Jun 2011 | American politician Anthony Weiner (Democrat, New York) resigned from the U.S. Congress after it was revealed that he had sent sexually explicit photos of himself to women via Twitter. In 2017 he was convicted of another charge of sending obscene material to a minor. He was sentenced to 21 months in prison, fined $10,000 and required to register as a sex offender. |

## JUNE 2026

| Ann. | Date | Event |
|---|---|---|
| 15 | 27 Jun 2011 | The former Governor of the U.S. state of Illinois, Rod Blagojevich, was convicted of corruption. He was sentenced to fourteen years in prison. U.S. President Donald Trump commuted his sentence to time served in 2020, and he was released. (Three other Governors of Illinois also served federal prison sentences.) |
| 10 | 3 Jun 2016 | Death of Muhammad Ali, American world heavyweight boxing champion. Regarded as the greatest heavyweight boxer of all time. |
| 10 | 6 Jun 2016 | Death of Peter Shaffer, British playwright, screenwriter and novelist. Best known for his plays *Equus* and *Amadeus*, which were both adapted into films. Twin brother of the writer Anthony Shaffer. |
| 10 | 10 Jun 2016 | Death of Gordie Howe, Canadian ice hockey player. Regarded as one of the greatest NHL players of all time. |
| 10 | 12 Jun 2016 | The Pulse nightclub shooting, Orlando, Florida, USA. A 29-year-old man entered the gay nightclub, which was hosting a Latin Night, and opened fire. He killed 49 people and injured 53. He was then shot dead in a gunfight with police. |
| 10 | 16 Jun 2016 | Death of Jo Cox, British Labour Party politician and campaigner against the Syrian civil war. Member of Parliament for Batley and Spen. (Murdered by a far-right extremist, aged 41.) |
| 10 | 23 Jun 2016 | The UK European Union (EU) membership referendum. 52 percent of voters chose to leave the EU. 48 percent voted to remain. The UK left the EU on 31st January 2020. |
| 10 | 26 Jun 2016 | The Panama Canal expansion project was completed and began commercial operation. The expansion doubled the canal's capacity. |
| 10 | 28 Jun 2016 | The Atatürk Airport attack, Istanbul, Turkey. Three terrorists wearing explosive belts entered Terminal 2, shot passengers, and then blew themselves up. 45 people were killed (plus the three terrorists) and more than 230 injured. The terrorists were believed to be from Russia and Central Asia. |

**JULY 2026**

| Ann. | Date | Event |
|------|------|-------|
| 1500 | 12 Jul 526 | Félix IV became Pope (until 530). |
| 1400 | 2 Jul 626 | The Xuanwu Gate Incident, Chang'an, China.<br>Li Shimin (Prince of Qin) led a successful coup and assassinated his brothers Crown Prince Li Jiancheng and Prince Li Yuanji.<br>He became Emperor Taizong of Tang on 4th September. |
| 750 | 27 Jul 1276 | Death of James I ('the Conqueror'), King of Aragon, Count of Barcelona and Lord of Montpellier (1213–76), King of Majorca (1231–76), King of Valencia (1238–76). Succeeded by his son, Peter III. |
| 500 | 14 Jul 1526 | Death of John de Vere, 14th Earl of Oxford, English peer and landowner. Lord Great Chamberlain of England. Regarded as an incompetent and extravagant wastrel, he was ordered by the king to moderate his habits. (Died aged 26.) |
| 500 | 31 Jul 1526 | Birth of Augustus, Elector of Saxony (1553–86).<br>The leader of Protestant Germany. |
| 400 | 13 Jul 1626 | Death of Robert Sidney, 1st Earl of Leicester, English statesman, patron of the arts and poet. |
| 250 | 2 Jul 1776 | American Revolution: the Second Continental Congress adopted the Lee Resolution (also known as The Resolution of Independence).<br>It was proposed by Richard Henry Lee from Virginia, and resolved that the Thirteen Colonies were free and independent states, separate from the British Empire. The resolution was formally announced on 4th July as the Declaration of Independence. |
| 250 | 4 Jul 1776 | American Revolution: the U.S. Declaration of Independence was adopted by the Second Continental Congress. |
| 250 | 8 Jul 1776 | American Revolution: the first public reading of the Declaration of Independence took place, in Philadelphia, Pennsylvania. |
| 250 | 12 Jul 1776 to 4 Oct 1780 | British explorer Captain James Cook's third and final voyage.<br>He travelled to New Zealand and Hawaii, where he was killed in a violent exchange with the local people. Charles Clerke then took command of the voyage, but died of tuberculosis on the return journey.<br>John Gore commanded the final stage of the return. |
| 250 | 29 Jul 1776 | The Domínguez–Escalante expedition set off on a journey of exploration from Santa Fe, New Mexico to their mission in Monterey, California.<br>The expedition was led by two Spanish Franciscan priests, Atanasio Domínguez and Silvestre Vélez de Escalante.<br>They travelled through unexplored areas of Colorado, Utah, and northern Arizona, mapping the route for future travellers. They endured numerous hardships along the way and were unable to reach California.<br>They returned to Santa Fe, arriving there on 2nd January 1777. |
| 200 | 4 Jul 1826 | Birth of Stephen Foster, ('the father of American music'), American songwriter and composer. His songs include *Oh! Susanna*, *Camptown Races*, *Swanee River*, and many others that are still popular today.<br>(Died 1864, aged 37 – possible suicide.) |

## JULY 2026

| Ann. | Date | Event |
|---|---|---|
| 200 | 4 Jul 1826 | Death of John Adams, 2nd President of the United States (1797–1801), 1st Vice President of the United States (1789–87). |
| 200 | 4 Jul 1826 | Death of Thomas Jefferson, 3rd President of the United States (1801–09), 2nd Vice President of the United States (1797–1801). |
| 200 | 5 Jul 1826 | Death of Sir Stamford Raffles, British statesman. Lieutenant-Governor of the Dutch East Indies (1811–16), Lieutenant-Governor of Bencoolen (now Bengkulu City, Sumatra) (1818–24). The founder of modern Singapore. |
| 200 | 11 Jul 1826 | Birth of John Fowler, British agricultural engineer. He pioneered the use of steam engines for ploughing and digging drainage channels. This significantly reduced the cost of ploughing, and allowed previously uncultivatable land to be drained and farmed. |
| 200 | 22 Jul 1826 | Death of Giuseppe Piazzi, Italian mathematician, astronomer and Catholic priest. Best known for discovering the dwarf planet Ceres. |
| 175 | 3 Jul 1851 | Birth of Charles Bannerman, British-born Australian cricketer (New South Wales and Australia) and umpire. He scored the first-ever run in Test cricket, and scored the first century in Test cricket. |
| 175 | 8 Jul 1851 | Birth of Arthur Evans, British archaeologist. Best known for unearthing the palace of Knossos on the island of Crete. He was also the first person to discover the Minoan writing systems known as Linear A and Linear B. (Linear A remains untranslated, Linear B was translated in the 1950s.) |
| 175 | 10 Jul 1851 | Death of Louis Daguerre, French photographer and artist who invented the daguerreotype photography process. He is regarded as one of the fathers of photography. |
| 175 | 11 Jul 1851 | Birth of Millie and Christine McKoy, American conjoined twins who were joined at the lower spine. The were born into slavery and exhibited as freaks. When slavery was abolished, they began a successful career as singers and entertainers, travelled the world, and were known as the Two-Headed Nightingale. |
| 175 | 23 Jul 1851 | The Treaty of Traverse des Sioux was signed by the USA and the Upper Dakota Sioux Indians in Minnesota Territory. The Native Americans agreed to sell 21 million acres of land to the USA for $1,665,000. The land now forms part of the U.S. states of Iowa, Minnesota and South Dakota. |
| 175 | 24 Jul 1851 | Window tax was abolished in England and Wales. The tax was introduced in 1696 and was based on the number of windows in a house. It led to many windows being bricked up. It was replaced by a tax on inhabited buildings. Scotland also had a window tax from 1748 to 1798, and France had one from 1798 to 1926. |
| 175 | 28 Jul 1851 | A total solar eclipse was photographed for the first time. The daguerreotype image was captured by Julius Berkowski at the Royal Observatory in Königsberg, Prussia (now Kaliningrad, Russia). |
| 150 | 2 Jul 1876 | Birth of Wilhelm Cuno, Chancellor of Germany (1922–23) and director of HAPAG (the Hamburg-America Line) – the world's largest shipping company at that time. |

## JULY 2026

| Ann. | Date | Event |
|---|---|---|
| 150 | 8 Jul 1876 to 9th | The Hamburg massacre (also known as the Red Shirt Massacre or the Hamburg riot), Hamburg, South Carolina, USA. White voters attempted to prevent black Republicans from voting in the upcoming 1876 U.S. presidential election Seven people were killed (one white, six black). |
| 150 | 17 Jul 1876 | Birth of Maxim Litvinov, Russian revolutionary and Soviet statesman and diplomat. A key figure in the introduction of the Kellogg–Briand Pact in the Soviet Union (the international agreement to renounce war as a means of settling disputes), and in the Allies' security policies against Nazi Germany. |
| 150 | 19 Jul 1876 | Birth of Joseph Fielding Smith, President of The Church of Jesus Christ of Latter-day Saints (1970–72). |
| 150 | 25 Jul 1876 | Birth of Elisabeth of Bavaria, Queen consort of the Belgians (1909–34). Wife of King Albert I. Mother of King Leopold III of Belgium and Queen Marie-José of Italy. Grandmother of King Baudouin and King Albert II of Belgium. |
| 150 | 31 Jul 1876 | The U.S. Coast Guard Academy was established near New Bedford, Massachusetts (as the School of Instruction of the Revenue Cutter Service). It relocated to New London, Connecticut in 1932. |
| 125 | 1 Jul 1901 | Birth of Irna Phillips, American screenwriter, scriptwriter, actress and casting agent. She pioneered daytime soap operas in the USA, and created the soap operas *Guiding Light*, *As the World Turns*, and *Another World*. |
| 125 | 3 Jul 1901 | Butch Cassidy's Wild Bunch carried out their last train robbery in the USA. They robbed a Great Northern Railway train near Wagner, Montana and stole more than $60,000 (equivalent to nearly $2 million today). Several members of the gang were captured or killed shortly afterwards. Cassidy and Harry Longabough (the Sundance Kid) fled to Argentina. |
| 125 | 4 Jul 1901 | William Howard Taft (later U.S. President) became Governor-General of the Philippines (until 1903). |
| 125 | 9 Jul 1901 | Birth of Dame Barbara Cartland, British romantic novelist. She wrote 723 novels, including 23 in a single year (1973). She was one of the best-selling authors of the 20th century, selling more than one billion copies of her books. |
| 125 | 24 Jul 1901 | American short story writer O. Henry was released from prison in Columbus, Ohio after serving three years for embezzling money from the bank where he worked. He had continued to submit stories for publication while he was in prison, using various pseudonyms and sending them via a friend, so no one would know he was a prisoner. |
| 125 | 28 Jul 1901 | Birth of Rudy Vallée, American pop singer, saxophonist, film and television actor, and radio host. |
| 125 | 31 Jul 1901 | Birth of Jean Debuffet, French artist and sculptor. Founder of the 'art brut' movement of self-taught/naïve artists who worked outside mainstream culture. |

## JULY 2026

| Ann. | Date | Event |
|------|------|-------|
| 100 | 1 Jul 1926 | Canada went back on the gold standard – meaning that its bank notes could be redeemed for the equivalent value in gold.<br>It had gone off the gold standard at the outbreak of WWI in 1914.<br>It went off it again in 1929 for the final time. |
| 100 | 2 Jul 1926 | The U.S. Army Air Service was renamed the U.S. Army Air Corps.<br>It became the U.S. Air Force in 1947. |
| 100 | 2 Jul 1926 | Death of Émile Coué, French psychologist and pharmacist.<br>Best known for pioneering psychotherapy and self-improvement by auto-suggestion (a form of self-hypnosis). |
| 100 | 8 Jul 1926 | Birth of Elisabeth Kübler-Ross, Swiss-American psychiatrist and writer. She pioneered near-death studies and is known for her book *On Death and Dying*, which includes the first description of the five stages of grief.<br>(Died 2004.) |
| 100 | 9 Jul 1926 to 29 Dec 1928 | The Chinese Nationalist Party (the National Revolutionary Army of the Kuomintang), led by Chiang Kai-shek, launched the Northern Expedition against the Beiyang government.<br>They successfully overthrew the government in December 1928, and reunified China. This led to the Chinese Civil War (1927–49). |
| 100 | 10 Jul 1926 | The Lake Denmark Naval Powder Depot in New Jersey, USA was struck by lightning. More than 600,000 tons of explosives detonated over two to three days, destroying nearly 200 buildings. 21 people were killed.<br>Little remained of the depot afterwards. |
| 100 | 10 Jul 1926 | Birth of Fred Gwynne, American stage, film and television actor, singer, children's writer and artist. Best known for his role as Herman Munster in the TV series *The Munsters*. (Died 1993.) |
| 100 | 12 Jul 1926 | Death of Gertrude Bell, British traveller, political administrator, archaeologist and writer. She helped explore and map Arabia, Asia Minor, Mesopotamia, Palestine and Syria; helped support the Hashemite dynasties in Jordan and Iraq; and played a leading role in establishing modern Iraq. (Overdose of sleeping pills, aged 57 ) |
| 100 | 14 Jul 1926 | Birth of Harry Dean Stanton, American film actor.<br>Known for his supporting roles. (Died 2017.) |
| 100 | 15 Jul 1926 | The first bus service began operating in Mumbai, India.<br>It was run by the Bombay Electric Supply & Tramway Company Limited. |
| 100 | 15 Jul 1926 | Birth of Leopoldo Galtieri, President/military ruler of Argentina (1981–82). He ordered Argentina's invasion of the Falkland Islands.<br>(Died 2003.) |
| 100 | 16 Jul 1926 | The world's first underwater colour photograph was published in *National Geographic* magazine. The photo of a hogfish was taken off the Florida Keys in the USA. The photographer detonated several pounds of magnesium flash powder on a raft to illuminate the scene fifteen feet beneath the surface. |
| 100 | 19 Jul 1926 | General Theodorus Pangalos became President of Greece.<br>He was deposed in a coup one month later. |
| 100 | 21 Jul 1926 | Birth of Bill Pertwee, British comedy actor. Best known for his role as the Chief ARP air raid warden William Hodges in the television sitcom *Dad's Army*. (Died 2013.) |

## JULY 2026

| Ann. | Date | Event |
|---|---|---|
| 90 | 5 Jun 1936 to Aug | A heatwave struck the USA. Temperature records were broken in Arkansas, Indiana, Kansas, Louisiana, Maryland, Michigan, Nebraska, New Jersey, North Dakota, Pennsylvania, South Dakota, Texas, West Virginia and Wisconsin. All of the records still stand apart from South Dakota (broken in 2006) and Texas (broken in 1994). |
| 90 | 6 Jul 1936 | Birth of Dave Allen, Irish comedian. (Died 2005.) |
| 90 | 7 Jul 1936 | American businessman Henry F. Phillips was granted five U.S. patents for the Phillips (cross-head) screw and screwdriver. (U.S. Patents 2,046,343 and 2,046,837–40.) |
| 90 | 11 Jul 1936 | The Triborough Bridge (now the Robert F. Kennedy Bridge) opened to traffic in New York City, USA. It links Manhattan, the Bronx and Queens. |
| 90 | 17 Jul 1936 to 1 Apr 1939 | The Spanish Civil War. Nationalist victory. On 26th July 1936, Germany and Italy joined the war, supporting General Francisco Franco's Nationalists. Portugal also joined later. The Soviet Union, Mexico and France supported the Republicans. |
| 90 | 18 Jul 1936 | Sicilian-born American mobster Charles 'Lucky' Luciano was sentenced to 30 – 50 years in prison after being convicted of 62 counts of compulsory prostitution. He was released in February 1946 and deported to Italy. |
| 90 | 18 Jul 1936 | The first Oscar Meyer Wienermobile was produced. The iconic hot dog-shaped vehicles advertise Oscar Meyer products in the USA and are still used today. |
| 90 | 18 Jul 1936 | The first episode of the experimental radio drama series *Columbia Workshop* was broadcast on CBS in the USA. It ran until 1943, and from 1946 to 1947. It later became *CBS Radio Workshop*, which ran from 1956 to 1957. |
| 90 | 20 Jul 1936 | The Montreux Convention was signed in Switzerland. It allowed Turkey to fortify the Dardanelles strait and to close the strait to warships when it was at war, and granted free passage to merchant ships. |
| 90 | 20 Jul 1936 | Birth of Alistair MacLeod, Canadian novelist, short story writer and creative writing teacher. Best known for his novel *No Great Mischief*, and for his short stories. (Died 2014.) |
| 90 | 21 Jul 1936 | Death of Georg Michaelis, Chancellor of Germany (1917). |
| 90 | 23 Jul 1936 | The Unified Socialist Party of Catalonia was founded in Spain when four left-wing groups merged. It was dissolved in 1997. |
| 90 | 24 Jul 1936 | The speaking clock telephone service was launched in the UK. (The world's first speaking clock service began in France in February 1933.) |
| 90 | 26 Jul 1936 | The Canadian National Vimy Memorial was unveiled in France by King Edward VIII – in one of his last official duties before he abdicated. It commemorates members of the Canadian Expeditionary Force killed in WWI and other Canadian soldiers killed (or presumed dead) in France who have no known grave. |
| 90 | 31 Jul 1936 | The International Olympic Committee announced that Tokyo, Japan would host the 1940 Olympics. In July 1938 Japan forfeited the games following the outbreak of the Second Sino–Japanese War. The 1940 Olympics were awarded to Helsinki, Finland instead, but they were eventually cancelled because of the outbreak of WWII. |

## JULY 2026

| Ann. | Date | Event |
|---|---|---|
| 80 | 1 Jul 1946 | Operation Crossroads, Bikini Atoll, Pacific Ocean. The USA conducted its first atomic bomb tests since the bombing of Nagasaki, Japan in 1945. The purpose of the tests was to determine the effect of nuclear explosions on warships. The first test ('Able') was conducted on 1st July. The bomb was detonated 520 feet (158 metres) above the fleet of warships monitoring the test. The second test ('Baker') was conducted on 25th July. The bomb was detonated 90 feet (27 metres) underwater. This was the first underwater nuclear explosion. |
| 80 | 1 Jul 1946 | Sarawak became a British Crown Colony. It joined the Federation of Malaysia in 1963. |
| 80 | 1 Jul 1946 | Birth of Mick Aston, British archaeologist. Best known as the resident academic on the television series *Time Team*. (Died 2013.) |
| 80 | 4 Jul 1946 | The Philippines gained its independence from the USA. |
| 80 | 4 Jul 1946 | The Kielce pogrom, Poland. An outbreak of anti-Jewish violence and rioting, initiated by the Polish Communist armed forces following a false accusation of child kidnapping. 42 Jews were killed. |
| 80 | 5 Jul 1946 | The first bikini two-piece swimsuit was unveiled at a fashion show in Paris, France. It was created by French designer Louis Réard. It was named after the U.S. atomic bomb test that took place at Bikini Atoll in the Pacific Ocean earlier that week (see 1st July). |
| 80 | 7 Jul 1946 | The first American saint, Mother Frances Xavier Cabrini, was canonised by Pope Pius XII. In 1900 she founded the Missionary Sisters of the Sacred Heart, which supported Italian immigrants to the USA. |
| 80 | 9 Jul 1946 | Birth of Bon Scott, Scottish-born Australian rock singer and songwriter (AC/DC). (Died 1980.) |
| 80 | 10 Jul 1946 | Hungary set the world record for hyperinflation: 348.46 percent per day. Prices doubled every eleven hours. By the end of the month, its currency, the pengo, was effectively worthless. A new currency, the forint, was introduced on 1st August. (1 forint equalled 400 octillion pengos.) |
| 80 | 11 Jul 1946 | Death of Paul Nash, British Surrealist artist, war artist and photographer. He played a leading role in the development of Modernism in British art and is regarded as one of the most important landscape artists of the first half of the 20th century. |
| 80 | 12 Jul 1946 | The first episode of the radio drama series *The Adventures of Sam Spade* was broadcast on ABC in the USA. It ran until 1951, transferring to CBS later in 1946 and to NBC in 1949. |
| 80 | 14 Jul 1946 | *The Common Sense Book of Baby and Child Care* by Benjamin Spock was published. It is one of the best-selling books in history (second only to the Bible in the USA during the 20th century). |
| 80 | 15 Jul 1946 | North Borneo became a British Crown Colony. It joined the Federation of Malaysia in 1963 as the state of Sabah. |
| 80 | 15 Jul 1946 | The Anglo–American loan: the USA loaned the UK $3.75 billion (£1.9 billion) to support its overseas expenditure following WWII. The UK made annual repayments, and repaid the loan in December 2006. |

## JULY 2026

| Ann. | Date | Event |
|---|---|---|
| 80 | 15 Jul 1946 | Death of Razor Smith, British cricketer. One of the leading bowlers of the early 20th century, but frequent injuries kept him out of many matches. |
| 80 | 21 Jul 1946 to 24 Jul 1948 | Bread and flour rationing was introduced in Britain. The country's wheat crop had been ruined by continual rain and there was a worldwide wheat shortage. |
| 80 | 21 Jul 1946 | The first successful landing and take-off of a jet aircraft on a U.S. aircraft carrier (the *USS Franklin D. Roosevelt*). |
| 80 | 21 Jul 1946 | Death of Gualberto Villarroel, President of Bolivia (1943–46). (Killed by anti-government rioters, aged 37.) Succeeded by interim President Néstor Guillén. |
| 80 | 22 Jul 1946 | The King David Hotel bombing, Jerusalem, Mandatory Palestine. The Irgun (a militant right-wing Zionist group) bombed the hotel which housed the British administrative headquarters for Palestine. 91 people were killed. |
| 80 | 24 Jul 1946 | American comedy duo Dean Martin and Jerry Lewis performed together for the first time, at Club 500 in Atlantic City, New Jersey. They were not well received, so on the second night they threw out their scripts and ad-libbed their performance – successfully. Their final show was on 24th July 1956 – exactly ten years after they started. |
| 80 | 26 Jul 1946 | Aloha Airlines began operations at Honolulu International Airport, Hawaii. It ceased operations in March 2008. |
| 80 | 27 Jul 1946 | Death of Gertrude Stein, American Modernist/avant-garde novelist, poet and playwright. A noted eccentric. She proclaimed herself 'the creative literary mind of the century'. |
| 80 | 28 Jul 1946 | Death of Alphonsa of the Immaculate Conception. Indian nun and educator. The first woman of Indian origin to be canonised as a saint. |
| 80 | 29 Jul 1946 | World War II: the Paris Peace Conference, France. The Allies negotiated treaties with Bulgaria, Finland, Hungary, Italy and Romania, which enabled those countries to resume their status as sovereign states. The treaties were signed on 10th February 1947. |
| 75 | 3 Jul 1951 | Birth of Jean-Claude Duvalier, ('Baby Doc'), President of Haiti (1971–86). Son of the previous president, François Duvalier ('Papa Doc'). (Died 2014.) |
| 75 | 5 Jul 1951 | American engineer William Shockley of Bell Laboratories announced that he had invented the junction transistor. (Patented 25th September 1951.) |
| 75 | 9 Jul 1951 | Death of Harry Heilmann, American baseball player (Detroit Tigers, Cincinnati Reds) and radio announcer (Detroit Tigers). |
| 75 | 10 Jul 1951 | Korean War: protracted armistice negotiations began in Kaesong, North Korea. Negotiations went on for two years – fighting continued throughout. |
| 75 | 13 Jul 1951 | The Great Flood, Kansas and Missouri, USA. Seventeen people were killed and more than half a million made homeless. |
| 75 | 13 Jul 1951 | Death of Arnold Schoenberg, Austrian-born American composer. One of the most influential composers of the 20th century. Leader of the Second Viennese School. The Nazi Party labelled his music 'degenerate' because he was Jewish. He emigrated to the USA. |

**JULY 2026**

| Ann. | Date | Event |
|------|------|-------|
| 75 | 14 Jul 1951 | The first sporting event to be broadcast in colour on U.S. television. CBS broadcast the Molly Pitcher Handicap horse race from Oceanport in New Jersey. |
| 75 | 15 Jul 1951 | Birth of Gregory Isaacs, Jamaican reggae singer and songwriter. (Died 2010.) |
| 75 | 16 Jul 1951 | King Léopold III of Belgium abdicated to solve the 'Royal Question' of whether his actions during WWII were contrary to the Belgian Constitution. He had been in exile since 1944, and his return to Belgium in 1950 was met with violence and strikes. He was succeeded by his son, Baudouin I, on 17th July. |
| 75 | 16 Jul 1951 | J. D. Salinger's novel *The Catcher in the Rye* was published. |
| 75 | 20 Jul 1951 | Death of Abdullah I, King of Jordan (1946–51). (Assassinated by a Palestinian nationalist.) Succeeded by his son, Talal, who ruled for only a year before abdicating because of mental illness. |
| 75 | 20 Jul 1951 | Death of Wilhelm, Crown Prince of Germany. The last Crown Prince of the German Empire and the Kingdom of Prussia. Eldest child of Wilhelm II, the last German Emperor. |
| 75 | 21 Jul 1951 | Birth of Robin Williams, American film and television actor and comedian (*Mork & Mindy, Good Morning, Vietnam, Dead Poets Society, Mrs. Doubtfire*, and many more). (Committed suicide in 2014.) |
| 75 | 23 Jul 1951 | Death of Philippe Pétain, Prime Minister of Vichy France during WWII. He was sentenced to death for treason in 1945, but it was commuted to life imprisonment because of his age and WWI service. |
| 75 | 26 Jul 1951 | The world première of the Walt Disney film *Alice in Wonderland*, in London, UK. Released USA: 28th July. UK: 20th August. |
| 75 | 29 Jul 1951 | The first Miss World beauty pageant was held in London, UK. The first pageant was known as the Festival of Britain Bikini Contest, but it became an annual event afterwards. |
| 70 | 4 Jul 1956 | Independence National Historical Park was established in Philadelphia, Pennsylvania, USA. The park contains Independence Hall, the Liberty Bell, the First Bank of the United States, and other historic buildings connected with the founding of the United States of America. It is known as 'America's most historic square mile'. |
| 70 | 7 Jul 1956 | The first successful ascent of Gasherbrum II (also known as K4) in the Karakoram mountain range (between Pakistan and China), by an Austrian team. It is the thirteenth-highest mountain in the world. |
| 70 | 9 Jul 1956 | The 1956 Amorgos earthquake and tsunami, Cyclades islands, Aegean Sea. The largest earthquake in Greece in the 20th century. It caused significant damage, particularly on the island of Santorini. 53 people were killed and 100 injured. |
| 70 | 13 Jul 1956 | Elvis Presley's hit song *Hound Dog* was released. He had performed the song on television for the first time on 5th June, to widespread press criticism. Critics accused him of influencing juvenile delinquency, and nicknamed him 'Elvis the Pelvis' for his exaggerated movements. |
| 70 | 15 Jul 1956 | Birth of Ian Curtis, British post-punk singer, songwriter and musician (Joy Division). (Committed suicide in 1980.) |

## JULY 2026

| Ann. | Date | Event |
|------|------|-------|
| 70 | 16 Jul 1956 | The Ringling Bros. and Barnum & Bailey Circus gave its final performance under the big top, in Pittsburgh, Pennsylvania, USA.<br>All future shows were held in indoor arenas and stadiums.<br>(It closed in 2017 but aims to relaunch in 2023 without animal performers.) |
| 70 | 17 Jul 1956 | The romantic musical comedy film *High Society* was released in the USA.<br>It was Grace Kelly's last film before she became Princess Grace of Monaco.<br>UK release: 20th December. |
| 70 | 19 Jul 1956 | The U.S. Secretary of State, John Foster Dulles, announced that the USA would not lend Egypt any money to construct the Aswan Dam, after the Soviet Union offered Egypt a $1.2 billion loan for its construction.<br>On 20th July, Britain also refused to lend Egypt any money for the dam.<br>In retaliation, the President of Egypt, Gamal Abdel Nasser, nationalised the Suez Canal. (See 26th July 1956.) |
| 70 | 24 Jul 1956 | Khartoum University College in Sudan was granted university status and became the University of Khartoum. |
| 70 | 25 Jul 1956 | The Italian ocean liner *SS Andrea Doria* sank after colliding with the Swedish American Line's *MS Stockholm* off Nantucket, Massachusetts, USA.<br>1,660 passengers and crew were rescued by other ships. 46 people died. |
| 70 | 26 Jul 1956 | The President of Egypt, Gamal Abdel Nasser, nationalised the Suez Canal, froze the assets of the Suez Canal Company, and closed the canal to Israeli shipping, after the USA and UK refused to finance the Aswan High Dam. This led to the Suez Crisis in October. |
| 70 | 30 Jul 1956 | The U.S. Congress adopted 'In God We Trust' as the official national motto of the United States. |
| 65 | 1 Jul 1961 | Haleakalā National Park was established in Hawaii, USA. |
| 65 | 1 Jul 1961 | Birth of Diana, Princess of Wales. (Killed in a car crash in 1997.) |
| 65 | 2 Jul 1961 | Death of Ernest Hemingway, American novelist and short story writer. Winner of the 1954 Nobel Prize in Literature. Best known for *For Whom the Bell Tolls*, *A Farewell to Arms* and *The Old Man and the Sea*. (Suicide.) |
| 65 | 4 Jul 1961 | The Soviet nuclear-powered submarine *K-19* suffered a complete loss of coolant to one of its two reactors during its maiden voyage.<br>The crew rigged up a secondary coolant system to prevent a meltdown, but they sacrificed their lives to do so: 22 of them died from radiation poisoning over the next two years.<br>(The submarine suffered so many accidents while in service that crew members nicknamed it 'Hiroshima'. It was decommissioned in 1990.) |
| 65 | 8 Jul 1961 | The Portuguese cargo liner *Save* ran aground and caught fire off Quelimane, Mozambique. 259 of the 549 passengers and crew were killed. |
| 65 | 9 Jul 1961 | Death of Whittaker Chambers, American writer, editor, Communist and Soviet spy. He famously testified against State Department official Alger Hiss in 'the trial of the century' in 1949–50. |
| 65 | 12 Jul 1961 | The city of Pune in India was flooded when the Panshet Dam and the Khadakwasla Dam burst. Around 1,000 people were killed.<br>(Cause: heavy rain caused the reservoir levels to rise so rapidly that the dams could not contain it.) |

## JULY 2026

| Ann. | Date | Event |
|---|---|---|
| 65 | 17 Jul 1961 | The Walt Disney drama film *Greyfriars Bobby* was released in the USA. UK: 31st July. |
| 65 | 17 Jul 1961 | Birth of Jeremy Hardy, British comedian. Best known for the radio panel shows *The News Quiz* and *I'm Sorry I Haven't a Clue*. (Died 2019.) |
| 65 | 17 Jul 1961 | Death of Ty Cobb, American baseball player. |
| 65 | 19 Jul 1961 to 23rd | Algerian War – the Bizerte Crisis, Tunisia. Tunisia blockaded the French naval base at Bizerte, aiming to force the French to leave. This led to a three-day battle in which 654 people were killed. The French captured the town on 23rd July. They returned the naval base to Tunisia in October 1963. |
| 65 | 20 Jul 1961 | The pop song *Take Good Care of My Baby* by Bobby Vee was released. |
| 65 | 21 Jul 1961 | Gus Grissom became the second American to travel into space. He made a 15-minute sub-orbital journey in the *Liberty Bell 7*. |
| 65 | 22 Jul 1961 | Women in Spain were legally guaranteed the same wage as their male counterparts. |
| 65 | 23 Jul 1961 | The Sandinista National Liberation Front (FSLN) was founded in Nicaragua. |
| 65 | 25 Jul 1961 | Cold War – the Berlin Crisis in Germany: U.S. President John F. Kennedy gave a televised speech in which he said he was willing to renew talks with the Soviet Union but would ask Congress to significantly increase military spending. He also announced that he was planning to triple the draft and call up reserves. And he warned that any attack on Berlin would be an attack on NATO. He said: 'We seek peace, but we shall not surrender.' |
| 65 | 25 Jul 1961 | British electronics engineer Clive Sinclair founded Sinclair Radionics. The company produced radios and hi-fi equipment, but later developed pocket calculators, digital watches, portable televisions and scientific equipment. He left the company in 1979. It is now known as Aim & Thurlby Thandar Instruments. |
| 65 | 26 Jul 1961 | Birth of Felix Dexter, St Kitts-born British television and radio actor and comedian. (Died 2013.) |
| 65 | 31 Jul 1961 | The first-ever tie in a Major League Baseball All-Star Game. Rain stopped play after nine innings at Fenway Park in Boston, Massachusetts, and the game was called at 1 – 1. |
| 60 | 1 Jul 1966 | The Medicare health insurance programme began operating in the USA. It offered health insurance to those aged 65 and older. |
| 60 | 1 Jul 1966 | Colour television broadcasts began in Canada. |
| 60 | 1 Jul 1966 | Joaquin Balaguer became President of the Dominican Republic for the second time (until 1978). He was also President in 1960–62 and 1986–96. |
| 60 | 1 Jul 1966 | The novelty song *They're Coming to Take Me Away, Ha-Haaa!* by Napoleon XIV was released. |
| 60 | 2 Jul 1966 | France carried out its first nuclear test in the Pacific, at Moruroa Atoll, French Polynesia. The bomb was code-named Aldébaran. |

# JULY 2026

| Ann. | Date | Event |
|---|---|---|
| 60 | 4 Jul 1966 | The Beatles declined an invitation to visit the presidential palace in Manila during their tour of the Philippines. There was a national backlash, and violence at the airport as they tried to leave the country at the end of their tour. The band was also annoyed that the audience had been so far from the stage, behind a wire fence, when they performed, and the sound was terrible. This was a major factor in their decision to stop performing live. Their final tour of the USA in August also went badly. Their final show was at Candlestick Park in San Francisco, California on 29th August. |
| 60 | 6 Jul 1966 | Malawi became a republic. Hastings Banda became its first President. |
| 60 | 6 Jul 1966 | Death of Sad Sam Jones, American baseball pitcher. |
| 60 | 8 Jul 1966 | Ntare V became the last King of Burundi after deposing his father, Mwambutsa IV Bangiriceng.<br>The monarchy was abolished in November and Burundi became a republic. Ntare V was executed during a Hutu uprising in 1972. |
| 60 | 10 Jul 1966 | Dr Martin Luther King Jr.'s Chicago Freedom Movement held its first large-scale rally, at Soldier Field in Chicago, Illinois, USA.<br>About 35,000 people took part (some sources say 60,000). |
| 60 | 11 Jul 1966 | The first episode of the television game show *The Newlywed Game* was broadcast on ABC in the USA. It ran until 2013. |
| 60 | 11 Jul 1966 | Birth of Melanie Appleby, British pop singer (Mel & Kim). (Died 1990.) |
| 60 | 13 Jul 1966 to 14th | American mass murderer Richard Speck killed eight student nurses in their residence in South Deering, Chicago, Illinois, USA.<br>He was convicted in April 1967 and sentenced to death, later commuted to life imprisonment. He died in prison in 1991. |
| 60 | 15 Jul 1966 | A ban on coloured guards and porters at London's Euston Station and St. Pancras Station ended. Asquith Xavier, a guard who had applied for a job at Euston and was refused, was finally given the job.<br>The lifting of the colour bar applied to all London stations. |
| 60 | 15 Jul 1966 to 3 Aug | Vietnam War – Operation Hastings.<br>U.S. and South Vietnamese forces launched a successful operation to push the North Vietnamese forces back across the Demilitarised Zone. |
| 60 | 18 Jul 1966 to 23rd | The Hough riots, Cleveland, Ohio, USA.<br>A riot broke out in the predominantly African-American neighbourhood, mainly because of racial tension and poverty. Up to a thousand residents were involved in the riots. Four people were killed, fifty injured and 275 arrested. There was widespread looting, arson and gunfire, and the Ohio National Guard was called in to assist police.<br>After the riots, many people moved away and the area went into decline. |
| 60 | 18 Jul 1966 | NASA launched its *Gemini 10* manned spacecraft, with astronauts John W. Young and Michael Collins on board.<br>It returned to Earth safely three days later after making 43 orbits. |
| 60 | 18 Jul 1966 | Death of Bobby Fuller, American rock singer, songwriter and guitarist (the Bobby Fuller Four). Best known for the songs *I Fought The Law* (later covered by The Clash) and *Love's Made a Fool of You*.<br>(Found dead in his car, aged 23. Possible accident, suicide or murder.) |

## JULY 2026

| Ann. | Date | Event |
|------|------|-------|
| 60 | 23 Jul 1966 | Death of Montgomery Clift, American stage and film actor. Noted for his emotional depth and sense of vulnerability in films such as *Red River, A Place in the Sun, I Confess, From Here to Eternity, The Young Lions* and *The Misfits*. |
| 60 | 25 Jul 1966 | The Motown pop song *You Can't Hurry Love* by The Supremes was released. |
| 60 | 29 Jul 1966 | American singer and musician Bob Dylan crashed his motorcycle and was seriously injured. He withdrew from public life while he recovered, also citing exhaustion. During this period, he recorded songs at his house and in a nearby basement with The Band (then known as the Hawks). The recordings were eventually released as *The Basement Tapes*. He resumed his recording career in October 1967, but didn't resume touring until 1974. |
| 60 | 29 Jul 1966 | Death of Johnson Aguiyi-Ironsi, Military Head of State of Nigeria (January – July 1966) who seized power during the 15th January coup. (Assassinated in the July Counter Coup.) |
| 60 | 30 Jul 1966 | The 1966 FIFA World Cup final. England beat Germany 4-2. English player Geoff Hurst became the first (and only) player to score a hat-trick in a World Cup final. At the time of writing this remains England's only World Cup win. |
| 50 | 1 Jul 1976 | Madeira was granted autonomy from Portugal. This is now celebrated as Madeira Day. |
| 50 | 1 Jul 1976 | The first Apple computer, the Apple I, went on sale (for $666.66) Buyers received a single circuit board and had to provide their own case, power supply, keyboard, TV (for display) and a cassette recorder for storage – though this required an add-on interface (sold separately). About 200 were built, of which about 175 were sold. |
| 50 | 2 Jul 1976 | North Vietnam and South Vietnam were reunited as the Socialist Republic of Vietnam, with Hanoi as its capital. Hanoi was formerly the capital of North Vietnam. |
| 50 | 2 Jul 1976 | The U.S. Supreme Court ruled that the death penalty did not violate the U.S. Constitution, provided that sentencing made provision for mercy claims. Mandatory death penalty was considered a 'cruel and unusual punishment' that violated the 8th and 14th Amendments. The capital punishment laws in Florida, Georgia and Texas were upheld, while those in Louisiana and North Carolina were rejected. (Gregg v. Georgia.) |
| 50 | 4 Jul 1976 | Operation Entebbe. Israeli commandos staged a counter-terrorist hostage-rescue mission at Entebbe Airport in Uganda following the hijacking of an Air France plane on 27th June. |
| 50 | 4 Jul 1976 | Former U.S. President George Washington was posthumously appointed General of the Armies of the United States. This made him the highest-ranking military officer in U.S. history. He was the 1st U.S. President, from 1789 to 1797. |

## JULY 2026

| Ann. | Date | Event |
|------|------|-------|
| 50 | 4 Jul 1976 | British punk rock band The Clash played their first live performance. They supported the Sex Pistols at the Black Swan bar/nightclub in Sheffield. |
| 50 | 6 Jul 1976 | The U.S. Naval Academy began admitting women. (See also: 7th July 1976.) |
| 50 | 7 Jul 1976 | The first female cadets were admitted to the U.S. Military Academy at West Point in New York. |
| 50 | 7 Jul 1976 | Death of Norman Foster, American film and television actor, film director and screenwriter. He directed many *Charlie Chan* and *Mr Moto* films. Husband of the actress Claudette Colbert. |
| 50 | 8 Jul 1976 | The first Indonesian satellite, *Palapa A1*, was launched. |
| 50 | 10 Jul 1976 | The Seveso disaster, northern Italy. An industrial accident at a chemical plant released a cloud of dioxins into residential areas, affecting around 120,000 people. 3,300 farm animals died and a further 80,000 were slaughtered. Some people suffered long-term health issues. |
| 50 | 11 Jul 1976 | The last slide rule in the USA was produced by Keuffel & Esser. It was presented to the Smithsonian Institution. The company had been making slide rules since 1891. They were rendered obsolete by electronic calculators. |
| 50 | 12 Jul 1976 | Death of Ted Mack, American broadcaster, musician and bandleader. Best known as the host of *The Original Amateur Hour* radio and TV series. |
| 50 | 12 Jul 1976 | The first episode of the television game show *Family Feud* was broadcast on ABC in the USA. There are many international versions. In the UK it is known as *Family Fortunes*. |
| 50 | 14 Jul 1976 | António Ramalho Eanes became President of Portugal (until 1986). |
| 50 | 15 Jul 1976 | Death of Paul Gallico, American novelist, short story writer and sports journalist. Best known for *The Snow Goose* and *The Poseidon Adventure*. |
| 50 | 15 Jul 1976 | The Chowchilla school bus kidnapping, California, USA. Kidnappers abducted a school bus driver and 26 children, and kept them captive in a quarry. The captives escaped unharmed after about sixteen hours. The quarry owner's son and two of his friends were convicted and sentenced to life imprisonment. (The two friends were released in 2015.) |
| 50 | 17 Jul 1976 | Indonesia annexed East Timor. It was not recognised by the international community. Indonesia relinquished its control in 1999. In May 2002, East Timor became the first new sovereign state of the 21st century. |
| 50 | 17 Jul 1976 to 1 Aug | The 1976 Summer Olympic Games were held in Montreal, Canada. Most African nations (and some others) boycotted the event because the International Olympic Committee refused to ban athletes who had competed in South Africa during apartheid. |
| 50 | 18 Jul 1976 | The International Convention on the Suppression and Punishment of the Crime of Apartheid came into effect. |
| 50 | 18 Jul 1976 | Romanian gymnast Nadia Comaneci, aged 14, became the first female to score a perfect 10 in an Olympic gymnastic event. She defected to the USA in 1989 and became a naturalised citizen in 2001. |

## JULY 2026

| Ann. | Date | Event |
|------|------|-------|
| 50 | 19 Jul 1976 | Sagarmatha National Park was established in Nepal. |
| 50 | 20 Jul 1976 | NASA's *Viking 1* lander successfully landed on Mars and sent back the first photo taken from the surface of Mars. |
| 50 | 21 Jul 1976 to 23rd | The first Legionnaire's Disease outbreak. The American Legion held its annual convention in Philadelphia, Pennsylvania. Within a week, 25 attendees had died from the first recognised cases of Legionnaire's Disease. 221 attendees contracted the disease and 34 of them eventually died (some sources give different figures). The bacterium was discovered in the hotel's air conditioning system, and was named *Legionella* after its first victims. |
| 50 | 21 Jul 1976 | Death of Christopher Ewart-Biggs, British Ambassador to Ireland (1976 for two weeks in July). (Assassinated by the IRA, aged 54.) |
| 50 | 22 Jul 1976 | Japan made its last reparation payment to the Philippines in respect of war crimes it committed during WWII. In 1956 it had been ordered to pay $550 million, spread over twenty years. Much (or all?) of this was paid in products and services rather than cash. |
| 50 | 25 Jul 1976 | NASA's *Viking 1* spacecraft took the famous photo of the 'Face on Mars'. NASA released the photo on 31st July. Images from more recent missions show that it was an optical illusion. |
| 50 | 25 Jul 1976 | The opera *Einstein on the Beach* by Philip Glass was performed for the first time, in Avignon, France. |
| 50 | 26 Jul 1976 | Capital punishment was abolished in Canada. The last execution in Canada was in 1962. |
| 50 | 28 Jul 1976 | The Tangshan earthquake, China. More than 240,000 people were killed (some sources claim at least 650,000, as the official figure only included those in the immediate area). Going by the larger estimate, it was the world's worst earthquake of the 20th century (by death toll) and the second-worst in recorded history. |
| 50 | 28 Jul 1976 | The official world airspeed record was broken by Captain Eldon W. Joersz and Major George T. Morgan in a Lockheed SR-71 Blackbird at Beale Air Force Base, California, USA. The record of 2,193.2 mph still stands. |
| 50 | 29 Jul 1976 | American serial killer David Berkowitz (the 'Son of Sam') killed his first victim in New York City. He killed his sixth and final victim in July 1977 and was arrested in August. In June 1978 he was given six life sentences. |
| 50 | 29 Jul 1976 | The pier-head of Southend Pier in Essex, England was destroyed by fire. It is the world's longest pier. It reopened in 1986, but shortly afterwards a tanker crashed into it, creating a seventy-foot gap. It reopened again in 1989. Two further fires in 1999 and 2005 caused significant damage. After restoration and redevelopment, it reopened in July 2012. |
| 50 | 31 Jul 1976 | The Big Thompson Canyon flash flood, Colorado, USA. A thunderstorm dumped 12 inches of rain in less than four hours, causing a 20-foot (6-metre) wall of water to sweep down the steep, narrow canyon. 143 people were killed. 418 houses and 52 businesses were destroyed, and part of the U.S. Route 34 highway was swept away. |

**JULY 2026**

| Ann. | Date | Event |
|---|---|---|
| 50 | 31 Jul 1976 | The soft rock song *If You Leave Me Now* by Chicago was released. It became the band's first No. 1 hit. |
| 40 | 3 Jul 1986 to 5th | Liberty Weekend, New York City, USA – a celebration of the centennial and restoration of the Statue of Liberty. The statue reopened to the public on 5th July, having been closed for restoration since 1984. |
| 40 | 3 Jul 1986 | Death of Rudy Vallee, American singer and bandleader. |
| 40 | 8 Jul 1986 | Kurt Waldheim, the former Secretary-General of the United Nations, became President of Austria (until 1992). His election was controversial as he had served in the Wehrmacht (Nazi Germany's armed forces) during WWII. He denied taking part in any war crimes or knowing they had taken place near where he was serving. Several countries, including the USA, refused to have any dealings with him. |
| 40 | 9 Jul 1986 | The Meese Report (the U.S. Attorney General's Commission on Pornography) was published. The controversial report linked hardcore porn to crime and recommended stricter enforcement of obscenity laws. |
| 40 | 9 Jul 1986 | New Zealand passed the Homosexual Law Reform Act, legalising homosexuality. |
| 40 | 10 Jul 1986 | Death of Patriarch Nicholas VI of Alexandria, Greek Orthodox Patriarch of Alexandria (1968–86). |
| 40 | 12 Jul 1986 | The Orange Parade riots, Portadown, County Armagh, Northern Ireland. |
| 40 | 14 Jul 1986 | The Plaza República Dominicana bombing, Madrid, Spain. The Basque separatist group ETA detonated a car bomb. Twelve people were killed and 32 injured. The twelve people who were killed were all members of the civil guard. |
| 40 | 14 Jul 1986 | The U.S. première of the science fiction action film *Aliens*. Released: 18th July. UK: 29th August. It was the sequel to the 1979 film *Alien*. Two more sequels were released in 1992 and 1997, a prequel series in 2012 and 2017, and a crossover series *Alien vs. Predator* in 2004 and 2007. A television series is due to begin in 2023. |
| 40 | 14 Jul 1986 | Death of Raymond Loewy, French-born American industrial designer. He designed the logos for numerous well-known companies and brands, including Shell, Exxon, TWA and BP, as well as the Air Force One livery, and the interiors of the Concorde supersonic airliner and NASA's *Skylab* space station. He also worked on locomotives and became known as the 'father of streamlining'. |
| 40 | 15 Jul 1986 | Death of Benny Rubin, American comedian and film actor. |
| 40 | 23 Jul 1986 | The marriage of Prince Andrew and Sarah Ferguson, in Westminster Abbey, London, UK. They became the Duke and Duchess of York. They were divorced in 1996 |
| 40 | 23 Jul 1986 | The U.S. Food and Drug Administration (FDA) approved the first genetically engineered vaccine for humans – a hepatitis B vaccine. The recombinant vaccine was derived from yeast and is still in use today. Previous hepatitis B vaccines were made from human blood, meaning that supply was low and there was a risk of contamination from HIV/AIDS and other infections. (Germany was the first to approve it in May 1986.) |

**JULY 2026**

| Ann. | Date | Event |
|------|------|-------|
| 40 | 24 Jul 1986 | Apartheid: South Africa's black citizens were no longer required to carry passbooks (internal passports) when travelling. Passbooks were designed to segregate the population, prevent black citizens from entering restricted areas or premises, and to prove they were lawfully employed. South Africa's pass laws were repealed in November 1986. |
| 40 | 25 Jul 1986 | Death of Vincente Minnelli, American film director. Best known for his musicals. Husband of the actress Judy Garland. Father of Liza Minnelli. |
| 40 | 25 Jul 1986 | Death of Ted Lyons, American baseball pitcher and manager (Chicago White Sox). |
| 40 | 26 Jul 1986 | Death of W. Averell Harriman, American statesman. A leading diplomat in relations between the USA and the Soviet Union during WWII and the Cold War. |
| 40 | 27 Jul 1986 | Greg Lemond became the first American cyclist to win the Tour de France. |
| 40 | 28 Jul 1986 | British estate agent Suzy Lamplugh failed to return from an appointment in London, sparking the biggest missing person investigation since Lord Lucan. She has never been found. |
| 30 | 1 Jul 1996 | The Rights of the Terminally Ill Act came into effect in Northern Territory, Australia, legalising voluntary euthanasia. It was overturned by the federal parliament in 1997. Four people died while the Act was in effect. |
| 30 | 1 Jul 1996 | Candidates taking the British driving test also had to pass a written exam for the first time. |
| 30 | 1 Jul 1996 | Death of Margaux Hemingway, American model and actress. Granddaughter of the writer Ernest Hemingway. (Suicide, aged 42.) |
| 30 | 1 Jul 1996 | Death of Steve Tesich, Serbian-born American screenwriter, playwright and novelist. Best known for *Breaking Away* and *The World According to Garp* |
| 30 | 2 Jul 1996 | Two American brothers, Lyle and Erik Menendez, were sentenced to life imprisonment for shooting and killing their wealthy parents in 1989. The brothers had argued that they had killed their father after suffering years of sexual and physical abuse. Prosecutors said they had killed their parents for their money. The trial was a national sensation when it was broadcast on Court TV. |
| 30 | 3 Jul 1996 | Boris Yeltsin was elected for a second term as President of Russia (until 1999), despite concerns about his health. |
| 30 | 4 Jul 1996 | Hotmail, one of the first webmail services, was launched. Microsoft acquired the company in December 1997. The service was replaced by Outlook.com in 2012–13. |
| 30 | 5 Jul 1996 to 18th | Hurricane Bertha hit the Leeward Islands, Puerto Rico, and North Carolina, the Mid-Atlantic States and New England in the USA. Twelve people were killed and it caused $335 million worth of damage. (There were also hurricanes named Bertha in 2008 and 2014.) |
| 30 | 5 Jul 1996 | Birth of Dolly the sheep, the first cloned mammal, at the Roslin Institute, in Edinburgh, Scotland. (Died 2003.) |

## JULY 2026

| Ann. | Date | Event |
|------|------|-------|
| 30 | 8 Jul 1996 | The Wolverhampton machete attack, England. A paranoid schizophrenic man entered St. Luke's Church of England infants' school during a teddy bears' picnic and attacked three children and four adults. In December he was sentenced to life imprisonment. Teacher Lisa Potts was awarded the George Medal for defending the children despite suffering severe injuries. |
| 30 | 8 Jul 1996 | British scientists Bob Sinden and Julian Crampton revealed their plan to use genetically engineered mosquitoes as 'flying syringes' that would immunise their victims against diseases such as malaria by biting them. A worldwide patent was granted in 2002. |
| 30 | 9 Jul 1996 | Lin Russell and her daughters Megan and Josie were savagely attacked by a schizophrenic man armed with a hammer at their home in Kent, UK. Lin and Megan died. Josie survived but suffered serious head injuries. Michael Stone was later convicted. |
| 30 | 9 Jul 1996 | A riot broke out at a football match in Tripoli, Libya when a team supported by the sons of Libyan leader Muammar Gadaffi scored a questionable goal that the referee allowed. Fans of the opposing team began shouting anti-Gadaffi slogans, prompting his sons and their bodyguards to fire their guns into the air and then into the crowd, causing a stampede and riot. Officially eight people were killed and 39 injured, but some sources say more than fifty were killed. |
| 30 | 9 Jul 1996 | Death of Melvin Belli, ('The King of Torts'), American lawyer who had many celebrity clients and was involved in several high-profile cases. He acted for Jack Ruby, who shot Lee Harvey Oswald, the accused assassin of U.S. President John F. Kennedy. |
| 30 | 10 Jul 1996 | NASA announced that its *Galileo* spacecraft had discovered a magnetic field around Jupiter's moon Ganymede. It is the only moon in the solar system known to have a magnetic field. Later analyses of *Galileo*'s data also found that Ganymede has an underground ocean. |
| 30 | 13 Jul 1996 | Death of Pandro S. Berman, American film producer (*The Hunchback of Notre Dame, National Velvet, The Picture of Dorian Gray, The Three Musketeers, Madame Bovary, The Prisoner of Zenda, Blackboard Jungle, Jailhouse Rock*). |
| 30 | 15 Jul 1996 | A Belgian Air Force Hercules plane crashed at Eindhoven Airport in the Netherlands and caught fire. The passengers included members of the Royal Netherlands Army marching band (Fanfarekorps). 34 people were killed and seven injured. (Cause: birds sucked into the engines.) |
| 30 | 15 Jul 1996 | MSNBC, the 24-hour television news channel, was launched in the USA. |
| 30 | 15 Jul 1996 | Death of Dana Hill, American film and television actress and voice actress. Best known for her role as Audrey Griswold in *National Lampoon's European Vacation*. (Diabetic coma and stroke, aged 32.) |
| 30 | 17 Jul 1996 | TWA Flight 800 exploded and crashed in the Atlantic shortly after taking off from John F. Kennedy International Airport in New York, USA. All 230 passengers and crew were killed. (Cause: faulty wiring caused a short circuit which ignited vapour in a fuel tank.) |
| 30 | 17 Jul 1996 | Death of Chas Chandler, British bass guitarist (The Animals), record producer and manager (Slade, Jimi Hendrix). |

**JULY 2026**

| Ann. | Date | Event |
|------|------|-------|
| 30 | 18 Jul 1996 to 25th | Sri Lankan Civil War – the Battle of Mullaitivu. Tamil Tiger victory. |
| 30 | 18 Jul 1996 | The Oakfield tornado, Wisconsin, USA. An F5 tornado hit the small town, injuring seventeen people and causing over $40 million worth of damage. |
| 30 | 18 Jul 1996 | The Israel general strike. Around 500,000 workers staged a general strike in protest of Prime Minister Benjamin Netanyahu's budget cuts, which targeted the poorest workers. The strike forced factories, banks and government offices to close, and also affected hospitals, utility services and airports. |
| 30 | 19 Jul 1996 to 20th | The Saguenay Flood, Quebec, Canada. Two weeks of heavy rain followed by a massive downpour led to the worst flood of the 20th century in Canada. Ten people were killed and it caused $1.5 billion worth of damage. It was one of the costliest natural disasters in Canadian history. |
| 30 | 19 Jul 1996 | Biljana Plavšić succeeded Radovan Karadžić as President of Republika Srpska in Bosnia and Herzegovina (until 1998). Karadžić became a fugitive until 2008. They were both later convicted of crimes against humanity for their roles in the Bosnian War. |
| 30 | 19 Jul 1996 to 4 Aug | The 1996 Olympic Games (also known as the Centennial Olympic Games) were held in Atlanta, Georgia, USA. (See also: 27th July 1996 – the Centennial Olympic Park bombing.) |
| 30 | 20 Jul 1996 | A bomb exploded at Reus airport in eastern Spain, injuring 35 people – mostly British tourists. The bomb was planted by Basque separatists. |
| 30 | 23 Jul 1996 | BSE ('mad cow disease'): British scientists reported that BSE could also be transmitted to sheep, according to laboratory tests. |
| 30 | 23 Jul 1996 | The first (experimental) high-definition (HD) television broadcasts in the USA were made by WRAL in Raleigh, North Carolina. |
| 30 | 23 Jul 1996 | Death of Jessica Mitford, American investigative journalist and writer. One of the six Mitford sisters. Known for her books *Hons and Rebels* and *The American Way of Death*. She was a member of Communist Party of the USA after WWII and refused to testify before the House Un-American Activities Committee. |
| 30 | 24 Jul 1996 | Terrorists from the Tamil Tigers organisation bombed a packed commuter train near Colombo, Sri Lanka. More than 60 people were killed and 400 injured. |
| 30 | 25 Jul 1996 | Pierre Buyoya became President of Burundi for the second time (until 2003) after Sylvestre Ntibantunganya was ousted in a military coup. |
| 30 | 27 Jul 1996 | The Centennial Olympic Park bombing, Atlanta, Georgia, USA. A bomb exploded during the 1996 Olympic Games. Two people were killed and more than 100 injured. |
| 30 | 28 Jul 1996 | The remains of Kennewick Man were discovered in Washington, USA. The skeleton of the prehistoric man, dating from around 7300 – 7600 BC, is one of the most complete ever found. Native American tribes claim him as one of their ancestors, but he is thought to be of Polynesian origin. |

## JULY 2026

| Ann. | Date | Event |
|---|---|---|
| 30 | 29 Jul 1996 | China carried out its last nuclear test.<br>It signed the Comprehensive Nuclear Test Ban Treaty on 24th September, but has not yet ratified it, and the Treaty has not yet come into force. China is one of eight nuclear powers that must ratify the Treaty before it comes into force. The USA has also not yet ratified it. |
| 30 | 30 Jul 1996 | Death of Claudette Colbert, French-born American stage and film actress. |
| 25 | 2 Jul 2001 | Barry George was convicted of killing British television presenter Jill Dando in April 1999. He was sentenced to life imprisonment.<br>He was acquitted in August 2008 and the case remains officially unsolved. |
| 25 | 2 Jul 2001 | American heart patient Robert Tools received the world's first self-contained artificial heart, the AbioCor. He survived for 151 days.<br>The AbioCor heart was implanted in fourteen other patients, but it was later abandoned. |
| 25 | 3 Jul 2001 | Vladivostok Air Flight 352 stalled and crashed on approach to Irkutsk Airport in Russia. All 145 passengers and crew were killed.<br>(Cause: pilot error.) (See also: 9th July 2005.) |
| 25 | 6 Jul 2001 | Former FBI agent Robert Hanssen pleaded guilty to fifteen counts of espionage. He passed classified information to Soviet and Russian intelligence services for 22 years.<br>He also betrayed a Soviet CIA informant who was later executed.<br>He was sentenced to life imprisonment in May 2002. |
| 25 | 7 Jul 2001 | The Bradford race riots, West Yorkshire, UK. 120 police officers were injured. |
| 25 | 15 Jul 2001 | The computer worm Code Red was discovered to be attacking computers running the Microsoft IIS web server. It defaced web pages.<br>It was the first successful large-scale mixed-threat attack on enterprise networks. The peak of the infection was on 19th July. |
| 25 | 16 Jul 2001 | China and Russia signed the Treaty of Good-Neighbourliness and Friendly Cooperation (also known as the Sino–Russian Treaty of Friendship). |
| 25 | 18 Jul 2001 to 23rd | The Howard Street Tunnel Fire, Baltimore, Maryland, USA.<br>A freight train derailed in the tunnel, sparking a chemical fire that burned for six days, and causing a burst water main that flooded streets above. The city centre had to be evacuated for several days, and there was major disruption to rail freight traffic. |
| 25 | 19 Jul 2001 | British politician and novelist Jeffrey Archer was convicted of committing perjury and perverting the course of justice during his 1986 libel trial against the *Daily Star* newspaper. He was sentenced to four years in prison. He was released in July 2003. |
| 25 | 20 Jul 2001 | The London Stock Exchange went public and began trading its shares on its own exchange. |
| 25 | 20 Jul 2001 | Studio Ghibli's animated fantasy film *Spirited Away* was released in Japan.<br>U.S. première: 31st August 2002, limited release: 20th September 2002, released: 28th March 2003.<br>UK première: 11th July 2003, released: 12th September 2003.<br>It became the first anime film to win an Academy Award. |

**JULY 2026**

| Ann. | Date | Event |
|---|---|---|
| 25 | 23 Jul 2001 | The President of Indonesia, Abdurrahman Wahid, was dismissed from office after being impeached for abuse of power.<br>He was succeeded by Megawati Sukarnoputri. |
| 25 | 23 Jul 2001 | Death of Eudora Welty, American short story writer and novelist. |
| 25 | 24 Jul 2001 | Simeon Saxe-Coburg-Gotha became Prime Minister of Bulgaria (until 2005). He was the last Tsar of Bulgaria (as Simeon II, 1943–46).<br>He is the only monarch in history to have regained power via democratic election to a different office. |
| 25 | 24 Jul 2001 | Sri Lankan Civil War: the Bandaranaike Airport attack.<br>Fourteen Tamil Tiger commandos launched one of the bloodiest attacks of the Civil War, destroying and damaging aircraft and killing seven members of the Sri Lankan Air Force. All fourteen commandos were killed.<br>The attack damaged the Sri Lankan economy, military and airline industry. |
| 25 | 24 Jul 2001 | American businessman Larry Silverstein acquired the World Trade Center complex in New York City on a 99-year lease worth $3.2 billion.<br>(This was seven weeks before the 9/11 terrorist attacks.)<br>In 2007, after several years of dispute, his insurers paid out $4.55 billion. |
| 25 | 27 Jul 2001 | The science fiction film *Planet of the Apes* was released in the USA.<br>UK: 17th August. |
| 25 | 28 Jul 2001 | Ian Thorpe of Australia became the first swimmer to win six gold medals at a single World Aquatics Championships.<br>(Three individual medals and three relay medals.) |
| 25 | 31 Jul 2001 | Death of Francisco da Costa Gomes, President of Portugal (1974–76). |
| 20 | 1 Jul 2006 | The Qinghai–Tibet Railway began operating.<br>The high-elevation railway links Xining, China to Lhasa, Tibet<br>Because of the line's altitude, the specially built trains have oxygen-rich carriages, personal oxygen supplies for every seat in case of emergency, UV protection, and a doctor on board. |
| 20 | 1 Jul 2006 | Death of Fred Trueman, British cricket player and broadcaster.<br>Regarded as one of the greatest bowlers in cricketing history. |
| 20 | 3 Jul 2006 | The Valencia metro derailment, Spain.<br>At least 43 people were killed and 47 injured.<br>(Cause unknown – possibly excessive speed on a bend, or the partial collapse of a tunnel wall.) |
| 20 | 4 Jul 2006 | Virgin Media was founded in the UK when Virgin Mobile merged with the cable company NTL:Telewest.<br>It was the UK's first quadruple-play media company, offering television, broadband, telephone and mobile phone services. |
| 20 | 5 Jul 2006 | North Korea tested seven missiles, including a long-range Taepodong-2 that U.S. intelligence services believed was capable of reaching Alaska.<br>It was the first North Korean missile with such a range.<br>It failed after about 40 seconds. |
| 20 | 5 Jul 2006 | Death of Kenneth Lay, American businessman. CEO and chairman of the energy company Enron.<br>He was convicted of fraud and conspiracy in the Enron corruption scandal and faced up to 45 years in prison, but died while awaiting sentencing. |

## JULY 2026

| Ann. | Date | Event |
|---|---|---|
| 20 | 6 Jul 2006 | Nathula La, a mountain pass between India and Tibet Autonomous Region, China, reopened after 44 years.<br>It was sealed by India in 1962 after the Sino–Indian War.<br>It is one of three open trading border posts between China and India and is an offshoot of the ancient Silk Road. |
| 20 | 7 Jul 2006 | Death of Syd Barrett, British rock singer, guitarist and songwriter (Pink Floyd). Noted for his secluded lifestyle and drug abuse. |
| 20 | 9 Jul 2006 | S7 Airlines Flight 778 overshot the runway and crashed as it attempted to land at Irkutsk International Airport in Russia.<br>125 people were killed and 63 injured. (Cause: pilot error.) |
| 20 | 10 Jul 2006 | Death of Shamil Basayev, Chechen terrorist.<br>One of the world's most-wanted terrorists. He was responsible for numerous guerrilla attacks and hostage-takings including the 2002 Moscow theatre crisis and the 2004 Beslan school siege. |
| 20 | 11 Jul 2006 | The Mumbai train bombings, India.<br>Seven terrorist bombs exploded in eleven minutes, killing more than 200 people and injuring over 700. |
| 20 | 11 Jul 2006 | Death of John Spencer, British snooker world champion and broadcaster. |
| 20 | 12 Jul 2006 to 14th | The 2006 Lebanon War (also known as the 2006 Israel–Hezbollah War).<br>Result: stalemate and ceasefire. |
| 20 | 12 Jul 2006 | The European Commission fined Microsoft €497 million ($794 million, £381 million) for failing to divulge information about its server products to rivals and for bundling Windows Media Player with its Windows operating system. It also fined the company an additional €1.5 million ($2.39 million, £1.14 million) per day from 16th December 2005 to 20th June 2006 for failing to comply after the deadline to do so had passed. |
| 20 | 12 Jul 2006 | Bigelow Aerospace launched *Genesis I* into orbit.<br>The unmanned inflatable space habitat's mission was designed to test the long-term viability of inflatable space structures.<br>It was the private American company's first structure to be sent into orbit. (At the time of writing it is expected to re-enter the atmosphere soon.) |
| 20 | 13 Jul 2006 | Death of Red Buttons, American stage, film and television actor and comedian. |
| 20 | 15 Jul 2006 | Twitter, the online micro-blogging service, was launched. |
| 20 | 17 Jul 2006 | The Pangandaran earthquake and tsunami, Java, Indonesia.<br>More than 600 people were killed and over 9,000 injured. |
| 20 | 17 Jul 2006 | Death of Mickey Spillane, American crime novelist.<br>Creator of the detective Mike Hammer. |
| 20 | 19 Jul 2006 | Death of Jack Warden, American film and television character actor (*12 Angry Men* [juror #7], *The Bachelor Party*, *All the President's Men*, *Being There*, *Shampoo*, *Heaven Can Wait*, and more). |
| 20 | 20 Jul 2006 | Tesla Motors, the American electric car manufacturer, unveiled its first model, the Tesla Roadster – the world's first fully electric sports car.<br>It went on sale in February 2008. |

## JULY 2026

| Ann. | Date | Event |
|------|------|-------|
| 20 | 21 Jul 2006 | NASA announced that radar images from its *Cassini* spacecraft showed liquid hydrocarbon (methane and ethane) lakes on Saturn's moon Titan. This was the first time currently existing lakes had been discovered outside Earth. In March 2007 liquid hydrocarbon seas were discovered in Titan's northern latitudes. |
| 20 | 28 Jul 2006 | Death of David Gemmell, British fantasy novelist. Noted for the violence of his stories, but also for the self-doubt, courage and honour of his main characters. Best known for *Legend*. |
| 20 | 30 Jul 2006 | The British pop music television show *Top of the Pops* ended after 42 years. It was the world's longest-running music show. |
| 20 | 31 Jul 2006 | Raúl Castro assumed office as President of Cuba after his brother Fidel Castro became too ill to continue. In February 2008 his temporary appointment was made permanent and Fidel officially retired. |
| 15 | 7 Jul 2011 | The world première of the fantasy film *Harry Potter and the Deathly Hallows: Part 2*, in London, UK. It was the final film in the eight-part series. UK release: 15th July. U.S. première: 11th July, released: 15th July. |
| 15 | 9 Jul 2011 | South Sudan gained its independence from Sudan. At the time of writing, it is the world's newest country. |
| 15 | 10 Jul 2011 | The last issue of the British Sunday tabloid newspaper the *News of the World* was published. It was shut down by its owners after a phone-hacking scandal led to a public backlash and the withdrawal of adverting It was replaced by *The Sun on Sunday* in February 2012. |
| 15 | 21 Jul 2011 | NASA's Space Shuttle programme ended when *Atlantis* landed at the end of its final mission. (*Atlantis* was launched on 8th July.) |
| 15 | 22 Jul 2011 | The Norway terrorist attacks. Anders Behring Breivik detonated a bomb in a van parked next to a tower block in Oslo. Two hours later he travelled to a summer camp on the island of Utøya and opened fire on the participants. A total of 77 people were killed and 319 injured. He was convicted of mass murder, causing a fatal explosion, and terrorism. |
| 15 | 24 Jul 2011 | Same-sex marriage was legalised in the U.S. state of New York. |
| 10 | 2 Jul 2016 | Death of Caroline Aherne, British actress, comedian and writer. Best known for her role as the mock chat show host Mrs Merton on *The Mrs Merton Show* and for the TV comedy shows *The Fast Show* and *The Royle Family*. (Lung cancer, aged 52.) |
| 10 | 2 Jul 2016 | Death of Elie Wiesel, Romanian-born American writer, Jewish rights activist, educator and Holocaust survivor. Winner of the 1986 Nobel Peace Prize. |
| 10 | 13 Jul 2016 | Theresa May became British Prime Minister (until 2019) after David Cameron resigned following the UK's referendum on leaving the European Union. |

## JULY 2026

| Ann. | Date | Event |
|------|------|-------|
| 10 | 26 Jul 2016 | Hillary Clinton became the first woman to be nominated for President of the United States by a major political party (Democrats). She lost to Donald Trump in the election in November. |
| 10 | 26 Jul 2016 | The Swiss solar-powered experimental aircraft *Solar Impulse 2* became the first solar-powered aircraft to circumnavigate the Earth. It took more than sixteen months to travel 26,000 miles. It was piloted by André Borschberg and Bertrand Piccard. |

## AUGUST 2026

| Ann. | Date | Event |
|------|------|-------|
| 1900 | 1 Aug 126 | Birth of Pertinax, Roman emperor (192–193 AD – assassinated). |
| 1500 | 30 Aug 526 | Death of Theodoric the Great, King of Italy (493–526), King of the Ostrogoths (475–526), King of the Visigoths (511–526). Succeeded by his grandson, Athalaric. |
| 750 | 18 Aug 1276 | Death of Pope Adrian V. (Died six weeks after being elected.) Succeeded by John XXI (who died after eight months). |
| 500 | 4 Aug 1526 | Death of Juan Sebastián Elcano, Spanish navigator. He completed the first circumnavigation of the Earth in 1519–22 (the Magellan–Elcano expedition), taking over from the Portuguese-born explorer Ferdinand Magellan, who was killed in a battle in the Philippines during the expedition. |
| 500 | 27 Aug 1526 | The Diet of Speyer in Germany ruled that the people of each state could determine their own beliefs. This reversed, but did not annul, the 1521 decision made by the Diet of Worms, which outlawed everything except Roman Catholicism and led to the Protestant expansion. In 1529 the second Diet of Speyer condemned this decision, but did not annul it. |
| 500 | 29 Aug 1526 | Ottoman–Hungarian Wars – the Battle of Mohács, Hungary. Ottoman victory leading to the partition of Hungary between the Ottoman Empire, the Habsburg Monarchy, and Transylvania. King Louis II of Hungary was killed during the battle. |
| 500 | 29 Aug 1526 | Death of Louis II, King of Hungary and Croatia (1516–26). Killed in the Battle of Mohács (see above), aged 20. Succeeded by the Holy Roman Emperor, Ferdinand I and/or John Zápolya – they both claimed the disputed title. |
| 400 | 27 Aug 1626 | Thirty Years' War – the Battle of Lutter, Germany. Holy Roman Empire/Catholic League victory over Denmark and Norway. |
| 250 | 2 Aug 1776 | American Revolution: the formal signing of the U.S. Declaration of Independence. |
| 250 | 25 Aug 1776 | Death of David Hume, Scottish philosopher, historian and economist. Best known for developing a system of philosophical empiricism, scepticism and naturalism. |
| 250 | 26 Aug 1776 | American Revolutionary War – the Battle of Long Island, New York. British victory – the British captured New York City and Long Island. |
| 200 | 19 Aug 1826 | The Canada Company was incorporated in the UK. It was formed to aid the colonisation of Upper Canada (now Ontario). |
| 175 | 12 Aug 1851 | American inventor Isaac Singer was granted a U.S. patent for his improved sewing machine. (U.S. Patent 8,294.) He set up I. M. Singer & Co. (later renamed the Singer Sewing Machine Company, now the Singer Corporation) to manufacture it. |
| 175 | 13 Aug 1851 | Birth of Felix Adler, American educator, religious leader and social reformer. Founder of the Ethical Culture movement. |

## AUGUST 2026

| Ann. | Date | Event |
|---|---|---|
| 175 | 14 Aug 1851 | Birth of Doc Holliday, American gambler, gunfighter and dentist. A close associate of the lawman Wyatt Earp. He was involved in the events surrounding the Gunfight at the O.K. Corral. |
| 175 | 22 Aug 1851 | The first America's Cup yacht race was held. The first year's event was a race around the Isle of Wight in the UK. It was won by the American schooner *America*. The trophy was named in honour of the first year's winner. The race is the oldest still-operating international sporting competition in any event. |
| 150 | 1 Aug 1876 | Colorado was admitted as the 38th state of the USA. |
| 150 | 2 Aug 1876 | Death of Wild Bill Hickok, American lawman, gambler and folk hero of the Old West. (Shot dead while playing poker, aged 39.) |
| 150 | 5 Aug 1876 | Birth of Mary R. Beard, American historian, writer, and women's rights activist and archivist. She wrote several books on women's role in history. |
| 150 | 7 Aug 1876 | Birth of Mata Hari, Dutch exotic dancer and courtesan. She was convicted of spying for Germany during WWI and executed by the French in 1917. |
| 150 | 8 Aug 1876 | American inventor Thomas Edison was granted a U.S. patent for his electric pen, which allowed writing to be duplicated. His system was a type of mimeograph. (U.S. Patent 180,857.) |
| 150 | 8 Aug 1876 | Birth of Varghese Payyappilly Palakkappilly, Indian priest. Founder of the Sisters of the Destitute. He was declared Venerable by Pope Francis in 2018. |
| 150 | 12 Aug 1876 | Birth of Mary Roberts Rinehart, American mystery novelist. Known as the 'American Agatha Christie'. She is credited with originating 'the butler did it' plot device. |
| 150 | 13 Aug 1876 to 17th | German composer Richard Wagner's complete *Ring cycle* (Der Ring des Nibelungen – The Ring of the Nibelung) was performed for the first time. It was performed over four nights at the Bayreuth Festspielhaus, which he built for the annual Bayreuth Festival. The playhouse is now dedicated solely to performances of his stage works. |
| 150 | 14 Aug 1876 | Prairie View A&M University was established in Texas, USA (as the Agricultural and Mechanical College for the Benefit of Colored Youth). |
| 150 | 14 Aug 1876 | Birth of Alexander I, King of Serbia (1889–1903 – assassinated). |
| 150 | 17 Aug 1876 | Birth of Eric Drummond, 7th Earl of Perth, British politician and diplomat. The first Secretary-General of the League of Nations (1920–33) |
| 150 | 19 Aug 1876 | Death of George Smith, British Assyriologist. Best known for discovering and translating the *Epic of Gilgamesh*, one of the oldest-known works of literature. (Dysentery, aged 36.) |
| 150 | 29 Aug 1876 | Birth of Charles Kettering, American inventor and automotive engineer. Head of research at General Motors (1920–47). Inventor of the electric starter motor. He also helped develop leaded fuel, two-stroke diesel engines, coloured paint for cars, the refrigerant Freon, and the first aerial missile. |

**AUGUST 2026**

| Ann. | Date | Event |
|---|---|---|
| 150 | 29 Aug 1876 | Birth of Kim Gu, President of the Provisional Government of the Republic of Korea (1926–27, 1940–47). |
| 150 | 31 Aug 1876 | The Sultan of the Ottoman Empire, Murad V, was deposed after three months because of his poor physical and mental health.<br>He was succeeded by his half-brother Abdul-Hamid II. |
| 125 | 3 Aug 1901 | Birth of Stefan Wyszyński, Polish cardinal. Bishop of Lublin (1946–48), Archbishop of Warsaw, Archbishop of Gniezno and Primate of Poland (1948–81). |
| 125 | 4 Aug 1901 | Birth of Louis Armstrong, ('Satchmo'), American jazz trumpeter and singer. |
| 125 | 5 Aug 1901 | Death of Victoria, Princess Royal. Daughter of Queen Victoria.<br>Empress consort of Germany and Queen consort of Prussia (1888).<br>Wife of Emperor Frederick III.<br>(Breast cancer, aged 60, a few months after her mother died.) |
| 125 | 8 Aug 1901 | Birth of Ernest Lawrence, American nuclear physicist.<br>Winner of the 1939 Nobel Prize in Physics for inventing the cyclotron, a type of particle accelerator.<br>He also worked on uranium isotope separation for the Manhattan Project that developed the nuclear bomb. He founded the Lawrence Berkeley National Laboratory and the Lawrence Livermore National Laboratory.<br>The chemical element lawrencium (Lr, 103) is named in his honour. |
| 125 | 10 Aug 1901 to 14 Sep | The U.S. Steel recognition strike of 1901.<br>The Amalgamated Association of Iron, Steel and Tin Workers attempted to gain union recognition in all U.S. Steel plants. It was unsuccessful. |
| 125 | 12 Aug 1901 | Death of Adolf Erik Nordenskiöld, Finnish-Swedish geologist, mineralogist, cartographer and explorer.<br>Known for leading the Vega Expedition (1878–79) – the first complete crossing of the North-East Passage between the Atlantic and Pacific Oceans. |
| 125 | 14 Aug 1901 | The first claimed powered flight (disputed).<br>German-born American aviation pioneer Gustave Whitehead is reported to have flown his flying machine *Number 21* in Connecticut, USA.<br>If this flight took place, as many witnesses and a newspaper report claim it did, then it would be the world's first sustained powered flight, beating the Wright Brothers by more than two years.<br>Whitehead died in relative obscurity in 1927. |
| 125 | 15 Aug 1901 | Birth of Arnulfo Arias Madrid, President of Panama (1940–41, 1949–51, 1968). His three presidencies were all ended by military coups. |
| 125 | 18 Aug 1901 | Birth of Arne Borg, Swedish swimmer. He broke 32 world records in the 1920s, and was a gold medallist at the 1928 Olympics (1500 m freestyle). |
| 125 | 20 Aug 1901 | Birth of Salvatore Quasimodo, Italian poet. One of the leading Italian poets of the 20th century. Winner of the 1959 Nobel Prize in Literature. |
| 125 | 21 Aug 1901 | The Thomasites, six hundred American teachers, arrived in Manila in the Philippines on the U.S. Army Transport Ship *Thomas*. They had been recruited to establish a new public school system, train Filipino teachers, and teach basic education. About 100 of them settled in the Philippines when their assignments were completed. (See also: 28th August 1901.) |

## AUGUST 2026

| Ann. | Date | Event |
|---|---|---|
| 125 | 25 Aug 1901 | Death of Clara Maass, American nurse. She died during a medical experiment to study yellow fever, aged 25. She allowed herself to be bitten by an infected mosquito in March and remained healthy. It was believed that she was now immune to the disease. She allowed a second infected mosquito to bite her in August, but this time she contracted yellow fever and died. |
| 125 | 26 Aug 1901 | Birth of Maxwell D. Taylor, American Army officer and diplomat. Commander of the 101st Airborne Division (the 'Screaming Eagles') during WWII. Chief of Staff of the Army (1955–59). Chairman of the Joint Chiefs of Staff (1962–64). U.S. Ambassador to South Vietnam (1964–65). |
| 125 | 27 Aug 1901 | Birth of Al Ritz, American comedian, actor and entertainer (the Ritz Brothers). |
| 125 | 28 Aug 1901 | Silliman University was established in Dumaguete in the Philippines (as Silliman Institute). It was the first American- and Protestant-founded institute of higher learning in Asia. |
| 125 | 31 Aug 1901 | Birth of Roy Wilkins, American civil rights leader. Executive Director of the National Association for the Advancement of Colored People (NAACP) (1955–77). |
| 100 | 1 Aug 1926 | Birth of Hannah Hauxwell, British farmer who lived alone and in poverty on a dilapidated farm in the Pennines. She was the subject of several television documentaries. (Died 2018.) |
| 100 | 6 Aug 1926 | The Japanese Broadcasting Corporation (NHK) was established when radio stations in Tokyo, Osaka and Nagoya merged. |
| 100 | 6 Aug 1926 | Gertrude Ederle of the USA became the first woman to swim across the English Channel. |
| 100 | 6 Aug 1926 | Warner Brothers released the first film to use the Vitaphone sound system. The film, *Don Juan*, had previously been released as a silent film. The Vitaphone version had a musical score and sound effects (but no spoken dialogue). |
| 100 | 7 Aug 1926 | The first British Grand Prix motor race was held at Brooklands in Surrey. |
| 100 | 12 Aug 1926 | Birth of John Derek, American actor and film director. Best known as the husband of his fourth wife, the actress Bo Derek. (Died 1998.) |
| 100 | 13 Aug 1926 | Birth of Fidel Castro, President of Cuba (1976–2008). First Secretary of the Central Committee of the Communist Party of Cuba (1965–2011). (Died 2016.) |
| 100 | 15 Aug 1926 | Birth of Konstantinos Stephanopoulos, President of Greece (1995–2005). (Died 2016.) |
| 100 | 17 Aug 1926 | Birth of George Melly, British jazz/blues singer; music, television and film critic; and writer and lecturer on art history, particularly Pop Art and Surrealism. (Died 2007.) |
| 100 | 22 Aug 1926 | The President/dictator of Greece, Theodoros Pangalos, was ousted after a month in office and imprisoned for two years. He was succeeded by former President Pavlos Kountouriotis. |

## AUGUST 2026

| Ann. | Date | Event |
|------|------|-------|
| 100 | 22 Aug 1926 | Death of Charles W. Eliot, American academic. President of Harvard University (1869–1909). He transformed Harvard from a provincial college into the USA's leading research university. |
| 100 | 23 Aug 1926 | Death of Rudolph Valentino, (the 'Great Lover'), Italian film actor. Noted for his romantic dramas (*The Four Horsemen of the Apocalypse, The Sheik, Blood and Sand, The Eagle, The Son of the Sheik*). (Sepsis following surgery for peritonitis, aged 31 – his death prompted a massive outpouring of grief and hysteria from his fans.) |
| 100 | 27 Aug 1926 | Birth of Pat Coombs, British film, television and radio character actress. Known for playing comically downtrodden women in several TV sitcoms. (Died 2002.) |
| 100 | 27 Aug 1926 | Birth of Kristen Nygaard, Norwegian computer scientist. Best known for co-inventing object-oriented programming and the programming language Simula. (Died 2002.) |
| 90 | 1 Aug 1936 to 16th | The 1936 Summer Olympic Games were held in Berlin, Germany. They were presided over by German leader Adolf Hitler. This was the last Olympics until 1948 because of WWII. |
| 90 | 1 Aug 1936 | Birth of Yves Saint-Laurent, Algerian-born French fashion designer. (Died 2008.) |
| 90 | 2 Aug 1936 | Death of Louis Blériot, French aviation pioneer, engineer and inventor. The first person to fly across the English Channel. |
| 90 | 4 Aug 1936 | The Prime Minister of Greece, Ioannis Metaxas, staged a self-coup, suspended parliament and the constitution, and established a dictatorship known as the 4th of August Regime (or the Metaxas Regime). |
| 90 | 7 Aug 1936 to 14th | The first Olympic basketball tournament was played. The USA beat Canada in the final. The tournament was played outside, and the weather was appalling, especially during the final. The next Olympic basketball tournament was in London, UK in 1948, when it was played indoors. (Basketball was a demonstration sport at the 1904 Olympics.) |
| 90 | 9 Aug 1936 | Sprinter Jesse Owens became the first American to win four gold medals at a single Olympic Games. German leader Adolf Hitler was using the 1936 Games in Berlin to demonstrate 'Aryan supremacy'. Owens, an African American, was the most successful athlete at the games, and is considered to have single-handedly crushed this myth. |
| 90 | 12 Aug 1936 | American diver Marjorie Gestring won the 3-metre springboard event at the 1936 Summer Olympics in Berlin, Germany. She was 13 years and 268 days old, and remains the youngest person to win an Olympic gold medal. |
| 90 | 14 Aug 1936 | The last public execution in the USA. Rainey Bethea was hanged for rape in Owensboro, Kentucky. |
| 90 | 19 Aug 1936 to 24th | The first of the Moscow show trials (the Trial of the Sixteen) was held. The 16 men were charged with forming a terror organisation that planned to kill Soviet leader Joseph Stalin and other Soviet leaders in order to restore capitalism. They were all found guilty, sentenced to death, and executed. There were two further show trials in January 1937 and March 1938. |

**AUGUST 2026**

| Ann. | Date | Event |
|------|------|-------|
| 90 | 19 Aug 1936 | Death of Federico García Lorca, Spanish poet, playwright and theatrical director. (Executed by Nationalist forces during the Spanish Civil War.) |
| 90 | 21 Aug 1936 | Birth of Wilt Chamberlain, American basketball player. (Died 1999.) |
| 90 | 24 Aug 1936 | The Australian Antarctic Territory was established. |
| 90 | 24 Aug 1936 | U.S. President Franklin D. Roosevelt secretly directed the Federal Bureau of Investigation (FBI) to investigate subversive activities and pursue fascists and communists. |
| 90 | 24 Aug 1936 | The British passenger liner *RMS Queen Mary* won the Blue Riband by crossing the Atlantic Ocean in the fastest-ever time. It held the record for only a year, but broke it again in 1938 and held it until 1952. |
| 90 | 26 Aug 1936 | The Anglo–Egyptian Alliance Treaty was signed in Cairo, Egypt, ending Britain's occupation of Egypt. |
| 90 | 29 Aug 1936 | Birth of John McCain, American politician. U.S. Senator from Arizona (1987–2018). U.S. presidential candidate (2008 – lost to Barack Obama). He suffered life-long disabilities in the Vietnam War. (Died 2018.) |
| 90 | 31 Aug 1936 | Radio Prague, the official international broadcasting station of the Czech Republic, began broadcasting. |
| 90 | 31 Aug 1936 | Elizabeth Cowell became the first female television announcer in the UK, as one of three BBC Television presenters at the Radiolympia Exhibition in London. BBC Television officially launched on 2nd November 1936. |
| 80 | 1 Aug 1946 | The leaders of the Russian Liberation Army (ROA) were executed for treason in Moscow, Russia. The ROA collaborated with Nazi Germany and fought alongside it during WWII. ROA soldiers were sentenced to detention in prison camps. |
| 80 | 1 Aug 1946 | The Atomic Energy Commission (AEC) was established in the USA. |
| 80 | 1 Aug 1946 | The Fulbright Program was established in the USA. It funds U.S. citizens to study or teach in a foreign country, and funds non-U.S. citizens to study or teach in the USA. It is the world's largest education exchange programme. |
| 80 | 1 Aug 1946 | Birth of Boz Burrell, British rock/blues/jazz singer, guitarist and bassist (King Crimson, Bad Company). (Died 2006.) |
| 80 | 3 Aug 1946 | Santa Claus Land, the world's first themed amusement park, opened in Santa Claus, Indiana, USA. In 1984 it became Holiday World & Splashin' Safari. |
| 80 | 3 Aug 1946 | Birth of Syreeta (Wright), American soul/R&B singer and songwriter. Best known for her work with Stevie Wonder (to whom she was married for eighteen months) and Billy Preston. (Died 2004.) |
| 80 | 4 Aug 1946 | The Dominican Republic earthquake and tsunami. About 100 people were killed by the earthquake and 20,000 made homeless. The tsunami caused widespread devastation across the Dominican Republic and Haiti, killing up to 1,800 people. |
| 80 | 4 Aug 1946 | Birth of Maureen Starkey, first wife of the Beatles' drummer Ringo Starr. (Died 1994.) |

## AUGUST 2026

| Ann. | Date | Event |
|---|---|---|
| 80 | 5 Aug 1946 | Death of Wilhelm Marx, Chancellor of Germany (1923–25, 1926–28). |
| 80 | 7 Aug 1946 to 30 May 1953 | The Turkish Straits crisis, Black Sea. The Soviet Union, which disputed Turkey's ownership of the Strait, pressured Turkey to allow its ships to pass through it freely to the Mediterranean Sea. Turkey refused, and the Soviets launched a show of naval strength that threatened to escalate. Turkey asked the USA to help protect it, and joined NATO, and the Soviet Union withdrew its demands. |
| 80 | 8 Aug 1946 | The Convair B-36 Peacemaker strategic bomber made its first flight. It was the first mass-produced nuclear weapon delivery vehicle, had the longest wingspan of any military aircraft, and was the first bomber with intercontinental range. It was used by the U.S. Air Force from 1949 to 1959. |
| 80 | 12 Aug 1946 | Birth of Terry Nutkins, British naturalist, television presenter and writer. Known for the children's TV series *Animal Magic* and *The Really Wild Show*. (Died 2012.) |
| 80 | 13 Aug 1946 | Death of H. G. Wells, British science fiction novelist (*The War of the Worlds*, *The Time Machine*, *The Invisible Man*, *The Island of Doctor Moreau*). |
| 80 | 14 Aug 1946 | Birth of Tom Walkinshaw, Scottish racing driver and founder of the Tom Walkinshaw Racing team (TWR). (Died 2010.) |
| 80 | 16 Aug 1946 | Direct Action Day (also known the Great Calcutta Killings), Kolkata, India. Muslim and Hindu mobs rioted across the city following the Muslim League's demand for the creation of Pakistan. More than 4,000 people were killed and 100,000 left homeless. The riots sparked further religious violence in other provinces, leading to the Partition of India in August 1947. |
| 80 | 16 Aug 1946 | The Japan Federation of Economic Organizations (Keidanren) was established. In May 2002 it merged with the Japan Federation of Employers' Associations to become the Japan Business Federation. |
| 80 | 17 Aug 1946 | Birth of Patrick Manning, Prime Minister of Trinidad and Tobago (1991–95, 2001–10). (Died 2016.) |
| 80 | 19 Aug 1946 | The Congress of Industrial Unions of Japan (Sanbetsu Kaigi) was established. It quickly grew, and had nearly 1.7 million members at its peak. But it began organising unsuccessful militant strike campaigns, and its popularity declined. It was dissolved in 1958. |
| 80 | 22 Aug 1946 | Death of Döme Sztójay, Prime Minister of Hungary (1944 for five months during WWII). |
| 80 | 23 Aug 1946 | The British Military Government in Germany abolished the former Prussian province of Schleswig–Holstein and made it a separate state. |
| 80 | 23 Aug 1946 | Birth of Keith Moon, British rock drummer (The Who). Noted for his eccentric style and self-destructive behaviour. (Died 1978.) |
| 80 | 24 Aug 1946 | Death of James Clark McReynolds, Associate Justice of the U.S. Supreme Court (1914–41), U.S. Attorney General (1913–14). |
| 80 | 25 Aug 1946 | The Golf Writers Association of America was founded, at Portland Golf Club in Oregon. (Some sources give the date as 18th August, but a plaque at the golf club says 25th August.) |

**AUGUST 2026**

| Ann. | Date | Event |
|---|---|---|
| 80 | 29 Aug 1946 | Birth of Demetris Christofias, President of Cyprus (2008–13). (Died 2019.) |
| 80 | 30 Aug 1946 | Birth of Peggy Lipton, American actress and model.<br>Best known for her role as Julie Barnes in the television crime drama *The Mod Squad*. Wife of the record producer and musician Quincey Jones. Mother of the actress Rashida Jones. (Died 2019.) |
| 75 | 1 Aug 1951 | Japan Airlines was founded. It commenced operations on 25th October. |
| 75 | 2 Aug 1951 | Birth of Andrew Gold, American singer, songwriter, musician and record producer. He played on numerous records by other artists, had a successful solo career with hits such as *Lonely Boy* and *Thank You for Being a Friend* (a cover version was used as the theme song for the TV sitcom *The Golden Girls*), and wrote music for film and television. (Died 2011.) |
| 75 | 8 Aug 1951 | Birth of Randy Shilts, American journalist and writer. (Died 1994.) |
| 75 | 9 Aug 1951 | Francisco Craveiro Lopes became President of Portugal (until 1953). |
| 75 | 10 Aug 1951 to 24th | Typhoon Marge hit Korea, China and Japan, causing widespread damage, flooding and devastation. It was the largest tropical cyclone ever recorded (until Typhoon Tip in 1979). |
| 75 | 11 Aug 1951 | The first Major League Baseball game to be televised in colour in the USA. WCBS-TV in New York City broadcast a game between the Brooklyn Dodgers and the Boston Braves. |
| 75 | 15 Aug 1951 | Death of Artur Schnabel, Austrian/Polish pianist and composer.<br>The first pianist to record the complete set of Beethoven's 32 piano sonatas. |
| 75 | 16 Aug 1951 | Birth of Umaru Musa Yar'Adua, President of Nigeria (2007–10 – died in office). |
| 75 | 21 Aug 1951 | Death of Constant Lambert, British composer and conductor.<br>A major figure in English ballet. |
| 75 | 23 Aug 1951 | Birth of Akhmad Kadyrov, President of the Chechen Republic (2003–04 – assassinated). |
| 75 | 30 Aug 1951 | The Mutual Defense Treaty Between the Republic of the Philippines and the USA was signed in Washington, D.C. |
| 70 | 1 Aug 1956 | The Social Security Act in the USA was amended to provide benefits to disabled workers aged 50–64, and disabled children (aged 18 or over) of retired or deceased workers if their disability began before the age of 18. The retirement age for widows and female parents was lowered to 62. |
| 70 | 3 Aug 1956 | Bedloe's Island in New York Harbor was renamed Liberty Island.<br>It is the site of the Statue of Liberty. |
| 70 | 6 Aug 1956 | The USA's DuMont Television Network ceased operations after ten years. |
| 70 | 7 Aug 1956 | The Cali explosion, Colombia.<br>Seven army ammunition trucks loaded with dynamite exploded  cause unknown). More than 1,300 people were killed and 4,000 injured.<br>(Some sources claim that 4,000 people were killed and 12,000 injured.)<br>The explosion caused an earthquake that destroyed numerous buildings. |

## AUGUST 2026

| Ann. | Date | Event |
|---|---|---|
| 70 | 8 Aug 1956 | Bois du Cazier coal mine disaster, Marcinelle, Hainaut Province, Belgium. Electric cables in a mine shaft ruptured and caused a fire, trapping miners underground. 262 miners died from smoke inhalation and carbon dioxide poisoning, and only twelve survived. Most of the miners were migrant workers from other countries. |
| 70 | 11 Aug 1956 | Death of Jackson Pollock, American abstract expressionist artist. Known for his drip paintings. (Car crash, aged 44.) |
| 70 | 14 Aug 1956 | Death of Bertolt Brecht, German poet, playwright and theatrical director/ reformer who developed the epic theatre style and promoted leftist/ Marxist causes. |
| 70 | 16 Aug 1956 | Death of Bela Lugosi, Hungarian-born American stage and film actor. Best known for his horror roles, most notably as Count Dracula. |
| 70 | 18 Aug 1956 | The Alexander Graham Bell Museum opened in Baddeck, Nova Scotia, Canada. In 1959 it became the Alexander Graham Bell National Historic Site. |
| 70 | 25 Aug 1956 | Death of Alfred Kinsey, American biologist, zoologist and entomologist. Best known for his work on human sexual behaviour. Founder of Indiana University's Kinsey Institute for Research in Sex, Gender and Reproduction. |
| 70 | 27 Aug 1956 | Britain's first nuclear power station, Calder Hall in Cumbria, began operating. It was officially opened on 17th October. It was the first nuclear power station in the world to generate power on an industrial scale, and formed part of the Sellafield complex. It closed in 2003 and was later demolished. (The world's first nuclear power station began operating in the Soviet Union in 1954, on an experimental basis, but its output was significantly lower than Calder Hall's.) |
| 70 | 30 Aug 1956 | The Lake Pontchartrain Causeway in Louisiana, USA opened. A second, parallel bridge opened alongside it in 1969. It is the world's longest continuous bridge over water. |
| 65 | 1 Aug 1961 | Six Flags Over Texas amusement park opened in Arlington, Texas, USA. It was the first park in the Six Flags chain. |
| 65 | 2 Aug 1961 | Birth of Pete de Freitas, Trinidad and Tobago-born rock drummer (Echo & the Bunnymen). (Killed in a motorcycle accident in 1989, aged 27.) |
| 65 | 3 Aug 1961 | The New Democratic Party was founded in Canada when the Cooperative Commonwealth Federation and the Canadian Labour Congress merged. |
| 65 | 6 Aug 1961 | Soviet cosmonaut Gherman Titov became the first person to spend an entire day in space, and the first to make more than one orbit. He orbited the Earth seventeen times in 25 hours on board *Vostok 2*. |
| 65 | 7 Aug 1961 | Birth of Walter Swinburn, British jockey and race horse trainer. (Died 2016 – fell from a window.) |
| 65 | 9 Aug 1961 | Death of Walter Bedell Smith, U.S. Army general. Chief of Staff during WWII. U.S. Ambassador to the Soviet Union (1946–48). Director of Central Intelligence (1950–53). Under Secretary of State (1953–54). |

## AUGUST 2026

| Ann. | Date | Event |
|------|------|-------|
| 65 | 10 Aug 1961 | Vietnam War: the U.S. Army began testing the use of herbicides and defoliants on crops and forests in South Vietnam to deprive the Viet Cong of food and cover.<br>The testing proved successful and led to Operation Ranch Hand (1962–71) in which 5 million acres of forest and 500,000 acres of crops were seriously damaged or destroyed.<br>The chemicals were sprayed at around 50 times the concentration used in agriculture. One of the chemicals was Agent Orange, which has since been found to cause long-term health issues. |
| 65 | 13 Aug 1961 | East Germany sealed the border between East and West Berlin to prevent an exodus of refugees to the West. Initially barbed wire fences were erected. Construction of the Berlin Wall began on 15th August.<br>The border was reopened in 1989. |
| 65 | 18 Aug 1961 | Death of Learned Hand, American Judge (1924–51), Chief Judge (1948–51) and Senior Judge (1951–61) of the U.S. Court of Appeals for the Second Circuit. |
| 65 | 21 Aug 1961 | The song *Please Mr. Postman* by The Marvelettes was released.<br>It became Motown's first #1 hit on the U.S. *Billboard* Hot 100 record chart. |
| 65 | 25 Aug 1961 | The President of Brazil, Jânio Quadros, resigned after seven months because of political instability. The country was thrown into chaos.<br>João Goulart succeeded him on 8th September but was ousted in a military coup in 1964. The resulting military dictatorship lasted until 1985. |
| 65 | 26 Aug 1961 | The Hockey Hall of Fame opened in Toronto, Canada. |
| 65 | 30 Aug 1961 | Death of Charles Coburn, American film actor.<br>Best known for his roles in *The Devil and Miss Jones*, *The More the Merrier* (Academy Award for Best Supporting Actor), *The Green Years*, *Monkey Business*, and *Gentlemen Prefer Blondes*. |
| 65 | 31 Aug 1961 | The Dutch National Ballet was founded when the Netherlands Ballet and the Amsterdam Ballet merged. |
| 60 | 1 Aug 1966 | The Cultural Revolution (also known as the Great Proletarian Cultural Revolution) began in China.<br>It was intended to preserve China's Maoist/Communist ideology by banishing capitalist and traditional elements from society.<br>Millions of people were persecuted or displaced and there were violent struggles throughout the country.<br>The Revolution ended after Mao Zedong's death in 1976. |
| 60 | 1 Aug 1966 | The University of Texas at Austin spree shooting, USA.<br>Engineering student Charles Whitman shot and killed fifteen people and wounded 31 others before being shot dead by police. In the early hours of the same morning, he had also killed his wife and mother.<br>It was the deadliest college campus shooting until 2007. |
| 60 | 3 Aug 1966 to 31 Jan 1967 | Vietnam War – Operation Prairie.<br>U.S. forces attempted to eliminate all North Korean forces south of the Vietnamese Demilitarised Zone, and prevent further North Korean forces from crossing the border. The operation was successful, but so many U.S. forces were involved that population centres were left under-protected. |

**AUGUST 2026**

| Ann. | Date | Event |
|------|------|-------|
| 60 | 3 Aug 1966 | Death of Lenny Bruce, American stand-up comedian, satirist and free speech activist. Noted for his black humour and controversial routines punctuated by obscenity. (Drug overdose, aged 40.) |
| 60 | 4 Aug 1966 and 5th | U.S. newspapers and radio stations republished an extract from a British newspaper article (dated March 1966) in which John Lennon of the Beatles said his band was 'more popular than Jesus'.<br>It provoked widespread protests. Radio stations in many states refused to play their records.<br>He apologised on 12th August during a press conference in Chicago, Illinois to promote the start of their final tour. |
| 60 | 5 Aug 1966 | The Beatles' album *Revolver* was released in the UK. (USA: 8th August.) |
| 60 | 6 Aug 1966 | Death of Cordwainer Smith, American science fiction short story writer.<br>He also wrote books on East Asian political science. (Heart attack, aged 53.) |
| 60 | 10 Aug 1966 | The Heron Road Bridge in Ottawa, Canada collapsed while it was being constructed. Nine workers were killed and more than sixty injured.<br>It was completed in 1967.<br>In 2016 it was renamed the Heron Road Workers Memorial Bridge. |
| 60 | 10 Aug 1966 | A spectacular meteor was seen in daylight over North America, from Utah in the USA to Canada. It is the only known case of a meteor entering the Earth's atmosphere and then leaving it again. |
| 60 | 10 Aug 1966 | NASA launched its *Lunar Orbiter I* spacecraft to the Moon to map its surface and photograph potential landing sites for the Apollo missions.<br>On 23rd August it took the first photo of the Earth from the Moon's orbit.<br>It was intended to spend a year studying the Moon, but it was deliberately crashed into the lunar surface on 29th October after it ran out of altitude-control gas, and to prevent it from interfering with transmissions from *Lunar Orbiter 2*. |
| 60 | 11 Aug 1966 | The Indonesia–Malaysia confrontation ended.<br>Commonwealth victory. Indonesia agreed to recognise Malaysia. |
| 60 | 12 Aug 1966 | The Shepherd's Bush murders, London, UK (also known as the Massacre of Braybrook Street). Three men shot and killed three police officers.<br>All three were given life sentences.<br>This event led to the founding of the Police Dependants' Trust. |
| 60 | 12 Aug 1966 to 29th | British rock band the Beatles performed their last concert tour, playing seventeen shows in the USA and two in Canada. Their final show was at Candlestick Park in San Francisco, California on 29th August.<br>Audiences were smaller than on previous tours following John Lennon's remark that the Beatles were 'more popular than Jesus' and the resulting media backlash. The band had already decided to retire from playing live shows by the end of the year, and to become a studio-only band. |
| 60 | 16 Aug 1966 | Vietnam War: the House Un-American Activities Committee began investigating Americans suspected of aiding the Viet Cong, with the intention of making such activities illegal.<br>The meeting was disrupted by anti-war protesters and fifty people were arrested. |

## AUGUST 2026

| Ann. | Date | Event |
|---|---|---|
| 60 | 17 Aug 1966 | NASA launched its *Pioneer 7* space probe to measure solar wind, the solar magnetic field, and cosmic rays.<br>In 1986 it also monitored the interaction between the solar wind and the tail of Halley's Comet. |
| 60 | 18 Aug 1966 | Vietnam War – the Battle of Long Tan. Australian victory. |
| 60 | 18 Aug 1966 to Sep | The Cultural Revolution in China – Red August, Beijing.<br>1,772 people were killed by Red Guards. Many of the victims were school teachers and principals. Over 30,000 homes were also ransacked and more than 85,000 families forced to leave the city. |
| 60 | 19 Aug 1966 | The Varto earthquake, eastern Turkey.<br>The whole town was devastated.<br>Between 2,300 and 3,000 people were killed and 1,400 to 1,500 injured. |
| 60 | 20 Aug 1966 | Birth of Dimebag Darrell, American heavy metal guitarist<br>(Pantera, Damageplan).<br>(Died 2004 – shot dead by a fan while performing on stage, aged 38.) |
| 60 | 22 Aug 1966 | The United Farm Workers Organizing Committee was formed in the USA. It is now part of the United Farm Workers. |
| 60 | 23 Aug 1966 | Death of Francis X. Bushman, American stage, film and television actor.<br>Billed as 'The Handsomest Man in the World' during the silent era. |
| 60 | 24 Aug 1966 | The Soviet Union launched its *Luna 11* space probe to study the Moon's chemical composition, gravity, meteorite concentration, and radiation. |
| 60 | 24 Aug 1966 | The science fiction film *Fantastic Voyage* was released in the USA.<br>UK: 14th October. |
| 60 | 26 Aug 1966 to 21 Mar 1990 | The Namibian War of Independence (also known as the South African Border War). SWAPO victory.<br>South-West Africa gained its independence from South Africa and became the Republic of Namibia. |
| 60 | 27 Aug 1966 to 28 May 1967 | British yachtsman Francis Chichester sailed his ketch *Gipsy Moth IV* from Plymouth, UK. He returned there 226 days later, becoming the first person to complete a solo circumnavigation of the world from West to East via the Capes. |
| 60 | 27 Aug 1966 | The garage rock song *96 Tears* by ? and the Mysterians was released.<br>It became a major hit in October, and is one of the songs that influenced the development of punk rock.<br>(?, the mysterious lead singer of the group, was Rudy Martínez.) |
| 60 | 29 Aug 1966 | The Beatles played their last live concert, at Candlestick Park in San Francisco, California, USA. |
| 60 | 29 Aug 1966 | Death of Sayyid Qutb, Egyptian writer, poet and Islamic theorist.<br>A leading member of the Muslim Brotherhood. (Executed for plotting the assassination of Egyptian President Gamal Abdel Nasser.) |
| 50 | 1 Aug 1976 | Trinidad and Tobago severed its links with the British monarchy and became an independent republic. |

## AUGUST 2026

| Ann. | Date | Event |
|---|---|---|
| 50 | 1 Aug 1976 | Austrian racing driver Niki Lauda suffered life-threatening burns and was left permanently disfigured when he crashed during the German Grand Prix. As a result of his accident, the Nürburgring circuit was declared too dangerous to race on. It was rebuilt and shortened. |
| 50 | 2 Aug 1976 | An intruder broke into a house in Fort Worth, Texas, USA and killed a twelve-year-old girl – the daughter of Priscilla Lee Childers who was in the process of divorcing oil heir T. Cullen Davis. The intruder then shot and serious wounded Childers, and killed her boyfriend, Stan Farr. Davis later became the wealthiest man ever to stand trial for murder. He was acquitted, and was also found not liable in a civil trial. Stan Farr's children sued him for wrongful death and were awarded $250,000. In a later trial he was cleared of hiring a hit-man to murder his ex-wife and a judge. |
| 50 | 2 Aug 1976 | Death of Fritz Lang, Austrian-born American film director. Best known for *Metropolis*, *M*, *The Big Heat* and the *Dr. Mabuse* series. |
| 50 | 4 Aug 1976 | Death of Roy Thomson, 1st Baron Thomson, Canadian-born British newspaper publisher and media magnate. Owner of Scottish Television, *The Scotsman* newspaper, *The Times* and *The Sunday Times*. He also formed a successful consortium to drill for oil in the North Sea. |
| 50 | 5 Aug 1976 | The American Basketball Association (ABA) merged with the National Basketball Association (NBA) and the ABA was dissolved. |
| 50 | 6 Aug 1976 | Death of Gregor Piatigorsky, Russian-born American cellist. |
| 50 | 7 Aug 1976 | NASA's *Viking 2* spacecraft went into orbit around Mars. Over the next two years it orbited Mars about 700 times and sent back 16,000 images. (It was deactivated in July 1978 after developing a leak in its propulsion system.) |
| 50 | 7 Aug 1976 | American biologists studying data returned from Mars by NASA's *Viking 1* spacecraft announced that the 'Labeled Release' experiment strongly indicated possible signs of life on Mars. Many scientists later concluded that the experiment had given a 'false positive' result. But the principal investigator, Gilbert Levin, insisted that the result was a true positive. He continued to contend this until his death in 2021. |
| 50 | 9 Aug 1976 | The Soviet Union launched its *Luna 24* space probe to collect soil samples from the Moon. It returned to Earth on 22nd August with 6 ounces (170 grams) of soil collected from the Mare Crisium. |
| 50 | 9 Aug 1976 to 15th | Hurricane Belle hit North Carolina, the Mid-Atlantic U.S. states, New England and eastern Canada. Three people were killed (plus a further nine indirectly), and it caused $100 million worth of damage. |
| 50 | 12 Aug 1976 | Lebanese Civil War: Syria intervened in the war. |
| 50 | 12 Aug 1976 | Lebanese Civil War – the Tel al-Zaatar massacre, Beirut. A Palestinian refugee camp was destroyed and approximately 2,000 people were killed in one of the bloodiest events of the war. (Some sources give different estimates of the number of deaths, ranging from 1,000 to 3,000, with as many as 4,000 wounded.) |

# AUGUST 2026

| Ann. | Date | Event |
|---|---|---|
| 50 | 14 Aug 1976 | The African Independence Party was founded in Senegal to take advantage of the newly introduced three-party system. |
| 50 | 16 Aug 1976 | The Moro Gulf earthquake and tsunami, Philippines. <br> Between 5,000 and 8,000 people were killed – mostly due to the tsunami. |
| 50 | 18 Aug 1976 | The axe murder incident, Korean Demilitarised Zone. <br> Two U.S. Army officers were killed by North Korean soldiers while they were cutting down a tree that was blocking UN observers' view. <br> This led to Operation Paul Bunyan on 21st August, in which U.S. and South Korean forces cut down the tree in a show of strength designed to intimidate the North Koreans but not provoke further escalation. |
| 50 | 19 Aug 1976 | Death of Alastair Sim, Scottish stage and film character actor. |
| 50 | 22 Aug 1976 | Death of Juscelino Kubitschek, President of Brazil (1956–61). |
| 50 | 25 Aug 1976 | The album *Boston* by the American rock band Boston was released. <br> It is one of the best-selling debut albums in history. It was played and recorded almost entirely by musician Tom Scholz in his basement. |
| 50 | 25 Aug 1976 | Death of Eyvind Johnson, Swedish novelist. <br> Joint winner of the 1974 Nobel Prize in Literature. |
| 50 | 27 Aug 1976 | Biologists at the Massachusetts Institute of Technology (MIT) announced that they had created the first man-made gene. It was an *E. coli* gene that corrected a harmful mutation that can occur in natural *E. coli*. |
| 50 | 27 Aug 1976 | British politician John Stonehouse resigned as a Member of Parliament after being sentenced to seven years in prison for fraud. <br> He is best known for his attempt to fake his own death in 1974. <br> In 2009 it was revealed that he had been a Czech spy during the 1960s, though he was never convicted. |
| 50 | 29 Aug 1976 | Death of Jimmy Reed, American blues singer, songwriter and musician. <br> His work influenced artists such as Elvis Presley, the Yardbirds, Van Morrison, the Grateful Dead, the Rolling Stones and Neil Young. |
| 50 | 30 Aug 1976 | The Notting Hill Carnival riot, London. <br> Black youths threw bottles, stones and other missiles at police officers, injuring more than 100 of them, and smashed windows and set fires. <br> It was a time of racial upheaval, and huge numbers of police attended the carnival anticipating trouble. They seemed ill-prepared for what they faced. |
| 40 | 1 Aug 1986 | American tennis player John McEnroe married actress Tatum O'Neal. <br> They were divorced in 1994. |
| 40 | 2 Aug 1986 | Death of Roy Cohn, American lawyer. <br> Best known as Senator Joseph McCarthy's chief counsel during the Army–McCarthy hearings in 1954. He was also the prosecutor in the espionage trial of Julius and Ethel Rosenberg, and was a mentor for future U.S. President Donald Trump. He was disbarred for unethical conduct in 1986 and died from an AIDS-related illness a few weeks later. |
| 40 | 3 Aug 1986 | Death of Beryl Markham, British-born Kenyan aviator, horse trainer, adventurer and writer. The first woman to fly solo from east to west across the Atlantic. Best known for her memoir *West with the Night*. |

# AUGUST 2026

| Ann. | Date | Event |
|---|---|---|
| 40 | 4 Aug 1986 | The United States Football League suspended operations. It had staked its future on a lawsuit against the NFL, which it claimed had a monopoly on football in the USA. Although it won its case, it was awarded only $1 in token damages. The suspension became permanent when it did not return for the planned 1987 season. (It had lost more than $163 million.) |
| 40 | 6 Aug 1986 | The Sydney flood, New South Wales, Australia.<br>A record 13 inches (328 mm) of rain fell on the city in 24 hours, flooding subways and causing massive disruption. |
| 40 | 7 Aug 1986 | Virgilio Barco Vargas became President of Colombia (until 1990). |
| 40 | 9 Aug 1986 | British rock band Queen performed their final live concert before the death of singer Freddie Mercury, at Knebworth Park in Stevenage, UK. |
| 40 | 9 Aug 1986 | The Headington Shark, a sculpture of a shark embedded head-first in the roof of a house, was erected in Oxford, England. |
| 40 | 17 Aug 1986 | Pixar released its first film, *Luxo Jr.*<br>The two-minute film stars a computer-animated desk lamp.<br>It was the first CGI film to be nominated for an Academy Award. |
| 40 | 20 Aug 1986 | The Edmond post office shooting, Oklahoma, USA.<br>Postal worker Patrick Sherrill shot twenty co-workers, killing fourteen of them, then committed suicide.<br>It was the deadliest incident of civilian workplace violence in U.S. history (until 2019), and inspired the phrase 'going postal'. |
| 40 | 21 Aug 1986 | The Lake Nyos gas disaster, Cameroon.<br>More than 1,700 people were killed when a cloud of carbon dioxide gas escaped from the volcanic lake. |
| 40 | 21 Aug 1986 | The first official explanation of the Chernobyl disaster (April 1986) was published. It blamed plant operators for violating rules and regulations. This explanation was later found to be erroneous – or at least partially so. In 1992, the IAEA Nuclear Safety Advisory Group's report found that the fault mostly lay with the reactor's construction, though human error was a contributing factor. |
| 40 | 22 Aug 1986 | The American energy company Kerr–McGee agreed to pay $1.38 million to former nuclear technician Karen Silkwood's estate in an out-of-court settlement.<br>As a union activist she had expressed concerns about health and safety at the plant where she worked, and in November 1974 abnormal levels of plutonium were found on her person and in her home. She was about to go public with the information when her car left the road in mysterious circumstances and she was killed. Her story is told in the film *Silkwood*. |
| 40 | 22 Aug 1986 | Death of Celâl Bayar, President of Turkey (1950–60). |
| 40 | 26 Aug 1986 | The Preppy Murder, Central Park, New York City, USA.<br>Robert Chambers strangled eighteen-year-old Jennifer Levin.<br>He was convicted of manslaughter and burglary, and sentenced to five to fifteen years in prison (released in February 2003).<br>In 2008 he was sentenced to nineteen years for drug-dealing. |

## AUGUST 2026

| Ann. | Date | Event |
|---|---|---|
| 40 | 27 Aug 1986 | The U.S. Air Force revealed that it had accidentally dropped a hydrogen bomb near Albuquerque, New Mexico in May 1957.<br>The non-nuclear trigger explosives detonated. No one was injured. |
| 40 | 28 Aug 1986 | U.S. Navy communications specialist Jerry Whitworth was sentenced to 365 years imprisonment and fined $410,000 for passing classified information to the Soviet Union between 1974 and 1985.<br>He was a member of the Walker family spy ring.<br>Judge John P. Vukasin called him 'one of the most spectacular spies of this century'. (See also: 6th November 1986.) |
| 40 | 31 Aug 1986 | The Soviet passenger liner *SS Admiral Nakhimov* sank after colliding with the bulk carrier *Pyotr Vasev* in the Black Sea. 423 people were killed. |
| 40 | 31 Aug 1986 | Death of Urho Kekkonen, President of Finland (1956–81). |
| 40 | 31 Aug 1986 | Death of Henry Moore, British sculptor. |
| 30 | 1 Aug 1996 | The novel *A Game of Thrones* by George R. R. Martin was published.<br>It was the first book in his *A Song of Ice and Fire* series, and was adapted into the television series *Game of Thrones*. |
| 30 | 1 Aug 1996 | Death of Mohamed Farrah Aidid, Somali military commander and faction leader. He played a key role in the ousting of President Mohamed Siad Barre during the Somali Civil War. He declared himself President of Somalia in June 1995 but was not recognised. |
| 30 | 1 Aug 1996 | Death of Frida Boccara, French singer.<br>Joint winner of the Eurovision Song Contest in 1969. |
| 30 | 4 Aug 1996 | Josia Thugwane became the first black South African to win an Olympic gold medal (men's marathon). |
| 30 | 4 Aug 1996 | Death of Geoff Hamilton, British gardener and broadcaster.<br>Best known as the presenter of the BBC television series *Gardener's World*. |
| 30 | 6 Aug 1996 | NASA reported that a meteorite (ALH 84001) found in Antarctica and believed to have come from Mars showed possible signs of primitive life.<br>It contained hydrocarbons, minerals and possible microfossils consistent with bacterial activity. |
| 30 | 6 Aug 1996 | American punk rock band the Ramones played their farewell concert, at The Palace in Hollywood, Los Angeles, California. |
| 30 | 7 Aug 1996 | An intense storm caused flash flooding and mudslides at a camp site near Biescas in the Spanish Pyrenees. 87 people were killed. |
| 30 | 9 Aug 1996 | Boris Yeltsin was sworn in as the President of Russia for a second term following the country's first post-independence election in June<br>Critics said the election had been rigged in his favour. |
| 30 | 9 Aug 1996 | Death of Sir Frank Whittle, British engineer and pilot.<br>Inventor of the jet engine. |

# AUGUST 2026

| Ann. | Date | Event |
|------|------|-------|
| 30 | 13 Aug 1996 | NASA announced that data returned from its *Galileo* space probe indicated the presence of 'warm ice' or liquid water on Jupiter's moon Europa.<br>Later evidence confirmed that the movement of the thick ice sheets was similar to plate tectonics on Earth.<br>NASA is planning to launch the *Europa Clipper* spacecraft in 2024 to study Europa in more detail. |
| 30 | 13 Aug 1996 | Microsoft released its Internet Explorer 3 web browser. It was the first widely used version and led to a browser war with Netscape Navigator. |
| 30 | 13 Aug 1996 | Death of António de Spínola, President of Portugal (1974).<br>He helped lead Portugal to democracy. |
| 30 | 16 Aug 1996 | Leonel Fernández became President of the Dominican Republic (until 2000) following the first democratic elections for about forty years.<br>He was President again from 2004 to 2012. |
| 30 | 16 Aug 1996 | A female gorilla, Binti Jua, rescued a three-year-old boy who had fallen into the primate enclosure at Brookfield Zoo near Chicago, USA. |
| 30 | 15 Aug 1996 | The Sigma Beta Rho fraternity was founded at the University of Pennsylvania in Philadelphia, USA. |
| 30 | 21 Aug 1996 | The Health Insurance Portability and Accountability Act came into effect in the USA. It simplified the administration of the health care system and protected the continuity of health care coverage for workers who changed or lost their jobs. |
| 30 | 22 Aug 1996 | U.S. President Bill Clinton signed the Welfare Reform Act into law.<br>It required welfare recipients to work in exchange for temporary relief, imposed a maximum limit of two years before returning to work or training, and a maximum limit of five years cumulatively. |
| 30 | 23 Aug 1996 | Saudi Arabian-born terrorist Osama bin Laden issued a fatwa entitled *A Declaration of War Against the Americans Occupying the Land of the Two Holy Places*. Few people knew who he was at that time, and it received little attention. (See also: 6th August 2001.) |
| 30 | 23 Aug 1996 | U.S. President Bill Clinton imposed far-reaching restrictions on advertising tobacco products to children, and announced an increase in tobacco taxation. |
| 30 | 24 Aug 1996 | Microsoft Windows NT 4.0 was released.<br>The operating system was designed for workstations and servers and had an almost identical graphical user interface to Windows 95.<br>It was succeeded by Windows 2000 in 1999. |
| 30 | 26 Aug 1996 | The former President of South Korea, Chun Doo-hwan, was sentenced to death after being convicted of insurrection, treason and embezzlement.<br>The Seoul High Court commuted his sentence to life imprisonment plus a massive fine (approximately £136 million/$185 million) in December.<br>In December 1997 his sentence was commuted to time served, and he was released. He had only paid a quarter of his fine, but he said he had no more money left to pay it, and the remainder was never collected.<br>He died in 2021. |

**AUGUST 2026**

| Ann. | Date | Event |
|------|------|-------|
| 30 | 26 Aug 1996 to 27th | The Sudan Airways Flight 150 hijacking. Seven Iraqis hijacked a passenger jet with 196 people on board, claiming that they were carrying grenades. They forced the plane to land at London Stansted Airport in the UK, where they demanded political asylum. Most of the passengers were released when the plane landed. After eight hours of negotiations, the hijackers were arrested by police, and the crew and remaining passengers were released. |
| 30 | 26 Aug 1996 | Death of Alejandro Agustín Lanusse, President of Argentina (1971–73). He was appointed by the military junta. |
| 30 | 28 Aug 1996 | Britain's Prince Charles and Princess Diana were divorced. Princess Diana could no longer be addressed as Her Royal Highness but would be known as Diana, Princess of Wales. |
| 30 | 30 Aug 1996 to 31st | The Revolutionary Armed Forces of Colombia (FARC) terrorist group destroyed Las Delicias military base, killing dozens of soldiers and kidnapping about sixty. |
| 30 | 30 Aug 1996 | British heavyweight boxer Frank Bruno announced his retirement. |
| 30 | 31 Aug 1996 | The First Chechen War ended. Chechen victory over Russian Federation forces. This led to the Second Chechen War (1999–2009) – Russian victory. |
| 25 | 1 Aug 2001 | The Chief Justice of the Alabama Supreme Court, Roy Moore, unveiled a 2.5-ton granite monument to the Ten Commandments in the rotunda of the judiciary building. Several groups filed a lawsuit calling for it to be removed, and a court ordered him to remove it by 20th August 2003. It was relocated to a side room on 27th August, and removed from the building in July 2004. As he had failed to remove it within the deadline, he was removed from office in November 2003. He was re-elected in 2012 and returned to office in January 2013. He was suspended in May 2016 and removed from office again in April 2017 for judicial misconduct. |
| 25 | 3 Aug 2001 | The Ealing bombing, London, UK. The Real IRA detonated a car bomb in Ealing Broadway shortly after midnight. Seven people were injured. This was the last Irish republican bombing outside Northern Ireland. |
| 25 | 3 Aug 2001 | Death of Christopher Hewett, British stage, film and television actor and theatre director. Best known for his lead role as the butler Lynn Aloysius Belvedere in the American TV sitcom *Mr. Belvedere*. |
| 25 | 4 Aug 2001 | Death of Lorenzo Music, American actor, voice actor, screenwriter and composer. Best known for playing the voice of the cartoon character Garfield the cat. He also co-created the TV sitcom *The Bob Newhart Show*, and was a writer and performer on *The Smothers Brothers Comedy Hour*. |
| 25 | 6 Aug 2001 | U.S. President George W. Bush received a daily briefing warning that the terrorist Osama bin Laden was determined to strike in the USA. This was six weeks before the 9/11 terrorist attack. |

## AUGUST 2026

| Ann. | Date | Event |
|------|------|-------|
| 25 | 6 Aug 2001 | The Erwadi fire incident, Tamil Nadu, India.<br>A fire began in a ramshackle shelter at a mental asylum where 45 inmates were chained to their beds. 28 of them died.<br>The cause of the fire remains unknown.<br>Chaining inmates to their beds was illegal.<br>All mental asylums of this type were closed the following week. |
| 25 | 6 Aug 2001 | Death of Larry Adler, American harmonica player. |
| 25 | 6 Aug 2001 | Death of Dorothy Tutin, British stage, film and television actress. |
| 25 | 7 Aug 2001 | Britain's National Health Service (NHS) bought the Heart Hospital in Harley Street, London. This was the first time that a private hospital had been re-nationalised. It was an NHS hospital from 1948 to 1989. |
| 25 | 9 Aug 2001 | The Sbarro restaurant suicide bombing, Jerusalem, Israel.<br>A Palestinian terrorist detonated a bomb in the pizzeria.<br>Fifteen people were killed (plus the bomber) and 130 injured. |
| 25 | 10 Aug 2001 | British politician Neil Hamilton and his wife Christine were arrested after being accused of raping a woman. The investigation was later dropped when it became apparent that the woman's accusations were entirely false. Mr Hamilton had previously been involved in other political scandals and was widely associated with sleaze. He had been forced to resign his ministerial post in 1994 after it was found that he had accepted bribes. |
| 25 | 10 Aug 2001 | Angolan Civil War – the 2001 Angola train attack.<br>UNITA forces detonated an anti-tank mine, causing a train to derail.<br>They then opened fire on the passengers.<br>252 people were killed and 165 injured. |
| 25 | 16 Aug 2001 | Princess Diana's former butler, Paul Burrell, was charged with theft after reportedly stealing 342 items worth £5 million from her estate.<br>The charges were dropped in November 2002 when the Queen came to his defence. |
| 25 | 20 Aug 2001 | Death of Sir Fred Hoyle, British mathematician, astronomer and writer. |
| 25 | 20 Aug 2001 | Death of Kim Stanley, American stage and television actress. |
| 25 | 22 Aug 2001 | Insurgency in Macedonia – Operation Essential Harvest was launched. NATO deployed 3,500 (later increased to 4,800) peacekeeping forces on a thirty-day mission to disarm the National Liberation Army and destroy their weapons.<br>The operation began on 27th August and was successful, although sporadic outbreaks of fighting continued into November.<br>A final ceasefire agreement was signed by both sides in January 2002. |
| 25 | 25 Aug 2001 | Death of Aaliyah, American R&B/hip hop singer and actress.<br>(Plane crash, aged 22.) |
| 25 | 25 Aug 2001 | Death of Ken Tyrrell, British Formula Two racing driver and founder of the Tyrrell Formula One team. He discovered and mentored drivers including Jackie Stewart, Jody Scheckter and John Surtees. |

# AUGUST 2026

| Ann. | Date | Event |
|------|------|-------|
| 25 | 27 Aug 2001 | The Peruvian Congress ruled that former President Alberto Fujimori was responsible for crimes against humanity.<br>On 5th September he was formally charged (in his absence as he had fled to Japan in November 2000).<br>In 2005 he declared that he was returning to Peru to run for election again. He flew to Chile, as there were no direct flights to Peru, and was immediately arrested and extradited.<br>In 2009 he was convicted of human rights violations and sentenced to 25 years in prison.<br>In later trials he was also convicted of embezzlement and bribery. |
| 20 | 3 Aug 2006 | Death of Dame Elisabeth Schwarzkopf, German-born Austrian/British soprano. |
| 20 | 4 Aug 2006 | The Muttur massacre, Sri Lanka.<br>Seventeen humanitarian aid workers employed by the French organisation Action Against Hunger were killed while working on reconstruction projects following the 2004 tsunami.<br>Sixteen of the employees were Tamils and one was a Muslim. Sri Lankan government forces were blamed for the massacre, though they deny it. |
| 20 | 5 Aug 2006 | Death of Susan Butcher, American sled dog racer and trainer. She won the Iditarod Trail Sled Dog Race four times between 1986 and 1990. |
| 20 | 7 Aug 2006 | Thermae Bath Spa opened in Bath, UK.<br>It features an open-air rooftop pool and an indoor pool, a large steam room and twenty treatment rooms and is fed by the only naturally hot, mineral-rich spring in the UK.<br>It replaced the municipal hot pools which closed in 1978 after an infectious organism was found in the aquifer that fed them. |
| 20 | 9 Aug 2006 | Terrorists attempted to detonate liquid explosives on board airliners travelling from the UK to the USA and Canada. The explosives were disguised as soft drinks.<br>The plot was discovered by British police during a surveillance operation and none of the explosives detonated. Many airlines immediately banned all liquids except baby milk formula and prescription medicine from passenger cabins.<br>The ban was relaxed in the following weeks, but at the time of writing many airlines still ban liquid containers larger than 100 ml. |
| 20 | 9 Aug 2006 | Death of James Van Allen, American physicist who discovered the Van Allen radiation belts surrounding the Earth. |
| 20 | 11 Aug 2006 | The Guimaras oil spill, Philippines.<br>The oil tanker *MT Solar 1* sank off the coast of Guimaras and Negros during a storm, spilling 110,000 gallons of oil into the gulf.<br>It was the worst oil spill in the Philippines' history.<br>The clean-up operation took three years. |
| 20 | 14 Aug 2006 | The Chencholai bombing, Sri Lanka.<br>The Sri Lankan Air Force bombed what it claimed was a rebel training camp, killing 61 Tamil girls aged between 16 and 18. |
| 20 | 15 Aug 2006 | Death of Dame Te Atairangikaahu, New Zealand Maori queen.<br>Queen of the Kingitanga (1966–2006). |

## AUGUST 2026

| Ann. | Date | Event |
|---|---|---|
| 20 | 16 Aug 2006 | Death of Alfredo Stroessner, President of Paraguay (1954–89). |
| 20 | 18 Aug 2006 | NASA announced that SpaceX and Rocketplane Kistler had been selected to provide cargo and crew demonstration flights to the International Space Station under the Commercial Orbital Transportation Services (COTS) programme.<br>SpaceX successfully completed its first demonstration flight (COTS Demo Flight 1) in December 2010.<br>Rocketplane Kistler failed meet its financial milestones for 2006 and 2007 and NASA terminated its funding. |
| 20 | 20 Aug 2006 | Death of Joe Rosenthal, American photographer.<br>Best known for his iconic WWII photograph *Raising the Flag on Iwo Jima*. |
| 20 | 23 Aug 2006 | Austrian kidnapping victim Natascha Kampusch escaped from captivity after eight years.<br>She was kidnapped by Wolfgang Priklopil at the age of ten and held in a secret cellar beneath his garage in Strasshof an der Nordbahn. |
| 20 | 24 Aug 2006 | Pluto was downgraded from a planet to a dwarf planet when the International Astronomical Union (IAU) redefined the term 'planet'. |
| 20 | 25 Aug 2006 | Death of Noor Hassanali, President of Trinidad and Tobago (1987–97). |
| 20 | 26 Aug 2006 | Death of Clyde Walcott, West Indian cricket player and administrator.<br>Regarded as the best batsman of his era. |
| 20 | 31 Aug 2006 | NASA awarded Lockheed Martin and its associates a multi-billion-dollar contract to develop the Orion Crew Exploration Vehicle that would carry astronauts to the Moon and Mars.<br>The first unmanned launch (*Artemis 1*) is expected to take place during the summer of 2022, and the first manned mission (a ten-day lunar fly-by in *Artemis 2*) is scheduled for May 2024. |
| 15 | 3 Aug 2011 to 2 Jun 2012 | The former President of Egypt, Hosni Mubarak, went on trial for corruption, abuse of power, and failing to halt the killing of peaceful protestors. He was sentenced to life imprisonment on 2nd June 2012.<br>An appeals court overturned the sentence in January 2013, but he was convicted again in a second trial in 2014.<br>The appeals court acquitted him again in March 2017. He died in 2020. |
| 15 | 20 Aug 2011 | Libyan Civil War – the Battle of Tripoli.<br>National Transitional Council victory. The rebels seized control of the capital and the government collapsed. Libya's leader, Muammar Gaddafi, fled, but was captured and killed on 20th October. |
| 15 | 21 Aug 2011 | Hurricane Irene hit the Caribbean, and made landfall in North Carolina, USA on 27th August.<br>49 people were killed and it caused over $14 billion worth of damage. |
| 15 | 24 Aug 2011 | Steve Jobs resigned as CEO of Apple Inc. because of ill health (pancreatic tumour). He died on 5th October. |
| 10 | 1 Aug 2016 | Death of Queen Anne of Romania. Wife of King Michael I of Romania.<br>They were married a year after he abdicated the throne, so she was never actually queen, though she was known by that title. |

## AUGUST 2026

| Ann. | Date | Event |
|---|---|---|
| 10 | 13 Aug 2016 | Death of Kenny Baker, British film and television actor.<br>Noted for his short stature (3 feet 8 inches).<br>He played the robot R2-D2 in six *Star Wars* films.<br>He also appeared in the films *The Elephant Man, Time Bandits, Willow, Flash Gordon, Amadeus,* and *Labyrinth*. |
| 10 | 22 Aug 2016 | Death of S. R. Nathan, President of Singapore (1999–2011). |
| 10 | 29 Aug 2016 | Death of Gene Wilder, American film actor, comedian, screenwriter and film director (*Willy Wonka & the Chocolate Factory, Everything You Always Wanted to Know About Sex (But Were Afraid to Ask), The Producers, Blazing Saddles, Young Frankenstein, Stir Crazy,* and more.)<br>Husband of the comedian and actress Gilda Radner. |
| 10 | 31 Aug 2016 | The first female President of Brazil, Dilma Rousseff, was impeached and removed from office for breaking budgetary laws.<br>She was succeeded by Vice President Michel Temer, who had been Acting President since 12th May. |

## SEPTEMBER 2026

| Ann. | Date | Event |
|------|------|-------|
| 1400 | 4 Sep 626 | Following the Xuanwu Gate Incident (a palace coup) in July, Emperor Gaozu of the Tang dynasty in China retired and passed the throne to Emperor Taizong. |
| 750 | 8 Sep 1276 | Pope John XXI became Pope (until 1277) following Adrian V's death in August. |
| 750 | 29 Sep 1276 | Birth of Christoffel II, King of Denmark (1320–26, 1329–32). |
| 300 | 2 Sep 1726 | Birth of John Howard, British philanthropist and prison reformer. |
| 250 | 5 Sep 1776 to 12th | The Pointe-à-Pitre Guadeloupe Hurricane. One of the deadliest Atlantic hurricanes in history. It hit Martinique on 5th September and Guadeloupe on 6th, and sank a convoy of French and Dutch merchant ships that were transporting goods to Europe. More than 6,000 people were killed. |
| 250 | 7 Sep 1776 | American Revolutionary War: the first reported use of a submarine in combat. The American submarine *Turtle* attempted to attach explosives to the hulls of British ships including *HMS Eagle* in New York Harbor. The explosives failed to attach and the mission failed. |
| 250 | 8 Sep 1776 | American Revolutionary War: American Patriot and solder Nathan Hale volunteered for an intelligence-gathering mission, spying on the British behind enemy lines in New York City. He was captured by the British and executed on 22nd September, aged 21. He was declared an American hero, and is the state hero of Connecticut. |
| 250 | 9 Sep 1776 | American Revolution: the Second Continental Congress adopted the name United States, which replaced the previous name United Colonies. |
| 250 | 11 Sep 1776 | American Revolutionary War – the Staten Island Peace Conference, New York. British diplomats met the leaders of the Second Continental Congress. The conference lasted only three hours, as the British Admiral Lord Richard Howe had limited powers to negotiate and was unable to grant the Americans recognition of their Declaration of Independence. The military campaign immediately resumed, and the war continued for another seven years. |
| 250 | 15 Sep 1776 | American Revolutionary War – the Landing at Kip's Bay, Manhattan, New York. British ships fired on the inexperienced American militia, who fled. The British then landed unopposed, forcing the Continental Army to withdraw to Harlem Heights (now Morningside Heights). (See also: 16th September 1776.) |
| 250 | 16 Sep 1776 | American Revolutionary War – the Battle of Harlem Heights (now Morningside Heights), Manhattan, New York. British forces who had landed at Kip's Bay the previous day pursued the Americans towards Harlem Heights. General George Washington launched a counter-attack and forced the British to retreat. |
| 250 | 17 Sep 1776 | The Presidio of San Francisco was established by the Spanish in what is now California, USA. |
| 250 | 24 Sep 1776 | The first St Leger Stakes horse race was held at Doncaster Racecourse, UK. The St Leger is the final leg of the English Triple Crown. |

## SEPTEMBER 2026

| Ann. | Date | Event |
|------|------|-------|
| 200 | 3 Sep 1826 | The U.S. warship *USS Vincennes* set off from New York, and returned on 8th June 1830. It was the first U.S. Navy ship to circumnavigate the world. |
| 200 | 5 Sep 1826 | Birth of John Wisden, British cricketer (Kent, Middlesex, Sussex) and founder of *Wisden's Cricketers' Almanac*. |
| 200 | 11 Sep 1826 | Former Freemason William Morgan, who was planning to release a book detailing the Masons' secrets, was arrested in Batavia, New York, USA for theft and the non-payment of a loan. He was put in a debtors' prison but released when one of his financial backers paid his debt. He was swiftly arrested again for the non-payment of a bar bill. A group of friends helped him escape from jail. He disappeared shortly afterwards. Some believe he was taken on a boat into the Niagara River and thrown overboard, while others believe the Masons killed him in some other way – a sheriff and three Masons were convicted of this, though they received minimal sentences. The Masons said they had paid him $500 to leave the country, though there were no confirmed sightings of him after this. His backers published his book and it became a bestseller, and there were protests against the Freemasons. |
| 200 | 13 Sep 1826 | Birth of Anthony Drexel, American banker and philanthropist He played a leading role in the rise of modern global finance. Co-founder of Drexel, Morgan & Co. (later J. P. Morgan & Co.). Founder of Drexel University. First president of the Association for Public Art. |
| 200 | 17 Sep 1826 | Birth of Bernhard Riemann, German mathematician. He made important contributions to the fields of analysis, number theory and differential geometry. |
| 200 | 22 Sep 1826 | Death of Johann Peter Hebel, German short story writer, poet and theologian. |
| 175 | 4 Sep 1851 | Birth of John Dillon, Irish politician and nationalist. Leader of the Irish Parliamentary Party (1918). |
| 175 | 11 Sep 1851 | The Christiana Riot, Pennsylvania, USA – one of several key events that led to the American Civil War. A federal marshal and a slave owner led a raid on the house of an escaped slave with the intention of recapturing four other slaves who had escaped from Maryland. The slave owner was killed in the riot, and the marshal and his raiders were driven away by gunfire. Many of the African Americans involved in the riot fled to Canada. |
| 175 | 13 Sep 1851 | Birth of Walter Reed, U.S. Army physician. Best known for proving that yellow fever was transmitted by mosquitoes, which led to the growth of epidemiology and biomedicine. Several medical facilities were named in his honour, including the Walter Reed National Military Medical Center in Bethesda, Maryland. |
| 175 | 14 Sep 1851 | Death of James Fenimore Cooper, American historical romance novelist, short story writer and travel writer. Best known for his novel *The Last of the Mohicans*. His father, William Cooper, founded Cooperstown in New York. |
| 175 | 18 Sep 1851 | The first edition of *The New York Times* newspaper was published in the USA (as the *New-York Daily Times*). |

## SEPTEMBER 2026

| Ann. | Date | Event |
|---|---|---|
| 175 | 19 Sep 1851 | Birth of William Lever, 1st Viscount Leverhulme, British industrialist, philanthropist and politician. <br> Co-founder of Lever Brothers (now Unilever) with his brother James. |
| 150 | 5 Sep 1876 | Death of Manuel Blanco Encalada, first (provisional) President of Chile (1826). |
| 150 | 7 Sep 1876 | The Northfield, Minnesota Raid, USA. <br> The James-Younger Gang of outlaws attempted to rob the First National Bank of Northfield. They shot and killed one civilian in the street, and the bank's assistant cashier who refused to open the safe. <br> When local people realised a robbery was in progress, they took weapons from local hardware stores and began shooting the outlaws. <br> Every member of the gang was shot, and two of them were killed. <br> The wounded survivors fled. The Younger brothers were wounded in another gunfight two weeks later, and were arrested and sentenced to life imprisonment. Jesse James formed a new gang, and was shot dead in 1882. |
| 150 | 9 Sep 1876 | Death of American Horse (the elder), Native American warrior chief. <br> Noted for his alliance with Crazy Horse during Red Cloud's War and the Battle of the Little Bighorn. <br> (Killed during the Battle of Slim Buttes during the Great Sioux War.) |
| 150 | 15 Sep 1876 | Birth of Frank Gannett, American publisher. <br> Founder of Gannett, the largest newspaper publisher in the USA, which publishes *USA Today* and many others. |
| 150 | 15 Sep 1876 | Birth of Bruno Walter, German-born American pianist, composer and conductor. Regarded as one of the greatest conductors of the 20th century. He worked closely with the composer Gustav Mahler. |
| 150 | 18 Sep 1876 | Birth of James Scullin, Prime Minister of Australia (1929–32). |
| 150 | 19 Sep 1876 | American entrepreneur and inventor Melville Reuben Bissell was granted a U.S. patent for the modern carpet sweeper. (U.S. Patent 182,346.) <br> He formed the Bissell corporation to manufacture and sell it. |
| 150 | 20 Sep 1876 | The Ottawa Rough Riders Canadian Football League team was formed. <br> It was dissolved in 1996. Ottawa's current football team, the Ottawa Redblacks, was founded in 2010. |
| 125 | 4 Sep 1901 | Birth of William Lyons, British car manufacturer and businessman. <br> Co-founder of Jaguar Cars. |
| 125 | 5 Sep 1901 | Minor League Baseball was founded in North America <br> (as the National Association of Professional Baseball Leagues). |
| 125 | 7 Sep 1901 | The Boxer Rebellion in China ended with the signing of the Boxer Protocol by China and the Eight-Nation Alliance. Allied victory. |
| 125 | 8 Sep 1901 | Birth of Hendrik Verwoerd, Prime Minister of South Africa (1958–66). <br> Minister of Native Affairs (1950–58). <br> He developed and implemented apartheid. (Assassinated in 1966.) |
| 125 | 9 Sep 1901 | Death of Henri de Toulouse-Lautrec, French artist and illustrator. <br> Particularly known for his posters for the Moulin Rouge and his paintings of theatrical life in Paris. Noted for his short legs, alcoholism and affinity for prostitutes. (Died from alcoholism and syphilis, aged 36.) |

## SEPTEMBER 2026

| Ann. | Date | Event |
|------|------|-------|
| 125 | 14 Sep 1901 | Death of William McKinley, 25th President of the USA (1897–1901) (Fatally shot by an anarchist on 6th September, aged 58.) Succeeded by Vice President Theodore Roosevelt. |
| 125 | 15 Sep 1901 | Birth of Donald Bailey, British civil engineer. Inventor of the Bailey bridge, which made an important contribution to ending WWII. |
| 125 | 17 Sep 1901 | Second Boer War – the Battle of Blood River Poort, South Africa. Boer victory. |
| 125 | 17 Sep 1901 | Second Boer War – the Battle of Elands River, near Tarkastad, South Africa. Boer victory. |
| 125 | 17 Sep 1901 | Birth of Francis Chichester, British yachtsman, aviator and businessman. Best known for being the first person to sail single-handed around the world via the clipper route in *Gypsy Moth IV* in 1966–67. |
| 125 | 19 Sep 1901 | Birth of Joe Pasternak, Hungarian-born American film producer. Known for his MGM musicals. |
| 125 | 22 Sep 1901 | Birth of Charles Huggins, Canadian-born American physician, physiologist and cancer researcher. Winner of the 1966 Nobel Prize in Physiology or Medicine for discovering that hormones could control the spread of cancer. |
| 125 | 23 Sep 1901 | Birth of Jaroslav Seifert, Czech poet, writer and journalist. Winner of the 1984 Nobel Prize in Literature. |
| 125 | 28 Sep 1901 | The American Safety Razor Company was founded by King Camp Gillette. He changed the name to the Gillette Safety Razor Company in July 1902. The company began producing razors and razor blades in 1903. |
| 125 | 28 Sep 1901 | Birth of William S. Paley, American broadcasting pioneer and executive. As the chief executive of CBS, he built the company from a small radio network into one of the biggest radio and television broadcasters in the USA. |
| 125 | 28 Sep 1901 | Birth of Ed Sullivan, American television host, sports reporter and columnist. Best known for hosting the variety show *Talk of the Town/ The Ed Sullivan Show* (1948–71), which brought many famous performers to national attention. |
| 125 | 29 Sep 1901 | Birth of Enrico Fermi, Italian-born American physicist who created the first nuclear reactor and demonstrated the first self-sustaining nuclear chain reaction. Known as the 'architect of the nuclear age' and the 'architect of the nuclear bomb'. He also made important contributions to other fields including quantum theory, particle physics and statistical mechanics. Winner of the 1938 Nobel Prize in Physics. |
| 100 | 1 Sep 1926 | The Lebanese Republic (now Lebanon) was established by France. Lebanon declared its independence from France in 1943. |
| 100 | 4 Sep 1926 | Birth of George William Gray, British organic chemist who developed the first liquid crystals, which led to the creation of liquid crystal displays (LCDs). (Died 2013.) |
| 100 | 7 Sep 1926 | Birth of Patrick Jenkin, Baron Jenkin of Roding, British politician who had several roles in Margaret Thatcher's cabinet. Secretary of State for the Environment (1982–85), Secretary of State for Industry (1981–83), Secretary of State for Health and Social Services (1979–81). (Died 2016.) |

## SEPTEMBER 2026

| Ann. | Date | Event |
|------|------|-------|
| 100 | 8 Sep 1926 | Germany was admitted to the League of Nations. Spain immediately withdrew in protest, as Brazil had done in June. |
| 100 | 10 Sep 1926 | Birth of Beryl Cook, British artist. Known for her instantly recognisable scenes of plump people enjoying themselves. (Died 2008.) |
| 100 | 11 Sep 1926 | The Aloha Tower in Honolulu Harbor, Hawaii was officially opened. The lighthouse is one of the most important landmarks in Hawaii. |
| 100 | 16 Sep 1926 to 22nd | The Great Miami Hurricane. The hurricane hit the Turks and Caicos Islands, the Bahamas, and the U.S. states of Florida, Alabama, Mississippi and Louisiana, and caused massive destruction. The exact death toll is unknown, but is believed to between 372 and over 539. |
| 100 | 19 Sep 1926 | Birth of Duke Snider, ('the Silver Fox', 'the Duke of Flatbush'), American baseball player. (Died 2011.) |
| 100 | 23 Sep 1926 | Birth of André Cassagnes, French inventor, toy maker and kite designer. Best known for inventing the Etch A Sketch. (Died 2013.) |
| 100 | 23 Sep 1926 | Birth of John Coltrane, American jazz saxophonist, bandleader and composer. (Died 1967.) |
| 100 | 25 Sep 1926 | Birth of Aldo Ray, American film and television actor. His portrayals inspired contemporary filmmakers, including Quentin Tarantino. |
| 100 | 26 Sep 1926 | Birth of Julie London, American jazz/pop singer and film and television actress. Known for the song *Cry Me a River* and for her role as nurse Dixie McCall in the TV series *Emergency!* (Died 2000.) |
| 90 | 2 Sep 1936 | Birth of Andrew Grove, Hungarian-born American businessman and engineer. CEO of Intel, which he transformed into the world's largest semiconductor manufacturer. (Died 2016.) |
| 90 | 3 Sep 1936 | Birth of Zine El Abidine Ben Ali, President of Tunisia (1987–2011 – ousted during the Tunisian Revolution). (Died 2019.) |
| 90 | 6 Sep 1936 | British aviation pioneer Beryl Markham became the first person to fly non-stop from Britain to North America, and the first woman to fly solo from east to west across the Atlantic Ocean. |
| 90 | 7 Sep 1936 | The last surviving thylacine (Tasmanian tiger or Tasmanian wolf) died at Hobart Zoo in Tasmania, Australia, and the species became extinct. |
| 90 | 7 Sep 1936 | Birth of Buddy Holly, American rock and roll singer and songwriter (*Peggy Sue*, *That'll be the Day*, *Oh Boy!*). (Killed in a plane crash in 1959.) |
| 90 | 9 Sep 1936 | German leader Adolf Hitler revealed his Four-Year Plan in a speech before the Labour Front in Nuremberg. He said Germany was overpopulated and could not feed itself from its own resources. It should extend its living space and/or the source of its food. In order to achieve this, the German Army must become operational within four years and the German economy must become fit for war within four years. Hermann Göring was put in charge of the implementing the plan on 18th October, and was granted extraordinary powers. |
| 90 | 11 Sep 1936 | The Boulder Dam (now the Hoover Dam) in Nevada, USA was dedicated by U.S. President Franklin D. Roosevelt. |

# SEPTEMBER 2026

| Ann. | Date | Event |
|---|---|---|
| 90 | 14 Sep 1936 | American neurologists Walter Freeman and James Watts performed the first prefrontal lobotomy in the USA. |
| 90 | 14 Sep 1936 | Birth of Terence Donovan, British photographer and film/video/TV commercial director. Director of the video for Robert Palmer's song *Addicted to Love*. (Died 1996.) |
| 90 | 16 Sep 1936 | Death of Irving Thalberg, American film producer (*Grand Hotel*, *A Night at the Opera*, *Mutiny on the Bounty*, and more). Known as 'The Boy Wonder' in the U.S. film industry. He discovered numerous film stars including Lon Chaney, Greta Garbo, Lionel Barrymore, Joan Crawford, Clark Gable, Jean Harlow, Spencer Tracy, and Norma Shearer. (Pneumonia, aged 37.) |
| 90 | 19 Sep 1936 | Birth of Al Oerter, American discus thrower.<br>The first athlete to win a gold medal for the same event at four consecutive Olympic Games (1956, 1960, 1964, 1968). (Died 2007.) |
| 90 | 21 Sep 1936 | Death of Frank Hornby, British inventor and businessman. He invented and founded Meccano, Hornby Model Railways, and Dinky Toys. |
| 90 | 24 Sep 1936 | Birth of Jim Henson, American puppeteer. Creator of the Muppets. (Died 1990.) |
| 90 | 25 Sep 1936 | Birth of Juliet Prowse, Indian-born South African actress and dancer. (Died 1996.) |
| 90 | 26 Sep 1936 | Birth of Winnie Madikizela-Mandela (Winnie Mandela), South African anti-apartheid activist and politician. Wife of Nelson Mandela. (Died 2018.) |
| 90 | 27 Sep 1936 | Birth of Gordon Honeycombe, Indian-born British radio broadcaster, television newscaster (ITV), stage and film actor, and playwright. (Died 2015.) |
| 90 | 30 Sep 1936 | Pinewood Studios in Buckinghamshire, England was officially opened. |
| 80 | 1 Sep 1946 | Greece held a referendum on maintaining the monarchy.<br>The results were in favour, although observers noted significant fraud by monarchists.<br>King George II returned from exile on 26th September but died on 1st April 1947. He was succeeded by his younger brother, Paul (until 1964), and then by Constantine.<br>The monarchy was abolished in 1973. |
| 80 | 1 Sep 1946 | Birth of Roh Moo-hyun, President of South Korea (2003–08). (Committed suicide in 2009.) |
| 80 | 2 Sep 1946 | The Interim Government of India was formed.<br>Its role was to assist India and Pakistan's transition from British rule to independence (in August 1947). |
| 80 | 2 Sep 1946 | Birth of Billy Preston, American R&B/rock/soul/funk/gospel keyboard player, singer and songwriter. He worked with acts including Little Richard, Syreeta, Sam Cooke, the Beatles, Sly & the Family Stone, the Rolling Stones, Ray Charles, and Eric Clapton, and was a successful solo artist. (Died 2006.) |
| 80 | 5 Sep 1946 | Birth of Freddie Mercury, Zanzibar-born British rock singer and songwriter (Queen). (Died 1991.) |

## SEPTEMBER 2026

| Ann. | Date | Event |
|---|---|---|
| 80 | 6 Sep 1946 | The first game in the All-America Football Conference was played (Cleveland Browns v. Miami Seahawks). The Conference was established as a rival to the National Football League (NFL) but ceased operating in 1949. |
| 80 | 7 Sep 1946 | Birth of Willie Crawford, American baseball player. (Died 2004.) |
| 80 | 8 Sep 1946 | Bulgaria held a referendum on whether to abolish the monarchy and become a republic. Over 95 percent of voters favoured the republic, and the monarchy was abolished on 15th September.<br>The last tsar, Simeon Saxe-Coburg-Gotha, went into exile.<br>He became Prime Minister in 2001 (until 2005). |
| 80 | 18 Sep 1946 | The Faroe Islands declared its independence from Denmark following a referendum held on 14th September.<br>On 20th September, King Christian X of Denmark annulled the declaration as the majority of voters had not supported independence.<br>He also dissolved the Faroe Islands' parliament on 24th September.<br>Denmark granted the Faroe Islands self-rule in 1948. |
| 80 | 19 Sep 1946 | Former British Prime Minister Winston Churchill gave a speech at the University of Zurich, Switzerland in which he called for a United States of Europe and the creation of a Council of Europe.<br>The Council of Europe was founded in May 1949.<br>The European Union was formed in 1993.<br>(Churchill was Prime Minister again from 1951 to 1955.) |
| 80 | 19 Sep 1946 | Birth of Michael Elphick, British stage, film and television actor.<br>Best known for his lead role in the TV detective drama series *Boon*.<br>He also played Harry Slater in the soap opera *EastEnders*. (Died 2002.) |
| 80 | 20 Sep 1946 to 5 Oct | The first Cannes Film Festival was held. |
| 80 | 24 Sep 1946 | Cathay Pacific Airways was founded in Hong Kong. |
| 80 | 26 Sep 1946 | The first edition of *Tintin* magazine was published in Belgium.<br>It was published weekly until 1993 when it ceased publication. |
| 80 | 26 Sep 1946 | Birth of Andrea Dworkin, American radical feminist, anti-pornography activist, and writer. (Died 2005.) |
| 80 | 26 Sep 1946 | Death of William Strunk Jr., American educator. Best known for his book *The Elements of Style*, which was later revised and expanded by his former student E. B White and is commonly known as Strunk and White. |
| 80 | 27 Sep 1946 | Birth of Robin Nedwell, British stage and television actor.<br>Best known for his role as Duncan Waring in the TV comedy series *Doctor in the House*. Also known for the TV series *The Lovers*, the comedy drama *Shillingbury Tales* and more. (Died 1999.) |
| 80 | 29 Sep 1946 | The BBC Third Programme was launched.<br>The national radio network became one of the leading cultural and intellectual forces in Britain. It was incorporated into BBC Radio 3 in 1970. |
| 75 | 1 Sep 1951 | The ANZUS Pact, a mutual security treaty, was signed by the USA, Australia and New Zealand. |
| 75 | 1 Sep 1951 | Birth of David Bairstow, British cricketer (Yorkshire and England), football player (Bradford City), and radio commentator. (Died 1998.) |

## SEPTEMBER 2026

| Ann. | Date | Event |
|---|---|---|
| 75 | 3 Sep 1951 | The first episode of the long-running TV soap opera *Search for Tomorrow* was broadcast on CBS in the USA. It ran for 35 years until 1986. |
| 75 | 4 Sep 1951 | The first live coast-to-coast television broadcast in the USA: U.S. President Harry S. Truman's opening speech from the Japanese peace treaty conference in San Francisco, California. (See also: 8th September 1951.) |
| 75 | 8 Sep 1951 | The San Francisco Peace Treaty (also known as the Treaty of San Francisco, or the Treaty of Peace with Japan) was signed by 49 countries. |
| 75 | 10 Sep 1951 | Britain began an economic boycott of Iran following Iran's nationalisation of the Anglo–Iranian Oil Company. |
| 75 | 11 Sep 1951 | Igor Stravinsky's opera *The Rake's Progress* was performed for the first time, in Venice, Italy. |
| 75 | 11 Sep 1951 | Florence Chadwick of the USA became the first woman to swim the English Channel in both directions. She completed the France–England stage on 8th August 1950, and the more difficult England–France stage on 11th September 1951. She broke the women's record for swimming the channel on both occasions. |
| 75 | 13 Sep 1951 to 15 Oct | Korean War – the Battle of Heartbreak Ridge. United Nations victory. |
| 75 | 14 Sep 1951 | Britain's largest oil refinery opened at Fawley, Hampshire. |
| 75 | 18 Sep 1951 | The U.S. première of the science fiction film *The Day the Earth Stood Still*. Released: 28th September. UK: 13th December. |
| 75 | 18 Sep 1951 ? | Birth of Dee Dee Ramone, American punk rock musician and songwriter (The Ramones). (Died 2002.) (Some sources give his year of birth as 1952 but this appears to be incorrect.) |
| 75 | 22 Sep 1951 | The first live coast-to-coast television broadcast of a sporting event in the USA. NBC broadcast a college football game between Duke University and the University of Pittsburgh. |
| 75 | 23 Sep 1951 | King George VI of the United Kingdom had surgery to remove his left lung, which had developed cancer after years of heavy smoking. He never fully recovered, and died on 6th February 1952. |
| 75 | 28 Sep 1951 | Birth of Jim Diamond, Scottish pop/rock singer, songwriter and musician. Lead singer of PhD (best known for their hit song *I Won't Let You Down*) and solo artist (best known for his hit song *I Should Have Known Better*). (Died 2015.) |
| 75 | 30 Sep 1951 | The first episode of the comedy/variety TV series *The Red Skelton Show* was broadcast on NBC in the USA. It ran until 1971, transferring to CBS for most of its run. |
| 70 | 2 Sep 1956 | The Mahbubnagar bridge collapse, India. The bridge collapsed as a train was passing over it, and two carriages fell into the river. At least 112 people were killed and 22 injured. |
| 70 | 3 Sep 1956 | Birth of Pat McGeown, Northern Irish political figure. Best known for taking part in a 1981 hunger strike while in prison for his role in an IRA bombing in Belfast. He resumed his political activities upon his release. (Died in 1996 from heart disease caused by the hunger strike.) |

## SEPTEMBER 2026

| Ann. | Date | Event |
|------|------|-------|
| 70 | 4 Sep 1956 | IBM introduced the world's first commercial hard disk drive – the 350 Disk Storage Unit. It could hold 5 Mb of data on a tower of fifty 24-inch magnetised platters.<br>On 14th September IBM launched the 305 RAMAC computer – the first commercial computer to be equipped with a hard disk drive. |
| 70 | 5 Sep 1956 | The Robinson train crash, New Mexico, USA.<br>Two Santa Fe express trains collided when a railway employee threw a lever prematurely and switched one train into the path of the other. Twenty people were killed. |
| 70 | 8 Sep 1956 | Elvis Presley's hit song *Blue Suede Shoes* was released. |
| 70 | 8 Sep 1956 | The album *Calypso* by Harry Belafonte was released.<br>It remained #1 on the Billboard album chart for 31 weeks, and was the first LP record to sell over 1 million copies.<br>It included the song *Day-O (The Banana Boat Song)*. |
| 70 | 8 Sep 1956 | Birth of Fad Gadget (real name: Frank Tovey), British avant-garde electronic musician and singer. Noted for his bleak lyrics, expressionless voice, and mechanised industrial sounds. (Died 2002.) |
| 70 | 9 Sep 1956 | Elvis Presley made his first appearance on the American television show *The Ed Sullivan Show*. |
| 70 | 11 Sep 1956 | Death of Billy Bishop, Canadian WWI fighter pilot.<br>The top Canadian fighter ace of the war – he shot down 72 enemy aircraft. He was awarded the Victoria Cross.<br>He also helped found the Royal Canadian Air Force. |
| 70 | 12 Sep 1956 | Quiz-rigging scandal: the first episode of the television quiz show *Twenty-One* was broadcast in the USA. Producer Dan Enright called it 'a dismal failure' as neither contestant could answer the questions. Subsequent episodes were rigged – the contestants were given a coaching session ahead of each broadcast, which included the answers they were expected to give. The show later became the subject of a Senate investigation that almost led to the demise of the TV quiz show genre. The film *Quiz Show* is based on these events. |
| 70 | 12 Sep 1956 | Birth of Leslie Cheung, Hong Kong singer and film actor.<br>He was enormously popular throughout Asia, and was one of the founders of Cantopop. (Died 2003.) |
| 70 | 13 Sep 1956 | Russian composer Igor Stravinsky's *Canticum Sacrum* was performed for the first time, in Saint Mark's Cathedral in Venice, Italy.<br>The piece is Stravinsky's tribute to Venice and its patron saint, Saint Mark. |
| 70 | 13 Sep 1956 | Birth of Joni Sledge, American singer and songwriter (Sister Sledge). (Died 2017.) |
| 70 | 14 Sep 1956 | Birth of Ray Wilkins, British football player, manager and sports broadcaster. He played for several British and European teams, and the England national team (1976–86). (Died 2018.) |
| 70 | 16 Sep 1956 | The first regular television service began in Australia (TCN9 Sydney).<br>It was officially opened on 27th October. |

## SEPTEMBER 2026

| Ann. | Date | Event |
|---|---|---|
| 70 | 16 Sep 1956 | Play-Doh modelling compound went on sale in the USA. It was originally sold as a wallpaper cleaning compound. It was relaunched as a modelling compound when the inventor's nephew discovered that nursery school children were using it to make Christmas ornaments. |
| 70 | 19 Sep 1956 | The First Congress of Black Writers and Artists was held, in Paris, France. |
| 70 | 22 Sep 1956 | Death of Frederick Soddy, British chemist. Winner of the 1921 Nobel Prize in Chemistry for his investigations of radioactive substances and for his contributions to the theory of isotopes. He was also a co-discoverer of plutonium. |
| 70 | 23 Sep 1956 | Birth of Paolo Rossi, Italian footballer. The leading goal-scorer and player of the tournament in the 1982 FIFA World Cup. (Died 2020.) |
| 70 | 25 Sep 1956 | The first undersea transatlantic telephone cable, *TAT-1*, went into service. It could carry 36 simultaneous calls (later increased to 48 and then to 72). It was retired in 1978. Earlier cables had only carried telegraph signals. |
| 70 | 27 Sep 1956 | U.S. Air Force test pilot Milburn G. Apt became the first person to exceed Mach 3 (three times the speed of sound), flying a Bell X-2 rocket plane over Edwards Air Force Base in California. The plane tumbled and crashed on its way back to base after the flight, and he was killed. |
| 70 | 27 Sep 1956 | Death of Babe Didrikson Zaharias, American sportswoman. One of the greatest athletes of the 20th century. A star of basketball, track and field, and golf. |
| 70 | 28 Sep 1956 | Elvis Presley's hit song *Love Me Tender* was released. |
| 70 | 28 Sep 1956 | Death of William Boeing, American aviation pioneer and aircraft manufacturer. Founder of the Boeing Company. |
| 70 | 30 Sep 1956 to 24 Sep 1957 | Algerian War – the Battle of Algiers. The National Liberation Front (FLN) launched a year-long campaign of guerrilla warfare against the French authorities in Algeria. Result: French tactical victory, FLN strategic victory. |
| 65 | 1 Sep 1961 to May 1991 | The Eritrean War of Independence. Eritrean victory: Eritrea gained its independence from Ethiopia. |
| 65 | 1 Sep 1961 | The Non-Aligned Movement was established at the Conference of Heads of State or Government of Non-Aligned Countries. It is a group of 120 nations that are not formally aligned with (or against) any major power bloc. |
| 65 | 5 Sep 1961 | Aircraft hijacking became a federal crime in the USA, and carried the death sentence. |
| 65 | 7 Sep 1961 to 22nd | Typhoon Nancy caused widespread devastation in Guam, the Ryūkyū Islands and Japan. It remains one of the most intense tropical cyclones ever recorded. Nearly 200 people were killed and thousands injured, particularly in Japan. |
| 65 | 7 Sep 1961 | Death of Pieter Sjoerds Gerbrandy, Prime Minister of the Netherlands (1940–45). He led the Dutch government-in-exile, which was based in the UK during WWII. |

# SEPTEMBER 2026

| Ann. | Date | Event |
|---|---|---|
| 65 | 10 Sep 1961 | The deadliest crash in Formula One history. German driver Wolfgang von Trips collided with British driver Jim Clark on the second lap of the Italian Grand Prix. Von Trips' car flipped over and rolled into the crowd, killing him and fifteen spectators. |
| 65 | 11 Sep 1961 | Hurricane Carla devastated the coast of Texas, USA, killing more than forty people and causing billions of dollars' worth of damage. |
| 65 | 11 Sep 1961 | The World Wildlife Fund (now the World Wide Fund for Nature) was founded in Switzerland. |
| 65 | 12 Sep 1961 | The African and Malagasy Union was founded. It promoted cooperation between newly independent French-speaking countries in Africa. It was disbanded in 1985. |
| 65 | 17 Sep 1961 | The Civic Arena (later known as the Mellon Arena) opened in Pittsburgh, Pennsylvania, USA. It was the first major sports venue with a retractable roof. Operating costs and maintenance issues meant that the roof remained permanently closed from 2001. The arena closed in 2010 and was demolished in 2011–12. It was replaced by a new arena across the street. |
| 65 | 17 Sep 1961 | The newly formed Minnesota Vikings played their first NFL game, defeating the Chicago Bears 37–13. |
| 65 | 17 Sep 1961 | The first episode of the police-based TV sitcom *Car 54, Where Are You?* was broadcast on NBC in the USA. It ran for two seasons until 1963. |
| 65 | 13 Sep 1961 | Birth of James Gandolfini, American stage, film and television actor and producer. Best known for his role as Tony Soprano in the Mafia-based TV crime drama series *The Sopranos*. (Died 2013.) |
| 65 | 18 Sep 1961 | Death of Dag Hammarskjöld, Swedish economist and statesman. Secretary-General of the United Nations (1953–61). (Plane crash while travelling to cease-fire negotiations in the Congo.) |
| 65 | 20 Sep 1961 | Antonio Abertondo of Argentina became the first person to swim across the English Channel and back again, non-stop. He took just over 43 hours. |
| 65 | 21 Sep 1961 | Boeing's CH-47 Chinook tandem-rotor transportation helicopter made its first flight. |
| 65 | 22 Sep 1961 | The country song *Big Bad John* by Jimmy Dean was released. It is regarded as one of the best country songs of all time, and also became a #1 hit on the *Billboard* pop music chart. |
| 65 | 23 Sep 1961 | Birth of Willie McCool, American astronaut. (Killed in the Space Shuttle *Columbia* disaster in 2003.) |
| 65 | 28 Sep 1961 | The Syrian coup d'état. Syrian Army officers staged an uprising that resulted in the break-up of the United Arab Republic (the union between Egypt and Syria). Syria immediately seceded from the union and regained its independence. Egypt continued to be known as the United Arab Republic until 1971. |
| 65 | 28 Sep 1961 | The first episode of the medical drama television series *Doctor Kildare* was broadcast on NBC in the USA. It ran for five seasons until 1966. |
| 65 | 28 Sep 1961 | The first episode of the television sitcom *Hazel* was broadcast on NBC in the USA. It ran for five seasons until 1966. |

## SEPTEMBER 2026

| Ann. | Date | Event |
|------|------|-------|
| 60 | 6 Sep 1966 | Death of Margaret Sanger, American nurse and birth control activist. She opened the first birth control clinic in the USA and coined the term 'birth control'. |
| 60 | 6 Sep 1966 | Death of Hendrik Verwoerd, Prime Minister of South Africa (1958–66). He developed and implemented apartheid. (Assassinated.) Succeeded by John Vorster. |
| 60 | 8 Sep 1966 | The Severn Bridge was officially opened. It links England and Wales, spanning the River Severn and River Wye. |
| 60 | 8 Sep 1966 | The first episode of the science fiction television series *Star Trek* was broadcast on NBC in the USA. It ran for three seasons until 1969. |
| 60 | 8 Sep 1966 | The first episode of the television series *Tarzan* was broadcast on NBC in the USA. It ran for two seasons until 1968. |
| 60 | 9 Sep 1966 | The National Traffic and Motor Vehicle Safety Act was signed into law in the USA following an alarming increase in deaths and injuries on the roads. It led to the creation of the National Highway Traffic Safety Administration, which introduced many important safety-related changes to road and vehicle design and driver behaviour. |
| 60 | 11 Sep 1966 | Death of Collett E. Woolman, American airline entrepreneur. The principal founder, chairman and first CEO of Delta Air Lines. He led the company from its early days as a small crop-dusting operation (Huff Daland Dusters) and oversaw its growth into one of the USA's major airlines. |
| 60 | 12 Sep 1966 | NASA launched its *Gemini 11* manned spacecraft with astronauts Pete Conrad and Dick Gordon on board. It returned to Earth safely on 15th September after performing tethering, docking, space walk, and artificial gravity tests. |
| 60 | 12 Sep 1966 | The first episode of the musical television sitcom *The Monkees* was broadcast on NBC in the USA. It ran until March 1968 and launched the music career of the pop/rock band The Monkees. |
| 60 | 12 Sep 1966 | The first episode of the television sitcom *Family Affair* was broadcast on CBS in the USA. It ran until September 1971. |
| 60 | 14 Sep 1966 to 25th | Vietnam War – Operation Attleboro. The U.S. 196th Light Infantry Brigade launched a mission to find North Vietnamese and Viet Cong bases in South Vietnam and force them to fight. The operation damaged the North Vietnamese supply line into South Vietnam, and the system was later used in larger operations, including Cedar Falls (January 1967) and Junction City (February 1967). |
| 60 | 14 Sep 1966 | Death of Gertrude Berg, American actress, producer and screenwriter. Best known for the comedy drama series *The Rise of the Goldbergs* (later known as *The Goldbergs*) which appeared on radio, TV, stage and film. |
| 60 | 14 Sep 1966 | Death of Hiram Wesley Evans, American white supremacist. Imperial Wizard of the Ku Klux Klan (1922–39). |
| 60 | 14 Sep 1966 | Death of Cemal Gürsel, President of Turkey (1960–66 – presidency terminated due to ill health). |

## SEPTEMBER 2026

| Ann. | Date | Event |
|---|---|---|
| 60 | 15 Sep 1966 | *HMS Resolution*, the first of the British Royal Navy's Resolution-class nuclear-powered ballistic missile submarines, was launched.<br>Its sister submarines were the *Repulse, Renown* and *Revenge*.<br>They were decommissioned in the mid-1990s and succeeded by the Vanguard-class submarine. |
| 60 | 16 Sep 1966 | The Metropolitan Opera House was officially opened at the Lincoln Center for the Performing Arts in New York City, USA. |
| 60 | 17 Sep 1966 | The first episode of the action/adventure television series *Mission: Impossible* was broadcast on CBS in the USA. It ran until 1973, and then from 1988 to 1990. It then became a popular film series. |
| 60 | 17 Sep 1966 | Death of Fritz Wunderlich, German tenor.<br>He was famous for singing works by Mozart and Wagner, but his career was cut short when he fell from a stairway while on holiday, aged 35. |
| 60 | 20 Sep 1966 | NASA launched its lunar lander *Surveyor 2* on a mission to achieve a soft landing on the Moon and photograph its surface for the Apollo missions. The mission failed: a mid-course correction failure caused the spacecraft to start tumbling, and it crashed into the Moon on 23rd September. |
| 60 | 21 Sep 1966 | Death of Paul Reynaud, Prime Minister of France (1940 for three months).<br>He attempted (unsuccessfully) to save France from Nazi occupation. |
| 60 | 25 Sep 1966 | Soviet composer Dmitri Shostakovich's *Cello Concerto No. 2* was performed for the first time, in Moscow. It was his 60th birthday. |
| 60 | 27 Sep 1966 to 11 Oct | Hurricane Inez hit the Caribbean, Bahamas, the U.S. state of Florida, and Mexico. 700 – 900 people were killed, thousands were left homeless and crops were destroyed. |
| 60 | 28 Sep 1966 | Death of André Breton, French writer and poet.<br>One of the key founders of Surrealism. |
| 60 | 29 Sep 1966 | The Chevrolet Camaro went on sale in the USA.<br>It was a designed to compete with the Ford Mustang. |
| 60 | 30 Sep 1966 | Botswana gained its independence from the UK.<br>Seretse Khama became its first president. |
| 60 | 30 Sep 1966 | Nazi war criminals Albert Speer and Baldur von Schirach were released from Spandau Prison after twenty years.<br>Their release was a worldwide media event.<br>Spandau Prison then held just one remaining prisoner, Deputy Führer Rudolf Hess. He remained there until his death in 1987. The prison was then demolished to prevent it from becoming a neo-Nazi shrine. |
| 50 | 1 Sep 1976 to 3rd | Hull Prison riot, UK.<br>More than 100 prisoners were involved in the three-day riot over staff brutality. Much of the prison was destroyed. It took a year to repair it. |
| 50 | 1 Sep 1976 | Meadowlands Racetrack opened in East Rutherford, New Jersey, USA. |
| 50 | 3 Sep 1976 | NASA's *Viking 2* lander landed on Mars. It photographed the surface, analysed soil samples and searched for signs of life. As was the case with *Viking 1*, the Labeled Release experiment gave a positive result for signs of life, but this is now disputed and is generally considered a 'false positive'. |

**SEPTEMBER 2026**

| Ann. | Date | Event |
|---|---|---|
| 50 | 4 Sep 1976 | The novelty disco song *Disco Duck* by Rick Dees and His Cast of Idiots was released. |
| 50 | 5 Sep 1976 ? | The first episode of the television series *The Muppet Show* was broadcast on ITV in the UK (after failing to get picked up by U.S. networks). Various dates are given for the first episode including 5th, 13th and 19th September. The 5th and 13th might be the dates when two pilot shows made in 1974 and 1975 were broadcast, with Series 1 beginning on 19th, but we're not entirely sure. It ran for five series until March 1981. |
| 50 | 6 Sep 1976 | Soviet Air Defence Forces pilot Viktor Belenko landed his MiG-25 jet interceptor aircraft at Hakodate Airport in Hokkaido, Japan and defected to the West. His defection caused the Soviet Union significant embarrassment and damage, and the Western military were able to study the aircraft in detail. |
| 50 | 9 Sep 1976 | Death of Mao Zedong, (Chairman Mao), Chinese communist leader. The founding father and head of state of the People's Republic of China. His funeral was held on 18th September in Tiananmen Square, Beijing and was attended by millions of people. |
| 50 | 10 Sep 1976 | The Zagreb mid-air collision, Yugoslavia (now Croatia). British Airways Flight 476 travelling from London, UK to Istanbul, Turkey collided with Inex-Adria Aviopromet Flight 550 travelling from Split, Yugoslavia (now Croatia) to Cologne, West Germany. All 176 people on board the two planes were killed. It was the world's deadliest mid-air collision at that time. (Cause: Zagreb air traffic control error.) |
| 50 | 10 Sep 1976 | Death of Dalton Trumbo, American screenwriter and novelist. Best known for *Kitty Foyle*, *Thirty Seconds over Tokyo*, *The Brave One*, *Exodus* and *Spartacus*. He was blacklisted by Hollywood for refusing to testify about alleged communist involvement. During that time he wrote under pseudonyms and won an Academy Award. |
| 50 | 16 Sep 1976 | The Episcopalian Church in the USA approved the ordination of women as priests and bishops. The first women (the Philadelphia 11) had already been ordained in July 1974, though the church had labelled their ordination invalid and irregular. |
| 50 | 16 Sep 1976 | Shavarsh Karapetyan, the world champion finswimmer, saved the lives of twenty passengers on a trolleybus that crashed into Yerevan Lake in Armenia and sank. He was seriously injured during the rescue and it ended his sports career. (He also famously rescued several people from a burning building in February 1985.) |
| 50 | 17 Sep 1976 | NASA unveiled its first Space Shuttle, *Enterprise*. It was only used for testing, did not have an engine or heat shield, and was incapable of space flight. Its first test flight was on 18th February 1977. The first shuttle to travel into space, *Columbia*, was launched in April 1981. |
| 50 | 18 Sep 1976 | The Reverend Sun Myung Moon held a 'God Bless America' festival and rally at the Washington Monument in Washington, D.C., USA About 300,000 people attended. |

# SEPTEMBER 2026

| Ann. | Date | Event |
|---|---|---|
| 50 | 19 Sep 1976 | Turkish Airlines Flight 452 crashed into a hill in Karatepe, Turkey. All 154 passengers and crew on board were killed. (Cause: pilot error – he mistook lights on a highway for the runway at the airport, even though he was nowhere near the airport.) |
| 50 | 21 Sep 1976 | Death of Orlando Letelier, Chilean economist, politician and diplomat. He lived in exile in Washington D.C., USA. (Assassinated by agents from Chile's secret police.) |
| 50 | 22 Sep 1976 | The first episode of the crime drama television series *Charlie's Angels* was broadcast on ABC in the USA. It ran for five seasons until 1981. |
| 50 | 24 Sep 1976 | The Government of Rhodesia agreed to introduce black majority rule within two years. It was introduced on 1st June 1979. Rhodesia was renamed Zimbabwe–Rhodesia the same day. It became Zimbabwe in April 1980. |
| 50 | 24 Sep 1976 | American newspaper heiress Patty Hearst was sentenced to seven years in prison for taking part in a bank robbery in 1974. She had famously joined the Symbionese Liberation Army which had kidnapped her. Her sentence was commuted by U.S. President Jimmy Carter and she was released in February 1979. She was pardoned by U.S. President Bill Clinton in 2001. |
| 50 | 28 Sep 1976 | Stevie Wonder's album *Songs in the Key of Life* was released. |
| 40 | 4 Sep 1986 | Death of Hank Greenberg, ('Hammerin' Hank'), American baseball player. The first Jewish baseball superstar. |
| 40 | 5 Sep 1986 | The Pan Am Flight 73 hijacking, Karachi Airport, Pakistan. Members of the Palestinian Abu Nidal Organisation hijacked a Pan Am jet with approximately 360 passengers on board. 22 people were killed and over 150 injured when authorities stormed the plane. (See also: 6th September 1986.) |
| 40 | 5 Sep 1986 to 17th | A wave of Middle Eastern terrorist bombings hit Paris, France. There were five attacks, on a post office, restaurant, bar, police headquarters, and a clothing store. 11 people were killed and 159 injured. |
| 40 | 6 Sep 1986 | Terrorists from the Abu Nidal Organisation killed 22 people in the Neve Shalom synagogue in Istanbul, Turkey. |
| 40 | 6 Sep 1986 | Death of Blanche Sweet, American silent film actress. |
| 40 | 7 Sep 1986 | Desmond Tutu became the first black Archbishop of Cape Town in South Africa. He remained in office until 1996. |
| 40 | 7 Sep 1986 | The first use of instant replay during a National Football League (NFL) game in the USA. The Cleveland Browns asked for a play to be reviewed during their game against the Chicago Bears. |
| 40 | 7 Sep 1986 | The President of Chile, General Augusto Pinochet, escaped with minor injuries when his motorcade was attacked in an assassination attempt near Santiago. Five of his bodyguards were killed. |
| 40 | 8 Sep 1986 | Nissan's first European car factory opened in Sunderland, UK. The factory was opened by Prime Minister Margaret Thatcher. The first car was produced at the factory in July 1986. |

## SEPTEMBER 2026

| Ann. | Date | Event |
|---|---|---|
| 40 | 8 Sep 1986 | The first episode of the television talk show *The Oprah Winfrey Show* was broadcast in the USA. It ran for 25 seasons until 2011. |
| 40 | 9 Sep 1986 | American educator Frank Reed, director of the Lebanese International School in Beirut, Lebanon, was taken hostage by Islamic militants. He was released in April 1990. |
| 40 | 11 Sep 1986 | Death of Panagiotis Kanellopoulos, Prime Minister of Greece (1967 – deposed by the military junta after eighteen days in office). |
| 40 | 12 Sep 1986 | Joseph Cicippio, the acting controller of the American University of Beirut, Lebanon, was kidnapped by members of Islamic Jihad. He was released in December 1991. |
| 40 | 15 Sep 1986 | The first episode of the legal drama television series *LA Law* was broadcast on NBC in the USA. It ran for eight seasons until 1994. |
| 40 | 16 Sep 1986 | The Kinross gold mine fire, South Africa. 177 people were killed and more than 200 injured. |
| 40 | 16 Sep 1986 | Unisys, the information technology company, was founded when the Sperry and Burroughs corporations merged. |
| 40 | 17 Sep 1986 | Death of Pat Phoenix, British stage, film and television actress. Known for her role as Elsie Tanner in the TV soap opera *Coronation Street*. |
| 40 | 19 Sep 1986 | The Colwich rail crash, Staffordshire, UK. Two express trains collided at high speed. One driver was killed, and 75 passengers were injured. (Cause: driver error and confusion over procedures at the junction.) |
| 40 | 22 Sep 1986 | A U.S. District Court in California ruled that computer code was protected by the same copyright laws as literary works. The court also ruled that reverse-engineering a computer chip's embedded microcode did not infringe its copyright. (NEC Corp. v. Intel Corp.) |
| 40 | 26 Sep 1986 | William Rehnquist became Chief Justice of the United States (until his death in 2005). |
| 40 | 26 Sep 1986 | Antonin Scalia became an Associate Justice of the U.S. Supreme Court (until his death in 2016). |
| 40 | 27 Sep 1986 | Death of Cliff Burton, American heavy metal bass guitarist (Metallica). (Killed when the band's tour bus crashed in Sweden, aged 24.) |
| 40 | 28 Sep 1986 | The Democratic Progressive Party (DPP) was founded in Taiwan. At that time, it was an illegal opposition party to the Kuomintang (KMT). The DPP was legalised in 1987, and its candidate Chen Shui-bian won the presidency in 2000, ending 91 years of KMT rule. |
| 40 | 30 Sep 1986 | Mordechai Vanunu, an Israeli nuclear technician, was kidnapped in Rome, Italy by members of Mossad, an Israeli intelligence agency. He was later sentenced to eighteen years in prison for revealing details of Israel's secret nuclear weapons programme to the British press. (The details were published in *The Sunday Times* on 5th October 1986). |

## SEPTEMBER 2026

| Ann. | Date | Event |
|------|------|-------|
| 30 | 2 Sep 1996 | Moro conflict: the 1996 Final Peace Agreement (the Jakarta Accord) was signed by the Government of the Philippines and the Moro National Liberation Front.<br>A breakaway faction, the Moro Islamic Liberation Front, rejected the agreement and became the dominant rebel group in the Philippines. |
| 30 | 3 Sep 1996 | Ruth Perry became the first female head of state of Liberia.<br>She was Chairperson of the interim Council of State until August 1997. |
| 30 | 3 Sep 1996 | Death of Emily Kame Kngwarreye, Australian artist. One of the most prominent and successful contemporary Aboriginal artists. |
| 30 | 3 Sep 1996 | Death of Og Mandino, American writer and speaker.<br>Best known for his best-selling book *The Greatest Salesman in the World*. |
| 30 | 4 Sep 1996 | The insurance company Lloyd's of London was forced to restructure to prevent itself from becoming insolvent following a series of huge payouts, particularly for asbestosis compensation in the USA.<br>A new reinsurance company, Equitas, was founded, which took over Lloyd's pre-1993 liabilities and was split off as a separate company. |
| 30 | 5 Sep 1996 to 10th | Hurricane Fran hit the east coast of the USA.<br>22 people were killed and it caused over $5 billion worth of damage. |
| 30 | 5 Sep 1996 | Pakistani terrorist Ramzi Ahmed Yousef was convicted of planning the Bojinka plot, including the assassination of Pope John Paul II and the bombing of several U.S. passenger flights.<br>He and two co-conspirators were sentenced to life in prison.<br>In January 1998 he was also convicted of the 1993 World Trade Center bombing in New York City, USA, and was sentenced to life plus 240 years. |
| 30 | 9 Sep 1996 | Death of Bill Monroe, ('the father of bluegrass'), American bluegrass singer, songwriter and mandolin player. |
| 30 | 10 Sep 1996 | The United Nations adopted the Comprehensive Nuclear-Test-Ban Treaty. It has not yet come into effect as it still needs to be ratified by China, Egypt, India, Iran, Israel, North Korea, Pakistan and the USA. |
| 30 | 11 Sep 1996 | Union Pacific Railroad in the USA acquired Southern Pacific Railroad. |
| 30 | 12 Sep 1996 | Death of Ernesto Geisel, President of Brazil (1974–79). |
| 30 | 13 Sep 1996 | Death of Tupac Shakur (also known as 2Pac), American rapper and actor. (Died from injuries suffered in a drive-by shooting in Las Vegas, Nevada on 7th September, aged 25.) |
| 30 | 14 Sep 1996 | Death of Juliet Prowse, Indian-born South African–British stage, film and television actress and dancer. Best known for the films *G. I. Blues* and *Can-Can*. Noted for her relationships with Frank Sinatra and Elvis Presley. Soviet leader Nikita Khrushchev proclaimed her dancing 'immoral'. |
| 30 | 16 Sep 1996 | Death of McGeorge Bundy, U.S. National Security Advisor (1961–66).<br>One of the main architects of U.S. foreign policy during the Kennedy and Johnson administrations. Best known for his role in the escalation of the USA's involvement in the Vietnam War. |

## SEPTEMBER 2026

| Ann. | Date | Event |
|------|------|-------|
| 30 | 17 Sep 1996 | American talk show host Oprah Winfrey launched her television book club. *Oprah's Book Club* recommended a new book each month for fifteen years. Most titles became huge bestsellers, often selling millions of copies. |
| 30 | 17 Sep 1996 | Death of Spiro Agnew, Vice-President of the United States (1969–73). |
| 30 | 20 Sep 1996 | Death of Paul Erdős, Hungarian mathematician who produced the most mathematical papers ever. Known for his work in number theory and combinatorics. He was also a legendary eccentric. |
| 30 | 21 Sep 1996 | The Defense of Marriage Act came into effect in the USA.<br>It allowed states to refuse to recognise same-sex marriages that had taken place in other states.<br>Section 3 of the Act, which denied same-sex partners the same federal recognition and rights to benefits as heterosexual partners, was declared unconstitutional in 2013. |
| 30 | 21 Sep 1996 | John F. Kennedy Jr., son of former U.S. President John F. Kennedy, married Carolyn Bessette on Cumberland Island, Georgia, USA.<br>They were both killed in a plane crash in 1999. |
| 30 | 22 Sep 1996 | Death of Bob Dent, Australian cancer sufferer. The first person in the world to lawfully end his life by means of voluntary euthanasia. |
| 30 | 22 Sep 1996 | Death of Dorothy Lamour, American film actress and WWII pin-up.<br>Best known for the *Road to…* comedies with Bing Crosby and Bob Hope. |
| 30 | 23 Sep 1996 | The Metropolitan Police in London raided several suspected IRA houses and warehouses. One terrorist suspect was shot dead and five were arrested. About 10 tons of home-made explosives and weapons were seized, preventing suspected imminent attacks. |
| 30 | 25 Sep 1996 | The last Magdalene Laundry (also known as Magdalene Asylums) was closed in Ireland. The laundries housed thousands of 'fallen women', removing them from society. They were forced to work long hours in commercial laundries for no pay, and were often abused. Those who died were buried in mass graves. The nuns who ran the laundries often didn't know the women's names and kept no records.<br>Ireland issued a formal apology in 2013 and launched a compensation scheme for survivors.<br>There were also Magdalene Laundries/Asylums in Australia, Canada, England and the USA. Those in Ireland were the last to close. |
| 30 | 27 Sep 1996 | The Taliban seized control of Kabul, the capital of Afghanistan, ousted President Burhanuddin Rabbani, and executed former President Mohammad Najibullah. Mullah Omar was installed as Head of the Supreme Council of Afghanistan, and became head of state (until 2001). |
| 30 | 27 Sep 1996 | The *Julie N.* oil spill, Portland, Maine, USA.<br>A Liberian oil tanker crashed into the Million Dollar Bridge, ripping a 30-foot hole in its hull. More than 179,600 gallons (679,860 litres) of heating oil was spilled into the Fore River, causing widespread contamination. |

## SEPTEMBER 2026

| Ann. | Date | Event |
|------|------|-------|
| 30 | 27 Sep 1996 | Scientists at the U.S. National Cancer Institute reported that a common genetic mutation found only in white people could slow the progress of AIDS and sometimes provided complete immunity. About 1 in 5 people have the mutation and 1 in 100 have a double dose that gives them complete immunity. Their report was published in the journal *Science*. |
| 30 | 27 Sep 1996 | Death of Mohammad Najibullah, President of Afghanistan (1987–92). (Killed by the Taliban, aged 49.) |
| 30 | 29 Sep 1996 | The Nintendo 64 video game system was released in the USA. Japan: 23rd June. Europe: 1st March 1997. |
| 30 | 29 Sep 1996 | Death of Leslie Crowther, British comedian, television presenter and game show host. Best known for *Crackerjack* and *The Price is Right*. |
| 30 | 30 Sep 1996 | Lucent Technologies was founded in the USA when AT&T spun off AT&T Technologies as a separate company. Lucent included Western Electric and Bell Labs. It merged with Alcatel in 2006 to form Alcatel-Lucent, which was then acquired by Nokia in 2016. |
| 30 | 30 Sep 1996 to 2 Oct | British woman Mandy Allwood gave birth to octuplets. She was only 19 weeks pregnant and none of the babies survived. She had refused selective reduction in favour of having all eight babies. The case provoked a storm of media controversy. Only one recorded set of octuplets has survived infancy: the Suleman octuplets, born in the USA in 2009. (Allwood died in 2022.) |
| 25 | 1 Sep 2001 | Death of Brian Moore, British football commentator and television presenter. |
| 25 | 2 Sep 2001 | Death of Christiaan Barnard, South African surgeon who performed the first human heart transplant. |
| 25 | 2 Sep 2001 | Death of Troy Donahue, American actor. A teen idol of the 1950s and 60s. |
| 25 | 4 Sep 2001 | Tokyo DisneySea, a nautical exploration-based theme park opened at the Tokyo Disney Resort in Japan. It is now the fourth most-visited theme park in the world. |
| 25 | 9 Sep 2001 | The Pärnu methanol tragedy, Estonia. Two employees stole 1.6 tonnes of methanol from an industrial processing plant and sold it to a counterfeit drinks manufacturer, claiming it was laboratory-grade alcohol. The manufacturer used it in counterfeit versions of several popular drink brands. Hundreds of people were subsequently poisoned. 68 died and 43 became severely disabled. (Sentencing was unexpectedly lenient.) |
| 25 | 9 Sep 2001 | Death of Ahmad Shah Massoud, Minister of Defence of Afghanistan (1992–2001). Leader of the Northern Alliance. (Assassinated by two Al-Qaeda suicide bombers under the orders of Osama bin Laden.) |
| 25 | 10 Sep 2001 | Former British Army major Charles Ingram won £1 million ($1.3 million) on the television quiz show *Who Wants to be a Millionaire?* He was subsequently found to have cheated (an accomplice in the audience coughed when the correct answer was read out from the available choices). Ingram, his wife, and the accomplice were given suspended prison sentences and substantial fines. |

# SEPTEMBER 2026

| Ann. | Date | Event |
|------|------|-------|
| 25 | 11 Sep 2001 | 9/11 – the September 11th terrorist attacks on the USA. Al-Qaeda terrorists hijacked four planes and crashed them into the World Trade Center's twin towers in New York City, the Pentagon, and a field in Pennsylvania (following a passenger revolt – the intended target was in Washington, D.C.) 2,973 people were killed. |
| 25 | 11 Sep 2001 | Death of David Angell, American television producer and screenwriter. Best known for the sitcoms *Cheers* and *Frasier*. (A victim of 9/11.) |
| 25 | 12 Sep 2001 | Following the 9/11 terrorist attacks, U.S. President George W. Bush vowed that the USA would use all of its resources to avenge the attacks. On 20th September he declared a 'war on terror'. |
| 25 | 12 Sep 2001 | In response to the 9/11 terrorist attacks on the USA, Article 5 of the North Atlantic Treaty was invoked for the first time. It declares that an armed attack against one member state is considered an armed attack against all member states. This ensured that the USA had the full support of its NATO allies in dealing with the terrorist attacks. |
| 25 | 12 Sep 2001 | The Australian airline Ansett Australia ceased trading due to the global airline depression following the 9/11 terrorist attacks. |
| 25 | 13 Sep 2001 | The USA named Al-Qaeda leader Osama bin Laden the prime suspect in the 9/11 terror attacks. |
| 25 | 13 Sep 2001 | Iain Duncan Smith became Leader of the Conservative Party in the UK following William Hague's resignation. Conservative MPs passed a vote of no confidence in him in November 2003 as they felt he was not capable of winning the next election. He resigned and was succeeded by Michael Howard. |
| 25 | 13 Sep 2001 | Death of Dorothy McGuire, American stage, film, radio and television actress. Best known for her film roles in *Gentleman's Agreement* and *Friendly Persuasion*, and for her role as the mother in *Swiss Family Robinson*. |
| 25 | 14 Sep 2001 | Nintendo's GameCube video game console was released in Japan. (North America: 18th November. Europe: 3rd May 2002.) |
| 25 | 16 Sep 2001 to 18th | Typhoon Nari hit Taiwan, causing massive flooding and mudslides. 104 people were killed. Parts of Taipei's metro system were put out of action for three months. |
| 25 | 16 Sep 2001 | Death of Samuel Z. Arkoff, American film producer. Known for his B movies. |
| 25 | 18 Sep 2001 to 9 Oct | Anthrax attacks in the USA. Contaminated letters were sent to two U.S. Senators and various news and media organisations in New York and Florida. Five people died and at least twelve were infected. Dozens of buildings were contaminated and had to be fumigated, and staff were given powerful antibiotics as a precaution. Senate offices, the U.S. Capitol and the Supreme Court were shut down for testing in October, and traces were found in the State Department and CIA Headquarters. The total cost of the damage was put at $1 billion (£625 million). |

## SEPTEMBER 2026

| Ann. | Date | Event |
|------|------|-------|
| 25 | 19 Sep 2001 | The USA began sending combat troops, aircraft and ships to the Persian Gulf and Indian Ocean in response to the September 11th terrorist attacks. Air strikes in Afghanistan began on 7th – 8th October. |
| 25 | 21 Sep 2001 | The U.S. Congress approved a $15 billion bailout to help the U.S. airline industry, which was struggling after the 9/11 terrorist attacks. |
| 25 | 22 Sep 2001 | The U.S. space probe *Deep Space 1* flew within 1,400 miles of Comet Borrelly and sent back images of its nucleus. |
| 25 | 22 Sep 2001 | Death of Isaac Stern, Ukrainian-born American violin virtuoso. |
| 25 | 25 Sep 2001 | Following the 9/11 terrorist attacks on the USA, U.S. President George W. Bush ordered an immediate freeze on the U.S. assets of suspected Islamic terrorist groups and individuals. He also declared that sanctions would be imposed on banks in other countries that provided the terrorists with access to the international financial system. |
| 25 | 27 Sep 2001 | U.S. President George W. Bush announced that the federal government would take over airport security following the 9/11 terrorist attacks. He also announced a range of airline security measures including reinforcing cockpit doors, banning passengers from entering the cockpit, and placing air marshals on commercial flights. |
| 25 | 27 Sep 2001 | The Zug massacre, Switzerland. A man entered the local parliament building, opened fire, detonated a home-made bomb, and then killed himself. Fourteen people (plus the perpetrator) were killed and eighteen injured. His suicide note stated that he believed there was a plot against him. It was the first assault of this type in Switzerland. |
| 25 | 29 Sep 2001 | Death of Nguyen Van Thieu, President of South Vietnam (1967–75). He was President for the second half of the Vietnam War. |
| 20 | 2 Sep 2006 | Death of Bob Mathias, American athlete and politician. Gold medallist at the 1948 and 1952 Olympics (decathlon). U.S. Congressman representing California (1967–75). |
| 20 | 3 Sep 2006 | The European Space Agency's lunar probe *SMART-1* was deliberately crashed into the Moon at 4,500 mph to simulate a meteor impact and to expose underground materials, such as water ice, for analysis. (It was launched in September 2003 and had orbited and studied the Moon since November 2004.) |
| 20 | 3 Sep 2006 | American tennis player Andre Agassi announced his retirement due to back problems. He was the former world number one player and the 1996 Olympic champion. |
| 20 | 4 Sep 2006 | Death of Steve Irwin, ('the Crocodile Hunter'), Australian wildlife conservationist and television personality. Noted for his exuberant personality and reckless enthusiasm. Best known for hosting the television series *The Crocodile Hunter*. (Stung in the chest by a stingray while filming *The Ocean's Deadliest*.) |

## SEPTEMBER 2026

| Ann. | Date | Event |
|------|------|-------|
| 20 | 6 Sep 2006 | U.S. President George W. Bush publicly admitted that the CIA operated a system of secret prisons (known as CIA black sites) around the world. They were used to detain enemy combatants in the War on Terror. He also said that fourteen key terrorism suspects had been transferred from black sites to Guantanamo Bay in Cuba to stand trial. |
| 20 | 10 Sep 2006 | Death of Patty Berg, American golfer. A founding member and first president of the Ladies Professional Golf Association (LPGA). Winner of 15 major women's titles – still the record. |
| 20 | 10 Sep 2006 | Death of Taufa'ahau Tupou IV, King of Tonga (1965–2006). |
| 20 | 11 Sep 2006 | Microsoft launched its search engine, Windows Live Search. It replaced MSN Search, which was launched in 1998. It was rebranded as Live Search in 2007 and Bing in 2009. |
| 20 | 15 Sep 2006 | Death of Raymond Baxter, British radio and television presenter. Best known for presenting the science and technology TV series *Tomorrow's World*. He was also a BBC radio commentator who covered the funerals of King George VI and Winston Churchill, the coronation of Queen Elizabeth II, and the first flight of Concorde. |
| 20 | 17 Sep 2006 | Fourpeaked Mountain in Alaska, USA erupted for the first time in over 10,000 years. |
| 20 | 19 Sep 2006 | Military coup in Thailand. Prime Minister Thaksin Shinawatra was ousted and replaced by the Commander-in-chief of the Royal Thai Army, Sonthi Boonyaratglin. |
| 20 | 21 Sep 2006 | Wal-Mart Stores in Tampa Bay, Florida, USA launched a $4 generic drug programme. Around 300 generic drugs were available on prescription at $4 for a 30-day supply. The test was soon expanded to cover the whole state. On 28th November it was expanded to the entire USA. Many competing stores later launched similar programmes. |
| 20 | 21 Sep 2006 | Death of Boz Burrell, British rock bassist (King Crimson, Bad Company). |
| 20 | 22 Sep 2006 | OneWebDay was held for the first time. The annual event takes place on 22nd September each year and celebrates the internet and how it affects people's lives. |
| 20 | 23 Sep 2006 | Death of Etta Baker, American folk/blues guitarist. |
| 20 | 26 Sep 2006 | Death of Tokyo Rose (Iva Toguri D'Aquino), American broadcaster of Japanese propaganda to Allied troops stationed in the South Pacific during WWII. She was convicted of treason and served 6 years in prison. |
| 20 | 27 Sep 2006 | The Global Warming Solutions Act of 2006 was signed into law in California, USA. California was the first U.S. state to set greenhouse gas emission targets and commit to a programme to reduce it. |
| 20 | 29 Sep 2006 | Gol Flight 1907 collided with an ExcelAire plane over Mato Grosso, Brazil. 154 people were killed. Investigators found the ExcelAire's transponder was switched off, and air traffic control radars had lost contact with it. Following the crash, the poor state of Brazil's aviation infrastructure and working conditions were made public, and air traffic controllers began working to rule. This triggered a crisis that lasted until July 2007. |

## SEPTEMBER 2026

| Ann. | Date | Event |
| --- | --- | --- |
| 15 | 17 Sep 2011 | The Occupy Wall Street movement began in Zuccotti Park, New York City, USA.<br>Protestors were forced out of the park on 15th November and began occupying other establishments, including banks, corporate headquarters, and college/university campuses. |
| 15 | 18 Sep 2011 | The 2011 Sikkim earthquake, India and Nepal.<br>At least 111 people were killed. There was structural damage in north-east India, Nepal, Bangladesh, Bhutan and southern Tibet. |
| 15 | 20 Sep 2011 | The USA repealed its eighteen-year 'Don't ask, don't tell' compromise policy on homosexual and bisexual people serving in the military.<br>They were now allowed to serve openly. |
| 15 | 28 Sep 2011 | Borders, the book and music retailer, went out of business. |
| 10 | 2 Sep 2016 | Death of Islam Karimov, first President of Uzbekistan (1991–2016).<br>Noted for his repressive authoritarian regime and human rights abuses. Succeeded by Shavkat Mirziyoyev. |
| 10 | 8 Sep 2016 | NASA launched *OSIRIS-Rex*, its first mission to study an asteroid, collect a sample from it, and return it to Earth.<br>It reached the asteroid 101955 Bennu in December 2018, landed and collected a sample from it in October 2020, and began its return to Earth in May 2021.<br>It is expected to return with the sample on 24th September 2023.<br>(The Japanese space probes *Hayabusa* and *Hayabusa2* successfully returned samples from asteroids in 2010 and 2020 respectively.) |
| 10 | 25 Sep 2016 | Death of Arnold Palmer, American golfer. Regarded as one of the greatest golfers in history, and its first star of the television era. |
| 10 | 28 Sep 2016 | Death of Shimon Peres, President of Israel (2007–14).<br>Prime Minister of Israel (1984–86, 1995–96). |
| 10 | 30 Sep 2016 to 9 Oct | Hurricane Matthew caused widespread devastation in Haiti, the Bahamas, and the Lesser Antilles. It also affected Jamaica and other Caribbean islands, as well as the south-eastern U.S. states.<br>603 people were killed, and it caused over $16 billion worth of damage. |

# OCTOBER 2026

| Ann. | Date | Event |
|------|------|-------|
| 800 | 3 Oct 1226 | Death of Saint Francis of Assisi, Italian friar, deacon and mystic. One of the most venerated religious figures in Christianity. Founder of the Franciscan Order. |
| 750 | 4 Oct 1276 | Birth of Margaret of Brabant, Queen consort of Germany (1308–11). Wife of Henry VII, Count of Luxembourg, King of Germany and Holy Roman Emperor. |
| 400 | 4 Oct 1626 | Birth of Richard Cromwell, English statesman. The last Lord Protector of the Commonwealth of England, Scotland and Ireland (1658–59). Son of the first Lord Protector, Oliver Cromwell. |
| 400 | 30 Oct 1626 | Death of Willebrord Snell (known in Dutch as Snellius), Dutch astronomer and mathematician. Best known for Snell's law, which describes the refraction of light. |
| 300 | 28 Oct 1726 | Jonathan Swift's novel *Gulliver's Travels* was published. |
| 250 | 9 Oct 1776 | Mission San Francisco de Asís (commonly known as Mission Dolores) was founded in what is now San Francisco, California, USA. It is the oldest surviving structure in San Francisco. |
| 250 | 11 Oct 1776 | American Revolutionary War – the Battle of Valcour Island, Lake Champlain, New York, USA. British victory. Most of the American ships were captured or destroyed, but the battle delayed the British forces' progress to the upper Hudson Valley. The site of the battle is now a National Historic Landmark. |
| 250 | 28 Oct 1776 | American Revolutionary War – the Battle of White Plains, New York. British victory – the Americans were forced into a significant retreat. |
| 250 | 31 Oct 1776 | American Revolutionary War: King George III of the United Kingdom gave his first speech before the British Parliament since the USA declared independence. He acknowledged that all was not going well for Britain in the war. |
| 200 | 7 Oct 1826 | The first commercial railway in the USA began operating. The gravity-powered Granite Railway ran for three miles from Quincy to Milton in Massachusetts. It carried granite to construct the Bunker Hill Monument in Boston. Most of the route is now part of the Southeast Expressway. |
| 200 | 18 Oct 1826 | The last English State Lottery was held (until 1994). State lotteries were then abolished until the National Lottery was launched in 1994. |
| 175 | 1 Oct 1851 | Hawaii's first postage stamps (known as the Hawaiian Missionaries) went on sale. |
| 175 | 2 Oct 1851 | Birth of Ferdinand Foch, French field marshal and military theorist. Supreme Allied Commander during WWI. He successfully coordinated the British, French and American forces, halted Germany's offensive, and launched an Allied counter-attack that won the war. |
| 175 | 18 Oct 1851 | Herman Melville's novel *Moby-Dick; or The Whale* was published in the UK. (USA: 14th November.) |
| 175 | 24 Oct 1851 | British astronomer William Lassell discovered two of Uranus's moons, Ariel and Umbriel. |

# OCTOBER 2026

| Ann. | Date | Event |
|------|------|-------|
| 150 | 1 Oct 1876 | Death of James Lick, American land owner, property investor and philanthropist. His business (and wealth) boomed as a result of the California gold rush, and he became the richest man in the state. |
| 150 | 2 Oct 1876 | The first classes began at Texas A&M University in the USA. At that time, it was known as the Agricultural and Mechanical College of Texas. It was the first public college in Texas. |
| 150 | 6 Oct 1876 | The American Library Association was founded. It is the world's oldest and largest library association. It promotes libraries and library education. |
| 150 | 7 Oct 1876 | Birth of Louis Tancred, South African cricketer. He played for South Africa's national team from 1902 to 1913, and was captain for three years. |
| 150 | 9 Oct 1876 | The first two-way long-distance telephone call was made, between Boston and Cambridge, Massachusetts, USA. Scottish-born American inventor Alexander Graham Bell conversed with his assistant, Thomas A. Watson, over a distance of two miles. |
| 150 | 18 Oct 1876 | Death of Francis Preston Blair, American journalist, newspaper editor and presidential adviser. Editor-in-Chief of the *Washington Globe*. |
| 150 | 19 Oct 1876 | Birth of Mordecai Brown, ('Three Finger Brown'), American baseball pitcher and manager. One of the greatest pitchers of his era. |
| 150 | 31 Oct 1876 | The Great Backerganj Cyclone (also known as the Bengal Cyclone), Bengal (now Bangladesh). One of the deadliest tropical cyclones in history. Around 200,000 people were killed in a storm surge and subsequent famine. |
| 125 | 1 Oct 1901 | Death of Abdur Rahman Khan, Emir of Afghanistan (1880–1901). He is regarded as a military genius, but a despotic ruler, and his period of rule has been called a 'reign of terror'. He ordered the executions of 100,000 people, and thousands more died when he forced tribes to migrate. Succeeded by his son, Habibullah Khan. |
| 125 | 2 Oct 1901 | The British Royal Navy's first submarine, *HMS Holland 1*, was launched. It remained in service until 1913 when it was lost while under tow. It was recovered in 1982 and is now on display at the Royal Navy Submarine Museum in Gosport, Hampshire. |
| 125 | 3 Oct 1901 | The Victor Talking Machine Company was incorporated. It merged with the Radio Corporation of America in 1929 and became RCA Victor. It later became RCA Records, which is now owned by Sony Music Entertainment. |
| 125 | 7 Oct 1901 | Birth of Frank Boucher, Canadian ice hockey player (Ottawa Senators, New York Rangers, Vancouver Maroons), coach, and manager (New York Rangers). |
| 125 | 10 Oct 1901 | Birth of Alberto Giacometti, Swiss sculptor and artist. |
| 125 | 10 Oct 1901 | Birth of Frederick D. Patterson, American educator. President of Tuskegee University (1935–53). Founder of the United Negro College Fund. |
| 125 | 10 Oct 1901 | Death of Lorenzo Snow, President of The Church of Jesus Christ of Latter-day Saints (1898–1901). |

## OCTOBER 2026

| Ann. | Date | Event |
|------|------|-------|
| 125 | 12 Oct 1901 | U.S. President Theodore Roosevelt renamed the Executive Mansion the White House. It is the official residence and workplace of the U.S. President. |
| 125 | 19 Oct 1901 | British composer Edward Elgar's *Pomp and Circumstance March No. 1* and *March No. 2* were performed for the first time, in Liverpool, UK. (*March No. 3* was first performed in 1904, *No. 4* in 1907, *No. 5* in 1930, and *No. 6* was completed by Anthony Payne in 2006.) |
| 125 | 19 Oct 1901 | Brazilian aviation pioneer Alberto Santos-Dumont won the Deutsch de la Meurthe prize in his *Santos-Dumont Number 6* airship, in Paris, France. He was the first person to fly an airship from Parc Saint Cloud, circle the Eiffel Tower, and return to the Parc within thirty minutes. He became one of the most famous people of the early 20th century. (He is a national hero in Brazil, where it is believed he built and flew a practical plane before the Wright Brothers.) |
| 125 | 19 Oct 1901 | Birth of Arleigh Burke, U.S. Navy admiral. Chief of Naval Operations under U.S. Presidents Eisenhower and Kennedy. The guided-missile destroyer *USS Arleigh Burke* was named in his honour. |
| 125 | 20 Oct 1901 | Birth of Adelaide Hall, American-born British jazz singer and entertainer. She released material over a span of eight decades and was listed in *Guinness World Records* as the world's most enduring recording artist. |
| 125 | 23 Oct 1901 | Death of Georg von Siemens, German banker and politician. Co-founder of the Deutsche Bank and the Indo-European Telegraph Company. He also helped finance several international railways, including the Northern Pacific and the Baghdad Railway. |
| 125 | 24 Oct 1901 | American schoolteacher Annie Edson Taylor, aged 63, became the first person to survive going over Niagara Falls in a barrel. She performed the stunt for financial reasons as she had fallen on hard times. |
| 125 | 27 Oct 1901 | French composer Claude Debussy's *Nocturnes* (also known as the *Three Nocturnes*) was performed in its complete form for the first time, in Paris. The first two movements had already been performed on 9th December 1900, but the female lead was unavailable on that date, so the third movement was not performed until October 1901. |
| 125 | 29 Oct 1901 | Death of Leon Czolgosz, American assassin of U.S. President William McKinley. (Executed.) |
| 125 | 30 Oct 1901 | Second Boer War – the Battle of Bakenlaagte, Mpumalanga, South Africa. Boer victory – the Boers attacked Britain's No. 3 Flying Column as it marched to its base camp. |
| 100 | 4 Oct 1926 | The city of San Francisco in California, USA adopted the dahlia as its official flower. |
| 100 | 8 Oct 1926 | Austro-Hungarian-born American physicist and electrical engineer Julius Edgar Lilienfeld filed the first patent for a field-effect transistor. The patent was granted in January 1930. (U.S. Patent 1,745,175.) He never built a transistor, as high-purity semiconducting materials were not available at that time, and he never became famous for his invention. However, his patent complicated things for later physicists who were able to build them. He also never published any details of his invention in official journals, which further confused matters. |

**OCTOBER 2026**

| Ann. | Date | Event |
|------|------|-------|
| 100 | 11 Oct 1926 | Birth of Jean Alexander, British television actress. Best known for her roles as Hilda Ogden in the soap opera *Coronation Street* and Auntie Wainwright in the comedy series *Last of the Summer Wine*. (Died 2016.) |
| 100 | 14 Oct 1926 | The children's book *Winnie-the-Pooh* by A. A. Milne was published |
| 100 | 15 Oct 1926 | Birth of Michel Foucault, French philosopher, historian of ideas and literary critic. (Died 1984.) |
| 100 | 15 Oct 1926 | Birth of Ed McBain (pen name of Evan Hunter), American crime/mystery novelist, short story writer and screenwriter. Best known for his *87th Precinct* police procedural novels. (Died 2005.) |
| 100 | 15 Oct 1926 | Birth of Karl Richter, German conductor, choirmaster, organist and harpsichordist. Leader of the Munich Bach Orchestra. (Died 1981.) |
| 100 | 18 Oct 1926 to 28th | The Havana-Bermuda hurricane devastated large parts of Cuba and Bermuda, and also affected the Bahamas and the U.S. state of Florida. 709 people were killed. |
| 100 | 18 Oct 1926 | Birth of Chuck Berry, American rock and roll singer, songwriter and guitarist. He pioneered the development of rock and roll and was a major influence on rock music. His hit songs include *Roll Over Beethoven* and *Johnny B. Goode*. He was sentenced to three years in prison for transporting a young girl across state lines for sexual intercourse. He was also sentenced for tax evasion. (Died 2017.) |
| 100 | 18 Oct 1926 | Birth of Klaus Kinski, German stage and film actor. Known for his roles as intense villains, especially in films directed by Werner Herzog (*Aguirre, the Wrath of God*, *Nosferatu the Vampyre*, *Woyzeck*, *Fitzcarraldo*, *Cobra Verde* and more). He was also noted for his violent outbursts on set. Father of the actors Pola, Nastassja and Nikolai Kinski. (Died 1991.) |
| 100 | 20 Oct 1926 | Death of Edward Douglas-Scott-Montagu, 3rd Baron Montagu of Beaulieu, British politician and founder of the National Motor Museum. He was imprisoned for homosexuality in 1954. (Died 2015.) |
| 100 | 21 Oct 1926 | Birth of Leonard Rossiter, British stage, film and television actor. Best known for his roles as the landlord Rigsby in the sitcom *Rising Damp* and the title character in *The Fall and Rise of Reginald Perrin*. (Died 1984.) |
| 100 | 24 Oct 1926 | Birth of Y. A. Tittle, American football player (Baltimore Colts, San Francisco 49ers, New York Giants). (Died 2017.) |
| 100 | 27 Oct 1926 | Birth of H. R. Haldeman, American advertising executive, political aide and campaign manager. White House chief of staff during Richard Nixon's administration. Best known for his involvement and conviction in the Watergate scandal. (Died 1993.) |
| 100 | 31 Oct 1926 | Birth of Jimmy Savile, British radio DJ and television presenter. Best known for the television series *Top of the Pops* and *Jim'll Fix It*. He was widely praised for his charity work and noted for his eccentricity. After his death, he was discovered to have been one of Britain's most prolific predatory sex offenders. (Died 2011.) |

# OCTOBER 2026

| Ann. | Date | Event |
|---|---|---|
| 100 | 31 Oct 1926 | Death of Harry Houdini, Hungarian-born American magician and escape artist. (Peritonitis, aged 52.)<br>He had recently been punched repeatedly in the stomach, during an incident in his dressing room. Some historians believe he did not seek medical treatment for appendicitis because the pain from the punches was masking it. Others believe the punches ruptured his appendix. |
| 90 | 1 Oct 1936 | General Francisco Franco was proclaimed head of state of Spain (until 1975). |
| 90 | 3 Oct 1936 | Death of John Heisman, American football player and coach.<br>The Heisman Trophy is named in his honour. It is awarded annually to the most outstanding college football player. |
| 90 | 4 Oct 1936 | The Battle of Cable Street, east London. UK.<br>The British Union of Fascists, led by Oswald Mosley, held a march through the East End of London. The marchers were dressed in their 'Blackshirt' uniforms. Anti-fascist demonstrators and local people forced them to retreat, and there were violent clashes with the Metropolitan Police who were there to protect the marchers.<br>175 people were injured and 150 arrested. The march was eventually called off, and the police escorted the marchers back to central London.<br>Afterwards, the wearing of political uniforms in public was banned, and organisers of political marches had to seek police permission first. |
| 90 | 5 Oct 1936 to 31st | The Jarrow March (also known as the Jarrow Crusade).<br>200 men set off from Jarrow in north-east England to Westminster in London to draw attention to the severe unemployment and poverty in their area following the closure of a shipyard. |
| 90 | 5 Oct 1936 | Birth of Václav Havel, Czech playwright, poet and political dissident.<br>President of Czechoslovakia (1989–1993).<br>First President of the Czech Republic (1993–2003). (Died 2011.) |
| 90 | 5 Oct 1936 | Death of J. Slauerhoff, Dutch poet.<br>One of the most important Dutch-language writers. |
| 90 | 7 Oct 1936 | Birth of Michael Hurll, British television producer.<br>He produced many of Britain's most popular comedy and light entertainment series, including *The Two Ronnies*, *Top of the Pops* and *Blind Date*. Founder of the British Comedy Awards. (Died 2012.) |
| 90 | 8 Oct 1936 | Death of Ahmet Tevfik Pasha, the last Grand Vizier (Prime Minister) of the Ottoman Empire (1920–22). |
| 90 | 9 Oct 1936 | The Boulder Dam (now the Hoover Dam) on the Colorado River in the USA went fully online and began generating electricity. |
| 90 | 14 Oct 1936 | Spanish Civil War: the first group of International Brigades volunteers arrived in Albacete, Spain, where they were sorted according to their experience and dispatched to combat units.<br>The first group of 500 volunteers were mostly French, plus a few exiled Poles and Germans.<br>Up to 35,000 volunteers took part in the war as members of the International Brigades. (No more than 20,000 were active at any one time.) |
| 90 | 14 Oct 1936 | The first Social Security office in the USA opened in Austin, Texas. |

**OCTOBER 2026**

| Ann. | Date | Event |
|---|---|---|
| 90 | 16 Oct 1936 | Birth of Andrei Chikatilo, (the 'Rostov Ripper'), Soviet-Ukrainian serial killer. (Executed 1994.) |
| 90 | 19 Oct 1936 | Birth of James Bevel, American civil rights leader and minister.<br>An influential adviser to Martin Luther King Jr.<br>He helped organise non-violent protests and notable marches.<br>He was an unsuccessful Vice-Presidential candidate in 1992.<br>He was also convicted of having an incestuous relationship with his daughter. (Died 2008.) |
| 90 | 19 Oct 1936 | Death of Lu Xun, Chinese writer, poet and critic.<br>Considered the greatest Chinese writer of the 20th century, and the founder of modern Chinese literature. |
| 90 | 20 Oct 1936 | Death of Anne Sullivan Macy, American teacher.<br>Known for efforts to educate Helen Keller, who became the first blind and deaf person to earn a Bachelor of Arts degree. |
| 90 | 21 Oct 1936 | Pan Am launched the first commercial passenger flight from the U.S. mainland (San Francisco, California) to Hawaii.<br>The *Hawaii Clipper* carried seven passengers, along with cargo and airmail. More than 1,000 people applied for the first seven tickets |
| 90 | 25 Oct 1936 | Germany and Italy signed a friendship treaty that would later become the Rome–Berlin Axis. |
| 90 | 30 Oct 1936 | Birth of Polina Astakhova, Soviet-Ukrainian gymnast.<br>Gold medallist at the 1956, 1960 and 1964 Olympics. (Died 2005.) |
| 90 | 31 Oct 1936 | The Boy Scouts of the Philippines was established. |
| 90 | 31 Oct 1936 | Birth of Michael Landon, American television actor, director and producer (*Bonanza, Little House on the Prairie, Highway to Heaven*). (Died 1991.) |
| 80 | 1 Oct 1946 | The International War Crimes Tribunal in Nuremberg, Germany ended.<br>Twelve Nazi leaders were sentenced to death for war crimes committed during WWII. Ten were hanged on 16th October.<br>(One was already dead, and one committed suicide the day before the execution.) (See also: 15th and 16th October 1946.) |
| 80 | 1 Oct 1946 to mid-Nov | The Autumn Uprising (also known as the Daegu Uprising or the October Incident), southern Korea.<br>A peasant uprising against the U.S. Army Military Government.<br>U.S. forces successfully put down the uprising.<br>274 people were killed and many others were arrested and tortured. |
| 80 | 1 Oct 1946 | Mensa International, the high IQ society, was founded. |
| 80 | 1 Oct 1946 to 3rd | The first-ever tie-breaker series in Major League Baseball in the USA.<br>The National League teams St. Louis Cardinals and the Brooklyn Dodgers had identical win-loss records for the season. The Cardinals won the play-off and went on to beat the Boston Red Sox in the World Series. |
| 80 | 2 Oct 1946 | The world's first commercial car telephone service began operating in Chicago, Illinois, USA. |

## OCTOBER 2026

| Ann. | Date | Event |
|---|---|---|
| 80 | 2 Oct 1946 | The first episode of the soap opera *Faraway Hill* was broadcast on the Dumont Television Network in the USA. It was the first network television soap opera in the USA. It ran until December. |
| 80 | 6 Oct 1946 | Birth of Tony Greig, South African-born British/Australian cricketer and commentator. (Died 2012.) |
| 80 | 9 Oct 1946 | Eugene O'Neill's play *The Iceman Cometh* premièred on Broadway. |
| 80 | 9 Oct 1946 | The first automatic electric blankets went on sale in Virginia, USA. They cost $37.50 (equivalent to around $540 today). |
| 80 | 10 Oct 1946 | Birth of Giant Haystacks, British professional wrestler. (Known as the Loch Ness Monster in the USA and Canada.) (Died 1998.) |
| 80 | 15 Oct 1946 | Death of Hermann Goering, German Nazi leader. He was sentenced to death at the Nuremberg trials (see 1st October 1946), but poisoned himself with cyanide on the eve of his execution. |
| 80 | 16 Oct 1946 | The Nuremberg executions. Ten prominent leaders of Nazi Germany were hanged for war crimes they committed during WWII. |
| 80 | 20 Oct 1946 | The puppet character Muffin the Mule made his first television appearance on the BBC series *For the Children*. He proved popular and was given his own series, *Muffin the Mule*, which ran from 1952 to 1955. (The series also ran on ITV from 1956 to 1957.) |
| 80 | 20 Oct 1946 | Birth of Chris Woodhead, Britain's Chief Inspector of Education, Children's Services and Skills (1994–2000). He was a controversial figure, who attacked schools and teachers for being 'mediocre' and overruled his inspectors. This sometimes had catastrophic results for the schools, teachers and students. Teachers' unions demanded that he be replaced, and he resigned in 2000. (Died 2015.) |
| 80 | 21 Oct 1946 | Birth of Lux Interior, American punk/rock/psychobilly singer (The Cramps). (Died 2009.) |
| 80 | 22 Oct 1946 | Operation Osoaviakhim. Soviet forces captured more than 2,200 German technical specialists and their families from the Soviet occupation zone in Germany and forcibly relocated them to work in the Soviet Union. The USA did the same thing (Operation Paperclip) but far less aggressively. |
| 80 | 24 Oct 1946 | The first photo of the Earth from space (altitude 65 miles) was taken by U.S. scientists using a V-2 rocket captured from Germany after WWII. |
| 80 | 27 Oct 1946 | The French Fourth Republic was established. The current French Fifth Republic was established in October 1958. |
| 80 | 29 Oct 1946 | Birth of Peter Green, British blues/rock singer, songwriter and guitarist. The founder of Fleetwood Mac. He was also a member of John Mayall & the Bluesbreakers, and later formed the Peter Green Splinter Group. (Died 2020.) |
| 75 | 2 Oct 1951 | Television broadcasts began in the Netherlands. |
| 75 | 3 Oct 1951 | The Shot Heard 'Round the World. In one of the greatest moments in baseball history, Bobby Thomson of the New York Giants hit a game-winning home run, and the Giants won the National League pennant. Their opponents, the Brooklyn Dodgers, had seemed certain to win the pennant for almost the entire season. |

## OCTOBER 2026

| Ann. | Date | Event |
|------|------|-------|
| 75 | 3 Oct 1951 to 12th | Korean War – Operation Commando. United Nations victory over China. |
| 75 | 6 Oct 1951 | Soviet leader Joseph Stalin announced that the Soviet Union had developed and successfully tested an atomic bomb. In fact, it had successfully tested its first atomic bomb (*Joe-1*) in August 1949. The U.S. Air Force detected it on 1st September 1949, and U.S. President Harry S. Truman announced it to the public at the end of that month. |
| 75 | 6 Oct 1951 | Malayan Emergency: the British High Commissioner in Malaya, Henry Gurney, was ambushed and killed by communist guerrillas. |
| 75 | 6 Oct 1951 | Death of W. K. Kellogg, American breakfast cereal manufacturer. Founder of the Kellogg company. |
| 75 | 7 Oct 1951 | Death of Anton Philips, Dutch businessman. Co-founder of the Philips electronics company with his brother Gerard. |
| 75 | 10 Oct 1951 | The Mutual Security Administration was established in the USA. It supervised all foreign aid programmes, including military assistance and economic programmes that bolstered the defence capabilities of the USA's allies. |
| 75 | 11 Oct 1951 | Birth of Louise Rennison, British writer and comedian. Best known for her *Confessions of Georgia Nicolson* series of books for teenagers, including *Angus, Thongs and Full-Frontal Snogging*, which was adapted into a 2008 film. (Died 2016.) |
| 75 | 14 Oct 1951 | The Organization of Central American States was established. |
| 75 | 15 Oct 1951 to 17th | The first party election broadcasts were televised in the UK. The three main parties were each allocated fifteen minutes. The Liberal Party broadcast theirs on 15th October, the Conservative Party on 16th October and the Labour Party on 17th October. The General Election was held on 25th October. |
| 75 | 15 Oct 1951 | Mexican chemistry student Luis Miramontes synthesised the first oral contraceptive at the Syntex pharmaceutical company in Mexico City. |
| 75 | 15 Oct 1951 | The first episode of the television sitcom *I Love Lucy* was broadcast on CBS in the USA. It ran for six seasons until 1957. |
| 75 | 16 Oct 1951 | Death of Liaquat Ali Khan, first Prime Minister of Pakistan (1947–51). (Assassinated.) Succeeded by Khawaja Nazimuddin. |
| 75 | 18 Oct 1951 | Snowdonia National Park was established in Wales. It was Britain's third national park. |
| 75 | 19 Oct 1951 | World War II: U.S. President Harry S. Truman officially terminated the state of war with Germany. |
| 75 | 26 Oct 1951 | Winston Churchill became Prime Minister of the UK for the second time (until 1955). He was also Prime Minister from 1940 to 1945. |
| 75 | 30 Oct 1951 | Dartmoor National Park was established in the UK. |
| 75 | 31 Oct 1951 | Zebra crossings were introduced in Britain. The first one was in Slough, Berkshire. |

## OCTOBER 2026

| Ann. | Date | Event |
|------|------|-------|
| 70 | 1 Oct 1956 | The rock and roll song *Singing the Blues* by Guy Mitchell was released. |
| 70 | 2 Oct 1956 | Death of George Bancroft, American film actor. |
| 70 | 3 Oct 1956 | The Bolshoi Ballet performed in Britain for the first time, at the Royal Opera House in Covent Garden, London. |
| 70 | 4 Oct 1956 | The first episode of the television drama anthology series *Playhouse 90* was broadcast on CBS in the USA. It ran for four seasons until 1960. |
| 70 | 6 Oct 1956 | Death of Charles E. Merrill, American stock broker and philanthropist. Co-founder of Merrill Lynch & Company (now Merrill, the investment and wealth management division of Bank of America). |
| 70 | 7 Oct 1956 | Death of Clarence Birdseye, American businessman and inventor who founded the modern frozen food industry. |
| 70 | 8 Oct 1956 | American baseball pitcher Don Larsen pitched the first (and only) perfect game in the history of the World Series. (Game 5 of the 1956 World Series: New York Yankees v. Brooklyn Dodgers.) |
| 70 | 14 Oct 1956 | Indian politician and social reformer B. R. Ambedkar converted to Buddhism. He then converted 500,000 of his Dalit followers (some sources say 350,000) who had attended the public ceremony. The Dalits (also known as the untouchables) were considered the lowest members of India's caste-based society. Their conversion to Buddhism was designed to allow them to escape this stigma. |
| 70 | 16 Oct 1956 | William J. Brennan Jr. became an Associate Justice of the U.S. Supreme Court (until 1990). |
| 70 | 16 Oct 1956 | Death of Jules Rimet, French football administrator. President of FIFA (1921–54). The first FIFA World Cup trophy was named the Jules Rimet Trophy in his honour. It was permanently awarded to Brazil after they won the World Cup for the third time in 1970. |
| 70 | 17 Oct 1956 | Britain's first nuclear power station, Calder Hall in Cumbria, was officially opened. It closed in March 2003 after operating for nearly 47 years. (See also: 27th August 1956.) |
| 70 | 19 Oct 1956 | The Soviet–Japanese Joint Declaration was signed. It officially ended the state of war that had existed between the two countries since August 1945, and restored diplomatic relations. |
| 70 | 19 Oct 1956 | Birth of Carlo Urbani, Italian physician and epidemiologist who first identified SARS and notified the World Health Organization, allowing it to be contained. His response saved millions of lives – though he died from the disease himself in 1993. |
| 70 | 21 Oct 1956 | The Mau Mau Uprising in Kenya: British forces captured rebel leader Dedan Kimathi, marking the end of Britain's military campaign. However, the uprising continued, led by ethnic units, until Kenya gained its independence in 1960. |
| 70 | 21 Oct 1956 | Birth of Carrie Fisher, American film and television actress, screenwriter and script doctor. Best known for her role as Princess Leia in *Star Wars*. (Died 2016.) |

## OCTOBER 2026

| Ann. | Date | Event |
|---|---|---|
| 70 | 23 Oct 1956 to 10 Nov | The Hungarian Revolution (also known as the Hungarian Uprising). A spontaneous nationwide revolt against Communist/Soviet rule was crushed when Soviet forces intervened with tanks. At least 2,500 Hungarians and 700 Soviet troops were killed. |
| 70 | 23 Oct 1956 | The first use of videotape on a U.S. network television show. *The Jonathan Winters Show* broadcast a video recording of a song performed by Dorothy Collins. (See also: 30th November 1956.) |
| 70 | 25 Oct 1956 | Death of Risto Ryti, President of Finland (1940–44), Prime Minister of Finland (1939–40). |
| 70 | 29 Oct 1956 to 7 Nov | The Suez Crisis. Israel invaded Egypt in an attempt to regain Western control of the Suez Canal and remove President Gamal Abdel Nasser from power. Britain and France joined the invasion, but were forced to withdrew by the United Nations, the USA and the USSR, leaving Sinai under Israeli occupation until March 1957. British Prime Minister Anthony Eden resigned in January 1957. Many commentators consider the Suez Crisis the end of Britain's role as a major world power. |
| 70 | 29 Oct 1956 | The city of Tangier was reintegrated into Morocco. It had been an international zone since 1924. |
| 70 | 29 Oct 1956 | The first episode of *The Huntley–Brinkley Report* was broadcast on NBC TV in the USA. It was NBC's flagship evening news show until July 1970. |
| 70 | 31 Oct 1956 | American naval officer George J. Dufek become the first person to land a plane at the South Pole. He and his crew of six were also the first Americans to set foot on the South Pole. (A Norwegian team led by Roald Amundsun first reached the South Pole in December 1911.) |
| 65 | 1 Oct 1961 | The Federal Republic of Cameroon was founded when the southern part of British Cameroons merged with French Cameroun. |
| 65 | 1 Oct 1961 | The United States Defense Intelligence Agency (DIA) was formed. It collects information on the military capabilities and intentions of foreign governments and non-state groups and individuals. |
| 65 | 1 Oct 1961 | Soviet-Russian composer Dmitri Shostakovich's *Symphony No. 12* was performed for the first time, in Saint Petersburg. |
| 65 | 2 Oct 1961 | The first episode of the medical drama television series *Ben Casey* was broadcast on NBC in the USA. It ran for five seasons until 1966. |
| 65 | 3 Oct 1961 to 20th | 120,000 members of the United Auto Workers (UAW) union staged a seventeen-day strike at Ford plants across the USA, demanding better working conditions. |
| 65 | 3 Oct 1961 | The first episode of the television sitcom *The Dick Van Dyke Show* was broadcast on CBS in the USA. It ran for five seasons until 1966. |
| 65 | 6 Oct 1961 | Cold War: U.S. President John F. Kennedy advised Americans to build bomb shelters to protect themselves from nuclear fallout in the event of an attack by the Soviet Union. |

# OCTOBER 2026

| Ann. | Date | Event |
|---|---|---|
| 65 | 10 Oct 1961 | The entire population of Tristan da Cunha was evacuated to the UK following a volcanic eruption. Most of them returned home two years later. |
| 65 | 11 Oct 1961 | Death of Chico Marx, American comedian (the Marx Brothers). |
| 65 | 14 Oct 1961 | Frank Loesser's musical *How to Succeed in Business without Really Trying* opened on Broadway. It ran until 1965, and was adapted into a 1967 film. |
| 65 | 17 Oct 1961 | Algerian War – the Paris massacre.<br>French police attacked Algerian protesters staging a peaceful demonstration in Paris. The exact number of Algerians killed is unknown – at least forty, but possibly several hundred. |
| 65 | 17 Oct 1961 | The Museum of Modern Art in New York City, USA famously hung Henri Matisse's artwork *Le Bateau* upside-down.<br>No one noticed for 47 days. It was hung the right way up on 3rd December. |
| 65 | 20 Oct 1961 | Elvis Presley's album *Blue Hawaii* was released. It was the soundtrack to his musical romantic comedy film of the same name. |
| 65 | 25 Oct 1961 | The first issue of the British satirical magazine *Private Eye* was published. |
| 65 | 26 Oct 1961 | Death of Peter Jensen, Danish-born American engineer, inventor and entrepreneur. Inventor of the first loud speaker.<br>Founder of the Magnavox electronics company. |
| 65 | 27 Oct 1961 | NASA's Saturn I rocket made its maiden flight.<br>It was NASA's first dedicated heavy-lift space launch vehicle.<br>After three further successful test flights it entered service in 1964.<br>It was succeeded by the Saturn IB in 1966. |
| 65 | 30 Oct 1961 | The Soviet Union exploded the *Tsar Bomba*, a 50-megaton hydrogen bomb, in a test at Novaya Zemlya in the Arctic Ocean.<br>It is currently the largest nuclear weapon ever built. |
| 65 | 30 Oct 1961 | Death of Luigi Einaudi, President of Italy (1948–55). |
| 65 | 31 Oct 1961 | Hurricane Hattie hit Belize. 307 people were killed and seventy percent of the buildings in Belize City were damaged, leaving 10,000 homeless.<br>The government was forced to relocate to the new city of Belmopan.<br>The hurricane also caused damage and a small number of deaths elsewhere in the Caribbean and Central America. |
| 65 | 31 Oct 1961 | De-Stalinisation: former Soviet leader Joseph Stalin's body was removed from Lenin's mausoleum in Red Square, Moscow and reburied within the Kremlin walls, out of public view.<br>The city of Stalingrad was renamed Volgograd on 10th November. |
| 60 | 4 Oct 1966 | Lesotho (formerly Basutoland) gained its independence from the UK. |
| 60 | 5 Oct 1966 | Fermi 1, a prototype fast breeder reactor at the Enrico Fermi Nuclear Generating Station in Michigan, USA, suffered a partial meltdown.<br>No radioactive material was released. |
| 60 | 6 Oct 1966 | The psychedelic drug LSD was banned in California, USA.<br>It was banned throughout the entire USA in 1967. |
| 60 | 7 Oct 1966 | Death of Johnny Kidd, British rock and roll singer and songwriter (Johnny Kidd & the Pirates). Best known for his hit song *Shakin' All Over*. (Car crash, aged 30.) |

**OCTOBER 2026**

| Ann. | Date | Event |
|---|---|---|
| 60 | 9 Oct 1966 | The Binh Tai Massacre, South Vietnam.<br>South Korean forces set fire to homes in the village of Binh Tai and shot the residents who fled the burning buildings. 68 people were killed. |
| 60 | 10 Oct 1966 | The Beach Boys' hit song *Good Vibrations* was released.<br>It was the most expensive single ever recorded at that time, costing around $75,000 (about $650,000 today). It used 90 hours' of tape recorded at four different studios over a period of seven months. |
| 60 | 10 Oct 1966 | The album *Parsley, Sage, Rosemary and Thyme* by Simon and Garfunkel was released. |
| 60 | 11 Oct 1966 | Birth of Luke Perry, American film and television actor. Best known for his role as Dylan McKay in *Beverley Hills, 90210*. (Died 2019.) |
| 60 | 13 Oct 1966 | The newly formed Jimi Hendrix Experience played their first live performance: a fifteen-minute set at the Novelty in Evreux, France. |
| 60 | 13 Oct 1966 | Death of Clifton Webb, American stage and film actor, dancer and singer. Best known for his roles in the films *Laura, The Razor's Edge* and *Sitting Pretty*. |
| 60 | 14 Oct 1966 | The Montreal Metro system in Quebec, Canada began operating. |
| 60 | 15 Oct 1966 | The Black Panther Party, a black nationalist and socialist organisation, was founded in the USA. (It was dissolved in 1982.) |
| 60 | 17 Oct 1966 | The 23rd Street Fire, Manhattan, New York City, USA.<br>Twelve firefighters were killed when a floor of the building collapsed while they were fighting a fire.<br>It was the biggest loss of life in the New York City Fire Department's history (until the 9/11 terrorist attacks in 2001.) |
| 60 | 18 Oct 1966 | Death of Elizabeth Arden, Canadian-born American businesswoman who founded the Elizabeth Arden cosmetics and fragrance empire. She was one of the wealthiest women in the world and a prominent racehorse owner. |
| 60 | 18 Oct 1966 | Death of S. S. Kresge, American merchant who founded a chain of discount stores that later became Kmart. |
| 60 | 19 Oct 1966 | Gulf + Western Industries purchased the Paramount Picture Corporation. |
| 60 | 21 Oct 1966 | The Aberfan disaster, South Wales.<br>A colliery spoil tip (also known as a slag heap) collapsed and fell onto the village. Worst hit was Pantglas Junior School.<br>116 children and 28 adults were killed. |
| 60 | 22 Oct 1966 | George Blake, one of Britain's most notorious double-agents, escaped from Wormwood Scrubs prison in London and fled to the Soviet Union. He had been sentenced to 42 years in prison in 1961. The escape was masterminded by fellow prisoner Sean Bourke, who believed the long sentence was inhumane. Their story is told in the play *Cell Mates* |
| 60 | 22 Oct 1966 | The Soviet Union launched its *Luna 12* spacecraft to photograph and study the Moon. It reached the Moon on 25th October and went into orbit around it. It operated successfully until January 1967. |
| 60 | 22 Oct 1966 | The album *The Supremes A' Go-Go* by The Supremes became the first album by an all-female group to top the *Billboard* album chart in the USA. |

# OCTOBER 2026

| Ann. | Date | Event |
|---|---|---|
| 60 | 24 Oct 1966 to 25th | Vietnam War: the Manila Summit Conference was held in the Philippines, and was attended by the leaders of Australia, Korea, New Zealand, the Philippines, South Vietnam, Thailand, and the USA.<br>They discussed the escalating war, and pledged to withdraw their forces from Vietnam within six months if North Vietnam withdrew its forces from South Vietnam. The war continued until 1975. |
| 60 | 26 Oct 1966 | Vietnam War: the U.S. Navy aircraft carrier *USS Oriskany* caught fire in the Gulf of Tonkin when a magnesium flare was accidentally ignited.<br>44 people were killed. An investigation found that the crewman who accidentally ignited the flare panicked and threw it into a weapons locker containing other flares. Had he thrown it over the side of the ship, the fire would not have started. |
| 60 | 26 Oct 1966 | The first Pacific communications satellite, *Intelsat II F-1* (Blue Bird), was launched. It could relay 240 telephone calls or two television channels.<br>It failed to reach its intended geostationary orbit, and was only used for tests and limited communications.<br>A further three Intelsat II satellites were launched in 1967, and they all operated successfully. They had a life-span of about four years. |
| 60 | 26 Oct 1966 | Death of Alma Cogan, British pop singer. One of the biggest stars of the 1950s and early 60s. (Ovarian cancer, aged 34.) |
| 60 | 30 Oct 1966 | Birth of Abu Musab al-Zarqawi, Jordanian-born Iraqi Islamic terrorist.<br>A prominent leader of the militant group Al-Qaeda and a close associate of its leader, Osama bin Laden. He was responsible for numerous terrorist attacks, bombings and hostage executions during the Iraq war.<br>(Killed in a U.S. air strike in 2006.) |
| 50 | 4 Oct 1976 | The InterCity 125 High Speed Train service began operating in the UK. |
| 50 | 4 Oct 1976 | Barbara Walters became the first woman to anchor a network television evening news show in the USA. She joined the *ABC Evening News* alongside Harry Reasoner. (Their relationship was described as 'difficult'.) |
| 50 | 6 Oct 1976 | The Thammasat University massacre, Bangkok, Thailand.<br>Students demonstrating against the return of former dictator Thanom Kittikachorn were attacked by police, government forces and right-wing paramilitary groups. 46 people were killed (official figure) though the real number is thought to be over 100. |
| 50 | 6 Oct 1976 | China's 'Gang of Four' were arrested.<br>On 21st October a massive media campaign was launched against them, accusing them of crimes against the state, and there were public celebrations of their arrest.<br>The Gang of Four included Mao Zedong's last wife, Jiang Qing, and her close associates. They were tried and convicted in 1981. All four received long prison sentences. |
| 50 | 6 Oct 1976 | Cubana de Aviación Flight 455 crashed in Bridgetown, Barbados after two bombs exploded. All 78 people on board were killed.<br>CIA-linked anti-Castro terrorists and the Venezuelan secret police were implicated. |

## OCTOBER 2026

| Ann. | Date | Event |
|------|------|-------|
| 50 | 7 Oct 1976 | Hua Guofeng became Chairman of the Communist Party of China, succeeding Mao Zedong who died in September.<br>He was also Premier of the People's Republic of China from 4th February 1976 until September 1980. |
| 50 | 8 Oct 1976 | British punk rock group the Sex Pistols signed with EMI for a two-year contract. The contract was ended in January 1977. |
| 50 | 11 Oct 1976 | The Toxic Substances Control Act came into effect in the USA.<br>It regulates the production, testing and sale of chemical substances. |
| 50 | 12 Oct 1976 | Indian Airlines Flight 171 crashed at Chhatrapati Shivaji Maharaj International Airport in Mumbai, India shortly after take-off, and while returning to the airport for an emergency landing. All 95 passengers and crew were killed. (Cause: engine failure and fire caused by metal fatigue.) |
| 50 | 14 Oct 1976 | The last manual telephone exchange in the UK closed down (Portree, Isle of Skye, Scotland). |
| 50 | 14 Oct 1976 | Death of Dame Edith Evans, British stage and film actress.<br>One of the finest stage actresses of her era. Particularly noted for playing haughty aristocratic women, though she played many other roles too. |
| 50 | 15 Oct 1976 | The first televised U.S. Vice-Presidential debate:<br>Walter Mondale (Democrat) and Bob Dole (Republican).<br>(The first U.S. Presidential debate was in 1960.) |
| 50 | 15 Oct 1976 | Death of Carlo Gambino, Italian-born American gangster.<br>Head of the Gambino organised crime family and reputed 'boss of bosses' of the American mafia. |
| 50 | 19 Oct 1976 | Lebanese Civil War – the Battle of Aishiya.<br>Forces from the Palestine Liberation Organisation and a Communist militia attacked an isolated Maronite village. Their first (daylight) attack was repelled by Israeli Defense Forces, but the attackers returned that night, forcing the villagers to flee. (The villagers returned in 1982.) |
| 50 | 20 Oct 1976 | The *MV George Prince* ferry disaster, Mississippi River, Louisiana, USA.<br>The ferry was hit by the Norwegian tanker *SS Frosta* and capsized immediately, killing 78 people. |
| 50 | 24 Oct 1976 | The first World Jewish Film and Television Festival opened in Jerusalem, Israel |
| 50 | 25 Oct 1976 | The National Theatre in London, UK was officially opened. |
| 50 | 26 Oct 1976 | Transkei gained its (nominal) independence from South Africa, though it was unrecognised internationally.<br>It reintegrated with South Africa in 1994 as part of its Eastern Cape province. |
| 50 | 31 Oct 1976 | The first VHS-format videocassette recorder (the JVC HR-3300) went on sale in Japan.<br>The first VHS-format VCR in the USA (the RCA VBT200) went on sale in August 1977.<br>The first VHS-format VCR in the UK (the JVC HR-3300EK) went on sale in 1978. |

## OCTOBER 2026

| Ann. | Date | Event |
|------|------|-------|
| 40 | 1 Oct 1986 | Former U.S. President Jimmy Carter's presidential library opened in Atlanta, Georgia. |
| 40 | 2 Oct 1986 | The Comprehensive Anti-Apartheid Act came into effect in the USA. It imposed sanctions on South Africa. U.S. President Ronald Reagan vetoed the bill, calling it 'economic warfare', but his veto was overridden by the U.S. Congress. Most of the sanctions were repealed in July 1991, and the remainder were repealed in November 1993. |
| 40 | 3 Oct 1986 | The Tandem Accelerator Superconducting Cyclotron (TASCC) began operating at Chalk River Laboratories in Ontario, Canada. It was the world's first tandem accelerator. It was decommissioned in 1996. |
| 40 | 3 Oct 1986 | Death of Vince DiMaggio, American baseball player. Brother of Joe DiMaggio and Dom DiMaggio. |
| 40 | 5 Oct 1986 | *The Sunday Times* newspaper in the UK published details of Israel's secret nuclear weapons programme. Mordechai Vanunu, the former nuclear technician who leaked the details, was abducted by the Israeli intelligence agency Mossad and served eighteen years in prison. He was released in 2004, but has been arrested and imprisoned several times since then, allegedly for violating the terms of his parole. |
| 40 | 5 Oct 1986 | Iran–Contra Scandal: former U.S. Marine Eugene Hasenfus was captured by Nicaraguan Sandinistas after his plane was shot down. As a result, it was discovered that the USA was illegally selling arms to Iran and using the money to fund covert operations in Nicaragua. |
| 40 | 5 Oct 1986 | Death of Hal B. Wallis, American film producer (*The Maltese Falcon, Casablanca, Gunfight at the O.K. Corral, Rooster Cogburn,* and more). |
| 40 | 6 Oct 1986 | Cold War: the Soviet nuclear submarine *K-219* sank in the Atlantic Ocean after an explosion in one of its missile tubes. Four crew members were killed and two more died later. There is a great deal of controversy surrounding this incident. The Soviet Union claimed a U.S. submarine (the *USS Augusta*) collided with the *K-219*, which the USA denied. The *K-219*'s captain may have deliberately scuttled the vessel. The 1997 film *Hostile Waters* claims to tell the story of the incident. (In 2001 the captain of the *K-219* successfully sued the film-maker, saying he had not given his permission to use his story or character.) |
| 40 | 7 Oct 1986 | The first issue of the British newspaper *The Independent* was published. In March 2016 its final printed edition was published and it became an online-only publication. |
| 40 | 9 Oct 1986 | Fox Broadcasting Company launched in the USA. |
| 40 | 9 Oct 1986 | Andrew Lloyd Webber's musical *The Phantom of the Opera* premièred in London, UK. |
| 40 | 10 Oct 1986 | The San Salvador earthquake, El Salvador. Approximately 1,500 people were killed. |
| 40 | 10 Oct 1986 | The spy comedy film *Jumpin' Jack Flash* was released in the USA. UK: 1st May 1987. |

## OCTOBER 2026

| Ann. | Date | Event |
|---|---|---|
| 40 | 10 Oct 1986 | The Near-Earth asteroid *3753 Cruithne* was discovered. It orbits the Sun but is affected by the Earth's gravity, giving it a bean-shaped or horseshoe-shaped orbit when observed from the Earth. |
| 40 | 11 Oct 1986 to 12th | Cold War: the Reykjavik summit in Iceland, aimed at reducing the nuclear arsenals of the USA and Soviet Union, ended in failure. U.S. President Ronald Reagan and Soviet leader Mikhail Gorbachev failed to reach agreement on the USA's Strategic Defence Initiative (SDI – also known as 'Star Wars'). |
| 40 | 12 Oct 1986 | Queen Elizabeth II became the first British monarch to visit China. |
| 40 | 16 Oct 1986 | Researchers from the Massachusetts Institute of Technology (MIT) in the USA announced the discovery of the first tumour suppressor gene. The gene (Rb) acts to prevent the development of retinoblastoma (a rare form of cancer that affects the eye) in humans. The team was led by Dr. Robert A. Weinberg. |
| 40 | 16 Oct 1986 | Italian mountaineer Reinhold Messner became the first person to climb all fourteen eight-thousanders (mountains whose summits are over 8,000 metres above sea level). |
| 40 | 16 Oct 1986 | Death of Arthur Grumiaux, Belgian violinist. |
| 40 | 17 Oct 1986 | Iran-contra scandal: the U.S. Congress approved a $100 million package of military and humanitarian aid for the Contras in Nicaragua. The sale of weapons to Iran (which was subject to an arms embargo) to provide funding for the Contras was made public in November. |
| 40 | 19 Oct 1986 | Death of Dele Giwa, Nigerian journalist. Founder of *Newswatch* magazine. (Assassinated, aged 39. There are several conspiracy theories about why he was killed and who did it.) |
| 40 | 19 Oct 1986 | Death of Samora Machel, the first President of Mozambique (1975–86). (Plane crash, aged 53.) Succeeded by Joaquim Chissano. |
| 40 | 21 Oct 1986 | The Marshall Islands signed a Compact of Free Association with the USA. |
| 40 | 21 Oct 1986 | The Electronic Communications Privacy Act came into effect in the USA. It protects citizens from unauthorised government access to telephone systems, email, and other electronic communications. |
| 40 | 21 Oct 1986 | American writer Edward Tracy was kidnapped by terrorists in Beirut, Lebanon. (He was released in August 1991.) |
| 40 | 22 Oct 1986 | The Tax Reform Act of 1986 came into effect in the USA. It was a major simplification of the income tax code. |
| 40 | 22 Oct 1986 | Death of Jane Dornnacker, American rock singer, actress, comedian and radio traffic reporter. (Helicopter crash while reporting on traffic for WNBC in New York City, aged 39.) |
| 40 | 22 Oct 1986 | Death of Albert Szent-Györgyi, Hungarian physiologist and biochemist. Winner of the 1937 Nobel Prize in Physiology or Medicine for discovering the role of vitamin C in the oxidation of nutrients. |
| 40 | 24 Oct 1986 | Britain broke off diplomatic relations with Syria when it was revealed that Syrian officials were involved in a plot to blow up an El Al airliner. |

**OCTOBER 2026**

| Ann. | Date | Event |
|---|---|---|
| 40 | 27 Oct 1986 | Big Bang Day, City of London, UK. The British financial market was deregulated and the London Stock Exchange switched to a computerised trading system. |
| 40 | 27 Oct 1986 | BBC One in the UK launched its new daytime television service, including the popular Australian soap opera *Neighbours*. |
| 40 | 28 Oct 1986 | British serial killer Jeremy Bamber was sentenced to life imprisonment for killing five members of his family. |
| 40 | 28 Oct 1986 | Death of John Braine, British novelist. Best known for *Room at the Top*. |
| 40 | 29 Oct 1986 | The M25 orbital motorway around Greater London was officially opened. |
| 40 | 30 Oct 1986 | The first fibre-optic undersea telecommunications cable across the English Channel went into service. |
| 40 | 31 Oct 1986 | Death of Robert Sanderson Mulliken, American chemist and physicist. Winner of the 1966 Nobel Prize for Chemistry for his work on the chemical bonds and electronic structure of molecules. |
| 30 | 1 Oct 1996 | Death of Pat McGeown, Northern Irish political figure. Best known as a member of the IRA who took part in a 1981 hunger strike while in prison for his role in a bombing in Belfast. He resumed his political activities upon his release. (Died from heart disease caused by the hunger strike.) |
| 30 | 2 Oct 1996 | The Electronic Freedom of Information Act Amendments were signed into law by U.S. President Bill Clinton. All U.S. government agencies were required to make their newly created records available in electronic format from 1st November 1996, put those records online if they had the ability to, create a searchable index of all material previously released under Freedom of Information requests, and make the index available online by the end of 1999. |
| 30 | 2 Oct 1996 | Former Los Angeles Police Department (LAPD) detective Mark Fuhrman admitted that he had committed perjury while giving his testimony during O. J. Simpson's murder trial. He pleaded no contest and was sentenced to three years' probation and fined $200. |
| 30 | 2 Oct 1996 | Death of Andrey Lukanov, Prime Minister of Bulgaria (1990). (Assassinated.) |
| 30 | 5 Oct 1996 | Yao Wenyuan, the last surviving member of the Chinese Communist political faction the 'Gang of Four', was released from prison after twenty years. (He died in 2005.) |
| 30 | 5 Oct 1996 | Death of Seymour Cray, American electrical engineer and designer of supercomputers. (Died from injuries suffered in a car crash in September, aged 71.) |
| 30 | 7 Oct 1996 | The IRA exploded two car bombs at the British Army's headquarters in Lisburn, Northern Ireland. One person was killed and 31 injured. |
| 30 | 7 Oct 1996 | Fox News Channel launched in the USA. |
| 30 | 8 Oct 1996 | Palestinian President Yasser Arafat made his first public visit to Israel, for talks with Israeli President Ezer Weizman. |
| 30 | 9 Oct 1996 | Death of Walter Kerr, American theatre critic, playwright, writer and director. |

## OCTOBER 2026

| Ann. | Date | Event |
|------|------|-------|
| 30 | 11 Oct 1996 | Time Warner merged with Turner Broadcasting System. |
| 30 | 12 Oct 1996 | Death of René Lacoste, French tennis player and founder of the Lacoste sportswear company. |
| 30 | 13 Oct 1996 | British racing driver Damon Hill won the 1996 Formula One world championship. He clinched victory in the final race of the season in Japan. |
| 30 | 13 Oct 1996 | Death of Beryl Reid, British stage, film, radio and television character actress. Best known for *The Killing of Sister George*, *Entertaining Mr. Sloane*, *Tinker, Tailor, Soldier, Spy*, *Smiley's People* and *The Beiderbecke Tapes*. |
| 30 | 14 Oct 1996 | American pop singer and actress Madonna gave birth to her first child, Lourdes Maria Ciccone Leon. |
| 30 | 16 Oct 1996 | The Mateo Flores Stadium disaster, Guatemala City, Guatemala. More than 80 football fans were killed and 150 injured in a stampede/ crush. Authorities had allowed in thousands more people than the stadium could handle. |
| 30 | 16 Oct 1996 | Death of Eric Malpass, British novelist. |
| 30 | 18 Oct 1996 | The academic journal *Science* published the first study that showed a causal link between a toxin found in tobacco smoke and the development of lung cancer. |
| 30 | 21 Oct 1996 | Death of Eric Halsall, British television presenter, writer and farm manager. Best known for his commentary for the sheepdog trial television series *One Man and His Dog*. |
| 30 | 22 Oct 1996 | Mercury Communications merged with three other UK cable companies to form Cable & Wireless Communications. It sold its cable division to NTL (now Virgin Media) in 2000. |
| 30 | 23 Oct 1996 | The civil trial of American football star and actor O. J. Simpson opened. In February 1997 he was found liable for the wrongful deaths of his ex-wife Nicole Brown Simpson and her friend Ron Goldman. He was ordered to pay the victims' families $33.5 million in damages. |
| 30 | 23 Oct 1996 | The W. M. Keck Observatory in Mauna Kea, Hawaii, USA was completed and the Keck II telescope began operating. The two 33-foot (10-metre) astronomical telescopes are among the largest in the world. |
| 30 | 25 Oct 1996 | The adventure video game *Tomb Raider* was released. |
| 30 | 28 Oct 1996 | Death of Morey Amsterdam, American television actor and comedian. Noted for his one-liners. Best known for playing Buddy Sorrell in *The Dick Van Dyke Show*. |
| 30 | 29 Oct 1996 to 30th | 8,000 unclaimed artworks looted by the Nazis during their WWII occupation of Austria (known as the Mauerbach collection) were auctioned by Christie's at the Austrian Museum of Applied Arts in Vienna. The auction raised $14.6 million (£9.1 million) for Austrian holocaust victims and their families. Many people considered the auction to be not so much about raising money but about remembering the lives and lifestyles the Nazis destroyed. |

## OCTOBER 2026

| Ann. | Date | Event |
|---|---|---|
| 25 | 1 Oct 2001 | Former U.S. President Bill Clinton was suspended from practising law for five years by the Supreme Court.<br>He resigned from the Supreme Court in November. |
| 25 | 1 Oct 2001 | The city of San Francisco in California, USA banned the use of internet filters on computers in its public libraries. The installation of filters had been ordered by the federal government to help keep children safe online. San Francisco's Board of Supervisors, supported by the American Library Association and others, said it restricted the freedom of adults, and was therefore unconstitutional.<br>The federal order mandating the installation of the filters was upheld by the U.S. Supreme Court in June 2003, which ruled that such filters do not violate free-speech rights. |
| 25 | 4 Oct 2001 | War on Terror: in response to the 9/11 terrorist attacks on the USA, NATO invoked Article 5 of its Treaty for the first time.<br>It states: 'an attack on any one member shall be considered an attack on all'. NATO launched eight separate military operations as a result. |
| 25 | 4 Oct 2001 | Siberia Airlines Flight 1812, flying from Tel Aviv, Israel to Novosibirsk, Russia, was accidentally shot down by the Ukrainian Air Force over the Black Sea. All 78 people on board were killed.<br>Ukraine eventually admitted that the incident was its fault – a missile went astray during a joint military exercise with Russia. It paid the victims' families $15 million in compensation ($200,000 per victim). |
| 25 | 7 Oct 2001 | War on Terror – Operation Enduring Freedom. The first U.S. and British forces arrived in Afghanistan to launch a military offensive following the 9/11 terrorist attacks. |
| 25 | 7 Oct 2001 | Death of Chris Adams, British wrestler, wrestling trainer, and judo champion.<br>(Shot dead in a brawl while awaiting trial for manslaughter, aged 46.) |
| 25 | 7 Oct 2001 | Death of Herbert Block, ('Herblock'), American newspaper cartoonist. |
| 25 | 8 Oct 2001 | War on Terror: the Office of Homeland Security (now the Department of Homeland Security) was established in the USA in response to the 9/11 terrorist attacks. Tom Ridge became its first director. |
| 25 | 8 Oct 2001 | The Linate Airport disaster, Milan, Italy.<br>Scandinavian Airlines System Flight 686 collided with a Cessna business jet during take-off, and exploded. All 114 people on both aircraft were killed, plus four people on the ground.<br>(Cause: the pilots of the Cessna got lost in fog and took a wrong turn onto the active runway. The airport's ground radar system was being replaced and was not operating.) |
| 25 | 9 Oct 2001 | American singer and entertainer Wayne Newton became Chairman of the United Service Organizations (USO) Celebrity Circle.<br>He replaced Bob Hope, who made 57 USO tours between 1941 and 1991. |
| 25 | 9 Oct 2001 | Death of Dagmar, American comic actress, model and television personality. |
| 25 | 11 Oct 2001 | The Polaroid Corporation went out of business.<br>The brand was acquired by the Impossible Project in 2008, and the company was renamed Polaroid in 2020. |

## OCTOBER 2026

| Ann. | Date | Event |
|------|------|-------|
| 25 | 12 Oct 2001 | War on Terror: following the 9/11 terrorist attacks on the USA, a special episode of the television show *America's Most Wanted* was broadcast. It featured the 22 most-wanted members of the terrorist organisation Al-Qaeda. The show was specially requested by the White House. |
| 25 | 12 Oct 2001 | Death of Quintin Hogg, Lord Hailsham, British lawyer and politician, Lord High Chancellor (1970–74, 1979–87). |
| 25 | 15 Oct 2001 | NASA's *Galileo* spacecraft flew within 112 miles of Jupiter's moon Io, and sent back images and data. |
| 25 | 16 Oct 2001 | Death of Etta Jones, American jazz singer and songwriter. |
| 25 | 17 Oct 2001 | Death of Rehavam Ze'evi, Israeli politician. Minister of Tourism. (Assassinated by terrorists from the Popular Front for the Liberation of Palestine (PFLP) in retaliation for Israel's assassination of PFLP leader Abu Ali Mustafa.) |
| 25 | 19 Oct 2001 | War on Terror: two U.S. military personnel were killed in a helicopter crash in Pakistan. They were the first American deaths in the War on Terror in Afghanistan. |
| 25 | 19 Oct 2001 | A dilapidated fishing boat (*SIEV-X*) carrying approximately 400 Middle Eastern asylum seekers sank near Java, Indonesia while en route to Christmas Island. 353 people were killed. |
| 25 | 19 Oct 2001 | Kjell Magne Bondevik became Prime Minister of Norway for the second time (until 2005). He was previously Prime Minister from 1997 to 2000. |
| 25 | 22 Oct 2001 | The action-adventure video game *Grand Theft Auto III* was released. It popularised the genre, and is considered one of the greatest video games of all time, but it also generated controversy about violence in video games. It was banned in Australia, and a modified version was later released there with some elements removed. |
| 25 | 22 Oct 2001 | The U.S. première of the science fiction film *Donnie Darko*. Limited release: 26th October. UK: 25th October 2002. |
| 25 | 23 Oct 2001 | Northern Ireland peace process: the IRA announced that it had begun decommissioning its weapons. |
| 25 | 23 Oct 2001 | Apple released its first iPod digital music player. |
| 25 | 23 Oct 2001 | Death of Josh Kirby, British artist who painted film posters, and magazine and book covers, particularly for science fiction. Best remembered for the covers of Terry Pratchett's *Discworld* novels. |
| 25 | 24 Oct 2001 | The Gotthard Road Tunnel fire, Switzerland. Two lorries crashed and caught fire in the tunnel, killing eleven people and injuring many more – mainly from smoke and gas inhalation. The tunnel was closed for two months for repairs. |
| 25 | 25 Oct 2001 | Microsoft released its Windows XP operating system. |
| 25 | 26 Oct 2001 | The USA Patriot Act was signed into law in the USA. Its name stands for: Uniting and Strengthening America by Providing Appropriate Tools Required to Intercept and Obstruct Terrorism. |

## OCTOBER 2026

| Ann. | Date | Event |
|---|---|---|
| 25 | 28 Oct 2001 | The Bahawalpur church shooting, Pakistan.<br>Six terrorists from the Lashkar-e-Jhangvi militant organisation in Afghanistan shot and killed a guard outside Saint Dominic's Church, then entered the building and opened fire, killing seventeen other Christians. (Non-Muslims in Pakistan are targeted by extremists because Pakistan backed the USA in the 2001 Invasion of Afghanistan following the 9/11 terrorist attacks.) |
| 25 | 28 Oct 2001 | The U.S. première of the computer-animated comedy film *Monsters, Inc.*<br>Released: 2nd November.<br>UK première: 17th November, released: 8th February 2002. |
| 20 | 1 Oct 2006 | Surayud Chulanont became Prime Minister of Thailand (until 2008) following a military coup on 19th September. |
| 20 | 1 Oct 2006 | All patents relating to the GIF image format (Graphics Interchange Format) expired and the format became free to use.<br>The GIF format was dogged by licensing issues between 1993 and 2004. |
| 20 | 2 Oct 2006 | The Amish school shooting, Nickel Mines, Pennsylvania, USA.<br>A gunman entered the village school and shot ten young girls, killing five of them, before committing suicide. The school was torn down a week later and rebuilt on another site, to a completely different design. |
| 20 | 3 Oct 2006 | The first International Day Against DRM (digital rights management) was held. It was organised by the campaign group Defective By Design and has been held annually since then. The campaign raises awareness of technology that restricts the use, modification and distribution of hardware and copyrighted works such as software, ebooks, videos and music files. It also encourages people to switch to DRM-free alternatives. |
| 20 | 4 Oct 2006 | WikiLeaks was launched by Australian activist Julian Assange.<br>The website publishes leaked news stories and classified media supplied by anonymous sources.<br>At the time of writing, Assange has been detained in a maximum-security prison in the UK since April 2019. Prior to that he spent seven years at the Embassy of Ecuador in London, where he was granted asylum on the grounds of political persecution. |
| 20 | 6 Oct 2006 | Death of Buck O'Neil, American baseball player, manager and coach (Kansas City Monarchs).<br>The first African American coach in Major League Baseball. |
| 20 | 7 Oct 2006 | Death of Anna Politkovskaya, American-born Russian investigative journalist. Noted for her reports on corruption and human rights abuses in Vladimir Putin's government, particularly during the Chechen War.<br>(Shot dead in her apartment building, aged 48, after receiving numerous death threats.) |
| 20 | 9 Oct 2006 | North Korea claimed to have tested its first nuclear device.<br>International commentators said the test was only partially successful. Some radiation was detected, but the explosion was small compared with similar tests by other countries. More successful underground tests were apparently conducted in 2009 and 2013 and 2016–17. |

## OCTOBER 2026

| Ann. | Date | Event |
|------|------|-------|
| 20 | 9 Oct 2006 | Russian and American scientists working at the Joint Institute of Nuclear Research (JINR) in Dubna, Russia, announced that they had created three atoms of oganesson (Og, 118). It is the heaviest man-made element but it exists for only a millisecond before decaying into livermorium (Lv, 116). |
| 20 | 9 Oct 2006 | Death of Ray Noorda, American computer networking pioneer and businessman. Co-founder, CEO and chairman of Novell. |
| 20 | 13 Oct 2006 | Death of Wang Guangmei, First Lady of China (1959–68). Wife of the Chinese leader Liu Shaoqi. She was imprisoned for twelve years during Mao Zedong's Cultural Revolution, but her reputation was later restored and she received compensation. |
| 20 | 14 Oct 2006 | Death of Freddy Fender, American country music/rock and roll singer and musician. Best known for his hit songs *Wasted Days and Wasted Nights* and *Before the Next Teardrop Falls*. He was also a member of the Texas Tornados and Los Super Seven. |
| 20 | 14 Oct 2006 | Death of Maurice Grosse, British paranormal investigator. Best known for his involvement in the Enfield Poltergeist case. |
| 20 | 16 Oct 2006 | The U.S. Army deactivated its last Mobile Army Surgical Hospital (MASH). It was deployed in Pakistan to support relief operations following the 2005 Kashmir earthquake. MASH units were replaced by Combat Support Hospitals. |
| 20 | 16 Oct 2006 | Death of Ross Davidson, Scottish stage and television actor. Best known for his roles in soap operas, most notably as Andy O'Brien in *EastEnders*. He also had roles in *Brookside*, *Pobol Y Cwm*, *Take the High Road* and *Hollyoaks*. |
| 20 | 17 Oct 2006 | The population of the USA reached 300 million people. It took just 39 years to grow from 200 million to 300 million. At the time of writing (2022) its population is about 329 million. |
| 20 | 20 Oct 2006 | Death of Jane Wyatt, American film and television actress. Best known for her roles as Margaret Anderson in the sitcom *Father Knows Best* and as Spock's mother in *Star Trek*. |
| 20 | 21 Oct 2006 | Death of Sandy West, American rock drummer, singer and songwriter (The Runaways). |
| 20 | 23 Oct 2006 | Jeffrey Skilling, the former CEO of Enron, the collapsed U.S. energy company, was sentenced to more than 24 years in prison (reduced to 14 years on appeal) and fined $45 million for conspiracy, fraud, insider trading, and making false statements to auditors. He was released in 2019 after serving twelve years. |
| 20 | 28 Oct 2006 | Death of Red Auerbach, American basketball coach. |
| 20 | 31 Oct 2006 | Death of P. W. Botha, first State President of South Africa (1984–89), Prime Minister of South Africa (1978–84). |
| 15 | 1 Oct 2011 | Divorce was legalised in Malta following a referendum in May. |

**OCTOBER 2026**

| Ann. | Date | Event |
|---|---|---|
| 15 | 3 Oct 2011 | American student Amanda Knox was released from prison in Italy after a court ruled that she was not guilty of killing British student Meredith Kercher in 2007. This followed the discovery that DNA evidence presented at her original trial was almost certainly contaminated.<br>A second trial was held from March 2013 to January 2014, and she and her former boyfriend, Raffaele Sollecito, were found guilty again.<br>This was overturned on appeal in March 2015, when the Supreme Court of Cassation ruled that the case was without foundation.<br>She was awarded compensation. |
| 15 | 5 Oct 2011 | The Mekong River massacre, Thailand.<br>Two Chinese cargo ships carrying amphetamines were hijacked.<br>All thirteen crew members were killed and dumped in the river.<br>A Chinese drug lord and three of his associates were later convicted and executed, and others were given prison sentences. |
| 15 | 20 Oct 2011 | The First Libyan Civil War: Libyan leader Muammar Gaddafi was captured by rebel forces and executed. The war ended on 23rd October.<br>The Second Libyan Civil War began in May 2014 (until October 2020) |
| 15 | 26 Oct 2011 | The Boeing 787 Dreamliner wide-bodied jet airliner went into service (with All Nippon Airways). |
| 15 | 31 Oct 2011 | The world's population reached 7 billion. |
| 10 | 13 Oct 2016 | Death of King Rama IX of Thailand (1946–2016).<br>Succeeded by his son, Rama X. |
| 10 | 13 Oct 2016 | Death of Dario Fo, Italian playwright, actor, theatrical director and composer. Winner of the 1997 Nobel Prize in Literature. |
| 10 | 14 Oct 2016 | Death of Jean Alexander, British television actress. Best known for her roles as Hilda Ogden in the soap opera *Coronation Street* and Auntie Wainwright in the comedy series *Last of the Summer Wine.* |
| 10 | 23 Oct 2016 | Death of Pete Burns, British pop/new wave singer, songwriter and television personality. Best known as the lead singer of Dead or Alive, and for their hit song *You Spin Me Round (Like a Record).*<br>He was also known for his extensive cosmetic surgery, which caused him serious health issues and led to his bankruptcy. |
| 10 | 24 Oct 2016 | Death of Jorge Batlle, President of Uruguay (2000–05). |
| 10 | 24 Oct 2016 | Death of Bobby Vee, American pop singer, songwriter and musician. |

**NOVEMBER 2026**

| Ann. | Date | Event |
|------|------|-------|
| 800 | 8 Nov 1226 | Death of Louis VIII ('The Lion'), King of France (1223–26). (Dysentery, aged 39.) Succeeded by his son, Louis IX. |
| 500 | 10 Nov 1526 | John Zápolya became King of Hungary (as John I) until 1540. His reign was disputed: Archduke Ferdinand I also claimed the title. |
| 400 | 18 Nov 1626 | St. Peter's Basilica in the Vatican City was completed. It is the largest church in the world (measured by its interior). |
| 400 | 21 Nov 1626 | Death of Edward Alleyn, English actor. A major figure of the Elizabethan stage. Founder of the College of God's Gift in Dulwich, South London (a charity that has since been divided into several separate organisations). |
| 300 | 13 Nov 1726 | Death of Sophia Dorothea of Celle. Wife of King George I of England (he was her first cousin – they divorced before he became king). Mother of King George II. She spent the last thirty years of her life in prison for having an alleged affair with a Swedish count. |
| 250 | 1 Nov 1776 | Mission San Juan Capistrano, a Roman Catholic church, was founded by Spanish missionaries in what is now California, USA. |
| 250 | 7 Nov 1776 | Richard Bache became Postmaster General of the USA (until 1782). He took over the role from his father-in-law, Benjamin Franklin. |
| 250 | 10 Nov 1776 to 29th | American Revolutionary War – the Battle of Fort Cumberland, Nova Scotia, Canada. (The site of the battle is now in New Brunswick.) A few hundred American forces attempted to storm the fort. They were successfully repelled, and British reinforcements arrived on 29th November to drive them off. The British then destroyed the homes and farms of local people who had supported the Americans in the siege. |
| 250 | 14 Nov 1776 | Birth of Henri Dutrochet, French physician, botanist, and physiologist. Best known for his investigations of osmosis. He also made many other important contributions to science. |
| 250 | 16 Nov 1776 | American Revolutionary War – the Battle of Fort Washington, Manhattan, New York. British victory – and one of the worst defeats of the war for the Americans. The British captured the fort and renamed it Fort Knyphausen in honour of Lieutenant General Wilhelm von Knyphausen, the officer who led the storming of the fort. |
| 200 | 24 Nov 1826 | Birth of Carlo Collodi, Italian children's writer, political humourist and journalist. Best known for his fairy tale *The Adventures of Pinocchio*. |
| 200 | 25 Nov 1826 | The American-built frigate *Hellas* was delivered to Greece and became the first flagship of the Revolutionary Hellenic Navy. While delivering the ship, the American crew had attempted to murder the captain and sell the ship in Colombia  They tried to sell it again when they arrived in Greece. Greek Admiral Andreas Miaoulis set fire to the ship and destroyed it in 1831 when the government ordered him to hand it over to the Russians. |
| 200 | 27 Nov 1826 | British chemist John Walker invented the first successful friction match. He refused to patent it, meaning that anyone was free to make them. |

# NOVEMBER 2026

| Ann. | Date | Event |
|---|---|---|
| 200 | 27 Nov 1826 | American explorer and frontiersman Jedediah Smith and his expedition reached the Mission San Gabriel Arcángel in California. They were the first Americans to cross the south-western USA, and the first to cross the Mojave Desert. (California was still part of Mexico at that time.) |
| 175 | 6 Nov 1851 | Birth of Charles Dow, American journalist and financial analyst. Co-founder of Dow Jones & Company and *The Wall Street Journal*. Inventor of the Dow Jones Industrial Average. |
| 175 | 11 Nov 1851 | American astronomer Alvan Clark was granted the first U.S. patent for a telescope. (U.S. Patent 8,509.) He established Alvan Clark and Sons, which ground lenses for refracting telescopes. The company created lenses for the world's largest refracting telescopes, including the 40-inch main telescope at Yerkes Observatory in Wisconsin, which was dedicated in 1897 and remains the world's largest. (Today's much larger telescopes are reflecting telescopes.) |
| 175 | 13 Nov 1851 | The first telegraph service between London, UK and Paris, France began operating. |
| 175 | 13 Nov 1851 | The Denny Party, a group of American pioneers, settled at Alki Point in Seattle, Washington. Over the next few years, they built a community at Elliott Bay that developed into what is now the city of Seattle. The date when they first arrived, 13th November 1851, is regarded as the date on which the city was founded. |
| 175 | 18 Nov 1851 | Death of Ernst August, King of Hanover (1837–51). Son of King George III of the UK. Succeeded by his son, George V, the last King of Hanover. |
| 175 | 20 Nov 1851 | Birth of Margherita of Savoy, Queen consort of Italy (1878–1900). Wife of King Umberto I. |
| 150 | 1 Nov 1876 | The North Sea Canal in the Netherlands was officially opened. It links Amsterdam to the North Sea. |
| 150 | 4 Nov 1876 | German composer Johannes Brahms' *Symphony No. 1* (Opus 63) was performed for the first time, in Karlsruhe, Germany. It took him 21 years to complete it. |
| 150 | 7 Nov 1876 | The 1876 U.S. presidential election. One of the most contentious elections in U.S. history. Rutherford B. Hayes was eventually elected as the 19th President of the USA after lengthy negotiations over disputed electoral votes. An electoral commission was appointed, which awarded all of the disputed votes to Hayes. He won the election by a single vote on 2nd March 1877. He was privately sworn into office on 3rd March and publicly inaugurated on 5th March. |
| 150 | 7 Nov 1876 | Edward Bouchet became the first African American to receive a PhD from an American college (Yale). |
| 150 | 23 Nov 1876 | William M. Tweed ('Boss' Tweed), the corrupt leader of the Tammany Hall political machine that ran New York, USA, was returned to New York after being captured in Spain. He had fled from prison during a home visit. He was returned to prison, and died there in 1878. |

# NOVEMBER 2026

| Ann. | Date | Event |
|---|---|---|
| 150 | 23 Nov 1876 | Birth of Manuel de Falla, Spanish composer and pianist.<br>One of the most important Spanish composers and musicians of the first half of the 20th century. |
| 150 | 24 Nov 1876 | Birth of Walter Burley Griffin, American architect.<br>Best known for designing Australia's capital city, Canberra. |
| 150 | 25 Nov 1876 | Birth of Princess Victoria Melita of Saxe-Coburg and Gotha.<br>Granddaughter of Queen Victoria.<br>Grand Duchess consort of Hesse and by Rhine (1894–1901).<br>Wife of Ernest Louis, Grand Duke of Hesse and by Rhine (her first cousin) – they divorced in 1901, causing a royal scandal. She then married another of her cousins, Grand Duke Kirill Vladimirovich of Russia. |
| 150 | 26 Nov 1876 | Birth of Willis Haviland Carrier, American engineer.<br>Best known for inventing the modern air conditioning system. |
| 150 | 29 Nov 1876 | Birth of Nellie Tayloe Ross, American politician.<br>The first female Governor of a U.S. state (Wyoming, 1925–27).<br>She won a special election to succeed her husband after he died in 1924.<br>She was also the first female Director of the U.S. Mint (1933–53). |
| 125 | 1 Nov 1901 | Sigma Phi Epsilon, one of the largest college fraternities in the USA, was founded at Richmond College in Virginia. |
| 125 | 3 Nov 1901 | Birth of Leopold III, King of the Belgians (1934–51 – abdicated). |
| 125 | 3 Nov 1901 | Birth of André Malraux, French novelist and statesman.<br>France's first Minister of Cultural Affairs (1959–69). |
| 125 | 5 Nov 1901 | Birth of Eddie Paynter, British cricketer (Lancashire 1926–45, Marylebone Cricket Club 1932–39, England 1931–39).<br>He has one of the highest batting averages of all time, and was a member of the England team during the infamous 'bodyline' tour of Australia. |
| 125 | 6 Nov 1901 | Death of Kate Greenaway, British illustrator of children's books. |
| 125 | 11 Nov 1901 | Birth of Sam Spiegel, Polish-born American film producer (*The African Queen, On the Waterfront, The Bridge on the River Kwai, Lawrence of Arabia* and more). |
| 125 | 12 Nov 1901 | German physicist Wilhelm Röentgen was awarded the first Nobel Prize in Physics, for discovering X-rays. (Prize presented on 10th December.) |
| 125 | 13 Nov 1901 | The Caister lifeboat disaster, Norfolk, UK.<br>The Caister-on-Sea lifeboat capsized during the Great Storm while attempting to reach a ship in distress. Nine lifeboatmen were killed. |
| 125 | 17 Nov 1901 | Birth of Walter Hallstein, German diplomat and statesman.<br>First President of the European Commission (1958–67). |
| 125 | 17 Nov 1901 | Birth of Lee Strasberg, Polish/Ukrainian-born American actor, theatrical director and teacher. The chief proponent of method acting in the USA. Director of the Actors Studio (1951–82). |
| 125 | 17 Nov 1901 | Birth of Joyce Wethered, Lady Heathcoat-Amery, British golfer.<br>British ladies' golf champion during the 1920s. |

## NOVEMBER 2026

| Ann. | Date | Event |
|---|---|---|
| 125 | 18 Nov 1901 | The Hay–Pauncefoot Treaty was signed by the USA and Great Britain. It authorised the USA to construct the Panama Canal.<br>A previous treaty (the Clayton–Bulwer Treaty of 1850) had ruled that building a canal such as this could not be undertaken by a single nation. |
| 125 | 18 Nov 1901 | Birth of George Gallup, American statistician and public-opinion surveyor who established the Gallup Poll. |
| 125 | 22 Nov 1901 | Birth of Joaquín Rodrigo, Spanish composer and piano virtuoso.<br>One of the most important Spanish composers of the 20th century.<br>Best known for the *Concierto de Aranjuez*. |
| 125 | 27 Nov 1901 | The U.S. Army War College was established at Washington Barracks (now Fort Lesley J. McNair) in Washington, D.C.<br>It moved to Carlisle Barracks in Pennsylvania in 1951. |
| 125 | 27 Nov 1901 | Death of Clement Studebaker, American wagon and carriage manufacturer and businessman. Co-founder of what became the Studebaker Corporation, which manufactured cars after his death. |
| 125 | 28 Nov 1901 | Austrian/Czech composer Gustav Mahler's *Symphony No. 4* was performed for the first time, in Munich, Germany. |
| 125 | 28 Nov 1901 | Death of Moses Dickson, American abolitionist, soldier and minister. Founder of the Knights of Liberty, which helped slaves escape to freedom through the Underground Railroad.<br>Co-founder of Lincoln University in Missouri. |
| 125 | 30 Nov 1901 | British inventor Frank Hornby was granted a UK patent for Meccano, a model construction system consisting of reusable parts.<br>(UK Patent 190,100,587.)<br>He sold it as 'Mechanics Made Easy'. It was renamed Meccano in 1907. |
| 125 | 30 Nov 1901 | Death of Edward John Eyre, British explorer of Australia, and colonial administrator. Controversial Governor of Jamaica (1862–65) where he spent much of his time devising punishments for non-whites and had several of his critics executed. |
| 100 | 3 Nov 1926 | Death of Annie Oakley, American markswoman who starred in Buffalo Bill's Wild West show. |
| 100 | 6 Nov 1926 | Birth of Frank Carson, Northern Irish comedian and entertainer. (Died 2012.) |
| 100 | 6 Nov 1926 | Birth of Zig Ziglar, American writer, salesman and motivational speaker. (Died 2012.) |
| 100 | 7 Nov 1926 | Birth of Dame Joan Sutherland, Australian operatic soprano. (Died 2010.) |
| 100 | 11 Nov 1926 | The United States Numbered Highway System was established, including the iconic Route 66 (Chicago, Illinois to Santa Monica, California).<br>The Interstate Highway System was established in June 1956 and supplemented or replaced many of the Numbered Highway System Routes. Route 66 was removed from the highway system in June 1985, but sections of it still remain in Illinois, Missouri, New Mexico and Arizona, where it is recognised as Historic Route 66. |
| 100 | 15 Nov 1926 | The National Broadcasting Company (NBC) radio network was launched in the USA. |

**NOVEMBER 2026**

| Ann. | Date | Event |
|---|---|---|
| 100 | 15 Nov 1926 | The Balfour Declaration was approved by delegates to the Imperial Conference of 1926. It declared that the UK and its Dominions in the British Empire were equal in status.<br>(The Imperial Conference of 1926 was held in London, UK and ran from 19th October to 23rd November.) |
| 100 | 20 Nov 1926 | Birth of John Gardner, British spy thriller novelist.<br>Best known for continuing Ian Fleming's *James Bond* series. (Died 2007.) |
| 100 | 20 Nov 1926 | Birth of Terry Hall, British ventriloquist and writer. One of the first to use an animal puppet. Known for his appearances with the bashful Lenny the Lion on children's TV series such as *The Lenny the Lion Show*.<br>He also helped children learn to read in the TV series *Reading with Lenny*, and appeared on numerous variety shows. (Died 2007.) |
| 100 | 25 Nov 1926 | The Late November tornado outbreak, southern USA.<br>107 people were killed and 451 injured. |
| 100 | 25 Nov 1926 | Birth of Poul Anderson, American science fiction and fantasy writer. (Died 2001.) |
| 100 | 26 Nov 1926 | Death of John Browning, American firearms designer and inventor. Founder of the Browning Arms Company. He pioneered the development of modern repeating, semi-automatic and automatic weapons. |
| 100 | 27 Nov 1926 | The First Treaty of Tirana (a five-year treaty of peace and security) was signed by Italy and Albania. It was followed by the Second Treaty of Tirana a year later, which established a secret twenty-year defence alliance. |
| 100 | 29 Nov 1926 | Birth of Beji Caid Essebsi, President of Tunisia (2014–19 – died in office). Tunisia's first democratically elected president. |
| 100 | 30 Nov 1926 | Birth of Richard Crenna, American film, television and radio actor (*Rambo, Body Heat, The Flamingo Kid, Our Miss Brooks, The Real McCoys*, and many more), director and producer. (Died 2003.) |
| 90 | 1 Nov 1936 | The Berlin–Rome Axis: Italian dictator Benito Mussolini first used the term 'axis' to describe the alliance between Italy and Germany. |
| 90 | 1 Nov 1936 | The Professional Rodeo Cowboys Association was founded.<br>It was originally called the Cowboys' Turtle Association, but it changed its name to the Rodeo Cowboys Association in 1945, and the Professional Rodeo Cowboys Association in 1975. |
| 90 | 2 Nov 1936 | The BBC Television Service was launched in the UK.<br>It was renamed BBC1 in 1964 and BBC One in 1997. |
| 90 | 2 Nov 1936 | The Canadian Broadcasting Corporation was established and its radio network was launched. |
| 90 | 3 Nov 1936 to Mar 1939 | Spanish Civil War – the Siege of Madrid.<br>The Nationalists staged an assault on Madrid, but were repelled by the Republicans. The Nationalists eventually seized the city in 1939. |
| 90 | 9 Nov 1936 | Birth of Mary Travers, American singer and songwriter (Peter, Paul and Mary). (Died 2009.) |

**NOVEMBER 2026**

| Ann. | Date | Event |
|---|---|---|
| 90 | 11 Nov 1936 | Birth of Jack Keller, American songwriter and record producer. He wrote songs for numerous artists including the Monkees, Crystal Gayle, Bill Medley, Jennifer Warnes, Ray Charles, B. B. King and Grover Washington Jr. Best known for the song *Venus in Blue Jeans* and the theme music for the television series *Bewitched*. (Died 2005.) |
| 90 | 12 Nov 1936 | The San Francisco–Oakland Bay Bridge (commonly known as Bay Bridge) opened to traffic. |
| 90 | 12 Nov 1936 | Birth of Mort Shuman, American songwriter, singer and pianist. He co-wrote (with Doc Pomus) many 1960s rock and roll hits, including *Viva Las Vegas*. (Died 1991.) |
| 90 | 14 Nov 1936 | Birth of Freddie Garrity, British singer (Freddie and the Dreamers) and children's television presenter. (Died 2006.) |
| 90 | 18 Nov 1936 | Birth of Don Cherry, American jazz trumpeter. (Died 1995.) |
| 90 | 20 Nov 1936 | Death of Buenaventura Durruti, Spanish anarchist. He helped co-ordinate the armed resistance during the early stages of the Spanish Civil War, but was shot and killed, aged 40. |
| 90 | 20 Nov 1936 | Death of Jose Antonio Primo de Rivera, Spanish politician. Founder of the Spanish Fascist party, the Falange. (Executed.) |
| 90 | 21 Nov 1936 | The first television gardening programme: *In Your Garden*, presented by Mr Middleton (C. H. Middleton), was broadcast by the BBC. |
| 90 | 23 Nov 1936 | The first issue of *Life* magazine was published in the USA. |
| 90 | 25 Nov 1936 | Germany and Japan signed the Anti-Comintern Pact, an agreement to collaborate against the threat of Soviet Communism. |
| 90 | 30 Nov 1936 | The Crystal Palace in London, UK was destroyed by a fire. |
| 90 | 30 Nov 1936 | Birth of Abbie Hoffman, American political activist. Founder of the Youth International Party. (Died 1989.) |
| 80 | 1 Nov 1946 | Karol Wojtyla (later Pope John Paul II) was ordained as a priest in Krakow, Poland. |
| 80 | 1 Nov 1946 | The first Basketball Association of America (BAA) game was played: the Toronto Huskies versus the New York Knicks. It was both teams' first-ever game. The Toronto Huskies disbanded in 1947. The New York Knicks are still playing today. The BAA became the National Basketball Association (NBA) in 1949. |
| 80 | 4 Nov 1946 | Birth of Robert Mapplethorpe, American photographer. Noted for his austere images, which often featured homoerotic or sadomasochistic themes. Some of the venues that exhibited his work were prosecuted for obscenity, and debates were held about public funding for controversial artworks. (Died 1989.) |
| 80 | 5 Nov 1946 | John F. Kennedy (later U.S. President) was elected to the House of Representatives in the 1946 midterm elections. He took his seat on 3rd January 1947. |

# NOVEMBER 2026

| Ann. | Date | Event |
|---|---|---|
| 80 | 5 Nov 1946 | The world's first mobile bank went into service on the Isle of Lewis in Scotland. It was operated by the National Bank of Scotland (now the Royal Bank of Scotland, which is part of the NatWest Group) and served crofters around Stornoway. |
| 80 | 5 Nov 1946 | Birth of Gram Parsons, American country/rock singer, songwriter and musician. Best known as a member of The Byrds. (Died 1973.) |
| 80 | 12 Nov 1946 | The U.S. première of Walt Disney's live action/animated film *Song of the South*. Released: 20th November. UK: December 1946. |
| 80 | 12 Nov 1946 | The first Autobank (drive-in bank) opened in Chicago, Illinois, USA. The Exchange National Bank (now part of the LaSalle Bank) had ten drive-up windows where motorists could pull up and do their banking from their cars. |
| 80 | 14 Nov 1946 | Death of Manuel de Falla, Spanish composer. |
| 80 | 20 Nov 1946 | Birth of Duane Allman, American rock/blues guitarist (the Allman Brothers Band). (Died 1971.) |
| 80 | 22 Nov 1946 | The first Biro ballpoint pens went on sale in the UK. |
| 80 | 23 Nov 1946 | First Indochina War: the French Navy bombarded the Vietnamese port city of Haiphong, killing at least 6,000 civilians. |
| 80 | 24 Nov 1946 | Birth of Ted Bundy, American serial killer and rapist. One of the most notorious criminals of the late 20th century. (Executed in 1989.) |
| 80 | 24 Nov 1946 | Birth of Penny Jordan, British romantic novelist. She wrote under the names Caroline Courtney, Annie Groves, Lydia Hitchcock, Penny Jordan, and Melinda Wright. More than 70 million copies of her books have been sold worldwide. (Died 2011.) |
| 80 | 29 Nov 1946 | Death of Johannes Vares, nominal head of state of Estonia (1940–41). (Suicide.) |
| 75 | 1 Nov 1951 | Exercise Desert Rock I/Operation Buster-Jangle, Nevada Test Site, USA. 5,000 U.S. Army soldiers from four units witnessed an atomic explosion at close range for the first time. They then entered the fallout zone to study the effects of the blast on fortifications they had built before the explosion. (See also: 29th November 1951.) |
| 75 | 2 Nov 1951 | Suez Crisis: 6,000 British troops arrived in Fayid, Egypt to quell unrest in the Canal Zone. It was the biggest airlift of troops since WWII. (See also: 20th November 1951.) |
| 75 | 5 Nov 1951 | The word 'Eurovision' was used for the first time, in an article in the *London Evening Standard* newspaper. The journalist, George Campey, was referring to a Dutch television show that was being broadcast by the BBC in the UK. The Eurovision Song Contest began in 1956. |
| 75 | 10 Nov 1951 | The Direct Distance Dialling telephone service was launched in the USA and area codes were introduced. For the first time, people could call each other right across the country without having to go through an operator. |

## NOVEMBER 2026

| Ann. | Date | Event |
|---|---|---|
| 75 | 14 Nov 1951 | Cold War: the USA supplied Yugoslavia with military and economic aid to exploit the growing rift between Yugoslavia and the Soviet Union. |
| 75 | 18 Nov 1951 | The first episode of the news/documentary television series *See It Now* was broadcast on CBS in the USA. It was the first live coast-to-coast TV broadcast in the USA. The series ran until 1958. |
| 75 | 20 Nov 1951 | Suez Crisis: the families of more than 1,000 British servicemen serving in Egypt's Canal Zone were sent back to Britain over fears for their safety. Five British servicemen were shot dead on 18th November and there was a strong anti-British sentiment in the area. |
| 75 | 20 Nov 1951 | The manufacture of colour televisions for sale to the public was banned by the USA's National Production Authority following the escalation of the Korean War. (Black and white televisions were not affected.) The ban was lifted in March 1953. |
| 75 | 23 Nov 1951 | Birth of David Rappaport, British dwarf actor. Best known for his role in the film *Time Bandits*. (Died 1990 – suicide.) |
| 75 | 24 Nov 1951 | The play *Gigi*, based on the novel by Colette, opened on Broadway. Audrey Hepburn (then an unknown actress) played the lead role. |
| 75 | 27 Nov 1951 | A surface-to-air missile shot down a plane for the first time, in a test at White Sands Missile Range, New Mexico, USA. The plane was an unmanned radio-controlled B-17 drone. The missile was a U.S. Army Nike Ajax, which went into service in 1954. |
| 75 | 29 Nov 1951 | Operation Buster-Jangle: the first U.S. underground atomic bomb test was carried out, at Frenchman Flat, Nevada. A 1.2 kiloton bomb ('Uncle') was detonated 16 feet (5 metres) below the ground. It created a crater 1,800 feet (550 metres) in diameter. |
| 75 | 29 Nov 1951 | The world's first business computer, the LEO I (Lyons Electronic Office), went into service, running business applications for J. Lyons & Co. It was based on the EDSAC computer developed at the University of Cambridge, which Lyons had helped finance. In 1954 Lyons formed LEO Computers and marketed the computer to other companies. LEO Computers later became part of ICL and then Fujitsu. |
| 70 | 1 Nov 1956 | The Springhill mining disaster of 1956, Nova Scotia, Canada. 39 miners were killed in a coal dust explosion at Springhill's Number 4 colliery. (125 miners were killed by a coal dust fire in the Number 1 and Number 2 collieries in 1891. 75 miners were killed in 1958 when part of the Number 2 colliery collapsed.) |
| 70 | 1 Nov 1956 | The States Reorganisation Act came into effect in India. State boundaries were altered, some states were merged, and the new states of Andhra Pradesh and Kerala were created. |
| 70 | 1 Nov 1956 | American physicists John Bardeen, Walter Brattain and William Shockley were jointly awarded the Nobel Prize for Physics for inventing the transistor. (Prize presented on 10th December.) |
| 70 | 1 Nov 1956 | The first Premium Bonds went on sale in the UK. The Lord Mayor of London bought the first one. |

## NOVEMBER 2026

| Ann. | Date | Event |
|------|------|-------|
| 70 | 4 Nov 1956 | The main phase of the Hungarian Revolution ended when Soviet forces crushed the rebellion. (See also: 11th November 1956.) |
| 70 | 4 Nov 1956 | Birth of James Honeyman-Scott, British rock/new wave guitarist and songwriter (The Pretenders). (Died 1982.) |
| 70 | 5 Nov 1956 | Death of Art Tatum, American virtuoso jazz pianist. Regarded as one of the greatest jazz pianists of all time and acclaimed for his technical proficiency. He was blind and self-taught. |
| 70 | 6 Nov 1956 | The Netherlands, Spain and Switzerland announced that they were boycotting the 1956 Summer Olympics in Melbourne, Australia in protest of the Soviet Union's brutal repression of the Hungarian Revolution. (See also: 11th November 1956.) |
| 70 | 7 Nov 1956 | The Suez Crisis ended after the United Nations ordered Britain, France and Israel to withdraw their forces. Two months later, the British Prime Minister, Anthony Eden, resigned – partly through ill health and partly because he had misled the House of Commons about the degree of Britain's collusion with France and Israel as they worked to end the crisis. |
| 70 | 11 Nov 1956 | The Hungarian Revolution of 1956 ended after the uprising was brutally repressed by the Soviet Union. 2,500 Hungarians and 700 Soviet Army soldiers were killed. 200,000 Hungarians fled to other countries as political refugees. |
| 70 | 12 Nov 1956 | The largest iceberg ever recorded was reportedly sighted in Antarctica. Reports said it measured 207 miles by 62 miles, with a surface area of over 12,000 square miles. However, as this measurement was only estimated, and taken before the advent of satellite imaging, it cannot be verified. The largest verified iceberg was B-15, recorded in 2000, which had a surface area of 4,209 square miles. |
| 70 | 13 Nov 1956 | The Montgomery bus boycott, Alabama, USA. The U.S. Supreme Court declared that Alabama's laws requiring the segregation of races on buses was unconstitutional, upholding the ruling made by a federal district court in Alabama in April (Browder v. Gayle). The boycott ended on 20th December. |
| 70 | 15 Nov 1956 | Elvis Presley's first feature film *Love Me Tender* was released. He made his acting debut in this film, and it was the only time he did not receive top billing. |
| 70 | 19 Nov 1956 | The Ford Motor Company established its Edsel brand, named in honour of founder Henry Ford's son, Edsel. The cars were regarded by customers as unattractive and low quality, and they were launched during a recession, so they did not sell well. The brand was discontinued in 1959 after making a loss of over $250 million (equivalent to more than $2 billion today). |
| 70 | 22 Nov 1956 to 8 Dec | The 1956 Summer Olympic Games were held in Melbourne, Australia. |
| 70 | 26 Nov 1956 | The first episode of the television game show *The Price Is Right* was broadcast on NBC in the USA. It ran until 1965, switching to ABC in 1963. The current version began in 1972. |

## NOVEMBER 2026

| Ann. | Date | Event |
|------|------|-------|
| 70 | 26 Nov 1956 | Death of Tommy Dorsey, American jazz/swing/big band trombonist, trumpet player and bandleader. He sometimes worked with his brother Jimmy Dorsey in the Dorsey Brothers Orchestra.<br>(Choked in his sleep after taking sleeping pills, aged 51.) |
| 70 | 27 Nov 1956 | The first Cy Young Award was presented to Don Newcombe of the Brooklyn Dodgers. The award honours the best pitchers in Major League Baseball. It was named in honour of pitcher Cy Young, who died in 1955. |
| 70 | 29 Nov 1956 | Suez Crisis: the British government announced that four months of petrol rationing would begin on 17th December. This triggered an immediate wave of panic-buying across the country, with many petrol stations running out and closing, or introducing their own rationing systems. Rationing actually lasted for five months. (See also: 17th December 1956.) |
| 70 | 29 Nov 1956 | The romantic musical comedy *Bells Are Ringing* opened on Broadway. It ran until 1959. It was adapted into a film in 1960. |
| 70 | 30 Nov 1956 | The first television show to be broadcast from videotape.<br>The *CBS Evening News* (also known as *Douglas Edwards with the News*) was broadcast live in New York City, USA and also fed to the West Coast where it was recorded and rebroadcast three hours later. |
| 65 | 2 Nov 1961 | Death of James Thurber, American writer, cartoonist and humourist. |
| 65 | 3 Nov 1961 | The U.S. Agency for International Development was founded. |
| 65 | 9 Nov 1961 | The Professional Golfer's Association (PGA) in the USA lifted its Caucasians-only rule after years of protest. |
| 65 | 9 Nov 1961 | Birth of Jill Dando, British television presenter. (Shot dead in 1999.) |
| 65 | 10 Nov 1961 | Joseph Heller's satirical anti-war novel *Catch-22* was published. |
| 65 | 11 Nov 1961 | The Russian city of Stalingrad was renamed Volgograd as part of Nikita Khrushchev's de-Stalinisation programme. |
| 65 | 16 Nov 1961 | Death of Sam Rayburn, Speaker of the U.S. House of Representatives (1940–47, 1949–53, 1955–61). |
| 65 | 19 Nov 1961 | Michael Rockefeller, the 23-year-old son of the Governor of New York (and later U.S. Vice President) Nelson Rockefeller, disappeared in Papua New Guinea. Some sources claim he was killed by natives when he swam ashore at their village. His body has never been found. |
| 65 | 21 Nov 1961 | The first revolving restaurant in the USA: La Ronde opened in Honolulu, Hawaii. It closed in the 1990s. It was then converted into offices and the revolving floor was welded into place so it no longer moved. |
| 65 | 23 Nov 1961 | Santo Domingo, the capital city of the Dominican Republic, had its original name restored. It had been known as Ciudad Trujillo (in honour of the dictator Rafael Trujillo) since it was rebuilt following a hurricane in 1930. (Trujillo was assassinated in May 1961.) |
| 65 | 28 Nov 1961 | American college football player Ernie Davis of Syracuse University became the first African American to win the Heisman Trophy.<br>He was diagnosed with leukaemia shortly afterwards and died in 1963, aged 23, without ever playing a professional game. |

## NOVEMBER 2026

| Ann. | Date | Event |
|------|------|-------|
| 65 | 29 Nov 1961 | Project Mercury: *Mercury-Atlas 5* mission.<br>The NASA spacecraft orbited the Earth twice and returned safely with Enos the chimp on board. He was the first U.S. animal to orbit the Earth.<br>(The first U.S. monkey to travel into space was Albert 1, who was launched on a sub-orbital flight in 1947 ) |
| 65 | 30 Nov 1961 | U Thant of Burma became Secretary-General of the United Nations (until 1971). He succeeded Dag Hammarskjöld, who was killed in a plane crash in September. |
| 60 | 2 Nov 1966 | The Cuban Adjustment Act came into effect in the USA. It allowed Cubans who had been officially admitted into the USA since 1959 and had lived there for at least two years to apply for permanent residence.<br>(The two-year residency requirement was reduced to one year in 1976.) |
| 60 | 2 Nov 1966 | Death of Mississippi John Hurt, American country-blues singer and guitarist. |
| 60 | 4 Nov 1966 | The Florence flood, Italy.<br>The Arno river burst its banks after days of intense rainfall.<br>The city was devastated, thousands were made homeless or lost their businesses, and 35 people were killed.<br>Millions of Renaissance books, manuscripts and artworks were damaged or destroyed. Restoration work is still ongoing to this day. |
| 60 | 6 Nov 1966 | NASA launched its *Lunar Orbiter 2* spacecraft to photograph safe landing sites on the Moon for the *Surveyor* and *Apollo* missions.<br>It successfully returned photos from 18th to 25th November, and returned gravity data until 7th December. It crashed into the Moon in October 1967. |
| 60 | 7 Nov 1966 | NBC became the first television network in the USA to broadcast all of its programming in colour. |
| 60 | 8 Nov 1966 | Edward Brooke of Massachusetts became the first African American elected to the U.S. Senate. He was inaugurated on 3rd January 1967. |
| 60 | 11 Nov 1966 | NASA launched its *Gemini 12* spacecraft with astronauts James A. Lovell and Buzz Aldrin on board. They carried out several science experiments and a space walk while in orbit, and returned to Earth safely on 15th November. It was Project Gemini's final flight. |
| 60 | 12 Nov 1966 | Eighteen-year-old American student Robert Benjamin Smith shot and killed five people at the Rose-Mar College of Beauty in Mesa, Arizona.<br>He said he did it 'to get known' after seeing reports of other mass-shootings on television. He also said he had hoped to kill ten times as many people, but he arrived at the college too early.<br>He was sentenced to death, but some of the testimony at his trial was later deemed unreliable. He was tried again and sentenced to life imprisonment. |
| 60 | 12 Nov 1966 | The pop/rock song *I'm a Believer* by the Monkees was released.<br>It was certified gold within two days of release and sold more than 10 million copies worldwide. |

## NOVEMBER 2026

| Ann. | Date | Event |
|---|---|---|
| 60 | 16 Nov 1966 | American neurosurgeon Sam Sheppard was cleared of killing his pregnant wife, Marilyn, in 1954. The U.S. Supreme Court had ordered a second trial after determining that the 'carnival atmosphere' surrounding his 1954 trial had made it impossible for due process to have been followed.<br>He had served ten years in prison.<br>(He died of liver failure caused by alcoholism in 1970, aged 46.) |
| 60 | 17 Nov 1966 | The Leonids meteor storm – one of the most spectacular meteor storms of the 20th century was seen over the Americas. A spectacular Leonids storm occurs roughly every 33 years. The next one is due in November 2033. |
| 60 | 17 Nov 1966 | Birth of Jeff Buckley, American folk/rock/pop singer, songwriter and guitarist. Considered one of the greatest singers of all time. (Died 1997.) |
| 60 | 20 Nov 1966 | The musical *Cabaret* opened on Broadway. |
| 60 | 22 Nov 1966 | The first chess match between two computers.<br>Programs running at the Massachusetts Institute of Technology (MIT) in the USA and the Institute for Theoretical and Experimental Physics (ITEP) in Moscow, Soviet Union played a correspondence match via telegraph.<br>It took nine months to complete four games. The Soviet Union won 3 – 1.<br>(The head of ITEP's computer lab was fired for wasting computer time.) |
| 60 | 23 Nov 1966 to 26th | New York City smog, USA.<br>Thick smog covered the city for four days over the Thanksgiving weekend. Around ten percent of the population suffered health issues including stinging eyes, respiratory problems and coughing.<br>168 deaths were directly attributed to the smog. |
| 60 | 23 Nov 1966 | Death of Seán T. O'Kelly, President of Ireland (1945–59). |
| 60 | 26 Nov 1966 | The world's first tidal power station was inaugurated on the Rance estuary in Brittany, France. |
| 60 | 28 Nov 1966 | The Burundi coup.<br>Prime Minister Michel Micombero overthrew the monarchy and installed himself as Burundi's first president (until 1976 when he was ousted in another coup). He died in exile in Somalia in 1983, aged 42.<br>(The former king, Ntare V, was executed in 1972, aged 24.) |
| 60 | 30 Nov 1966 | Barbados gained its independence from the UK. |
| 50 | 2 Nov 1976 | Jimmy Carter was elected as the 39th President of the United States.<br>(Inaugurated 20th January 1977.) |
| 50 | 3 Nov 1976 | The limited release of the supernatural horror film *Carrie* in the USA.<br>It was based on Stephen King's novel of the same name.<br>Full release: 16th November. UK: 13th January 1977. |
| 50 | 6 Nov 1976 | Birth of Pat Tillman, American football player who abandoned his career to enlist in the U.S. Army following the 9/11 terrorist attacks.<br>(Killed in a friendly fire incident in Afghanistan in 2004, aged 27.) |
| 50 | 7 Nov 1976 | Argentina established a clandestine naval base (Corbeta Uruguay) on Thule Island in the South Sandwich Islands (a British overseas territory). This was part of its attempt to legitimise its claim over the Falkland Islands. (Britain destroyed the base at the end of the Falklands War.) |

## NOVEMBER 2026

| Ann. | Date | Event |
|---|---|---|
| 50 | 11 Nov 1976 | Death of Alexander Calder, American sculptor and artist who invented the mobile. He was also known for his wire figures. |
| 50 | 12 Nov 1976 | Death of Mikhail Gurevich, Soviet military aircraft designer who developed MiG fighter planes with Artem Mikoyan. (The M and G in MiG are their initials.) |
| 50 | 12 Nov 1976 | Death of Walter Piston, American classical composer, music theorist and educator. |
| 50 | 15 Nov 1976 | Death of Jean Gabin, French film actor. A key figure in French cinema. |
| 50 | 18 Nov 1976 | The Spanish Parliament approved a bill to establish a constitutional democracy after 37 years of dictatorship under General Francisco Franco. The bill was approved by the public in a referendum on 15th December. A new democratic constitution was adopted on 6th December 1978. |
| 50 | 18 Nov 1976 | Death of Man Ray, American Modernist photographer, artist and film-maker. He played a major role in the Dada and Surrealist movements. |
| 50 | 19 Nov 1976 | Death of Sir Basil Spence, Indian-born British architect. Best known for designing the new Coventry cathedral, which replaced the one that was destroyed in WWII. |
| 50 | 20 Nov 1976 | The U.S. première of the sports drama film *Rocky*. Released: 3rd December. UK: 7th January 1977. |
| 50 | 22 Nov 1976 | The first *Cathy* comic strip by Cathy Guisewhite was published in the USA. It ran until 2010, and appeared in more than 1,400 daily newspapers at its peak. |
| 50 | 24 Nov 1976 | The 1976 Çaldıran–Muradiye earthquake, eastern Turkey. 4,000–5,000 people were killed and there was widespread damage. |
| 50 | 26 Nov 1976 | British punk rock band the Sex Pistols' debut single *Anarchy in the UK* was released. |
| 40 | 2 Nov 1986 | American hospital administrator David Jacobsen was released by Islamic Jihad in Beirut, Lebanon after being held hostage for seventeen months. |
| 40 | 3 Nov 1986 | Details of the Iran–Contra scandal were made public for the first time. The Lebanese magazine *Ash-Shiraa* reported that the USA had secretly sold arms to Iran in the hope of securing the release of seven American hostages. U.S. President Ronald Reagan confirmed on national television on 13th November that arms shipments had been made, but said it was to improve relations with Iran, not to free the hostages. (See also: 21st November 1986.) |
| 40 | 3 Nov 1986 | The Federated States of Micronesia become self-governing, but retained ties with the USA, particularly for defence and financial support. |
| 40 | 4 Nov 1986 | Rose Bird, the Chief Justice of the Supreme Court of California, USA, was removed from office by voters over her opposition to the death penalty. She was the first (and only) Chief Justice in California's history to be voted out of office. |
| 40 | 5 Nov 1986 | Death of Bobby Nunn, American R&B singer (The Coasters, The Robins). |

## NOVEMBER 2026

| Ann. | Date | Event |
|------|------|-------|
| 40 | 6 Nov 1986 | The Sumburgh disaster, Shetland Islands, Scotland. A Chinook helicopter suffered a mechanical failure and crashed in the North Sea near Sumburgh Airport while ferrying workers from the Brent oil field. 45 people were killed. |
| 40 | 6 Nov 1986 | Former U.S. Navy communications specialist John Anthony Walker Jr. was sentenced to life imprisonment after he admitted being the head of the Walker family spy ring. The family passed classified information to the Soviet Union between 1974 and 1985. |
| 40 | 8 Nov 1986 | Death of Vyacheslav Molotov, Russian statesman and diplomat. As Soviet foreign minister he represented the Soviet Union at Allied conferences during WWII. The Molotov cocktail (an improvised incendiary bomb made by filling a glass bottle with flammable liquid – usually petrol) was named after him, as he had claimed in propaganda that Soviet bombing missions over Finland were actually dropping food supplies. |
| 40 | 10 Nov 1986 | Death of Sir Gordon Richards, British jockey. The first to ride 4,000 winners. |
| 40 | 11 Nov 1986 | Unisys, the American information technology company, was founded when Sperry and Burroughs merged. |
| 40 | 13 Nov 1986 | Apartheid: South Africa repealed the pass laws, which had restricted the movements of blacks within the country and required them to carry passbooks (internal passports). |
| 40 | 15 Nov 1986 | American financier Ivan Boesky was fined $100 million by the Securities and Exchange Commission for insider trading. He also served two years in prison and was permanently barred from working in the securities industry. He famously claimed 'Greed is healthy'. The character Gordon Gekko in the film *Wall Street* was partly based on him. |
| 40 | 16 Nov 1986 | Death of Siobhan McKenna, Irish stage and film actress. |
| 40 | 17 Nov 1986 | Death of Georges Besse, French business executive. Head of the Renault car company. (Assassinated.) |
| 40 | 20 Nov 1986 | U.S. President Ronald Reagan declared the rose the National Flower of the USA. |
| 40 | 21 Nov 1986 to 25th | Iran–Contra Affair: U.S. National Security Council staff member Oliver North and his secretary shredded, altered and removed documents relating to the sale of arms to Iran. He was fired on 25th November. |
| 40 | 21 Nov 1986 | The world première of the science fiction film *Star Trek IV: The Voyage Home*, in Canada. USA: 26th November. UK: 10th April 1987. |
| 40 | 21 Nov 1986 | Death of Jerry Colonna, American musician, actor, comedian, singer and songwriter. He played numerous comical characters on Bob Hope's radio shows and was the voice of the March Hare in the Disney film *Alice in Wonderland*. |
| 40 | 22 Nov 1986 | American boxer Mike Tyson became the youngest-ever WBC world heavyweight champion at the age of 20. |

## NOVEMBER 2026

| Ann. | Date | Event |
|---|---|---|
| 40 | 22 Nov 1986 | Death of Scatman Crothers, American actor, voice actor, singer and dancer. Best known as the voice of *Hong Kong Fooey* in the TV cartoon series. |
| 40 | 24 Nov 1986 | Susan Sontag's acclaimed short story *The Way We Live Now* was published in *The New Yorker* magazine. It describes the beginnings of the AIDS crisis. |
| 40 | 25 Nov 1986 | Iran–Contra Affair: U.S. Attorney General Edwin Meese admitted that profits from the sale of arms to Iran had been used to assist the Contra rebels in Nicaragua. National Security Adviser John Poindexter resigned the same day. |
| 40 | 25 Nov 1986 | The King Fahd Causeway opened. It links Saudi Arabia and Bahrain across the Persian Gulf. |
| 40 | 25 Nov 1986 | Birth of Amber Hagerman, American kidnapping and murder victim. Her death in 1996 led to the creation of the AMBER Alert child abduction system. |
| 40 | 26 Nov 1986 | Ukrainian-born American car factory worker John Demjanjuk went on trial in Israel after being misidentified as 'Ivan the Terrible', a notoriously cruel guard at the Treblinka extermination camp. He was found guilty in April 1988 and sentenced to death. The decision was overturned on appeal in 1993. In 2009 he was deported to Germany for a second trial. In May 2011 he was convicted of being a camp guard at Sobibor extermination camp and was sentenced to five years in prison. He was released pending appeal and died in a nursing home in 2012, aged 91. |
| 40 | 29 Nov 1986 | The Moiwana massacre, Suriname. At least 35 inhabitants of the village were killed – mostly women and children. The attack was carried out by the Surinamese military, led by Dési Bouterse, and he is suspected of having directed the massacre. (He was President of Suriname from 2010 until 2020. He was convicted of drug trafficking and the execution of fifteen military opponents.) |
| 40 | 29 Nov 1986 | Death of Cary Grant, British-born American film actor (*Bringing Up Baby, Gunga Din, His Girl Friday, The Philadelphia Story, To Catch A Thief, North by Northwest*, and more). |
| 30 | 1 Nov 1996 | The first DVD Video player, the Toshiba SD-3000, went on sale in Japan. At that time there were only three DVD Video discs available. (USA: 31st March 1997. UK: June 1997.) |
| 30 | 1 Nov 1996 | Death of J. R. Jayewardene, President of Sri Lanka (1978–89). |
| 30 | 2 Nov 1996 | Death of Eva Cassidy, American folk/soul/blues/pop singer who gained international recognition after her early death from melanoma. Best known for the song *Over the Rainbow* and the album *Songbird*. |
| 30 | 3 Nov 1996 | Death of Jean-Bédel Bokassa, President of the Central African Republic (1966–76). Self-proclaimed Emperor of the Central African Empire (1976–79). |
| 30 | 4 Nov 1996 | Ffyona Campbell, the first woman to walk around the world, revealed that she had accepted lifts from her support crew when she fell ill during the American stage of her walk. (She later walked that section again.) |

## NOVEMBER 2026

| Ann. | Date | Event |
|------|------|-------|
| 30 | 5 Nov 1996 | The President of Pakistan, Farooq Leghari, dismissed Prime Minister Benazir Bhutto and dissolved the National Assembly because of economic mismanagement, corruption, and a decline in law and order. |
| 30 | 7 Nov 1996 | An international team of scientists reported in the journal *Nature* that they had found the unmistakable chemical signature of primitive life in a rock formation that was at least 3.85 billion years old. This meant that life on Earth evolved at least 400 million years earlier than previously thought. The rocks were found on Akilia Island in south-west Greenland. More recent studies suggest that life may have formed as early as 4.41 billion years ago, but the data is currently disputed. |
| 30 | 7 Nov 1996 | NASA launched *Mars Global Surveyor*, which mapped the entire planet and studied its atmosphere. It also identified landing sites for Mars rovers, and provided data links back to Earth. It operated until 2006 when a series of faulty software updates resulted in the spacecraft orientating towards the Sun, causing its battery to overheat. |
| 30 | 10 Nov 1996 | Death of Marjorie Proops, British agony aunt for the *Daily Mirror* newspaper. |
| 30 | 11 Nov 1996 | The Vietnam Veterans Memorial Fund in the USA unveiled a half-size replica of the Vietnam Veterans Memorial, known as 'The Wall That Heals'. The 250-foot (76-metre) replica wall and museum visits around 24 U.S. cities each year. It honours members of the U.S. armed forces who served, died or were unaccounted for in the Vietnam War, and lists 58,195 names. The full-size memorial is in Washington, D.C. |
| 30 | 12 Nov 1996 | The world's deadliest mid-air collision: the Charkhi Dadri mid-air collision, India. Saudia Flight 763, flying from Delhi, India to Dhahran, Saudi Arabia collided with Kazakhstan Airlines Flight 1907, flying from Chimkent, Kazakhstan to Delhi, India. All 349 people on both planes were killed. (Cause: the pilot of the Kazakhstan Airlines plane failed to follow air traffic control instructions that were being relayed to him by a radio operator sitting behind him.) |
| 30 | 12 Nov 1996 | The European Court of Justice ordered Britain to comply with the EU mandate of a maximum 48-hour working week. |
| 30 | 14 Nov 1996 | Death of Cardinal Joseph Bernardin, Archbishop of Chicago (1982–96). The highest-ranking figure in the Roman Catholic Church in the USA. |
| 30 | 15 Nov 1996 | Death of Alger Hiss, U.S. State Department official who was convicted of perjury after being accused of being a member of a Soviet spy ring. (Whether or not he was actually a spy is still debated, though there are increasing suspicions that he was.) Senator Joseph McCarthy's claim that the State Department had been infiltrated by communists was given added weight by this case. |
| 30 | 16 Nov 1996 | Microsoft launched its Windows CE operating system for handheld computers. (CE = Consumer Electronics.) It was later replaced by Windows Embedded Compact. The last version was released in 2013 and it has now been discontinued. |

## NOVEMBER 2026

| Ann. | Date | Event |
|------|------|-------|
| 30 | 18 Nov 1996 | The Channel Tunnel fire.<br>A truck caught fire while on board a Heavy Goods Vehicle shuttle travelling through the tunnel. It caused considerable damage and the tunnel was closed for six months for repairs.<br>There was another serious fire in September 2008, and part of one of the tunnels was closed for five months. |
| 30 | 18 Nov 1996 | The U.S. première of the science fiction film *Star Trek: First Contact*.<br>Released: 22nd November. UK: 13th December. |
| 30 | 19 Nov 1996 | Pope John Paul II held a historic first meeting with Cuban leader Fidel Castro at the Vatican. |
| 30 | 21 Nov 1996 | Death of Abdus Salam, Pakistani theoretical/nuclear physicist.<br>Joint winner of the 1979 Nobel Prize for Physics for his work on weak nuclear forces and electromagnetism. He was the first Pakistani to win a Nobel Prize, and the first Muslim to win a Nobel science prize. |
| 30 | 22 Nov 1996 | Death of Terence Donovan, British photographer and film/video/TV commercial director.<br>Director of the video for Robert Palmer's song *Addicted to Love*. |
| 30 | 23 Nov 1996 | The Ethiopian Airlines Flight 961 hijacking.<br>A passenger jet was hijacked en route to Nairobi, Kenya, and the pilot was ordered to fly to Australia. He told the hijackers there was not enough fuel on board to do this, but he was ignored.<br>The plane crashed in the Indian Ocean, killing 125 people. |
| 30 | 23 Nov 1996 | The first Tamagotchi handheld virtual pets were released by Bandai in Japan. (Rest of the world: 1st May 1997.) |
| 30 | 23 Nov 1996 | Death of Mohamed Amin, Kenyan photojournalist and TV cameraman.<br>His reports on the 1984 famine in Ethiopia attracted international attention and led to fundraising events such as Live Aid.<br>(Plane crash – Ethiopian Airlines Flight 961 – see above.) |
| 30 | 24 Nov 1996 | The first NASCAR event to be held in Japan:<br>the 1996 NASCAR Thunder Special Suzuka.<br>The race was won by American driver Rusty Wallace. |
| 30 | 24 Nov 1996 | Death of Sorley MacLean, Scottish poet.<br>Regarded as the greatest Gaelic poet of the 20th century. |
| 30 | 26 Nov 1996 | Death of Michael Bentine, British radio and television comic actor and writer. Best known for *The Goon Show*.<br>He also presented children's TV shows including *The Bumblies*, *It's a Square World* and *Michael Bentine's Potty Time*.<br>He and his family also carried out extensive research into the paranormal. |
| 30 | 26 Nov 1996 | Death of Paul Rand, American Modernist graphic designer and art director.<br>Best known for his corporate logos including IBM, UPS, Enron, Westinghouse, ABC, NeXT and more. |
| 30 | 28 Nov 1996 | Algeria adopted a revised constitution.<br>The presidency was limited to two terms and political parties based on religion, regionalism, gender or language were banned. |

# NOVEMBER 2026

| Ann. | Date | Event |
|------|------|-------|
| 30 | 29 Nov 1996 | Dražen Erdemovic, a soldier in the Bosnian Serb army, was sentenced to ten years in prison for his enforced participation in the 1995 Srebrenica massacre in which 1,200 Muslims were killed.<br>He was the first person to be sentenced by the International Criminal Tribunal for the former Yugoslavia, and the first person convicted of war crimes since WWII. He had pleaded guilty.<br>In March 1998 his sentence was reduced to five years. |
| 30 | 29 Nov 1996 | Death of Dan Flavin, American minimalist artist. Known for his installations formed from arrays of fluorescent lighting tubes. |
| 30 | 30 Nov 1996 | England officially returned the Stone of Scone (also known as the Stone of Destiny) to Scotland after 700 years. It was the coronation stone of the Scottish and (later) the English and British monarchs. It was removed from Scotland in 1296 during King Edward I's invasion of Scotland, and was then kept in Westminster Abbey. Scotland agreed to loan the Stone to Westminster Abbey for future coronations. It currently resides in Edinburgh Castle but is due to be relocated to Perth City Hall by 2024. |
| 30 | 30 Nov 1996 | Death of Tiny Tim, American entertainer. Best known for his falsetto rendition of the song *Tiptoe through the Tulips* while strumming a ukulele. |
| 25 | 4 Nov 2001 | Hurricane Michelle caused $2 billion worth of damage across Central America, particularly Cuba. 17 people were killed, 26 reported missing, and thousands of homes were destroyed. (See also: 16th December 2001.) |
| 25 | 4 Nov 2001 | The Police Service of Northern Ireland was established and the Royal Ulster Constabulary was dissolved. |
| 25 | 4 Nov 2001 | The world première of the fantasy film *Harry Potter and the Philosopher's Stone* (USA: *Harry Potter and the Sorcerer's Stone*), in London, UK.<br>It was the first film in the Harry Potter series.<br>U.S. première: 11th November, released 16th November.<br>UK release: 16th November. |
| 25 | 5 Nov 2001 | Death of Roy Boulting, British film-maker who worked with his twin brother, John. Their films include *Private's Progress, Lucky Jim I'm All Right, Jack, There's a Girl in My Soup*, and more. |
| 25 | 7 Nov 2001 | Concorde, the British/French supersonic passenger jet, returned to service.<br>It had been grounded since the crash in Paris, France on 25th July<br>It was retired in 2003. |
| 25 | 7 Nov 2001 | Belgium's national airline, Sabena, went out of business.<br>It assets were acquired by Brussels Airlines, which became Belgium's national airline in March 2007. |
| 25 | 8 Nov 2001 | Twelve British and two Dutch plane-spotters were arrested in Greece and charged with spying. Some were given three-year prison sentences at their trial in April 2002. Their convictions were overturned in November 2002. |
| 25 | 9 Nov 2001<br>to 10th | War in Afghanistan – the Battle of Mazar-e-Sharif.<br>Northern Alliance/U.S. victory – the Taliban's first major defeat.<br>(See also: 12th November 2001.) |

## NOVEMBER 2026

| Ann. | Date | Event |
|------|------|-------|
| 25 | 9 Nov 2001 | The Dolby Theatre opened in Hollywood, Los Angeles, California, USA (as the Kodak Theatre). It is the venue for the annual Academy Awards ceremony. |
| 25 | 9 Nov 2001 | Death of Dorothy Dunnett, Scottish historical novelist. |
| 25 | 10 Nov 2001 | Death of Ken Kesey, American writer. Best known for his novel *One Flew Over the Cuckoo's Nest*. |
| 25 | 12 Nov 2001 | War in Afghanistan – the fall of Kabul. Afghanistan's ruling Taliban abandoned the capital without a fight as a coalition of U.S./NATO and Northern Alliance troops entered the city. |
| 25 | 12 Nov 2001 | American Airlines Flight 587 crashed in Queens, New York City, USA shortly after take-off. All 260 people on the plane were killed, plus five on the ground. As this was only a month after the 9/11 terrorist attacks, there were fears that this was another terrorist attack. (Cause: the first officer's [co-pilot's] aggressive overuse of the rudder controls while fighting against turbulence caused the vertical stabiliser to detach from the plane.) |
| 25 | 13 Nov 2001 | War on terrorism: U.S. President George W. Bush signed an Executive Order which stated that foreign nationals suspected of committing or planning terrorist acts against the USA would be subject to military tribunals rather than civilian trials. |
| 25 | 13 Nov 2001 | Death of Peggy Mount, British stage, film and television actress. |
| 25 | 14 Nov 2001 | Death of Charlotte Coleman, British film and television actress (*Four Weddings and a Funeral, Oranges Are Not the Only Fruit, Worzel Gummidge, Marmalade Atkins*). (Asthma attack, aged 33.) |
| 25 | 15 Nov 2001 | Microsoft released its first Xbox video games console. (Europe: 14th March 2002.) |
| 25 | 17 Nov 2001 | Death of Michael Karoli, German musician and composer. A founding member of the krautrock band Can. |
| 25 | 19 Nov 2001 | The Aviation and Transportation Security Act was passed in the USA following the 9/11 terrorist attacks. It created the Transportation Security Administration, which is responsible for screening passengers at airports and placing armed Federal Air Marshals on planes. Before the Act was passed, airlines were responsible for screening passengers, and many of them contracted it out to third-party organisations. |
| 25 | 21 Nov 2001 | Death of Salahuddin Abdul Aziz Shah, King of Malaysia (1999–2001.) Succeeded by Sirajuddin of Perlis. |
| 25 | 22 Nov 2001 to 9 Dec | War in Afghanistan – the Fall of Kandahar. Coalition forces ousted the Taliban from the last major city under their control. This marked the end of the Taliban regime's control of Afghanistan (until August 2021 when it seized control of the country again following NATO's withdrawal). |
| 25 | 22 Nov 2001 | Death of Mary Kay Ash, American founder of Mary Kay cosmetics. |

**NOVEMBER 2026**

| Ann. | Date | Event |
|------|------|-------|
| 25 | 23 Nov 2001 | Death of Mary Whitehouse, British social activist who campaigned against harmful and offensive content in the mainstream British media. She established the Clean Up TV campaign and later became the founder and first president of the National Viewers' and Listeners' Association. (The association later became Mediawatch-UK. It closed down in 2021.) |
| 25 | 24 Nov 2001 | Death of Arthur Hailey, British-Canadian novelist. Best known for *Hotel*, *Airport*, *Wheels* and *The Moneychangers*. |
| 25 | 27 Nov 2001 | NASA announced the discovery of the first atmosphere to be detected on an extrasolar planet. The Hubble Space Telescope detected sodium in the atmosphere of extrasolar planet HD 209458b (Osiris). Hydrogen, oxygen and carbon have also been detected since then |
| 25 | 29 Nov 2001 | Death of George Harrison, British rock guitarist, singer and songwriter (the Beatles). |
| 25 | 30 Nov 2001 | The Green River Killer, Gary Ridgeway, was arrested in Seattle, Washington, USA. He was convicted of killing 49 women in Washington in the 1980s and 90s, and confessed to killing 71. He was sentenced to life imprisonment in January 2004. |
| 20 | 1 Nov 2006 | Death of William Styron, American novelist and essayist whose works examine tragic themes. (*Lie Down in Darkness*, *The Long March*, *The Confessions of Nat Turner* and *Sophie's Choice*.) |
| 20 | 5 Nov 2006 | Saddam Hussein, the former President of Iraq, was sentenced to death for his role in the massacre of 148 Iraqi Shi'ites in 1982. He was executed on 30th December. (His co-defendants, Barzan Ibrahim al-Tikriti and Awad Hamed al-Bandar, were also sentenced to death. They were executed on 15th January 2007.) |
| 20 | 7 Nov 2006 | Keith Ellison from Minnesota became the first Muslim elected to the U.S. Congress. He was inaugurated on 3rd January 2007 and remained in office until 2019 when he became Attorney General of Minnesota |
| 20 | 10 Nov 2006 | NASA's *Cassini* spacecraft filmed a hurricane-like storm on Saturn's south pole. It was the first time a hurricane had been seen on another planet. In April 2013 it also recorded a hurricane on Saturn's north pole. |
| 20 | 10 Nov 2006 | The National Museum of the Marine Corps opened near MCB Quantico in Triangle, Virginia, USA. |
| 20 | 10 Nov 2006 | Death of Diana Coupland, British stage, film and television actress and singer. Best known for her role as Jean Abbott in the sitcom *Bless This House*. |
| 20 | 10 Nov 2006 | Death of Jack Palance, American stage, film and television actor. Generally known for his menacing roles. Best known for the film *City Slickers*. |
| 20 | 11 Nov 2006 | The New Zealand War Memorial was unveiled in London, UK. It commemorates New Zealand's military personnel who died in WWI and WWII. |
| 20 | 11 Nov 2006 | Sony's PlayStation 3 video games console was released in Japan (USA: 17th November. Europe: 23rd March 2007.) |
| 20 | 13 Nov 2006 | Google acquired the online video-sharing service YouTube. |

## NOVEMBER 2026

| Ann. | Date | Event |
|------|------|-------|
| 20 | 14 Nov 2006 | Microsoft released its Zune portable media player. It was discontinued in October 2011. |
| 20 | 15 Nov 2006 | The Middle Eastern television news channel Al Jazeera English launched worldwide. |
| 20 | 15 Nov 2006 | Death of Ana Carolina Reston, Brazilian fashion model. (Anorexia, aged 21.) |
| 20 | 16 Nov 2006 | Death of Milton Friedman, American economist, statistician and educator. Leader of the Chicago school of economics. Winner of the 1976 Nobel Prize in Economics. |
| 20 | 17 Nov 2006 | Paul Gibbons was sentenced to 2.5 years in prison for the first 'web rage' attack in Britain. He had pleaded guilty to unlawful wounding. Police advised internet users not to put details online that would allow them to be traced. |
| 20 | 17 Nov 2006 | Death of Ruth Brown, ('Miss Rhythm', 'the Queen of R&B'), American singer, songwriter and actress. Her success in the 1950s helped establish Atlantic Records. |
| 20 | 17 Nov 2006 | Death of Ferenc Puskás, Hungarian football player and manager. Regarded as one of the greatest players of all time, and the sport's first international superstar. |
| 20 | 18 Nov 2006 | American actor Tom Cruise married actress Katie Holmes in a Scientologist wedding ceremony in Italy. They divorced in 2012. |
| 20 | 19 Nov 2006 | The Nintendo Wii video games console was released in the USA. (Japan: 2nd December. Europe: 8th December.) |
| 20 | 20 Nov 2006 | Death of Robert Altman, American film director. Noted for the stylised realism of his work. Best known for *M*A*S*H, McCabe and Mrs. Miller* and *Nashville*. |
| 20 | 21 Nov 2006 | The Nepalese Civil War ended with the signing of the Comprehensive Peace Accord. |
| 20 | 23 Nov 2006 | Death of Betty Comden, American lyricist and screenwriter. Known for her collaborations with Adolph Green on highly successful Broadway and Hollywood musicals. Best known for the film *Singin' in the Rain*. |
| 20 | 23 Nov 2006 | Death of Alexander Litvinenko, Russian-born British intelligence agent, journalist and writer. A prominent critic of the Putin regime in Russia, which he described as a 'mafia state'. (Poisoned by radioactive polonium. His death is believed to have been ordered by the President of Russia, Vladimir Putin. Russia refused to cooperate with the investigations into his death.) |
| 20 | 27 Nov 2006 | Death of Alan ('Fluff') Freeman, Australian-born British disc jockey and radio personality. Best known for hosting *Pick of the Pops*, and for his catchphrases 'Hi there, pop pickers!' and 'Not 'arf!' |
| 20 | 29 Nov 2006 | Death of Allen Carr, British anti-smoking campaigner, therapist and writer. Best known for his book *The Easy Way To Stop Smoking*. (Lung cancer, aged 72.) |

## NOVEMBER 2026

| Ann. | Date | Event |
|---|---|---|
| 15 | 12 Nov 2011 | The Prime Minister of Italy, Silvio Berlusconi, resigned (with effect from 16th November) over Italy's debt crisis. He was succeeded by Mario Monti. |
| 15 | 26 Nov 2011 | NASA launched its *Curiosity* rover.<br>It landed in Gale Crater on Mars in August 2012.<br>It was designed to operate for one Mars year (approximately two Earth years), but at the time of writing (2022) it is still operating. |
| 15 | 29 Nov 2011 | American pop singer Michael Jackson's personal doctor, Conrad Murray, was convicted of involuntary manslaughter for administering a lethal dose of propofol.<br>He was sentenced to four years in prison. (He served two years.) |
| 10 | 4 Nov 2016 | The Paris Agreement on Climate Change (also known as the Paris Climate Accords) came into effect. |
| 10 | 7 Nov 2016 | Death of Leonard Cohen, Canadian folk/soft rock singer, songwriter and poet. |
| 10 | 7 Nov 2016 | Death of Janet Reno, U.S. Attorney General (1993–2001). |
| 10 | 7 Nov 2016 | Death of Jimmy Young, British disc jockey, radio presenter and singer.<br>One of the first DJs on BBC Radio 1.<br>He also presented shows on Radio 2 for nearly thirty years. |
| 10 | 8 Nov 2016 | Donald Trump was elected as the 45th President of the USA.<br>(Inaugurated 20th January 2017.) |
| 10 | 11 Nov 2016 | Death of Robert Vaughn, American stage, film and television actor.<br>Best known for his TV roles as Napoleon Solo in *The Man from U.N.C.L.E.*, Harry Rule in *The Protectors*, and Albert Stroller in *Hustle*.<br>He also appeared in films including *The Magnificent Seven*, *Bullitt*, and *Superman III*. |
| 10 | 16 Nov 2016 | Death of Jay Wright Forrester, American computer scientist, engineer and writer. Best known for inventing magnetic core memory. |
| 10 | 18 Nov 2016 | Death of Denton Cooley, American heart surgeon.<br>Best known for implanting the first artificial human heart.<br>Founder of the Texas Heart Institute. |
| 10 | 23 Nov 2016 | Death of Andrew Sachs, German-born British television actor and playwright. Best known for his role as the Spanish waiter Manuel in the TV sitcom *Fawlty Towers*. |
| 10 | 25 Nov 2016 | Death of Fidel Castro, President of Cuba (1976–2008),<br>Prime Minister of Cuba (1959–76). |

## DECEMBER 2026

| Ann. | Date | Event |
|---|---|---|
| 900 | 13 Dec 1126 | Death of Henry IX, Duke of Bavaria (1120–26). |
| 600 | 31 Dec 1426 | Death of Thomas Beaufort, Duke of Exeter.<br>English naval commander during the Hundred Years' War.<br>Lord Chancellor (1410–12). |
| 500 | 12 Dec 1526 | Birth of Álvaro de Bazán, 1st Marquis of Santa Cruz, Spanish admiral.<br>He was never defeated in battle. |
| 400 | 15 Dec 1626 | Death of Adriaen de Vries, Dutch Mannerist sculptor.<br>The most famous European sculptor of his era. Noted for his fine modelling, bronze casting, and his manipulation of patina. |
| 400 | 18 Dec 1626 | Birth of Christina, Queen of Sweden (1632–54 – abdicated).<br>Noted for her intelligence and her interest in writing, religion, science, mathematics, philosophy, and art. She never married and is believed to have had a relationship with a close female friend. She also secretly converted to Catholicism, and moved to Rome after her abdication. |
| 250 | 5 Dec 1776 | Phi Beta Kappa, the oldest academic honour society in the USA, and the first Greek-letter fraternity, was founded, at the College of William and Mary in Williamsburg, Virginia. |
| 250 | 19 Dec 1776 | The first of Thomas Paine's pamphlets *The American Crisis* was published in the *Pennsylvania Journal* newspaper in the USA.<br>He published thirteen pamphlets in 1776–77, and three more in 1777–83, aiming to boost the American colonists' morale during the American Revolutionary War. |
| 250 | 26 Dec 1776 | American Revolutionary War – the Battle of Trenton, New Jersey.<br>American victory. General George Washington's first major win of the war, against Hessian auxiliaries who were caught off-guard.<br>The win boosted the Americans' flagging morale. |
| 200 | 3 Dec 1826 | Birth of George McClellan, American military officer, civil engineer, railway executive and politician.<br>He commanded forces in the Mexican–American War and the American Civil War and was the Commanding General of the U.S. Army (1861–62). He is also known for his disagreement with U.S. President Abraham Lincoln, which led to him being removed from his command.<br>He ran against Lincoln in the 1864 presidential election, but lost. |
| 200 | 7 Dec 1826 | Death of John Flaxman, British Neoclassical sculptor.<br>He was particularly noted for his funerary monuments, several of which are in Westminster Abbey and St. Paul's Cathedral.<br>He also designed decorations for Buckingham Palace's facades. |
| 200 | 21 Dec 1826 to 31 Jan 1827 | The Fredonian Rebellion, Nacogdoches, Texas.<br>American settlers in Texas, which was then part of Mexico, declared their independence as the Republic of Fredonia. The Texas Militia and Mexican soldiers restored order, and the organisers of the rebellion fled to the USA. |
| 175 | 2 Dec 1851 | The President of France, Louis-Napoléon Bonaparte, staged a coup to avoid having to leave office when his term ended in 1852. He had himself crowned Emperor Napoleon III, granted himself dictatorial powers, and dissolved the National Assembly. He dissolved the French Second Republic in December 1852 and ruled the Second French Empire until 1870. |

## DECEMBER 2026

| Ann. | Date | Event |
|------|------|-------|
| 175 | 8 Dec 1851 | Chilean Revolution – the Battle of Loncomilla. Government victory. The decisive battle of the Revolution, which ended on 31st December. |
| 175 | 10 Dec 1851 | Birth of Melvil Dewey, American librarian who created the Dewey Decimal system of library classification. A founding member of the American Library Association. Also noted for the many allegations of sexual harassment and racism made against him, which led to his resignation. |
| 175 | 19 Dec 1851 | Death of J. M. W. Turner, British Romantic artist. Noted for his landscapes and marine paintings. |
| 175 | 22 Dec 1851 | India's first train began operating. The steam engine *Jenny Lind* had been shipped over from the UK to help transport materials for the construction of the Ganges Canal. It ran for about 4.7 miles between Roorkee and Piran Kaliyar. (India's first passenger train began operating in 1853.) |
| 175 | 24 Dec 1851 | The Library of Congress in Washington, DC, USA was devastated by a fire. It destroyed 35,000 books (about two-thirds of its collection). Two-thirds of former U.S. President Thomas Jefferson's personal library was lost. The Library had purchased this after its previous collection was destroyed by the British during the War of 1812. Librarians eventually managed to find replacements for all but 300 of the lost books. |
| 175 | 29 Dec 1851 | The first YMCA (Young Men's Christian Association) opened in the USA, in Boston, Massachusetts. The world's first YMCA was established in London, UK in 1844. |
| 175 | 30 Dec 1851 | Birth of Asa Griggs Candler, American businessman and politician. He founded the Coca-Cola Company in 1892 after purchasing the recipe from its inventor, the chemist John Pemberton. He then developed the company into one of the world's biggest brands. He was also Mayor of Atlanta, Georgia (1917–19.) |
| 150 | 5 Dec 1876 | The Brooklyn Theatre fire, New York, USA. A fire broke out during a play when a lamp set fire to part of the canvas set on the stage. Stage hands were unable to contain the fire and it spread to the ceiling. More than 1,000 people were in the audience, and many were trapped in the upper circle. At least 278 people were killed (some sources say more than 300). The site of the theatre is now a park next to the New York Supreme Court. |
| 150 | 6 Dec 1876 | The first cremation in the USA took place, at the LeMoyne Crematory in North Franklin Township in Pennsylvania. (It closed in 1901.) |
| 150 | 12 Dec 1876 | Birth of Alvin Kraenzlein, American athlete. Best known for developing the modern hurdling technique. In 1900 he became the first person to win four individual gold medals at a single Olympic Games (60 m, 110 m hurdles, 200 m hurdles, long jump), and he remains the only track-and-field athlete to achieve this. |
| 150 | 22 Dec 1876 | Birth of Filippo Tommaso Marinetti, Egyptian-born Italian poet, editor and art theorist. The founder of the Futurist movement. He wrote the first *Futurist Manifesto*, and co-wrote the *Fascist Manifesto*. |
| 150 | 23 Dec 1876 | The first constitution of the Ottoman Empire came into effect (until 1878, and again from 1908 to 1922). |

## DECEMBER 2026

| Ann. | Date | Event |
|---|---|---|
| 150 | 25 Dec 1876 | Birth of Muhammad Ali Jinnah, the founder of Pakistan.<br>He is known in Pakistan as the 'Father of the Nation', and his birthday is a national holiday.<br>He was the first Governor-General of Pakistan (1947–48 – died in office). |
| 150 | 29 Dec 1876 | The Ashtabula River railroad disaster, Ohio, USA.<br>The Ashtabula Bridge failed as the *Pacific Express* train was passing over it. The carriages plunged into the river, and oil lamps and heating stoves overturned and set the carriages on fire.<br>92 people were killed and 64 injured. |
| 150 | 29 Dec 1876 | Birth of Pablo Casals, Spanish/Puerto Rican cellist, composer and conductor. Regarded as one of the greatest cellists of all time. |
| 125 | 5 Dec 1901 | Birth of Walt Disney, American animator and film and television producer.<br>Co-founder (with his brother Roy) of the Walt Disney Company.<br>Creator of popular cartoon characters including Mickey Mouse and Donald Duck. Creator of Disneyland. |
| 125 | 10 Dec 1901 | The first Nobel Prize ceremony was held in Stockholm, Sweden.<br>Prizes were awarded for notable achievements in the fields of chemistry, literature, peace, physiology or medicine and physics.<br>The prizes were presented by the King of Sweden. |
| 125 | 11 Dec 1901 to 14th | The first table tennis (ping-pong) tournament was held, at the Royal Aquarium in London, UK. (See also: 6th December 1926.) |
| 125 | 12 Dec 1901 | The first radio transmission was sent across the Atlantic Ocean.<br>Italian physicist Guglielmo Marconi transmitted the letter 'S' in Morse code from Poldhu in Cornwall, UK to Newfoundland, Canada. |
| 125 | 14 Dec 1901 | Birth of Paul, King of Greece (1947–64).<br>First cousin of Prince Philip, Duke of Edinburgh. |
| 125 | 16 Dec 1901 | Birth of Margaret Mead, American anthropologist and broadcaster.<br>She was also noted for advocating the broadening of sexual conventions. |
| 125 | 20 Dec 1901 | Birth of Robert J. Van de Graaff, American physicist.<br>Best known for inventing the Van de Graaff generator, which generates high-voltage static electricity. |
| 125 | 25 Dec 1901 | Birth of Princess Alice, Duchess of Gloucester.<br>Wife of Prince Henry, Duke of Gloucester.<br>She was the oldest-living member of the British royal family when she died in 2004, aged 102. |
| 125 | 27 Dec 1901 | Birth of Marlene Dietrich, German-born American stage and film actress, singer, entertainer, and humanitarian.<br>One of the greatest Hollywood actresses of all time. |
| 125 | 27 Dec 1901 | Birth of Irene Handl, British stage, film and television actress.<br>Best known for her many comic roles on TV. |
| 100 | 1 Dec 1926 | Birth of Keith Michell, Australian stage, film and television actor.<br>He worked primarily in the UK, and is best known for playing King Henry VIII in several productions.<br>He also sang the hit song *Captain Beaky and His Band*. (Died 2015.) |

## DECEMBER 2026

| Ann. | Date | Event |
|------|------|-------|
| 100 | 5 Dec 1926 | Sergei Eisenstein's classic film *Battleship Potemkin* was released in the USA (but only in New York). (Soviet Union: December 1925.) |
| 100 | 5 Dec 1926 | Death of Claude Monet, French artist.<br>The leader of the Impressionist movement. |
| 100 | 6 Dec 1926 to 11th | The first World Table Tennis Championships were held, in London, UK. |
| 100 | 7 Dec 1926 | The Electrolux Servel gas refrigerator went on sale in the USA.<br>It remained on the market until the 1950s and was the only gas refrigerator available. It had no moving parts – a gas-fuelled flame caused the coolant to circulate. The process was invented by Swedish engineers Baltzar von Platen and Carl Munters. |
| 100 | 9 Dec 1926 | The United States Golf Association approved the use of steel-shafted golf clubs. Earlier clubs were made of hickory but were prone to twisting. |
| 100 | 11 Dec 1926 | Birth of Big Mama Thornton, American rhythm and blues singer and songwriter. Best known for the song *Hound Dog* (later recorded by Elvis Presley). (Died 1984.) |
| 100 | 16 Dec 1926 | Birth of James McCracken, American operatic tenor. (Died 1988.) |
| 100 | 16 Dec 1926 | Birth of A. N. R. Robinson, President of Trinidad and Tobago (1997–2003). (Died 2014.) |
| 100 | 17 Dec 1926 | Birth of Stephen Lewis, British stage, film and television actor, comedian, screenwriter and playwright. Best known for his TV roles as Blakey in *On the Buses* and Smiler in *Last of the Summer Wine*. (Died 2015.) |
| 100 | 18 Dec 1926 | The term 'photon' was coined by American physical chemist G. N. Lewis in a letter published in the journal *Nature*. |
| 100 | 19 Dec 1926 | Antanas Smetona became President of Lithuania (until June 1940 when Lithuania was occupied and annexed by the Soviet Union.) |
| 100 | 20 Dec 1926 | Birth of Geoffrey Howe, British Conservative politician.<br>A leading figure in Margaret Thatcher's cabinet, and her longest-serving Cabinet minister. Chancellor of the Exchequer (1979–83), Foreign Secretary (1983–89), Deputy Prime Minister and Leader of the House of Commons (1989–90). (Died 2015.) |
| 100 | 25 Dec 1926 | Death of Emperor Taishō of Japan (1912–26).<br>Succeeded by his son Hirohito (as Emperor Showa). |
| 100 | 28 Dec 1926 | The highest recorded first-class cricket innings: 1,107<br>(Victoria against New South Wales, Australia.) |
| 100 | 29 Dec 1926 | Death of Rainer Maria Rilke, Austrian/Czech poet and novelist.<br>Noted for his lyrical intensity. |
| 90 | 1 Dec 1936 | The first U.S. patent for a large-scale commercial hydroponics plant was awarded to Frank Farrington Lyons and Ernest Brundin.<br>(U.S. Patent 2,062,755.) It described how plants could be grown in soil-less medium with their roots suspended in mineral-rich water. |
| 90 | 2 Dec 1936 | Death of John Ringling, American circus founder (Ringling Brothers). |
| 90 | 3 Dec 1936 | New York City's classical music radio station WQXR was founded. |

# DECEMBER 2026

| Ann. | Date | Event |
|---|---|---|
| 90 | 5 Dec 1936 | The Soviet Union adopted a new constitution (the 'Stalin Constitution'). The Congress of Soviets was replaced by the Supreme Soviet. |
| 90 | 8 Dec 1936 | Birth of David Carradine, American actor and martial artist. Best known for the TV series *Kung Fu* and the films *Kill Bill: Vol 1* and *Vol 2*. Also noted for his troubled private life and drug abuse. (Died 2009.) |
| 90 | 11 Dec 1936 | King Edward VIII of the United Kingdom abdicated to marry Wallis Warfield Simpson, a divorcee. He became the Duke of Windsor. His younger brother, the Duke of York, became King George VI. |
| 90 | 12 Dec 1936 to 26th | Chinese Civil War – the Xi'an Incident. The Generalissimo of the Republic of China, Chiang Kai-shek, was kidnapped by two of his generals. They opposed his policy of fighting the Communists rather than Japan, which had invaded northern China. The Nationalists and Communists then united to fight Japan. |
| 90 | 18 Dec 1936 | The first live giant panda to be taken out of China arrived in San Francisco, California, USA. Named Su Lin, it had been captured as a nine-week-old cub by American socialite Ruth Harkness. She sold it to Brookfield Zoo in Chicago, Illinois. It died of pneumonia in 1938, by which time she had already brought a second panda from China. |
| 90 | 20 Dec 1936 | The prototype Junkers JU 88 aircraft made its first flight. It was one of Germany's principal bombers in the Battle of Britain during WWII. |
| 90 | 24 Dec 1936 | American physicist and physician John H. Lawrence administered the first radioisotope for medical treatment at the University of California, Berkeley. He used radioactive phosphorus-32 to treat a woman suffering from leukaemia. He became renowned for his pioneering treatment and is known as the 'father of nuclear medicine'. |
| 90 | 25 Dec 1936 | Birth of Ismail Merchant, Indian-born film producer. Best known for his collaboration with director James Ivory as Merchant Ivory Productions (*Room with a View*, *Howards End*, *The Remains of the Day*, and more). (Died 2005.) |
| 90 | 26 Dec 1936 | The Palestine Symphony Orchestra played its first concert. The Orchestra was mainly comprised of German Jews who had been denied the right to perform in Germany. The Orchestra later became the Israel Philharmonic Orchestra. |
| 90 | 29 Dec 1936 | Birth of Mary Tyler Moore, American stage, film and television actress and producer. Best known for her TV sitcom roles, including *The Dick Van Dyke Show* and *The Mary Tyler Moore Show*. (Died 2017.) |
| 90 | 29 Dec 1936 | Birth of Ray Nitschke, American football player. (Died 1998.) |
| 90 | 30 Dec 1936 | The United Automobile Workers (UAW) staged the first sit-down strike in the USA. This led to the unionisation of the U.S. car industry. |
| 90 | 31 Dec 1936 | Death of Miguel de Unamuno, Spanish writer and philosopher. |
| 80 | 2 Dec 1946 | Birth of Gianni Versace, Italian fashion designer. (Shot dead by American spree killer Andrew Cunanan in 1997.) |
| 80 | 5 Dec 1946 | U.S. President Harry S. Truman established the President's Committee on Civil Rights. |

## DECEMBER 2026

| Ann. | Date | Event |
|---|---|---|
| 80 | 7 Dec 1946 | The Winecoff Hotel fire, Atlanta, Georgia, USA.<br>119 people were killed, including the hotel's owners.<br>Many of those who died jumped or fell to their deaths in an effort to escape the fire. It remains the deadliest hotel fire in U.S. history.<br>(Cause: unknown.) |
| 80 | 9 Dec 1946 to 13 Apr 1949 | The Subsequent Nuremberg Trials were held before the International Military Tribunal following WWII. The twelve trials involved surviving members of Nazi Germany's leadership, doctors alleged to have been involved in human experimentation, Nazi death squads, and others.<br>Trial 1 was the doctors' trial and involved 23 defendants.<br>It ran from 9th December to 20th August 1947. Seven defendants were sentenced to death, nine were given prison sentences ranging from ten years to life, and seven were acquitted. |
| 80 | 9 Dec 1946 | The Constituent Assembly of India met for the first time, in New Delhi. Its purpose was to draft the Constitution of India, which came into effect on 26th January 1950 when India became an independent republic.<br>The Constituent Assembly was then dissolved and became the Provisional Parliament of India. |
| 80 | 9 Dec 1946 | The U.S. Military's experimental rocket-powered plane the XS-1 made its first powered flight. It became the Bell X-1 and was in service until 1958. |
| 80 | 10 Dec 1946 | Death of Walter Johnson, American baseball pitcher (Washington Senators) and manager (Washington Senators, Cleveland Indians).<br>Regarded as one of the greatest pitchers in baseball history.<br>Several of his records still stand today. |
| 80 | 10 Dec 1946 | Death of Damon Runyon, American journalist and short story writer.<br>Best known for the musical *Guys and Dolls*. It was based on his stories of the Broadway district of New York City following the prohibition era. |
| 80 | 11 Dec 1946 | UNICEF, the United Nations International Children's Emergency Fund, was established in New York City, USA. |
| 80 | 12 Dec 1946 | Tide laundry detergent was introduced in the USA.<br>It was initially sold in a few test markets but expanded nationwide by 1949 and quickly became the best-selling brand. |
| 80 | 13 Dec 1946 | The Knickerbocker Ice Company fire, Washington Heights, Manhattan, New York City, USA. An abandoned icehouse caught fire and destroyed an adjacent apartment building. 37 people were killed.<br>(The Knickerbocker Ice Company had ceased trading in 1924.) |
| 80 | 14 Dec 1946 | The United Nations voted to accept six blocks of land in Manhattan, New York City, USA, which had been gifted to it by John D. Rockefeller Jr. for its headquarters. |
| 80 | 14 Dec 1946 | Birth of Patty Duke, American stage, film and television actress (*The Miracle Worker, The Patty Duke Show, Valley of the Dolls*, and more).<br>She was also a mental health advocate, and President of the Screen Actors Guild (1985–88). (Died 2016.) |
| 80 | 18 Dec 1946 | Birth of Steve Biko, South African anti-apartheid activist.<br>Founder of the Black Consciousness Movement.<br>(Beaten to death by state security officers in 1977, aged 30.) |

# DECEMBER 2026

| Ann. | Date | Event |
|---|---|---|
| 80 | 19 Dec 1946 to 1 Aug 1954 | The First Indochina War (also called the French Indochina War). The Vietnamese fought the French, who opposed Vietnamese independence. Việt Minh victory, resulting in the partition of Vietnam into north and south. |
| 80 | 19 Dec 1946 | Birth of Robert Urich, American stage, film and television actor and television producer. Best known for his lead roles in the TV series *Vega$* and *Spenser: For Hire*. (Died 2002.) |
| 80 | 20 Dec 1946 (21 Dec in Japan) | The Nankai earthquake and tsunami, Nankaido, Japan. The earthquake caused extensive damage. At least 1,362 people were killed and 2,600 injured. More than 38,000 homes were destroyed. |
| 80 | 21 Dec 1946 | The U.S. première of Frank Capra's film *It's A Wonderful Life*. Released: 7th January 1947. UK première: 6th April 1947. |
| 80 | 21 Dec 1946 | Birth of Kevin Peek, Australian rock and classical guitarist and composer. Best known as a member of the instrumental rock band Sky. (Died 2013.) |
| 80 | 21 Dec 1946 | Birth of Carl Wilson, American surf rock guitarist, singer and songwriter (the Beach Boys). (Died 1998.) |
| 80 | 23 Dec 1946 | U.S. President Harry S. Truman established an amnesty board to review the cases of 15,000 conscientious objectors who had been imprisoned for refusing to serve in WWII. The board determined that 1,500 (ten percent of those imprisoned) were eligible for a presidential pardon as they were members of pacifist religious groups such as the Quakers. They were granted a pardon on 23rd December 1947. The remainder were classed as convicted criminals. |
| 80 | 23 Dec 1946 | Birth of John Sullivan, British screenwriter and television producer. Best known for his TV sitcoms including *Only Fools and Horses*, *Citizen Smith*, *Just Good Friends*, *Dear John*, *The Green Green Grass*, and more. (Died 2011.) |
| 80 | 25 Dec 1946 | The first nuclear reactor in Europe to achieve a self-sustaining nuclear chain reaction: the F-1 research reactor at the Kurchatov Institute in Moscow, Soviet Union. It continued operating for nearly seventy years. |
| 80 | 25 Dec 1946 | Death of W. C. Fields, American actor and comedian. |
| 80 | 26 Dec 1946 | The Flamingo Las Vegas hotel opened in Las Vegas, Nevada, USA. It was the first luxury hotel on the Las Vegas Strip. It was built by the mobster Bugsy Siegel. |
| 75 | 1 Dec 1951 | British composer Benjamin Britten's opera *Billy Budd* (Opus 50) was performed for the first time, in London, UK. (This was the original four-act version. He revised it into a two-act version, which was first performed in January 1964.) |
| 75 | 4 Dec 1951 | Mount Hibok-Hibok (also known as Catarman Volcano) erupted on Camiguin island in the Philippines. Lava flows, poisonous gas and landslides destroyed the surrounding area and killed more than 3,000 people. Afterwards, around half the island's population moved away. |
| 75 | 5 Dec 1951 | Death of Shoeless Joe Jackson, American baseball player. He was an exceptional player, but he was banned from playing at the prime of his career following his involvement in the Black Sox Scandal. |

## DECEMBER 2026

| Ann. | Date | Event |
|------|------|-------|
| 75 | 6 Dec 1951 | Death of Harold Ross, American journalist and publisher.<br>Co-founder and editor-in-chief of *The New Yorker*. |
| 75 | 10 Dec 1951 | Death of Algernon Blackwood, British novelist, short story writer and broadcaster. Noted for his ghost stories and weird fiction. |
| 75 | 11 Dec 1951 | American baseball star Joe DiMaggio (New York Yankies) announced his retirement after thirteen years. |
| 75 | 15 Dec 1951 | Death of Eric Drummond, 7th Earl of Perth, British politician and diplomat. First Secretary-General of the League of Nations (1920–33). |
| 75 | 16 Dec 1951 | The first episode of the crime drama television show *Dragnet* was broadcast on NBC in the USA. It ran for eight seasons until 1959.<br>A later version ran from 1967 to 1970. It was based on the radio series of the same name, which ran from 1949 to 1957. |
| 75 | 20 Dec 1951 | EBR-1 (Experimental Breeder Reactor 1) became the first nuclear reactor to generate electricity, at Argonne National Laboratory, Idaho, USA.<br>It generated enough electricity to power four light bulbs – though its output was gradually increased. |
| 75 | 23 Dec 1951 | The first National Football League (NFL) championship game to be televised live coast-to-coast in the USA: the Los Angeles Rams beat the Cleveland Browns 24–17. The DuMont Television Network paid the NFL $95,000 for the broadcast rights. |
| 75 | 24 Dec 1951 | Libya declared its independence from the UK and France.<br>Idris was proclaimed King of Libya. |
| 75 | 24 Dec 1951 | The first opera composed for television, *Amal and the Night Visitors* by Gian Carlo Menotti, was broadcast on NBC in the USA. |
| 75 | 30 Dec 1951 | The first episode of the Western television show *The Roy Rogers Show* was broadcast on NBC in the USA. It ran for six seasons until 1957.<br>A radio series of the same name also ran from 1944 to 1955. |
| 75 | 31 Dec 1951 | The Marshall Plan ended.<br>It was set up by the USA after WWII to help rebuild Europe, and distributed $13 billion in foreign aid.<br>By the time it ended, the economies of all participating countries had surpassed their pre-war levels. It was replaced by the Mutual Security Agency, which was established on 10th October 1951. |
| 70 | 1 Dec 1956 | *Mad* magazine's mascot Alfred E. Neuman appeared on the front cover for the first time. (Issue 30.) |
| 70 | 2 Dec 1956 | Cuban Revolution: 82 members of the 26th of July Movement landed in Cuba after sailing from Mexico with the aim of overthrowing Fulgencio Batista's dictatorship.<br>Their members included Fidel and Raúl Castro and Che Guevara.<br>They ousted Batista on 1st January 1959 and established a revolutionary socialist state.<br>In October 1965 the 26th of July Movement became the Communist Party of Cuba, which continues to govern Cuba. |

# DECEMBER 2026

| Ann. | Date | Event |
|------|------|-------|
| 70 | 4 Dec 1956 | The Million Dollar Quartet performed together for their one and only time. The quartet (Johnny Cash, Jerry Lee Lewis, Carl Perkins and Elvis Presley) held an impromptu jam session at Sun Studios in Memphis, Tennessee, USA. It is considered a seminal moment in rock and roll history.<br>The session was recorded, and some of the tracks were released in 1981. The complete session was released a few years later, after more of the recorded tracks were discovered. |
| 70 | 10 Dec 1956 | American physicists John Bardeen, Walter Brattain and William Shockley received the 1956 Nobel Prize in Physics for inventing the transistor. |
| 70 | 12 Dec 1956 | The IRA began its Border Campaign in Northern Ireland.<br>The campaign of guerrilla warfare aimed to overthrow British rule and establish a united Ireland.<br>The Campaign was officially called off on 26th February 1962, though it had long since petered out. |
| 70 | 14 Dec 1956 | Death of Juho Kusti Paasikivi, President of Finland (1946–56). |
| 70 | 17 Dec 1956 | The U.S. Supreme Court ruled that racial segregation on buses was unconstitutional, upholding the verdict of the federal district court of Alabama (see 13th June 1956).<br>On 20th December it ordered Alabama to desegregate its buses, and the twelve-month Montgomery bus boycott ended. |
| 70 | 17 Dec 1956 | Suez Crisis: petrol rationing was introduced in Britain.<br>Motorists were limited to 200 miles per month; businesses to 300; and farmers, religious ministers and essential local authority workers to 600. Doctors, surgeons, midwives and disabled drivers were exempt from rationing. Rationing ended on 14th May 1957. |
| 70 | 17 Dec 1956 | Death of Eddie Acuff, American stage and film actor.<br>Best known for his supporting roles. (Heart attack, aged 53.) |
| 70 | 18 Dec 1956 | The first episode of the television panel/game show *To Tell the Truth* was broadcast on CBS in the USA. It ended in December 2001 after 25 seasons. |
| 70 | 20 Dec 1956 | The Montgomery bus boycott in Alabama, USA ended when the U.S. Supreme Court ordered Alabama to desegregate its buses.<br>(See 17th December.) |
| 70 | 22 Dec 1956 | Suez Crisis: the Anglo–French Task Force withdrew from Port Said and Port Fuad in Egypt after being ordered to leave by the United Nations.<br>The task force was replaced by Danish and Colombian units from the United Nations Emergency Force. |
| 70 | 22 Dec 1956 | The first gorilla born in captivity was born at Columbus Zoo in Ohio, USA. The female gorilla, named Colo, lived until 2017 and became the oldest-known gorilla in the world. |
| 70 | 23 Dec 1956 | Birth of Michele Alboreto, Italian Formula One racing driver. (Died 2001.) |
| 70 | 31 Dec 1956 | The Romanian television network TVR began broadcasting. |
| 65 | 2 Dec 1961 | Cuban leader Fidel Castro declared that he was a Marxist-Leninist and announced that Cuba was going to adopt Communism. |
| 65 | 2 Dec 1961 | Anton Geesink of the Netherlands became the first non-Japanese judo world champion. |

**DECEMBER 2026**

| Ann. | Date | Event |
|------|------|-------|
| 65 | 4 Dec 1961 | Birth control pills became available on the NHS in the UK. |
| 65 | 9 Dec 1961 | Tanganyika gained its independence from the UK.<br>It retained the British monarch as its head of state for a year before becoming an independent republic within the Commonwealth on 9th December 1962.<br>In April 1964 it merged with Zanzibar and became Tanzania. |
| 65 | 10 Dec 1961 | American biochemist Melvin Calvin received the 1965 Nobel Prize in Chemistry for discovering how photosynthesis works. |
| 65 | 11 Dec 1961 | Vietnam War: 32 U.S. Army helicopters and 400 troops arrived in Saigon. This was the USA's first direct military support for South Vietnam's battle against the Vietcong. |
| 65 | 12 Dec 1961 | The first amateur radio satellite *OSCAR 1* was launched by the U.S. Department of Defense.<br>It was built by members of the TRW Radio Club in Redondo Beach, California, USA, with assistance from Foothill College.<br>It operated for 22 days, and simply transmitted the Morse code for 'HI'.<br>It re-entered the Earth's atmosphere and burnt up on 31st January 1962. |
| 65 | 13 Dec 1961 | Death of Grandma Moses, American folk artist. |
| 65 | 15 Dec 1961 | Holocaust: former Nazi official Adolf Eichmann was sentenced to death by an Israeli court for organising the deportation of Jews to concentration camps. He was executed on 31st May 1962. |
| 65 | 16 Dec 1961 | Birth of Bill Hicks, American stand-up comedian. (Died 1994.) |
| 65 | 17 Dec 1961 | The Niterói circus fire, Brazil.<br>A fire broke out during a performance with around 3,000 people in the circus tent. The tent was made from cotton treated with paraffin wax, and was highly flammable. More than 500 people were killed and more than 800 injured. (Cause: uncertain – possible electrical fault or arson.) |
| 65 | 19 Dec 1961 | Operation Vijay: India annexed the Portuguese territories of Goa, Daman, and Diu. |
| 65 | 19 Dec 1961 | The British government appointed the Committee of the Inquiry on Decimal Currency (the Halsbury Committee).<br>It published its report in 1963, which recommended the decimal coins Britain should use, a timetable for their introduction, and the cost of switching to decimal currency. The suggestions were approved in 1966.<br>Britain switched to decimal currency on 15th February 1971. |
| 65 | 20 Dec 1961 | Death of Moss Hart, American playwright, librettist and theatrical director. Best known for his collaborations with George S. Kaufman, including *You Can't Take It with You* and *The Man Who Came to Dinner*, and for directing the musical *My Fair Lady*. |
| 65 | 20 Dec 1961 | Death of Earle Page, Prime Minister of Australia (April 1939 following the death of Joseph Lyons). Leader of the Country Party (1921–39).<br>Treasurer of Australia (1923–29). Minister for Commerce (1940–41).<br>Minister for Health (1949–56). |
| 65 | 24 Dec 1961 | Death of Frank Richards, British writer.<br>Best known for creating the character Billy Bunter. |

## DECEMBER 2026

| Ann. | Date | Event |
|---|---|---|
| 65 | 28 Dec 1961 | Tennessee Williams' play *The Night of the Iguana* opened on Broadway. |
| 65 | 28 Dec 1961 | Death of Edith Wilson, First Lady of the United States (1915–21). Wife of U.S. President Woodrow Wilson. She married him during his first term in office, and managed his office after he suffered a stroke in 1919. |
| 65 | 30 Dec 1961 | Russian composer Dmitri Shostakovich's *Symphony No. 4* (Opus 43) was performed for the first time, in Moscow. It was originally scheduled to be performed in December 1936, but it was withdrawn (possibly by order of the Soviet leader Joseph Stalin or other Communist Party leaders). After it was withdrawn, Shostakovich refused to reschedule its performance until after Stalin's death. |
| 65 | 31 Dec 1961 | Ireland's state broadcaster RTÉ launched its television service. |
| 65 | 31 Dec 1961 | The Beach Boys played their first live performance, at the Ritchie Valens Memorial Dance in Long Beach, California, USA. |
| 60 | 1 Dec 1966 | Kurt Georg Kiesinger became Chancellor of West Germany (until 1969). |
| 60 | 7 Dec 1966 | The Erzurum army barracks fire, Turkey. 68 soldiers were killed and more than 100 injured when a fire swept through the barracks. |
| 60 | 8 Dec 1966 | The Greek car ferry *SS Heraklion* capsized and sank in the Aegean Sea. More than 200 people were killed. (Cause: a truck crashed against a loading door during a storm, forcing it open and allowing the sea in.) |
| 60 | 15 Dec 1966 | Saturns's 10th moon, Janus, was discovered by French astronomer Audouin Dollfus. Its 11th moon, Epimetheus, was discovered on 18th December by American astronomer Richard L. Walker. The two moons were thought to be the same object until 1978, as their orbits were virtually identical. Epimetheus was not officially named until 1983. |
| 60 | 15 Dec 1966 | Death of Walt Disney, American animator and film and television producer. Co-founder (with his brother Roy) of the Walt Disney Company. Creator of popular cartoon characters including Mickey Mouse and Donald Duck. Creator of Disneyland. |
| 60 | 16 Dec 1966 | The United Nations declared apartheid a crime against humanity. |
| 60 | 16 Dec 1966 | Foreign language versions (including English) of Chairman Mao's *Little Red Book* were published. It is one of the most-printed books in history. (Official title: *Quotations from Chairman Mao Tse-tung*.) It was originally published in Chinese in January 1964. |
| 60 | 16 Dec 1966 | The blues rock song *Hey Joe* by the Jimi Hendrix Experience was released. It was their first single. |
| 60 | 18 Dec 1966 | The animated television film *How the Grinch Stole Christmas* was broadcast for the first time, on CBS in the USA. It is based on the book of the same name by Dr. Seuss. |

## DECEMBER 2026

| Ann. | Date | Event |
|------|------|-------|
| 60 | 21 Dec 1966 | The Soviet Union launched its *Luna 13* spacecraft.<br>It landed on the Moon on 24th December and sent back panoramic television images of the landscape. It also measured the density of the lunar surface, the pressure exerted on the surface by the landing, and the temperature.<br>It operated until 28th December when its batteries became exhausted. |
| 60 | 26 Dec 1966 to 1 Jan 1967 | The first Kwanzaa celebration took place in the USA. It is an annual week-long celebration of African American culture and heritage. |
| 60 | 27 Dec 1966 | The largest known cave shaft in the world, the Cave of Swallows, was discovered in Aquismón, San Luis Potosí, Mexico. |
| 50 | 1 Dec 1976 | British punk rock band the Sex Pistols made their infamous appearance on Thames Television's *Today* show, in which the host, Bill Grundy (who later claimed he was drunk), encouraged them to use foul language.<br>The show was only broadcast in London, but made national headlines and the band became household names.<br>Grundy was suspended and the incident effectively ended his career.<br>The Sex Pistols' first national tour was due to begin on 3rd December, but only seven of the twenty scheduled concerts took place, as organisers and local authorities banned them from appearing and cancelled the shows. |
| 50 | 1 Dec 1976 | Birth of Matthew Shepard, American murder victim.<br>He was a student from the University of Wyoming who was beaten and left to die in 1998 because of his sexual orientation.<br>His death led to the introduction of the Hate Crimes Prevention Act in the USA (also known as the Matthew Shepard Act or the Shepard/Byrd Act).<br>His death also inspired books, films, songs, and other works. |
| 50 | 2 Dec 1976 | Fidel Castro became President of Cuba (until 2008). |
| 50 | 2 Dec 1976 | Death of Danny Murtaugh, American baseball player, manager and coach. Best known for his career with the Pittsburgh Pirates, where he was second baseman and manager. |
| 50 | 3 Dec 1976 | Patrick Hillery became President of Ireland (until 1990). |
| 50 | 3 Dec 1976 | Jamaican reggae singer Bob Marley, his wife, and his manager were shot and wounded in an attempted assassination.<br>They all made full recoveries.<br>The assault was thought to be politically motivated – he was due to play at a political concert two days later.<br>The concert went ahead, but he then spent a month recovering on Nassau before relocating to England for two years. |
| 50 | 4 Dec 1976 | British-American actress Elizabeth Taylor's 7th marriage:<br>to American politician John Warner.<br>They were divorced in 1982, as she found life as a politician's wife too boring and depressing. |
| 50 | 4 Dec 1976 | Death of Tommy Bolin, American rock guitarist and songwriter.<br>He was a member of several bands, including Deep Purple (1975–76) as well as being a solo artist and session musician.<br>(Drug and alcohol overdose, aged 25.) |

## DECEMBER 2026

| Ann. | Date | Event |
|---|---|---|
| 50 | 4 Dec 1976 | Death of Benjamin Britten, British composer, conductor and pianist. One of the leading British composers of the 20th century. Noted for his operas. Best known for *Peter Grimes* and *The Rape of Lucretia*, his choral work the *War Requiem*, and *The Young Person's Guide to the Orchestra*. |
| 50 | 5 Dec 1976 | The Rally for the Republic, a Gaullist and Conservative political party, was founded in France by Jacques Chirac (later President of France). It was dissolved in 2002. |
| 50 | 6 Dec 1976 | American stuntwoman Kitty O'Neil broke the women's land speed record. She drove the rocket car *SMI Motivator* at an average speed of 512.71 mph. Her record stood for more than forty years. (It was broken by American driver Jessi Combs in 2019 – though she was killed in a crash when a wheel failed during the attempt.) |
| 50 | 6 Dec 1976 | Death of João Goulart, President of Brazil (1961–64). |
| 50 | 8 Dec 1976 | The album *Hotel California* by the American rock band the Eagles was released. It was their biggest-selling studio album, and one of the best-selling albums of all time. It sold more than 32 million copies. |
| 50 | 15 Dec 1976 | The Liberian oil tanker *MV Argo Merchant* ran aground and sank off Nantucket Island, Massachusetts, USA. It spilled its entire cargo of 7.7 million gallons of oil into the sea – one of the biggest marine oil spills in history. The ship had been involved in more than a dozen incidents before this, under several different names. |
| 50 | 16 Dec 1976 | The swine flu mass-vaccination programme in the USA was scrapped after it caused Guillain-Barre syndrome (which can cause paralysis) in dozens of people. The U.S. government had planned to vaccinated everyone in the country, but only around twenty percent pf the population had been vaccinated by the time the programme was scrapped. Pharmaceutical companies settled hundreds of compensation claims over the next few years. |
| 50 | 17 Dec 1976 | WTCG (later WTBS) became the first 'superstation' in the USA – i.e. the first independently owned television channel to be available across the entire country. The station, owned by media mogul Ted Turner, was previously only available in Georgia and surrounding states. It paved the way for today's basic cable TV services. It is now called TBS. |
| 50 | 17 Dec 1976 | The musical romantic drama film *A Star is Born* was released in the USA. UK: March 1977. |
| 50 | 31 Dec 1976 | American rock band The Cars played their first live show, at the Pease Air Force Base in New Hampshire. |
| 40 | 1 Dec 1986 | Iran–Contra Affair: the Tower Commission was established to investigate matters surrounding the Iran–Contra Affair and to evaluate the National Security Council. On 19th December, former U.S. Deputy Attorney General Lawrence Walsh was appointed Independent Counsel to investigate the affair. |

## DECEMBER 2026

| Ann. | Date | Event |
|------|------|-------|
| 40 | 1 Dec 1986 | The Guinness share-trading scandal began in Britain.<br>The Government ordered an enquiry into the company's affairs and raided its headquarters. It led to one of the biggest trials of the 20th century. |
| 40 | 1 Dec 1986 | The Musée d'Orsay opened in Paris, France.<br>It is one of the largest art museums in Europe, and is housed in the former Gare d'Orsay railway station.<br>It displays French art dating from 1848 to 1914. |
| 40 | 1 Dec 1986 | Death of Lee Dorsey, American R&B singer. |
| 40 | 2 Dec 1986 | Death of Desi Arnaz, Cuban-born American actor, bandleader and television producer. Best known for his role in the TV sitcom *I Love Lucy* with his real-life wife Lucille Ball. |
| 40 | 7 Dec 1986 | Birth of Megan Kanka, American rape and murder victim whose death in 1994 led to the creation of Megan's Law. |
| 40 | 11 Dec 1986 | Apartheid: the South African government imposed sweeping new media restrictions (see 12th June for the initial restrictions). Reporters had to submit articles on restricted topics to the government for approval/censorship prior to publication. Restricted topics included: security force action, boycotts, banned meetings, and detainees.<br>Coverage of peaceful anti-apartheid protests was also banned. |
| 40 | 13 Dec 1986 | Death of Ella Baker, American civil rights activist. |
| 40 | 17 Dec 1986 | Davina Thompson became the world's first recipient of a heart, lung and liver transplant, at Papworth Hospital in Cambridge, UK. |
| 40 | 17 Dec 1986 | American serial killer Richard Kuklinski was arrested by officers from the Bureau of Alcohol, Tobacco, and Firearms after an eighteen-month operation (Operation Iceman). He was convicted of murdering five people who he had lured with offers of a business deal so he could rob them.<br>He claimed to have murdered up to 200 people, though no more than five murders could be verified.<br>He was sentenced to life imprisonment in 1988, and a further thirty years in 2003 after he confessed to killing a police officer.<br>He was the subject of the 2012 film *The Iceman*. |
| 40 | 19 Dec 1986 | Soviet dissident Andrei Sakharov was released from internal exile in Gorky and allowed to return to Moscow. |
| 40 | 22 Dec 1986 | Death of David Penhaligon, British politician.<br>President of the Liberal Party (1985–86). Member of Parliament for Truro (1974–86). (Killed in a car crash, aged 42.) |
| 40 | 23 Dec 1986 | The experimental American plane *Voyager*, piloted by Dick Rutan and Jeana Yeager, became the first aircraft to fly around the world without stopping or refuelling. |
| 40 | 29 Dec 1986 | Death of Harold Macmillan, 1st Earl of Stockton, British Prime Minister (1957–63). |
| 40 | 30 Dec 1986 | The British government announced that the use of canaries in coal mines was to be phased out in favour of hand-held electronic gas detectors.<br>British mines still used around 200 canaries at that time. |

## DECEMBER 2026

| Ann. | Date | Event |
|------|------|-------|
| 40 | 31 Dec 1986 | The Dupont Plaza Hotel and Casino arson attack, San Juan, Puerto Rico. Three employees set the building on fire. 97 people were killed and 140 injured. |
| 30 | 4 Dec 1996 | NASA launched its *Mars Pathfinder* spacecraft. It landed on Mars on 4th July 1997 and released *Sojourner*, the first successful rover to operate on another planet. The mission analysed the Martian atmosphere, climate, geology, and the composition of its rocks and soil. *Pathfinder* operated for 85 days and *Sojourner* for seven days. |
| 30 | 4 Dec 1996 | Jonathan Schmitz was sentenced to 25–50 years in prison. On 12th November he had been convicted of second-degree murder for shooting a man who revealed he had a crush on him on an episode of the U.S. television talk show *The Jenny Jones Show*. (He was released in 2017.) |
| 30 | 5 Dec 1996 | General Motors released the EV1 electric car. It was the first modern electric car from a major manufacturer, and the first to be mass-produced. It was only available to lease, not to buy. 1,117 cars were produced. Production ceased (somewhat controversially) in 1999, mainly because of its limited range (about 70 miles per charge). |
| 30 | 6 Dec 1996 | Death of Pete Rozelle, American sports executive. Commissioner of the National Football League (NFL) (1960–89). During his term in office he doubled the size of the league, negotiated lucrative deals with TV networks, and helped to create the Super Bowl. |
| 30 | 8 Dec 1996 | Death of Howard Rollins, American stage, film and television actor. Best known for the TV series *In the Heat of the Night* and the film *Ragtime*. Also noted for his drug/legal issues. (AIDS-related lymphoma, aged 46.) |
| 30 | 9 Dec 1996 | The United Nations Oil-for-Food Programme was implemented in Iraq. |
| 30 | 9 Dec 1996 | Death of Mary Leakey, British archaeologist and anthropologist. She discovered (with her husband Louis Leakey) several significant fossils in Africa that were important in the understanding of human evolution. |
| 30 | 10 Dec 1996 | The President of South Africa, Nelson Mandela, signed a new constitution, completing the transition from white minority rule to full democracy. (Effective from 4th February 1997.) |
| 30 | 11 Dec 1996 | Death of Willie Rushton, British satirist, comedian, cartoonist, writer and actor. Co-founder of *Private Eye* magazine. |
| 30 | 12 Dec 1996 | Uday Hussein, the son of Iraqi President Saddam Hussein, was seriously injured in an assassination attempt that left him partially paralysed. He and his brother, Qusay, were both killed in a gunfight against U.S. forces during the Iraq War in 2003. |
| 30 | 12 Dec 1996 | The U.S. première of the science fiction comedy film *Mars Attacks!* Released: 13th December. UK: 28th February 1997. |
| 30 | 12 Dec 1996 | Death of Vance Packard, American social critic, writer and journalist. Best known for his book *The Hidden Persuaders*, which explores the manipulative techniques used by advertisers and politicians. |
| 30 | 16 Dec 1996 | Death of Joe Coral, British bookmaker who founded the Coral chain of betting shops. |

**DECEMBER 2026**

| Ann. | Date | Event |
|---|---|---|
| 30 | 17 Dec 1996 | The Red Cross assassinations, Grozny, Chechnya.<br>Six staff from the International Committee of the Red Cross (ICRC) were assassinated by gunmen at the ICRC field hospital in Novye Atag<br>The staff were shot while they slept.<br>The ICRC immediately handed over responsibility for the hospital to the Chechen Ministry of Health and evacuated all of its staff.<br>(It is not known who was responsible for the attack, but they told the Chechen staff to get out of the way and deliberately targeted non-Chechens.) |
| 30 | 17 Dec 1996 | Peruvian guerrillas stormed the Japanese embassy in Lima and held 72 people hostage. They were held for four months until commandos stormed the embassy and rescued them. |
| 30 | 18 Dec 1996 | The school board of Oakland, California, USA passed a resolution recognising Ebonics (Black English or African American Vernacular English) as a legitimate language that should be taught in schools<br>The board later reversed its resolution. |
| 30 | 19 Dec 1996 | Death of Marcello Mastroianni, Italian film actor.<br>The most popular leading man in Italian cinema during the 1960s<br>Many of his films were directed by Federico Fellini. |
| 30 | 20 Dec 1996 | NeXT Software merged with Apple Computer.<br>Steve Jobs founded both companies. He re-joined Apple as part of the merger. |
| 30 | 20 Dec 1996 | Honda unveiled its P2 humanoid robot. It was the world's first autonomous walking humanoid robot. It later evolved into the ASIMO. |
| 30 | 20 Dec 1996 | Death of Carl Sagan, American astronomer, cosmologist, writer and broadcaster. He helped to popularise astronomy and the search for extra-terrestrial intelligence. |
| 30 | 21 Dec 1996 | Death of Margret Rey, American writer and illustrator of children's books. Best known for her *Curious George* series, which she wrote with her husband, H. A. Rey. |
| 30 | 23 Dec 1996 | The first women priests were ordained in the Anglican Church in Jamaica. |
| 30 | 23 Dec 1996 | Death of Ronnie Scott, British jazz saxophonist and jazz club owner. |
| 30 | 25 Dec 1996 or 26th | Death of JonBenét Ramsey, six-year-old American beauty queen<br>(Found brutally murdered at her family's home in Boulder, Colorado.) |
| 30 | 26 Dec 1996 | The United Nations Convention to Combat Desertification came into effect. It aims to combat desertification and mitigate the effects of drought, especially in Africa, via long-term strategies, national action programmes and international cooperation. |
| 30 | 27 Dec 1996 | The first genocide trial began in Rwanda following the 1994 civil war in which approximately 800,000 people were killed. |
| 30 | 29 Dec 1996 | The Guatemalan Civil War ended after 36 years with the signing of the Guatemala Peace Accords in Guatemala City. |
| 30 | 30 Dec 1996 | The Brahmaputra Mail passenger train bombing, Western Assam, India.<br>Terrorists detonated a bomb next to the track as the train passed by.<br>Three carriages were destroyed and a further six derailed. At least 33 people were killed. The terrorists were believed to be Bodo separatists. |

# DECEMBER 2026

| Ann. | Date | Event |
|------|------|-------|
| 30 | 30 Dec 1996 | Death of Lew Ayres, American film actor. Best known for *All Quiet on the Western Front* and for his leading role in eight *Dr. Kildare* films. |
| 25 | 1 Dec 2001 | Trans World Airlines (TWA) ceased operating after being acquired by American Airlines. |
| 25 | 2 Dec 2001 | Enron, the world's largest energy corporation, collapsed, sparking one of the biggest corporate accounting scandals in U.S. history. |
| 25 | 6 Dec 2001 to 17th | Invasion of Afghanistan – the Battle of Tora Bora. U.S. forces launched a major assault on the cave complex with the aim of capturing or killing Osama bin Laden, the leader of the terrorist organisation Al-Qaeda. Al-Qaeda's headquarters were believed to be located in the caves. U.S. victory, but Osama bin Laden escaped. He was killed in a covert operation by U.S. forces in Pakistan in 2011. |
| 25 | 6 Dec 2001 | The Canadian province of Newfoundland was renamed Newfoundland and Labrador. |
| 25 | 6 Dec 2001 | Death of Sir Peter Blake, New Zealand yachtsman and environmentalist. |
| 25 | 7 Dec 2001 | The Taliban regime in Afghanistan ended as they surrendered their final bastion in Kandahar. |
| 25 | 10 Dec 2001 | The UK première of the epic fantasy adventure film *The Lord of the Rings: The Fellowship of the Ring*. It was the first film in the trilogy. U.S. première: 13th December. Released: 19th December. |
| 25 | 11 Dec 2001 | Zacarias Moussaoui, a French citizen, became the first person to be indicted in connection with the 9/11 terrorist attacks on the USA. He was in custody for immigration violation at the time of the attacks, but was charged with conspiring to kill U.S. citizens. He admitted conspiracy and was sentenced to life imprisonment in May 2006. |
| 25 | 12 Dec 2001 | The Immanuel bus attack, West Bank. Palestinian militants ambushed a bus carrying Israeli civilians. Eleven passengers were killed and thirty injured. The following day, Israel sent troops into Palestine and launched air strikes in retaliation. There was another attack on a bus in Immanuel in July 2002, when nine Israeli civilians were killed and twenty injured. |
| 25 | 12 Dec 2001 | Phong Nha–Kẻ Bàng National Park was established in Vietnam. It is a UNESCO World Heritage Site, and was a nature reserve before it was made a national park. |
| 25 | 12 Dec 2001 | American actress Winona Ryder was arrested for shoplifting $5,500 worth of clothes and accessories from a Saks Fifth Avenue store in Beverly Hills, California. During her trial she was also found to be using prescription drugs without a valid prescription. She was sentenced to three years' probation, 480 hours' community service, fined $3,700, ordered to pay Saks Fifth Avenue $6,355, and ordered to attend drugs counselling. The doctor who supplied her medication had his licence revoked. |
| 25 | 13 Dec 2001 | The Pentagon released a videotape of Al-Qaeda leader Osama bin Laden in which he stated that the deaths and destruction achieved by the 9/11 terrorist attacks on the USA had exceeded his most optimistic expectations. |

**DECEMBER 2026**

| Ann. | Date | Event |
|---|---|---|
| 25 | 13 Dec 2001 | The Indian Parliament terrorist attack, New Delhi, India.<br>Five members of two Pakistani-based terrorist organisations broke through security in their vehicle, shot and killed six police officers, two security guards and a gardener, and wounded eighteen others.<br>The terrorists were killed by security forces outside the parliament building. |
| 25 | 13 Dec 2001 | U.S. President George W. Bush gave six months' notice that the USA was pulling out of the 1972 Anti-Ballistic Missile Treaty.<br>This led to the signing of the Strategic Offensive Reductions Treaty (SORT) in May 2002. |
| 25 | 15 Dec 2001 | The Leaning Tower of Pisa re-opened to the public. It had been closed since 1990 while work was carried out to prevent it from falling over. |
| 25 | 16 Dec 2001 | The first U.S. commercial food shipment for forty years arrived in Cuba following Hurricane Michelle (See 4th November 2001).<br>Cuba had refused to accept humanitarian aid from the USA, but accepted its proposal to purchase food supplies.<br>(The U.S. embargo on Cuba was imposed in October 1960.) |
| 25 | 16 Dec 2001 | The March on the Mound.<br>Thousands of people marched through Edinburgh, Scotland to protest against the handling of rural issues by the Scottish Parliament. |
| 25 | 16 Dec 2001 | Death of Stuart Adamson, British singer, songwriter and guitarist (The Skids, Big Country). (Suicide, aged 43.) |
| 25 | 18 Dec 2001 | The Cathedral of St. John the Divine in New York City, USA was damaged by a fire that swept through the north transept.<br>Renovations and repairs took seven years.<br>It was rededicated in November 2008. |
| 25 | 19 Dec 2001 | The highest barometric pressure ever recorded:<br>1085.6 millibars (32.06 inches of mercury) at Tosontsengel, Mongolia. |
| 25 | 21 Dec 2001 | Economic crisis in Argentina: President Fernando de la Rúa and Finance Minister Domingo Cavallo resigned.<br>Riots had erupted in Buenos Aires the previous day when the government restricted cash withdrawals from bank accounts.<br>On 23rd December Argentina suspended payments on its external debt.<br>It was the biggest debt default in history.<br>It defaulted for a second time in July 2014. |
| 25 | 21 Dec 2001 | Death of Dick Schaap, American sportswriter and broadcaster. |
| 25 | 22 Dec 2001 | Hamid Karzai became acting President of Afghanistan, heading the interim post-Taliban government.<br>He was inaugurated as the official President of Afghanistan on 7th December 2004 after winning the presidential election. |
| 25 | 22 Dec 2001 | British terrorist Richard Reid (the 'shoe bomber') attempted to blow up a transatlantic flight from Paris, France to Miami, Florida, USA using explosives hidden in his shoes.<br>A U.S. court sentenced him to life imprisonment in January 2003. |
| 25 | 22 Dec 2001 | Cc, the world's first cloned cat, was born at Texas A&M University, USA. |

# DECEMBER 2026

| Ann. | Date | Event |
|---|---|---|
| 25 | 26 Dec 2001 | Death of Sir Nigel Hawthorne, British actor. Best known for playing Sir Humphrey Appleby in the television series *Yes, Minister* and *Yes, Prime Minister*. |
| 25 | 29 Dec 2001 | The Lima fire, Peru. A firework sparked a massive fire in Lima's shopping district. Approximately 290 people were killed. |
| 20 | 1 Dec 2006 | The Federal Rules of Civil Procedure in the USA were updated to include electronic documents. From this date, all companies involved in federal litigation must produce electronically stored information and communications (including employees' emails and instant messages) as part of the discovery process of a trial. |
| 20 | 1 Dec 2006 | Felipe Calderón became President of Mexico (until 2012). |
| 20 | 4 Dec 2006 | The first Blu-ray Disc player to go on sale in North America was released: the Sony BDP-S1. (Blu-ray is the high-definition successor to DVD video.) |
| 20 | 4 Dec 2006 | A live adult giant squid was filmed for the first time, by Japanese zoologist Tsunemi Kubodera near the Bonin Islands in the Pacific Ocean. |
| 20 | 4 Dec 2006 | Death of Ross A. McGinnis, American soldier. He was posthumously awarded the Medal of Honor for his actions in Iraq. He threw himself on a grenade when it landed in his vehicle, saving the lives of his colleagues. |
| 20 | 5 Dec 2006 | The Fijian coup d'état. Frank Bainimarama, the Commander of the Fijian Military Force, overthrew the government. He took office as Prime Minister of Fiji on 5th January 2007. |
| 20 | 5 Dec 2006 | The New York City Board of Health voted to ban the use of artificial trans fats in restaurants (with effect from July 2007). It also ordered that restaurants must prominently display the calorie content of each item on their menus. It was the first major city in the USA to ban trans fats and order the calorie count to be displayed. (Trans fats raise levels of unhealthy forms of cholesterol and have been linked to heart disease.) |
| 20 | 6 Dec 2006 | NASA released photos from its *Mars Global Surveyor* mission which suggested that liquid water had flowed on Mars between 1999 and 2001 and might still be doing so. |
| 20 | 9 Dec 2006 to 15th | Typhoon Utor hit the Philippines and Malaysia. 38 people were killed. The typhoon also caused serious flooding that killed at least 118 people (see 18th December 2006). |
| 20 | 10 Dec 2006 | Christer Fuglesang became the first Swedish citizen (and the first Scandinavian) to travel into space. He was a Mission Specialist on the U.S. space shuttle *Discovery*. |
| 20 | 10 Dec 2006 | Death of Augusto Pinochet, President/dictator of Chile (1974–90). |
| 20 | 11 Dec 2006 | The Netherlands became the first country to complete the switch to digital terrestrial television. |
| 20 | 12 Dec 2006 | Death of Al Shugart, American computer engineer. Known for his work on the development of the hard disk drive. He also led the team that developed the floppy disk drive. Co-founder of Seagate Technology, the world's largest independent manufacturer of disk drives. |

## DECEMBER 2026

| Ann. | Date | Event |
|---|---|---|
| 20 | 13 Dec 2006 | *Time* magazine named its Person of the Year as 'You' – the general public – for contributing user-generated content to websites such as Facebook, Wikipedia, YouTube, and others. |
| 20 | 13 Dec 2006 | The baiji (the Chinese river dolphin or Yangtze River dolphin) was declared functionally extinct.<br>None were found in the 2006 survey. One may have been seen in 2007, but there are too few remaining for the species to survive.<br>The last confirmed living specimen was seen in 2002. |
| 20 | 14 Dec 2006 | Death of Ahmet Ertegün, Turkish-born American music executive.<br>Co-founder and president of Atlantic Records.<br>He helped drive the success of R&B and its performers, and was chairman of the Rock and Roll Hall of Fame. |
| 20 | 16 Dec 2006 to 20th | The first-ever parliamentary elections were held in the United Arab Emirates. Twenty members of the Federal National Council were elected by the public, and the other twenty members were appointed by the rulers of each Emirate. |
| 20 | 18 Dec 2006 to 13 Jan | The South-East Asian floods.<br>A series of floods affected the region, particularly Malaysia, following Typhoon Utor.<br>At least 118 people were killed and more than 400,000 displaced. |
| 20 | 18 Dec 2006 | Death of Joseph Barbera, American cartoon animator, director and producer. Known for his partnership with William Hanna (Hanna–Barbera Productions).<br>Their shows include *Tom and Jerry*, *The Flintstones*, *Yogi Bear*, *Scooby-Doo*, *Top Cat*, *The Smurfs*, *Huckleberry Hound*, and *The Jetsons*. |
| 20 | 21 Dec 2006 | Death of Saparmurat Niyazov, first President of Turkmenistan (1990–2006). |
| 20 | 23 Dec 2006 | Death of Charlie Drake, British stage and television slapstick comic and actor. Known for his catchphrase 'Hello, my darlings!' |
| 20 | 24 Dec 2006 | Death of Frank Stanton, American broadcasting executive.<br>President of CBS (1946–71). |
| 20 | 25 Dec 2006 | Death of James Brown, ('the Godfather of Soul'), American singer, songwriter, musician and record producer.<br>One of the founding fathers of funk.<br>His songs include *Papa's Got a Brand New Bag*, *I Got You*, *It's a Man's Man's Man's World*, *Get Up (I Feel Like Being a) Sex Machine* and *Living in America*. |
| 20 | 26 Dec 2006 | Death of Gerald Ford, 38th President of the United States (1974–77). |
| 20 | 29 Dec 2006 | Britain finished repaying the Anglo-American loan.<br>The USA loaned Britain $3.75 billion in 1946 following WWII, when Britain was virtually bankrupt. Canada loaned an additional $1.9 billion. |
| 20 | 30 Dec 2006 | The Madrid–Barajas Airport bombing, Spain.<br>A van bomb exploded in the Terminal 4 parking area, almost completely demolishing all five floors. Two people were killed and 52 injured.<br>It took rescuers five days to recover the bodies of those who died.<br>The Basque separatist organisation ETA claimed responsibility. |
| 20 | 30 Dec 2006 | The Indonesian ferry *MV Senopati Nusantara* sank in the Java Sea during a storm while travelling from Borneo to Java. 400 – 500 people were killed. |

## DECEMBER 2026

| Ann. | Date | Event |
|------|------|-------|
| 20 | 30 Dec 2006 | Death of Saddam Hussein, President/dictator of Iraq (1979–2003). (Executed for war crimes.) |
| 10 | 7 Dec 2016 | Death of Greg Lake, British rock musician. Best known as a founding member of the prog rock bands King Crimson and Emerson, Lake & Palmer. |
| 10 | 8 Dec 2016 | Death of John Glenn, American astronaut and politician. The first American to orbit the Earth, and the third American in space. The last surviving member of the Mercury Seven. U.S. Senator from Ohio (1974–99). Chair of the Senate Governmental affairs Committee (1987–99). |
| 10 | 18 Dec 2016 | Death of Zsa Zsa Gabor, Hungarian-born American stage, film and television actress and socialite. Miss Hungary 1936. She was married nine times. |
| 10 | 19 Dec 2016 | Death of Andrei Karlov, Russian Ambassador to Turkey (2013–16). (Assassinated, aged 62.) |
| 10 | 22 Dec 2016 | A medical trial in Guinea found that the VSV-EBOV vaccine against the Ebola was safe and highly effective. It was the first proven vaccine against Ebola. It was approved in the USA in 2019 under the brand name Ervebo. |
| 10 | 24 Dec 2016 | Death of Richard Adams, British novelist. Best known for *Watership Down*. |
| 10 | 24 Dec 2016 | Death of Rick Parfitt, British rock singer, guitarist and songwriter (Status Quo). |
| 10 | 24 Dec 2016 | Death of Liz Smith, British film and television actress. She had several roles in BBC sitcoms, including Nana in *The Royle Family*. |
| 10 | 25 Dec 2016 | Death of George Michael, British pop singer, songwriter, record producer and philanthropist. One of the best-selling recording artists of all time. A member of Wham!, he then had a successful solo career with hits including *Careless Whisper* and *Faith*. He was also noted for his troubled personal life and drug issues. |
| 10 | 27 Dec 2016 | Death of Carrie Fisher, American film and television actress, screenwriter and script doctor. Best known for her role as Princess Leia in *Star Wars*. Daughter of the actress Debbie Reynolds, who died the following day. |
| 10 | 28 Dec 2016 | Death of Debbie Reynolds, American stage, film and television actress, singer, dancer, and businesswoman. Mother of the actress Carrie Fisher. |

**Have you checked out our other books yet?**

- Our 35 **'ideas for writers'** books cover numerous genres, characters, plots, description, dialogue, storylines, and more. There are more than 5,000 ideas in total, so you'll always have something amazing to write about – and no more writer's block!

- **How to Win Short Story Competitions** tells you everything you need to know, including how judges score each story, and how to get the highest scores in each category. It's packed with hints, tips and insider secrets that will get you onto the shortlist every time.

- **The Fastest Way to Write Your Book** walks you through the whole process of writing a full length novel or non-fiction book in less than a month. You'll come up with your great idea, expand it into a full-length outline, and write your entire first draft – all in just twenty to thirty days, and with no loss of quality. It's packed with tried-and-tested tips that will enable you to complete each step in the fastest possible time. Why write just one book a year when you can write twelve? (*Expanded second edition.*)

- **The Fastest Ways to Edit, Publish and Sell Your Book** continues where *The Fastest Way to Write Your Book* ends. It's packed with ideas and tips to get your book polished, printed and into your readers' hands in the fastest time possible. It covers traditional publishing, self-publishing, printed books and e-books, and walks you through the fastest approaches for each of them.

**Full details at ideas4writers.com**

Printed in Dunstable, United Kingdom